Second Edition

Philosophical and Ideological Perspectives on Education

Gerald L. Gutek
Loyola University, Chicago

Allyn and Bacon
Boston • London • Toronto • Sydney • Tokyo • Singapore

Senior Editor: Virginia C. Lanigan
Editorial Assistant: Nihad M. Farooq
Senior Marketing Manager: Kathy Hunter
Production Administrator: Annette Joseph
Production Coordinator: Holly Crawford
Editorial-Production Service: Connie Leavitt, Bookwrights
Composition Buyer: Linda Cox
Manufacturing Buyer: Megan Cochran
Cover Administrator: Suzanne Harbison
Cover Designer: Susan Paradise

Library of Congress Cataloging-in-Publication Data

Gutek, Gerald Lee.
    Philosophical and ideological perspectives on education / Gerald
L. Gutek.—2nd ed.
      p. cm.
    Includes bibliographical references and index.
    ISBN 0-205-26106-X
    1. Education—Philosophy. 2. Philosophy. I. Title.
LB1025.3.G87   1997
370'.1—dc20   96-7676
                                     CIP

Printed in the United States of America
10 9 8 7 6 5 4 3 2   01 00 99 98

*This book is dedicated to the memory
of my uncle, Ralph Joseph Novotney,
a man who was excellent in all things.*

Contents

Preface

Philosophical and Ideological Perspectives on Education is a result of my teaching and research in Foundations of Education courses. As a teacher in teacher education programs, I have sought to understand and work with ideas that relate to the history, philosophy, and ideology of education. I have looked for contexts, or have attempted to create them, in order to examine ideas about education in terms of their origins, development, meaning, and relevance to teaching and learning. I believe that teacher education should be rooted in and nurtured by the cultural foundations that are part of its origins, in a time when cultural foundations are often neglected. I hope that my colleagues in the fields of history and philosophy of education who share my interest in educational ideas will find my approach congenial and useful.

Although focusing on philosophy of education, this book provides a three-dimensional introduction to educational ideas. First, it examines the major philosophical systems and ideologies that have shaped educational thought and practice. Second, it outlines certain ideas from the fields of philosophy and ideology to illustrate how these disciplines contribute to educational theory. Third, in seeking to provide a context for educational philosophy, ideology, and theory, it includes brief biographical sketches of principal originators or contributors of leading ideas about education. Since the book is intended for use in Philosophy of Education or Cultural Foundations of Education courses in teacher education programs, it provides discussion questions and inquiry projects that may lead students to further reading, research, and field study.

I would like to thank the reviewers of this manuscript for their helpful suggestions and comments: Mary K. Bary, Idaho State University; Jim Bowman,

University of Central Arkansas; George D. Gates, Idaho State University; Byron F. Radebaugh, Northern Illinois University; and David E. Washburn, Bloomsburg University.

Gerald L. Gutek

► 1

Philosophy and Education

During a person's first experience as a teacher, little time exists to examine the general or theoretical implications that result from his or her presence in a school. All too frequently, teaching is a hurried and frustrating series of episodes in which the teacher reacts to the immediate demands of students, parents, administrators, colleagues, and community and school organizations. In the first years of a teaching career, the teacher must meet the day-to-day demands of lesson planning, conducting classes, and attending conferences both in and out of school. Little time is free to reflect on education. For the teacher to become a genuine professional, however, exclusive attention to daily routine and detail is insufficient. Every teacher knows that education is a powerful instrument for the shaping of individual lives and society. When the teacher begins to reflect on his or her role, that person is beginning to pass from preoccupation with the immediately practical to an examination of the theory that underlies and sustains practice. Because it is a moral enterprise, teaching requires the careful blending of theory and practice. Theory without practice is insufficient; practice unguided by theory is aimless.

Blending theory and practice, teaching has both a reflective and an active dimension. It has effects that transcend the immediate instructional episodes of the classroom. The way in which teachers relate to their students depends on their conception of human nature. Instruction is about something; it is about a skill or about knowledge. One's view of reality shapes one's beliefs about knowledge. When the teacher begins to reflect on the conception of reality, of human nature, and of society, he or she is philosophizing about education. To provide a framework for such philosophizing, the sections that follow examine areas of both philosophy and education and also provide an introduction to philosophies of education.

AREAS OF PHILOSOPHY

In its most general terms, philosophy is the human being's attempt to think speculatively, reflectively, and systematically about the universe and the human relationship to that universe. Metaphysics, the study of the nature of ultimate reality, involves speculation about the nature of existence. It asks the question, After all the nonessentials of life have been stripped away, what is genuinely real? Our beliefs about the nature of reality determine how we perceive our relationships to the universe and to society. These beliefs raise our most important questions—what is and what is not real—and also begin to provide the answers to these questions. Is there a spiritual realm of existence or is reality material? What is the origin of the universe? Is it purposeful by its own nature or do we create our own purposes?

In their speculations into the nature of reality, metaphysicians have drawn varying conclusions. Whereas an Idealist defines reality in spiritual or nonmaterial terms, a Realist sees reality as an order of objects that exist independently of human beings. Conversely, a Pragmatist holds that the human conception of reality is based on experience.

Metaphysics relates to educational theorizing and practice in many ways. The subjects, experiences, and skills in the curriculum reflect the conception of reality held by the society that supports the school enterprise. Much formal schooling represents the attempt of curriculum-makers, teachers, and textbook authors to describe certain aspects of reality to students. For example, subjects such as history, geography, chemistry, and so on, describe certain dimensions of reality to students.

Epistemology, the theory of knowing and knowledge, is of crucial importance to educators. Defining the foundations of knowledge, epistemology considers such important questions as: (1) How do we know what we know? (2) On what process of knowing do we base our knowledge of the world and society? (3) What is the authority on which we base our claims to truth? (4) Do our knowledge claims derive from divine revelation, empirical evidence, or personal and subjective experience?

Historically, much authority has rested on a belief in God or the supernatural and revelations of divine truths to inspired men and women. Civilization's great religions—Judaism, Christianity, Islam, Hinduism, and Buddhism, for example—rest on knowledge claims that involve a holy book or scriptures, such as the Bible or the Koran. Implied is the believer's faith in a transcendent, universal, spiritual authority, which, while prior to and independent of human experience, is its true guide. These divinely revealed truths are universally valid in every time and place. While not necessarily religious, philosophies such as Idealism and Realism also claim a universal knowledge authority. Other philosophies, such as Pragmatism, base knowledge claims on human experience, especially publicly verifiable empirical evidence. Highly subjective, Existentialism roots knowledge in one's intuitive perception of one's own needs and psychological disposition.

Dealing with the most general and basic conceptions of knowing, epistemology is closely related to methods of teaching and of learning. For example, an Idealist may hold that knowing, or the cognitive process, is really the recall of ideas that are present latently in the mind. The appropriate educational method for Idealists would be the Socratic dialogue in which the teacher attempts to bring latent ideas to the student's consciousness by asking leading questions. Realists hold that knowledge originates in the sensations we have of objects in our environment. We arrive at concepts from these sensations. Through the abstraction of sensory data, we build concepts that correspond to these objects in reality. A teacher who wishes to structure instruction based on the Realist sensation–abstraction formula might use classroom demonstrations to explain natural phenomena to students. A Pragmatist, in contrast, holds that we create knowledge by interacting with our environment in problem-solving episodes. Thus, problem solving is the appropriate method of instruction for those who accept the Pragmatist's view of knowledge.

Axiology is concerned with value theory and attempts to prescribe what is good and right conduct. The subdivisions of axiology are ethics and aesthetics. Ethics refers to the philosophic study of moral values and conduct. Aesthetics is concerned with the study of values in the realm of beauty and art. Whereas metaphysics is concerned with attempts to describe the nature of ultimate reality, axiology refers to prescriptions of moral behavior and beauty. Educators have always been concerned with the formation of values in the young and with the encouragement of certain kinds of preferred behavior.

In a general way, each person is influenced by those who seek to shape his or her behavior along certain lines, Children are continually told that they should or should not do certain things. Statements such as "you should wash your hands before eating," "you should not break the school's windows," or "you should love your country" are all obvious value statements. In the process of growing to maturity, an individual encounters countless attempts to mold behavior along preferred modes of action. In a very direct way, parents, teachers, and society reward or punish behavior as it conforms to or deviates from their conceptions of correctness, goodness, or beauty.

In a very real way, modern men and women live in a world of clashing values. The nationalistic value patterns of the various nation-states have led to conflict and to war. Within nations, values clash along class or group lines.

Cultural ethos refers to the national value core that provides a sense of identity, purpose, and community to a society. In the contemporary United States, strong cultural divisions exist in defining the nation's ethos and character. James

Hunter, a noted author on American values, has found these divisions to be so deep that they constitute a veritable "culture war."[1] Among the divisive value issues that impact contemporary U.S. society are the following: Is the national character religious or secular? Should there be prayer in the schools? What is the role of women in U.S. society? What is the nature of the family? These fundamental issues are intertwined with issues of national identity. Is there and should there be a national character? Or, should the United States be a place of many diverse identities, cultures, and lifestyles? Further, how does this clash of values impact schooling? What is the role of schools in transmitting and cultivating values?[2]

The classical conflict in values can be identified as that of objective versus subjective value theory. Those who subscribe to an objective value theory assert that what is good is rooted in the universe itself and is applicable everywhere for all time. In contrast, subjectivists assert that values are group or personal preferences—likes or dislikes—that depend on particular circumstances, times, and places. For them, values are not universally valid but are relative in that they depend on particular situations.

The aesthetic dimension of life frequently has been overlooked in U.S. education. In its broadest sense, aesthetic theory refers to the cultivation of taste and a feeling for what is beautiful. Although aesthetic theory is concerned with the human attempt to objectify insights and feelings in various art forms, it is equally concerned with the cultivation of persons whose lives are harmonious, balanced, and beautiful. While aesthetic values have an obvious place in art, drama, music, and dancing classes, they are also relevant to the cultivation of the public taste and style of life.

Logic is concerned with the rules or patterns of correct and valid thinking. It examines the rules of valid inference that enable us to frame correctly our propositions and our arguments. Deductive logic refers to reasoning that moves from general statements or principles to particular instances and applications. Inductive logic is reasoning that moves from particular instances to generalizations.

EDUCATION

The word *education* refers very broadly to the total social processes that bring a person into cultural life. The human species reproduces biologically as do all other living organisms. Biological reproduction, however, is not cultural reproduction. By living and participating in a culture, the immature human being gradually becomes a recipient of and a participant in a culture. Many persons and social agencies are involved in the process of enculturation of the young. The family, the peer group, the community, the media, the church, and the state all have formative effects on the individual. By living with other people, the immature child learns how to deal with them. He or she takes on their language, their manners, and their behavior. Educational theorists and philosophers have long recognized the educative role of interactions of human beings and society, and they have tried to indicate the kind of social order that is based on and fulfills human potentiality.

Education, in a more formal and deliberate sense, takes place in the school, a specialized social agency established to cultivate preferred skills, knowledge, and values in the learner. The school is staffed by teachers who are regarded as experts in the learning processes. Informal education, or milieu, is related to formal education, or schooling. If the school is to succeed in its program of instruction, its curriculum and methods must be viable in relation to society.

Curriculum

As the vital center of the school's educational efforts, the curriculum is the locus of the sharpest controversies. Decision making in curricular matters involves considering, examining, and formulating the ends of education. Those concerned with curriculum planning and organization ask such questions as: What knowledge is of most worth? What knowledge should be introduced to the learner? What are the criteria for selecting knowledge? What is valuable for the learner as a person and as a member of society? The answers to these questions not only determine what is included and what is excluded from the school's instructional program, but also rest ultimately on assumptions about the nature of the universe, of human beings, of society, and of the good life. In the philosophies to be examined in this book, we will find a variety of basic and general assumptions that provide alternatives applicable to making the curriculum.

Curriculum has been defined in various ways. Throughout most of the history of education, the curriculum consisted of the basic skills of reading, writing, and mathematical computation at the primary or elementary level, and the arts and sciences at the secondary and higher levels. For many educators, the curriculum remains essentially a program of studies, skills, and subjects offered to a learner in a formal sequence. Since the appearance of the activity, experience, or process approach, many educators have moved to a more generalized conception of curriculum. For them, the curriculum includes all of the learner's experiences for which the school assumes responsibility.

In the broadest sense, the curriculum can be defined as the organized experiences that a student has under the guidance and control of the school. In a more precise but restricted sense, the curriculum is the systematic sequence of courses or subjects that forms the school's formal instructional program. These two major definitions of curriculum, as well as the variations that lie between them, are based on particular conceptions of knowledge and value. The philosophies of education examined in this book will be found to hold conceptions of the curriculum that range from the broad view that includes all of the learner's experiences, to the more restricted view that sees it as academic subject matter.

There can be no question that curriculum designers, regardless of their philosophical convictions, attempt to seek that which is of the greatest worth to the learner. The problem lies in identifying and agreeing on what is of the greatest truth, beauty, and goodness. This question has metaphysical, epistemological, axiological, and logical dimensions. Philosophers and educational theorists, however, have responded to this question with different answers, and their disagreements have resulted in a variety of curricula.[3]

For the Idealist, Realist, and Thomist philosophers, as well as for the Essentialist and Perennialist theorists, the curriculum consists of skills and subject matters that are organized in a systematic and sequential fashion. They regard the learning of the basic skills as necessary tools that have generative power for the later study of the more sophisticated subjects based on such learned disciplines as mathematics, science, and history. For these more traditional philosophies, the preferred curricular design focuses on subject matter. Their major goal is the transmission and preservation of the cultural heritage. Scientists and scholars, through their research, have developed the learned disciplines that explain the various dimensions of reality. The curriculum, then, is the means of transmitting this heritage, in learnable units, to the immature so that they can participate in the culture. The survival of civilization is believed to hinge on the ability to transmit tested truth and value to the young. The subject-matter curriculum is a form of the conscious and deliberate transmission of the adult view of reality to children. Although children may be initially imposed on, the acquisition of knowledge will lead to their eventual freedom by multiplying their alternatives of action. The subject-matter curriculum is arranged in a hierarchy with priority given to subjects regarded as more general, and hence more significant, than other subjects. This arrangement of the subject-matter hierarchy depends on the particular conception of reality and values that is the background for constructing the curriculum.

In contrast to the subject-matter design, various other curricula have been proposed as desirable ways of organizing the school's instructional program. Experimentalists, Progressives, and Reconstructionists are more concerned with the process of learning than the acquisition of subject matter. This process-oriented curricular design is often called the activity, the experience, or the problem-solving curriculum. In contrast to the differentiated knowledge in the subject-matter curriculum, the process approach concentrates on developing methodological skills to work through and organize undifferentiated human experience. According to John Dewey's experimental mode of learning, the method of scientific inquiry can be applied to all human problems. The curriculum that evolved from Dewey's methodological premise is a series of problem-solving episodes based on the learner's needs and interests as well as on social situations and issues.

Methodology of Instruction

The method of instruction is closely related to the goals or ends specified in the curriculum. *Methodology* refers to the processes of teaching and learning by which the learner is brought into relationship with the skills and knowledge specified and contained in the curriculum. In the school, methods are the procedures a teacher uses to aid students in having an experience, mastering a skill or process, or acquiring an area of knowledge. If efficient and effective, the methods of instruction will achieve the desired end.

John Colman has defined method as, "An ordered system by which a teacher puts educative agents to work on humans to produce certain changes or results." He has identified five necessary elements in instructional methodology: (1) an aim, or the specific objective or purpose of instruction; (2) an introduction that relates the particular lesson to previous learning or experiences; (3) content, or the substance or subject of a lesson; (4) a summary to reinforce the particular learning; and (5) an evaluation that determines if the particular aim has been achieved by the learner.[4]

Because teaching implies the use of a technique to achieve a desired objective, educators are involved in methodological questions. In programs of teacher education, attention is given to courses in techniques and methods of teaching. For example, courses exist in teaching reading, language arts, science, social studies, mathematics, music, and art. Supervised student or practice teaching is designed to provide the prospective teacher with experience in integrating content and methodology in a classroom situation. Experienced teachers are involved in programs of in-service training designed to familiarize them with new methods. School administrators devote much of their time and resources to introducing and experimenting with methodological innovations. Even a cursory examination of the literature of professional education gives evidence of a keen interest in methodology. One will find articles on the Socratic method, the project method, the discovery method, the inquiry method, collaborative learning, and other approaches to instruction.

The methods of teaching and of learning are most closely related to epistemology, or knowing, and to logic, the correct patterns of thinking. Once again, the study of educational philosophy provides clues to learning strategies that relate to the conception of knowing embodied in the philosophical system. If knowledge, or ideas, are innately present in the mind, then the most effective instructional strategy is one that brings them to consciousness, such as the Socratic method. If, however, learning is transactional between the person and the environment, as Dewey asserts, then the most effective method is problem-solving.

Teachers and Learners

Formal education involves a teacher and a learner. The conception of the roles and functions of the teacher and the learner depends on one's view of human nature. The Thomists' view of a human being as an "incarnate spirit-in-the world" is very different from the Pragmatist conception of the human being as a biological-sociological-vocal phenomenon. The Existentialist view that the person creates his or her own essence differs from the philosophies that see the human being as a category in a metaphysical system. From each of these perspectives, the roles of the teacher and the learner would be seen quite differently.

The teacher–learner relationship also reflects the roles of the teacher and learner in the instructional process. In the subject-matter curriculum, the teacher is an authority figure who is expert in the content and teaching of a body of organized knowledge. In regard to that knowledge, the learner is an immature person who is present in the school to acquire and to master that knowledge. in such a curricular framework, the teacher–learner relationship depends substantially on the logic of the subject matter.

In contrast to the subject-matter approach, the process-oriented educator looks to the child's interests to provide the basis of the teacher–learner relationship. The child, not the subject matter, is the center of the relationship. The teacher is a guide to the learning process but does not dominate it.

The teacher's assumptions about learners influence his or her behavior toward learners and determine the curriculum he or she will plan for them. Assumptions about human nature influence the type of curriculum, the particular method of instruction, and the school's climate.

PHILOSOPHIES OF EDUCATION

Over time, a number of systematic philosophies have been developed. Idealism, Realism, and Thomism represent three of the major philosophies that have had a long history in Western civilization. They remain vital philosophies that guide educational processes and give substance to various curricular designs. Closely related to these more traditional philosophies are the educational theories of Perennialism, which emphasizes the human being's rationality, and Essentialism, which stresses basic skills and subjects.

In contrast to the more traditional philosophies, John Dewey's Pragmatism emphasizes the educational process as a transaction between the person and the environment. Among the educational theories that are related to Pragmatism are Progressivism and Reconstructionism. Progressivism, a reaction against traditionalism in schooling, stresses the liberation of the child's needs and interests. Reconstructionism urges that schools play a significant role in cultural criticism and change.

Two contemporary approaches to educational philosophy are Existentialism and Philosophical Analysis. The Existentialist is concerned about the rise of a mass society and bureaucratic schools that dehumanize students by reducing them to objects or functions. Philosophical Analysis seeks to establish meaning in the language that we use in both common and scientific discourse.

In addition to examining significant philosophies of education, in later chapters we will also examine several ideologies that have shaped the Western political, social, and educational perspective. Based on political and social contexts, ideologies such as Nationalism, Liberalism, Conservatism, Utopianism, Marxism, and Totalitarianism have shaped schools, curricula, and styles of teaching and learning. At times, elements of philosophical systems have been fused with particular ideologies. The definition of ideology and the relationship of ideology to education are treated in Chapter 9. The text concludes with a discussion of theories of education in Chapter 16 and then examines Essentialism, Perennialism, Progressivism, Social Reconstructionism, and Critical Theory as five significant theories of education.

CONCLUSION

It is valuable for teachers to recognize various philosophies of education and to identify curricula and methods in their relationship to particular philosophical positions. This competency helps educators to examine and to criticize educational policies and programs. For example, many of the proposals made in educational reports such as *A Nation at Risk* and *Education for Excellence* rest on philosophical and ideological assumptions.[5] In many respects, these proposals represent a revival of Essentialism and Perennialism. When educators are unable to recognize the philosophical and ideological perspective from which proposals emanate, they are unable either to criticize or to implement these proposals from a professional perspective.

Philosophical inquiry can aid the educator in examining decisions and problems. In turn, philosophy of education may draw heavily from the experiences, practices, and observations of the educator. For example, as we shall see in later chapters, educational goals, practices, methods, and ends can be extrapolated from such systems of philosophy as Idealism, Realism, and Thomism. The converse is also true, however. It is possible to create educational theories by examining educational practices and generalizing about their most general consequences for personal and social growth as the Essentialists, Progressives, and Perennialists have done.

Throughout history, and particularly in recent years, education has been the subject of much debate and conflict. In many ways, the presence of divergent views is a sign of vitality. As a social institution, the school is the focal point of conflicts. Numerous recommendations have been made for school reform. Some have even suggested that the school be abandoned as society's primary educational institution. Others argue that schools should deliberately instill religious and spiritual values in the young; still others plead for an emphasis on law and order. Some voices proclaim that schools must return to the intellectual virtues, to the liberal arts and sciences, or to basic education. Others see schools as agencies of social criticism or vehicles for initiating social and political reform. Behind these proposals lie assumptions about the nature of the universe, human life, and society. By examining these assumptions in their philosophical matrix, these various alternatives in education may be explored and illuminated.

It is hoped that the study of educational philosophy will stimulate teachers to think about education in terms sufficiently general so that they may resist the temptation of subscribing to the promises of panaceas or to propagandistic slogans. Perhaps an examination of the philosophy of education will aid teachers to recognize that organizational and instructional innovations can be used for many purposes and can have many consequences. Finally, it is hoped that the study of the philosophy of education will encourage teachers to examine and to formulate the broad personal and professional goals that should guide educational practice.

DISCUSSION QUESTIONS

1. How is teaching both reflective and active?

2. Define metaphysics, epistemology, axiology, and logic as subdivisions of philosophy.

3. Identify and define value conflicts that have an impact on schooling.

4. Provide examples of the clash between those who hold objective values and those who hold subjective values.

5. Define and cite examples of formal and informal education.

6. Examine the subject-matter curriculum in terms of its philosophical assumptions.

7. Examine the philosophical assumptions that support the process-oriented curriculum method.

INQUIRY PROJECTS

- In a paper, identify and analyze a current curriculum controversy with special attention to philosophical issues such as the nature of reality, human nature, and knowledge.

- Visit several elementary and secondary school classes. Direct special attention to the curricular and instructional strategies being used. In a report to the class, reflect on your observations in terms of underlying philosophical assumptions.
- Read and review a book that is used in teacher education in terms of the author's view of reality and human nature.
- Collect a number of articles about education from the popular press. Analyze these articles in terms of the view of human nature and the teaching–learning process that is expressed.
- Read a novel about teaching and analyze the author's perception of the teacher–learner relationship.
- Analyze several academic majors described in the catalogue of your college or university. What conceptions of knowledge are implied in the course requirements for these majors?

FURTHER READINGS

Apple, Michael W. "Producing Inequality: Ideology and Economy in the National Reports on Education," *Educational Studies,* 18, No. 2 (summer 1987); 195–220.

Bigge, Morris L. *Educational Philosophies for Teachers.* Columbus, OH: Chas. E. Merrill, 1982.

Coleman, John E. *The Master Teachers and the Art of Teaching.* New York: Pitman, 1967.

Fitzgibbons, Robert E. *Making Educational Decisions: An Introduction to Philosophy of Education.* New York: Harcourt Brace Jovanovich, 1981.

Hunter, James Davison. *Culture Wars: The Struggle to Define America.* New York: Basic Books, 1991.

Kaminsky, James S. *A New History of Educational Philosophy.* Westport, CT: Greenwood Press, 1993.

Kammen, Michael. *Contested Values: Democracy and Diversity in American Culture.* New York: St. Martin's Press, 1995.

Kelly, Elizabeth A. *Education, Democracy & Public Knowledge.* Boulder, CO: Westview Press, 1995.

Kliebard, Herbert M. *The Struggle for the American Curriculum 1893–1958.* Boston: Routledge & Kegan Paul, 1986.

Kneller, George F. *Movements of Thought in Modern Education.* New York: John Wiley, 1984.

Knight, George R. *Philosophy & Education: An Introduction in Christian Perspective.* Berrien Springs, MI: Andrews University Press, 1980.

Knight, George R. *Issues and Alternatives in Educational Philosophy.* Berrien Springs, MI: Andrews University Press, 1982.

Soltis, Jonas, ed. *Philosophy of Education Since Mid-Century.* New York: Teachers College Press, Columbia University, 1981.

Spring, Joel. *Wheels in the Head: Educational Philosophies of Authority, Freedom, and Culture from Socrates to Paulo Freire.* New York: McGraw-Hill, 1984.

Welker, Robert. *The Teacher as Expert: A Theoretical and Historical Examination.* Albany: State University of New York Press, 1992.

ENDNOTES

1. James Davison Hunter, *Culture Wars: The Struggle to Define America* (New York: Basic Books, 1991), pp. 3–29.

2. Ibid., p. 44.

3. For an analysis of the interplay of the forces that shape curriculum, see Herbert M. Kliebard, *The Struggle for the American Curriculum 1893–1958* (Boston: Routledge & Kegan Paul, 1986).

4. John E. Colman, *The Master Teachers and the Art of Teaching* (New York: Pitman, 1967), pp. 5–11.

5. Michael W. Apple, "Producing Inequality: Ideology and Economy in the National Reports on Education," *Educational Studies,* 18, No. 2 (summer 1987): 195–220.

▶ 2

Idealism and Education

Idealism, which asserts that reality is essentially spiritual or ideational, is one of humankind's oldest and most enduring systems of thought. The belief that the world and human beings within it are part of an unfolding universal spirit has long been a cosmic principle in oriental religions such as Hinduism and Buddhism. It was probably through cultural interactions between East and West that Idealist concepts found their way into Western thought.

In the Western educational tradition, Idealism's origins are usually traced to the ancient Greek philosopher Plato. Although only a few contemporary philosophers of education are Idealists, an examination of Idealism provides a valuable cultural and educational perspective. Despite its contemporary eclipse, Idealism has often dominated philosophical discourse in the past. In eighteenth- and nineteenth-century Germany, Idealists such as Johann Gottlieb Fichte (1762–1814), Friedrich Schelling (1775–1854), and Georg Wilhelm Friedrich Hegel (1770–1831) dominated philosophy.[1] Hegel's monumental work, *The Philosophy of History,* influenced philosophical thought both in Germany and abroad. It should be remembered that both Karl Marx (1818–1883) and John Dewey (1859–1952) studied Idealism in their education as philosophers. Friedrich Froebel (1782–1852), the founder of the kindergarten, created a method of early childhood education based on Idealist philosophy.

In the United States, Idealism has also had its time of philosophical popularity. The New England Transcendentalists—Ralph Waldo Emerson (1803–1882) and Henry David Thoreau (1817–1862)—used Idealist metaphysical propositions as the basis of their concepts of the Oversoul, or Macrocosm, and of Nature. The nineteenth-century school administrator William Torrey Harris (1835–1909) used Hegelian Idealism as a philosophical rationale for school organization and curriculum.

While Idealism is historically significant, certain current educational practices have their origin and rationale in the Idealist perspective. The notion that
education is a process of unfolding that which is present but latent in the child
is grounded in idealist epistemology. The concept of the teacher as a moral and
cultural model, or exemplar, also originated in Idealism, as did the Socratic
method, which includes the skillful asking of probing questions to stimulate the
student's recollection. Because Idealism has been a prominent philosophy that
has influenced present education, in this chapter we will (1) examine Plato as a
theorist who used an Idealist perspective in framing his educational doctrines;
(2) analyze the essential components of Idealism as a systematic philosophy in
terms of metaphysics, epistemology, and axiology; and (3) comment on Idealism's implications for education, curriculum, character formation, methodology
of instruction, and teacher–student relationships.

PLATO: FOUNDER OF WESTERN IDEALISM

As suggested earlier, the origins of Idealism in Western thought are generally
traced to Plato, the famous student of Socrates. Whereas Socrates raised fundamental questions about reality, knowledge, and human nature, Plato went beyond
his teacher in seeking to provide fundamental answers. Plato sought to answer
the metaphysical question, What is the nature of reality? and the epistemological
question, What is the nature of knowledge and how do we come to know? From
these fundamental questions, Plato moved into the axiological dimension by asking, What is the relationship between knowledge and the proper conduct of
human life in terms of ethical, moral, and aesthetic behavior?

In this section of the chapter, we will examine how Plato established the
basic philosophical foundation for Idealism that remains with us today. In Idealist education, the notion that the teacher is a learned master and that the student
is a disciple in learning the master's wisdom is a powerful concept that was true
in the case of Socrates, the master, and Plato, the disciple.

In ancient Athens, the intellectual gadfly and social critic, Socrates (469–
399 B.C.), had attracted a circle of students, one of whom was Plato.[2] Rejecting
the Sophists' materialistic opportunism and moral relativism, Socrates embarked
on a quest to discover the universal principles of truth, justice, and beauty that
governed all humankind. The basic conflict between Socrates and the Sophists
points out an issue that has been recurrent in education. The Sophists claimed
that ethical principles were relative to a given time and place, and given circumstances; in other words, morally correct behavior was a response to changing
circumstances. Socrates disputed this form of situational ethics, claiming that
what was true, good, and beautiful was the same throughout the world.

Socrates asserted that human beings should seek to live lives that were morally excellent. Rather than training people in a particular vocational or profes-

An engraving of Plato (427–347 B.C.), the Greek philosopher, who was a student of Socrates and a founder of Idealism.

sional skill as the Sophists claimed was necessary, Socrates argued that a genuine education aimed to cultivate the knowledge that every person needed as a human being. It was the kind of education that cultivated morally excellent persons who acted according to reason. Once again, Socrates' assertion that there was a general education for every free human being provides a strong argument for liberal education and against vocational training.

Unlike the Sophists, Socrates denied that true wisdom would result from merely telling a student about some body of information or training him or her in a particular technique. He asserted that concepts, the basis of true knowledge, existed within the mind and could be brought to consciousness. Probing questions would stimulate the learner to discover the truth that was in his or her mind by bringing latent concepts to consciousness.

Socrates' basic epistemological goal was that human beings define themselves in terms of the criteria of universal truth. Through rigorous self-analysis, each person should seek the truth that was universally present in all members of the human race. As a teacher, Socrates asked probing questions that stimulated his students to investigate the perennial human concerns about the meaning of life, truth, and justice.[3] Through dialogue, Socrates and his students dealt with basic questions by defining them, criticizing them, and developing more adequate and comprehensive definitions.

Socratic education involved discipleship—that is, a close personal relationship between teacher and student designed to create within the student's character an ethical predisposition to discover and use truth to order and govern his or her life. In the past, this kind of ethical development was called character formation. Contemporary educators refer to it as modeling. That is, the teacher personifies desirable character traits and dispositions that are worthy of the learner's imitation.

Our knowledge about Socrates comes from Plato (427–347 B.C.), who was Socrates' student and a speculative philosopher in his own right. Plato, who founded the Academy in Athens in 387 B.C., wrote a number of philosophical works that have established the foundations of Western philosophy. Among them were *Protagoras,* which examined the issue of virtue; *Phaedo,* which examined the immortality of the soul; and *The Republic* and the *Laws,* which looked at both political and educational issues.

Like his mentor Socrates, Plato rejected the Sophists' claims that ethical behavior was situationally determined and that education could be reduced to specialized vocational or professional training. Plato based his metaphysical beliefs on the existence of an ideal, hence unchanging, world of perfect ideas, such as universal and timeless concepts of truth, goodness, justice, and beauty.[4] The individual examples or cases of these general concepts were imperfect reflections or representations of the perfect form. In structuring a philosophy based on such an unchanging order or reality, Plato was attacking the Sophists' relativism and reliance on sensory perception. In contrast, he asserted that human beings were good and honorable when their conduct conformed to the ideal and universal concepts of truth, goodness, and beauty.

Plato's epistemology, or theory of knowledge, was based on the concept of "reminiscence" or recollection by which human beings recalled the truths that were latently but unconsciously present in their minds. Reminiscence implied that every human being possessed a soul, which prior to birth had lived in a spiritual world of perfect forms or ideas. With the shock of birth—actually, an imprisoning of the psyche in a material flesh-and-blood body—this knowledge of the perfect ideas was repressed within the unconscious part of the mind. However, the ideas of the perfect forms were still there and could be brought to consciousness. Knowing required effort, however. The learner had to be ready and willing to learn, had to discard false opinion, and had to seek truth in a conscious fashion.

Genuine knowledge, according to Plato, was immaterial, intellectual, and eternal as were the perfect forms on which it was based. There is but one idea of perfection that is common to all human beings regardless of where and when they live or the circumstances under which they live. Like truth itself, a genuine education is also universal and timeless. Because reality can only be discovered intellectually, the best kind of education is also intellectual in nature. Although Plato developed his educational philosophy in ancient Greece, his ideas have been reiterated many times since then. Defenders of Liberal education have often relied on Plato's ideas, which are also the basis for the contemporary educational theory of Perennialism. For example, Allan Bloom, in his noted attack on relativism in *The Closing of the American Mind,* calls Plato's *Republic* "the book on education" which really explains Bloom's own experience as a teacher.[5]

In his famous allegory of the cave, Plato depicted humans as prisoners, who, chained in a dark cave, can only glimpse shadows reflected against a wall, rather than the objects of which they are reflections. Like these shadows, the perceptions of our senses are not reality but distorted images of it. True knowledge comes as we escape the cave of sensation and opinion and go into the light where the sun, the light of reason, shows things as they truly are.

While his allegory of the cave encouraged human beings to liberate themselves by finding universal truth, Plato's Idealism also stressed the importance of the political state. Plato compared the well-ordered political state with the well-functioning human organism. The perfectly functioning political state and the perfectly functioning person both conformed to the form of justice. In *The Republic,* Plato wrote about a perfect society ruled by an intellectual elite of philosopher-kings.[6]

Plato's ideal state existed to cultivate truth and virtue in its citizens. His political and educational theory rested on the assumptions that only knowledgeable persons should govern society and that all the republic's residents should contribute, according to their aptitude, to the general welfare. Education and educational agencies would have a key role in determining the role and functions that the individual exercised in the community.

An examination of the class composition of Plato's republic provides an idea of the functioning of the organic state and education's role in ensuring that the state functioned properly. Plato divided the inhabitants of his republic into three basic classes: the philosopher-kings, who were the intellectual rulers of the state; the auxiliaries, who were the state's military defenders; and the workers, who performed the services and produced the economic goods that the state needed. By way of analogy, the philosopher-kings could be compared to the state's mind, the auxiliaries to its limbs, and workers to its stomach. Assignment to one of these three basic classes depended on one's intellectual ability.

In Plato's republic, the educational system exercised a selecting role as it assessed the person's intellectual potentiality. Once the individual's intellectual potentiality had been determined, he or she received the education appropriate to this ability and ultimately to the function to be exercised in the political state.

The philosopher-kings, the supreme rulers of the political state, were highly educated intellectuals who, after a long period of training in philosophy and dialectic, had attained a vision of the truth. In Plato's political design, the philosopher-kings were virtuous, intelligent, and talented persons who had the capacity for leadership. The philosopher-king had the important assignment of determining the kind of education a person should have for his or her future role in the state.

The auxiliaries, or warriors, who comprised the second class were subordinate to the state's intellectual rulers. More willful than intellectual, the auxiliaries—because of their courage—were to defend the republic. Based on their capacities, the education of the auxiliaries was primarily military. The third class of people, the workers, who produced the state's goods and services, had a limited capacity for intellectual abstraction. Their education consisted of vocational training.

Although much more could be said about Plato's political and educational philosophy, the following generalizations are useful in contributing to our understanding of Idealism as a philosophy of education:

1. Idealism is a comprehensive worldview that embraces many strains of thought; it is so comprehensive that it includes among its adherents those who have stressed personal liberation and self-definition as well as those who have argued for the creation of an organic society in which persons are primarily identified as exercising a specific role in the total state system.
2. Idealism has encouraged a hierarchical view of people, society, and knowledge. Both the position of a person in society and a subject in the curriculum are in ranked order based on the ability to abstract or to be abstracted.

From the foregoing historical discussion based on Plato as a founder of Idealism in the Western tradition, we turn now to the philosophy of Idealism.

IDEALISM AS A SYSTEMATIC PHILOSOPHY

In this section, we will treat the following components of Idealism: (1) its metaphysical rationale, (2) epistemology, and (3) axiology.

Idealist Metaphysics

Idealism asserts the primacy of the mental, the spiritual, and the ideal as the basis of reality. It affirms that reality is essentially spiritual or mental and denies the possibility of knowing anything except ideas. In explaining the universe, Idealism posits ultimate reality solely in the mind and argues that the universe is an expression of a highly generalized intelligence and will.[7]

In explaining human nature, the Idealist holds that the human being's spiritual essence is its essential and permanent characteristic. The mind provides the elemental life force that gives the person vitality and dynamism. Mind is evidenced by doubting; doubting is thinking; thinking gives evidence of the presence of intellect or of mind.

The person's real self is nonmaterial, spiritual, or mental. Selfhood, an integrating core of personal values, provides identity for the person because it separates that which *is* from that which *is not* the self.

Reality is spiritual in substance rather than material. Although it may exhibit nonmental entities, the universe definitely contains spiritual or mental realities that are irreducible and hence really existent. Spirit is more inclusive than matter and encompasses it. Matter is dependent on spirit for spirit both energizes and vitalizes matter.

Although the spiritual is ultimately real, it is possible to speak of the "real" world and the world of "appearance" in the Idealist's perspective. The real world of mind and ideas is eternal, permanent, regular, and orderly. Representing a perfect order of reality, the eternal ideas are unalterable because change is inconsistent and unnecessary in a perfect world. It is possible, then, to assert the existence of absolute, universal, and eternal truth and value in contrast to changing sensations or opinion.

In contrast to eternal truth, the "world of appearance" or of opinion is characterized by change, imperfection, irregularity, and disorder. In terms of the real and the apparent, the educational task is to redirect students from sensation and opinion to the reality of ideas. just as Socrates and Plato argued against the relativism of the Sophists, today's educators need to create in their students a readiness to undertake the continuous and arduous search for the truth. Today's students need to free themselves from the relativism and shoddiness of opinion that says anything goes. They need to embark on a Socratic-like journey to find the universal truths that are present but latent in their minds.

Idealist metaphysics involves a transition from the notion of an individual mind to the assumption that the entire universe is itself also a larger and more comprehensive spiritual mind. Through the principle of relationship, the individual mind is related to other minds and to the Universal Mind. In other words, the individual comes to realize that what is occurring in the universe is also occurring within the self. The subjective individual mind can know other minds and can understand them. To know and interpret other minds implies that an order of intelligibility exists that can be comprehended. This leads to the assumption that there is a Universal Self, an all-encompassing entity from which all reality comes. Thus, the individual human mind is related to and is of the same spiritual substance as the Universal Mind.

The principle of intelligibility or the relationships of mind to mind can be explained by the concepts of the Macrocosm and the Microcosm. Idealists have given various names to the concept of the World or Macrocosmic Mind such as the ground-of-being, the Absolute Self, the World Mind, the First Cause, or the Universal. Regardless of the name, the Macrocosmic or Absolute Mind transcends all limiting qualifications. Because the Absolute Mind is underived, complete, perfect, and unconditioned, it cannot be changed in any way. The universe is one all-inclusive and complete mind of which the lesser minds are limited parts. The Universal, or Macrocosmic Mind, is an absolute person, which is continually thinking, valuing, perceiving, and willing. The Macrocosmic Mind or Self is both a substance and a process. Although the language may seem vague or poetical, the Macrocosm can be said to be thought thinking, contemplation contemplating, and will willing.

Although composed of the same substance as the whole, the Microcosm is a limited part of the whole, an individual, lesser self. A qualitative relationship exists between the Absolute Mind and the individual Microcosmic Self. The individual self, or mind, is a complete entity insofar as it is a self. However, in relationship to the universe, it is part of the whole. In the sense that the part is less than the whole, the individual self is qualitatively less than the whole.

Although subtle metaphysical distinctions run through Idealism, the following constitute the underlying basis of Idealist philosophy: (1) the universe is spiritual and contains distinctively mental, or nonmaterial, realities; (2) these mental realities are personal; and (3) the universe is one all-inclusive and complete part in which the lesser selves are genuine and identical parts or constituent members.

Idealist Epistemology

In order to explain Idealist epistemology, it should be remembered that the Absolute Mind is eternally thinking. The Finite Mind, or the Microcosmic human mind, though of the same spiritual substance as the Absolute Mind, is limited in its completeness. Nevertheless, the individual mind can communicate with and share the ideas of the Absolute Self or the Macrocosmic Mind, whose knowledge is complete. The human mind is emergent but limited. As an emerging personality, the individual human mind is on a quest to be united in the Absolute.

In Idealism, knowing is recognition or reminiscence of latent ideas that are preformed in the mind. By reminiscence, the human mind may discover the ideas of the Macrocosmic Mind in its own thoughts. Through intuition, introspection, and insight, the individual looks within his or her own mind and therein finds a copy of the Absolute. What is to be known is already present in the mind. The challenge of teaching and learning is to bring this latent knowledge to consciousness.

For the Idealist, the basic logic underlying the metaphysical and epistemological processes is that of relating the whole and the part. Mind is essentially a process by which relationships are ordered on the basis of whole–part logic. Truth exists within the Macrocosm, or the Absolute, in an order or pattern that is logical, systematic, and related. Each proposition is related to a larger and more comprehensive higher proposition. While the whole includes the parts, the parts must be consistent with the whole.

According to the Idealists, truth is a set of closely related, orderly, and systematic relationships. To be, or to exist, means to be involved systematically in the whole–part, or Macrocosmic–Microcosmic, relationship. As an assimilator and arranger, mind locates consistency and exposes inconsistency. The properly functioning intellect seeks to establish a perspective based on relating the parts to the whole. The Whole Mind, or the Macrocosmic Mind, is contemplating the universe according to a total perspective that orders time and space. The properly functioning individual mind, striving to imitate the Universal Mind, seeks to fashion a coherent perspective into the universe. The consistent mind is able to relate the parts—time, space, circumstance, event—into a coherent pattern or whole. Inconsistency occurs when time, place, circumstance, and condition are unrelated and cannot be put into perspective.

Idealist Epistemology and the Educative Process

According to Idealist epistemology, education's major goal is to stimulate learners to achieve a more vital and fuller identification with the Absolute Mind, or the Macrocosm. Learning is a process by which students come into a gradually expanding mental awareness that leads to self-definition based on a comprehensive understanding or perspective of the universe.

As a highly intellectual process, learning is the recalling of and the working with ideas. Because reality is mental, education also is concerned with concepts or ideas. People become educated as they systematically bring ideas to consciousness and arrange them into a system in which the part, or the individual, is related to the whole.

Idealists support the subject-matter curriculum in which various ideas, or concepts, are organized in their relationship to each other. The various learned disciplines or subjects contain necessary concepts that are related to each other and that are referred to through symbols. For example, a word is a sign of something, or a symbol of it. Symbols refer to or point to concepts. Learning is a self-active process that occurs when the learner recalls the concept to which the symbol refers.

Throughout history, humankind has developed bodies of related concepts, or conceptual systems, such as the clusters of linguistic, mathematical, and aesthetic systems. Each conceptual system has symbols that refer to the various concepts. While many conceptual systems and their corresponding learned disciplines exist, these various subject matters form a larger synthesis. The various subject matters represent the varying dimensions of the Absolute that have unfolded and been discovered over time by human beings. However, their cause, origin, and culmination are in the underlying unity. For example, the liberal arts are arranged into many conceptual systems, or learned disciplines, such as history, language, philosophy, mathematics, chemistry, and so forth. However, the highest degree of knowledge is that which sees the relationships of these various subject matters as an integrated unity.

Idealist Axiology

In Idealist axiology, values are more than mere human preferences; they really exist and are inherent intrinsically in the universe. Value experience is essentially an imitation of the Good, which is present in the Absolute. As such, values are absolute, eternal, unchanging, and universal. It is lack of perspective produced by sensation, opinion, or confusion that causes people to be mistaken in their ethical decision making.

In our search for values, Idealists tell us to look to the ethical core found in the wisdom of the human race which has persisted over time. Ethical conduct grows out of the permanent aspects of a social and cultural tradition that in reality is the wisdom of the past functioning in the present. Rich sources of value education can be found in history, literature, religion, and philosophy.

For the Idealist, our aesthetic experience comes from the idealization of the world around us. Art portrays our ideas about reality. Art succeeds when it portrays the idealized representations of that which appears commonplace in our life. Good art—literature, drama, painting, sculpture—succeeds when it creates perspective and harmony. Like a work of art, an aesthetic personality is one of harmony and balance. In aesthetic education, the student should be exposed to the great works of art and literature and should try to find the essence that makes them timeless.

THE EDUCATIONAL IMPLICATIONS OF IDEALISM

In the following section, we examine (1) the educational goals of Idealism, (2) the school, (3) the Idealist curriculum, (4) the attitudinal dimension, (5) Idealist methodology, and (6) the teacher–learner relationship.

Idealism's Educational Goals

The overriding goal of an Idealist education is to encourage students to be truth seekers. To seek the truth and to live according to it means that people must first want to know the truth and then be willing to work to attain it through careful and rigorous study. Idealist education aims at a personal conversion to the good, true, and beautiful. Idealist education has the following objectives that are intended to help students become truth seekers:

1. The teaching–learning process should assist students to realize fully the potentialities inherent in their human nature.
2. The school, as a social institution, should expose students to the wisdom contained in the cultural heritage so that they can know, share in, and extend it through their own personal contributions.

The goal of an Idealist education may seem too abstract and altruistic for today's society. Just as Socrates and Plato combated the relativism of the Sophists in ancient Greece, so too do contemporary Idealists battle against materialism, acquisitiveness, and vocationalism. Idealists would challenge educational goal-setting, which is motivated by consumerism and a desire for status.

The Idealists see a genuine education as being general rather than training for a specific occupation or profession. The goal of vocationalism is expertise in job performance rather than wholeness and excellence as a human being. While Idealists would not oppose people being prepared to earn their livelihood and contribute to the economic well-being of society, they would oppose—as a matter of educational policy—giving vocational training priority over general education.

Acquisitiveness and a crude vocationalism stem from what Idealists would diagnose as a major ill of modern times—namely, a lack of wholeness caused by a myopic vision and a limited perspective. From the time of Plato, Idealists have condemned materialism as an obstacle to a true vision of reality. Such a true vision comes from establishing a proper distance from the sensory world of things so that one can see objects, causes, motives, and ambition in a broad and long-range vista and with a sense of relationship. Whether or not we agree with the metaphysical and epistemological underpinnings of Idealism, the sense of perspective and relationship that Idealism cultivates is a worthy educational goal.

The School

The role of the school, as an educational agency, derives from the Idealist's view of civilization and of how institutions promote progress.[8] Idealists see progress as the historical evolution of human culture from its primitive origins to successive and cumulative stages of higher and advanced levels of civilization. Throughout the centuries of human history, the corpus of knowledge has grown as each generation transmits and adds to it. The words *successive* and *cumulative* have a special meaning for the school. Its administrators and teachers are to arrange knowledge as a structured curriculum in which subjects, that is, organized bodies of knowledge, succeed each other in increasingly complex and sophisticated content. As students progress through schooling, their learning is cumulative in that the knowledge attained at one level or grade is added to in the next higher level.

Civilization preserves truth and knowledge by institutionalizing them. In this way, the achievements of each generation are transmitted to the succeeding generation. In particular, it is the task of the school to preserve past knowledge, skill, and discipline; it prepares children for the future by transmitting the cultural heritage in a deliberate fashion by way of systematically ordered, sequential, and cumulative curricula.

The Idealist Curriculum

Idealists maintain that the curriculum is a body of intellectual subject matters, or learned disciplines, that are basically ideational and conceptual. These various conceptual systems explain and are based on particular manifestations of the Absolute. However, all of these conceptual systems are derived from and lead eventually to the one unifying and integrating concept, idea, or cause.

Conceptual systems derived from the Universal Absolute constitute the cultural inheritance, a legacy that should be added to by each generation. The Idealist curriculum can be viewed as a hierarchy in which the summit is occupied by the most general disciplines, namely philosophy and theology, which explain humankind's most essential relationships to God and to the Cosmos. According to this hierarchical principle, the more particular subjects are justified by their relationship to the more general subjects. The more general subject matters are abstract and transcend the limitations of a particular time, place, and circumstance. Because they are general and abstract, they can transfer to a wide variety of situations. Mathematics, in its pure form, is a very useful discipline that provides the opportunities for dealing with abstractions. History and literature are also ranked high in the curriculum hierarchy. In addition to being cognitive stimuli, the historical and literary disciplines are value laden. History, biography, and autobiography can be examined as sources of moral and cultural models, exemplars, and heroines and heroes. History can be viewed as the record of the Absolute unfolding over time and in the lives of persons, especially those men and women of heroic dimension.

Somewhat lower in the curriculum hierarchy can be found the various sciences concerned with particular cause-and-effect relationships. As the key to communication, language, a necessary skill, is cultivated at the elementary level.

The Attitudinal Dimension of Education

Because the ethical core is contained within and is transmitted by the cultural heritage, subjects such as philosophy, theology, history, literature, and artistic criticism are also rich sources of value. These subjects, which fuse the cognitive and the axiological, are the bearers of the human moral tradition and represent the generalized ethical and cultural conscience of civilization. The humanities can be closely studied and used as sources of cognitive stimulation. At the same time, these historical and literary sources can be absorbed emotionally and used as the basis for the construction of models of value. Value education, according to the Idealist conception, requires that the student be exposed to worthy models and exemplars so that their styles might be imitated and extended. Therefore, the student should be exposed to and should examine critically the great works of art and literature that have endured through time.

Idealist Methodology

The Idealist conception of instructional method is derived from Idealism's concept of epistemology. The thought process is essentially that of recognition, an introspective self-examination in which the learner examines the contents of his or her own mind and therein finds the truth that is shared by all others because it reflects the universal truth present in the World Mind. Idealist educators such as Friedrich Froebel, the founder of the kindergarten, have emphasized the principle of the learner's own self-activity. The learning process is made more efficient by the stimulation offered by a teacher and school environment committed to intellectual activity. Immersion in the cultural heritage, via the curriculum, is part of formal schooling, according to Idealists.

The learner's own self-activity is related to the learner's interests and willingness to expend effort. Students have their own intuitive self-interests, which attract them to certain acts, events, and objects. With such intrinsic interests, no external prodding is needed. When interest is intrinsic, or internal to the learner, the positive attraction of the task is such that no conscious exertion is needed.

Although learners have their own interests, not all learning is easy. Students may be deluded by the world of appearance and may seek ends that are not genuinely related to their own self-development. At these times, effort may be required when the task does not elicit sufficient interest on students' parts. At such a time, the teacher, a mature model of cultural values, should encourage every student's redirection to truth. After an expenditure of interest and the application of self-discipline, the student may become interested in the learning task. Again, the cultural heritage comes into play to generate the student's interests. The broader the exposure to the cultural heritage, the more likely it is that the student will have many interests. The more interests that are present, the greater are the possibilities for further self-development.

Although no one particular method can be specified, the Socratic dialogue is certainly appropriate to the Idealist classroom. The Socratic dialogue is a process in which the mature person, the teacher, acts to stimulate the learner's awareness of ideas. The teacher must be prepared to ask leading questions about crucial human concerns. When using the Socratic dialogue in a classroom situation, the teacher must be able to use the group process so that a community of interest develops in which all students want to participate. The Socratic method requires skillful questioning on the part of the teacher and thus is not a simple recall of facts that have been memorized in advance. However, this may be a necessary first step so that the dialogue does not degenerate into a pooling of ignorant and uninformed opinion.

The use of the Socratic dialogue can be illustrated by the following example in which a high school English teacher is discussing Mark Twain's *Huckleberry Finn* with students. The class is examining the moral dilemma that Huck encounters when he must either follow the law of the state or the higher law of his conscience. Specifically, Huck must decide if he should surrender the escaped slave Jim to the authorities for return to his slave master, or if he should help Jim escape to a free state. Huck's dilemma reveals the apparent conflict between the more general and abstract values and those that are more immediate and particular.

The teacher uses *Huckleberry Finn,* a classic work of the American experience, to represent perennial values. It is important that the teacher place the story in its historical and literary context so that the students are aware of its relationship to the American experience. The relationships of the book to the history of the Dred Scott decision and the fugitive slave law should also be made clear.

It is important that students have read the book before discussing it. While welcoming a free-flowing discussion, the Idealist teacher does not encourage misinformation or permit unfounded opinion to obscure the real meaning of the learning episode. Once the students are aware of Mark Twain's own life, the context of the novel, the characters, and the plot, then the serious exploratory learning can take place through the asking of stimulating questions. Avoiding those questions that can be answered with a simple yes or no, the teacher's questions should lead to still other questions.

The conflict between civil law and higher law is a crucial issue that has persisted throughout human history. What should a person do when the law of the state and the dictates of his or her conscience conflict? Is there a distinction between the good person and the good citizen? Should the person follow his or her conscience and take the risks attendant to such a decision? Should he or she seek to change the law? Is the inner law of conscience part of a universal and higher law that binds all human beings?

Once the students have explored the theme of the human conflict presented by Huck's dilemma, other instances of the same conflict can be illustrated by pointing to examples of civil disobedience as practiced by Henry David Thoreau, Mohandas Gandhi, and Martin Luther King, Jr. The moral questions raised by the Holocaust during World War II and the Nuremberg trials of the Nazi leaders can be examined to illustrate the persistence of these broad moral issues.

Imitation of the model or exemplar is also a part of the Idealist methodology. Students are exposed to valuable lessons based on worthy models or exemplars from history, literature, religion, biography, and philosophy. They are encouraged to study and to analyze the model so that the particular person being studied serves as a source of value. The teacher is also a constant model in that he or she is a mature embodiment of the culture's highest values. Although the teacher should be selected for competency in both subject matter and pedagogy, he or she should be an aesthetic person who is worthy of imitation by students. Students imitate the model by incorporating the exemplar's value schema into their own lives. Emulation is not mimicry; rather, it is an extension of the good into one's own life.

The Teacher–Learner Relationship

In the teacher–learner relationship, emphasis is placed on the teacher's central and crucial role. As a mature person, the Idealist teacher should be one who has established a cultural perspective and has integrated various roles into an harmonious value orchestration. While the learner is immature and seeks the perspective that the culture can provide, this does not mean that the student's personality should be manipulated by the teacher. The student is striving to gain a mature perspective into his or her own personality. As in the case of all people, the learner's spiritual nature and personality are of great worth. Thus, the teacher should respect the learner and should assist the learner to realize the fullness of his or her own personality. Because the teacher is a model and mature representative of the culture, selection of the teacher is of great importance. The teacher should embody values, love students, and be an exciting and enthusiastic person.

J. Donald Butler, in *Idealism in Education,* has identified some of the desired qualities of the good teacher. According to Butler, the teacher should (1) personify culture and reality for the student; (2) be a specialist in human personality; (3) as an expert in the learning process, be capable of uniting expertise with enthusiasm; (4) merit students' friendship; (5) awaken students' desire to learn; (6) realize that teaching's moral significance lies in its goal of perfecting human beings; and (7) aid in the cultural rebirth of each generation.[9]

CONCLUSION

Idealism, a philosophy proclaiming the spiritual nature of the human being and the universe, asserts that the good, true, and beautiful are permanently part of the structure of a related, coherent, orderly, and unchanging universe. Idealist educators prefer a subject-matter curriculum that emphasizes truths gained from enduring theological, philosophical, historical, literary, and artistic works. The following concepts, rooted in Idealist philosophy, have a special relevance for educational practice:

1. Education is a process of unfolding and developing that which is a potential in the human person.
2. Learning is a discovery process in which the learner is stimulated to recall the truths present within the mind.
3. The teacher should be a moral and cultural exemplar or model of values that represent the highest and best expression of personal and humane development.

DISCUSSION QUESTIONS

1. Describe the metaphysics, epistemology, logic, and axiology associated with Idealism.

2. What is the philosophical rationale for the Idealist rejection of situational ethics?

3. Provide examples of and examine the conflict between absolute and relative values and ethics.

4. Examine the selective or sifting function that education exercises in Plato's *Republic*. Determine if contemporary schools exercise a similar role.

5. Identify your educational goals. Would an Idealist agree or disagree with them?

6. Analyze the role of the school according to Idealism.

7. Analyze the rationale used by Idealists in organizing the curriculum.

8. In your own educational experience, identify examples of modeling or imitation.

INQUIRY PROJECTS

- In a research paper, analyze the educational ideas of one of the following: Johann Gottlieb Fichte, Georg Wilhelm Friedrich Hegel, Ralph Waldo Emerson, William T. Harris, Friedrich Froebel.
- Examine the philosophical method used by Henry David Thoreau in *Walden*.
- Prepare a lesson plan based on the Socratic method.
- Read several autobiographical works or novels dealing with teaching. Determine the degree to which the principal character was a model for his or her students.
- Examine several textbooks used in teacher education programs. Determine how the authors of these books define the role of the school. Compare and contrast their definitions with the Idealist view of the school.
- Identify the subjects offered in the contemporary high school. Analyze these subjects in priority according to the Idealist rationale for curriculum organization.
- Identify a classic work of literature. Indicate how this book conforms to the Idealist orientation.

FURTHER READINGS

Brumbaugh, Robert S., and Nathaniel M. Lawrence. *Philosophers on Education: Six Essays on the Foundations of Western Thought*. Boston: Houghton Mifflin, 1963.

Butler, J. Donald. *Idealism in Education*. New York: Harper & Row, 1966.

Butler, J. Donald. *Four Philosophies and Their Practice in Education and Religion*. New York: Harper & Row, 1968.

Colman, John E. *The Master Teachers and the Art of Teaching*. New York: Pitman, 1967.

Eliot, Alexander. *Socrates, A Fresh Appraisal of the Most Celebrated Case in History*. New York: Crown Publishers, 1967.

Graham, William. *Idealism: An Essay, Metaphysical and Critical*. Bristol, England: Thoemmes, 1991.

Greene, Theodore M. "A Liberal Christian Idealist Philosophy of Education," in *Modern Philosophies of Education,* 54th Yearbook, Part I, National Society for the Study of Education. Chicago: University of Chicago Press, 1955.

Gulley, Norman. *The Philosophy of Socrates.* New York: St. Martin's Press, 1968.

Nettleship, Richard L. *The Theory of Education in the Republic of Plato.* New York: Teachers College Press, Columbia University, 1968.

The Republic of Plato. Translated by A. D. Lindsay. New York: J. M. Dent, 1950.

Rescher, Nicholas. *Human Knowledge in Idealistic Perspective.* Princeton, NJ: Princeton University Press, 1992.

Sacks, Mark. *The World We Found: The Limits of Ontological Talk.* London: Duckworth, 1989.

Samuelson, William G., and Fred A. Markowitz. *An Introduction to Philosophy in Education.* New York: Philosophical Library, 1987.

Schelling, Friedrich Wilhelm J. *Idealism and the Endgame of Three Essays.* Edited and translated by Thomas Pfau. Albany: University of New York Press, 1994.

Strain, John Paul. "Idealism: A Clarification of an Educational Philosophy," *Educational Theory,* 25, No. 3 (summer 1975): 263–271.

Taylor, A. E. *Socrates.* New York: Anchor Press, 1953.

Webb, Thomas E. *The Veil of Isis: A Series of Essays on Idealism.* Bristol, England: Thoemmes, 1990.

Weissman, David. *Intuition and Ideality.* Albany: State University of New York Press, 1987.

ENDNOTES

1. A recent publication is Friedrich Wilhelm J. von Schelling, *Idealism and the Endgame Theory: Three Essays,* ed. and trans. Thomas Pfau (Albany: State University of New York Press, 1994).

2. A. E. Taylor, *Socrates* (New York: Anchor Press, 1953). Also see Norman Gulley, *The Philosophy of Socrates* (New York: St. Martin's Press, 1968) and Alexander Eliot, *Socrates, A Fresh Appraisal of the Most Celebrated Case in History* (New York: Crown, 1967).

3. John E. Colman, *The Master Teachers and the Art of Teaching* (New York: Pitman, 1967), pp. 28–34.

4. Robert S. Brumbaugh and Nathaniel M. Lawrence, *Philosophers on Education: Six Essays on the Foundations of Western Thought* (Boston: Houghton Mifflin, 1963), pp. 10–48.

5. Allan Bloom, *The Closing of the American Mind* (New York: Simon and Schuster, 1987), p. 381.

6. *The Republic of Plato,* trans. A. D. Lindsay (New York: J. M. Dent, 1950) and Richard L. Nettleship, *The Theory of Education in the Republic of Plato* (New York: Teachers College Press, Columbia University, 1968).

7. For treatments of Idealism, see J. Donald Butler, *Idealism in Education* (New York: Harper & Row, 1966), and Sarvepalli Radhakrishnan, *An Idealist View of Life* (London: Unwin Books, 1932). An analysis is provided by John P. Strain, "Idealism: A Clarification of an Educational Philosophy," *Educational Theory,* 25 (summer 1975): 263–271.

8. Strain, "Idealism: Educational Philosophy," pp. 263–271.

9. Butler, *Idealism in Education,* p. 120.

▶ 3

Realism and Education

Like Idealism, Realism is among the Western world's most enduring philosophies. In contrast to Idealists, Realists assert that objects exist regardless of our perception of them. For example, this book that you are reading exists as an "object-in-itself," and its existence does not depend on your perception or use of it. Even if you were not reading it, this text would still exist. The essential doctrines of Realism are the following:

1. We live in a world of real existence in which many things, such as persons and objects, exist.
2. The objects of reality exist regardless of the uses we make of them.
3. By using our reason, it is possible for us to have some knowledge of these objects.
4. Knowledge about these objects, the laws that govern them, and their relationships to each other is the most reliable guide to human conduct.[1]

In summary, Realism can be defined as a philosophical position that asserts the existence of an objective order of reality and the possibility of human beings gaining knowledge about that reality. It further prescribes that our behavior should conform to this knowledge.

While it is difficult to find many manifestations of Idealism in contemporary schooling, one can find many examples of Realism. For instance, the subject-matter curricula found in many secondary schools and colleges consist of discretely organized bodies of knowledge, such as history, language, mathematics, science, and so forth. These various subject matters are construed to represent humankind's carefully organized and systematic exploration of reality. High school and college students will be found reading textbooks written by experts in the learned disciplines or attending classes taught by specialists in the various subject matters. In this chapter, we will examine the basic principles of Realist philosophy and analyze its educational implications. Before doing so, however, we will examine the historical origins of Realism as expressed by the ancient Greek philosopher Aristotle (384–322 B.C.).

ARISTOTLE: THE FOUNDER OF REALISM

As is true of Idealists, there are also varieties of Realists. For example, Classical Realists trace their philosophical origins to ancient Greek philosophizing; Scientific Realists see the natural sciences and the scientific method as the basis for understanding reality; Theistic Realists, among them the Thomists, envision a supernatural supreme being as the creator of the natural world.[2] These varieties of Realism have their common origin in Aristotle's work. In this section of the chapter, we will present a general overview of Aristotle's contribution to the history of ideas, and then examine his philosophical concepts that form the basis of Realist philosophy.

Aristotle in the History of Educational Ideas

Aristotle, a student of Plato, was for a time the tutor of Alexander the Great, the Greek king who conquered most of the known world. Of more educational significance, however, was that Aristotle founded the Lyceum, a philosophical school, in Athens in 334 B.C., and wrote on such philosophical matters as metaphysics, logic, and ethics, and on the natural sciences of astronomy, zoology, and botany.[3]

Aristotle's work in the natural sciences described an ascending order of natural progression. At the lowest level in the order came lifeless things, inanimate objects such as rocks and minerals. Upward, in the next higher order, came plants and vegetation, which, although alive in comparison to inanimate objects, lacked many of the powers of the animals. In the animal kingdom, there was a continuous scale of ascent upward to human beings, who were the highest in the hierarchy because of their rationality. In this brief description of natural phenomena, Aristotle's propensity to classify and categorize should be noted. This proclivity was followed by later Realists who saw classification as the most accurate and useful way of organizing our knowledge of the objects found in natural reality.

In the *Nicomachean Ethics,* Aristotle emphasized the Hellenic ideals of moderation, harmony, and balance, which became the core of Realist axiology or value theory. His *Politics,* like Plato's *Republic,* recognized that a reciprocal relationship existed between the good human being and the good citizen.[4]

A bust of Aristotle (384–322 B.C.), the Greek philosopher, who was a student of Plato and a founder of Realism.

Aristotle saw a basic duality in human nature in that human beings possess an immaterial soul or mind as well as a material body. Like the animals in the lower orders, human beings have appetites and physical needs that must be satisfied if they are to survive. Unlike animals, the human's mind or intellect gives one the power to think. The truly educated person exercises reason in guiding his or her ethical conduct and political behavior.

Aristotle's ethical theory was based on his conception of human rationality. Like the universe, humankind was moving to a prescribed goal. The goal of human life was to achieve happiness, which meant that the person had fully realized his or her potentiality. Educationally, the liberal arts and sciences—the studies intended for free persons—contributed to achieving this goal because they sharpened human reason.

In the medieval era, Aristotle was rediscovered by scholastic educators, such as Thomas Aquinas, who developed a synthesis of Aristotelian philosophy and

Christian theology. Contemporary humanist educators, such as Robert Hutchins, Mortimer Adler, and Harry Broudy, made Aristotle's Realism an important foundation for their own educational philosophies. From this general treatment of Aristotle's contribution to Western thought, we now proceed to a more detailed examination of his philosophy and its implications for education.

The Aristotelian Basis of Realism

While Plato was concerned with an abstract world of perfect forms or ideas, Aristotle used common-sense observation to investigate a public world of natural and social phenomena. As a result of empirical observation and research, Aristotle developed a metaphysical system that construed being to be a uniting of actuality and potentiality. Whereas actuality is complete and perfect, potentiality has the capability of being perfected. In his explanation of reality, Aristotle referred to four formal causes. He defined a cause as that which in any way influenced the production of something. The Material Cause, or matter, is that out of which a being is made. As the substratum of existence, matter is indeterminate but has the potential to become an object. Form, or the Formal Cause, is that into which a thing is made. Form, the principle of actuality, provides the design that shapes and gives structure to an object. In terms of knowing, form—the essence of a being—is the object of intellectual knowledge.

Essence refers to the qualities that are necessary for an object to be what it is; these defining qualities, or necessary conditions, remain unchanged despite alterations or changes in an object's accidental qualities.

For Aristotle, the union of form and matter constituted an individual concrete substance. From form came the object's essential or unalterable qualities; from matter came the object's imperfections, limitations, and individuating qualities. The Efficient Cause is the agency that brings about the action, or motion, from potentiality to actuality. For Aristotle, all natural processes were developmental actions that brought out the latent possibilities by bringing into actuality those perfections already contained as potency in matter. The Final Cause referred to the direction toward which the object is tending.

Throughout the Aristotelian metaphysical system is the pronounced predilection to dualism—the tendency to view reality as composed of two constituent elements. *Dualism* means that two related entities exist, neither of which can be reduced to the other. For example, mind and body are two separate entities. Metaphysical dualism asserts that the two essential components of reality, while related, remain distinct. Thus, Aristotle viewed existence as the uniting of the two elements of actuality and potentiality, of form and matter. As we will point out later, this dualistic conception of reality profoundly affected Western thought. Human beings are viewed as composite creatures composed of spirit and matter, or mind and matter. Such a dichotomous view of human nature leads to distinctions that have significant educational consequences. Knowledge can be separated into the theoretical and the practical arts; aesthetic experience can be viewed as dealing with either the fine or applied arts; education can be categorized as either liberal or vocational. In the context of these Aristotelian dualisms, that which was abstract, theoretical, fine, and liberal was given priority over that which was practical, applied, and vocational. In the chapter on Pragmatism, we will examine John Dewey's attack on dualism.

The Aristotelian conception of a dualistic universe can also be seen in the categories of substance and accident. Substance is the ultimate "element," that which exists of and by itself, of which any object is made; it is the underlying reality to which the primary qualities of an object adhere. Substance is the continuing essence of an object that remains constant through all the alterations in the object's accidental characteristics.

In contrast, *accident* refers to the variable changes that do not alter the essence of a being but individuate it. In various treatments of Pragmatism, one often encounters the statement that reality is constantly changing. The Realist would observe that to measure change, there must be some stable object that is changing. For the Realist, that which undergoes change is substantial, whereas the changes themselves are accidental. For example, all human beings share a common human nature, which is their essence. Particular persons, however, are of different races, ethnic groups, weights, and heights. These individualistic characteristics are in the category of the accident.

When Aristotelians refer to the essence of a human being, they mean those substantial elements that are unchanging, regardless of time, place, and circumstances. It is from these universals that educators should establish the curriculum. For example, Aristotelians define humans as rational beings who possess an intellect that enables them to abstract from experience and to frame and act on various choices. Regardless of their race, nationality, occupation, or sex, all human beings have the power to reason. Nevertheless, particular persons live at various times and in different places. Varying environmental and social conditions contribute to cultural variations within the common human experience. Although a particular person may be American, Chinese, Russian, or Nigerian because of the accident of being born in a particular place, all people share a common human nature. As a result of being born in a certain location, some people will speak a particular language, such as English, Russian, Swahili, or French. But regardless of their particular languages, all people use language as a means of communication.

The following quotation from Robert Hutchins, a modern follower of Aristotle's philosophy, clearly distinguishes between substance and accident. In *The Higher Learning in America,* Hutchins analyzed the educational implications of this Aristotelian distinction.

> *One purpose of education is to draw out the elements of our common human nature. These elements are the same in any time or place. The*

notion of educating a man to live in any particular time or place, to
adjust him to any particular environment, is therefore foreign to a true
conception of education.

Education implies teaching. Teaching implies knowledge. Knowl-
edge is truth. The truth is everywhere the same. Hence education should
be everywhere the same. I do not overlook the possibilities of differences
in organization, in administration, in local habits and customs. These
are details. I suggest that the heart of any course of study designed for
the whole people will be, if education is rightly understood, the same at
any time, in any place, under any political, social, or economic condi-
tions. Even the administrative details are likely to be similar because
all societies have generic similarity.[5]

Hutchins's comments reveal the Realist's overarching conception that the
human being is rational and should live according to reason. From this it follows
that the basic goal of education is to cultivate the human being's rational potentiality so that it might be actualized. In *De Anima* and the *Nichomachean Ethics,*
Aristotle asserted that certain general principles of human nature and behavior
were discernible. Along with other animals, humans share the functions of nutrition, locomotion, reproduction, and respiration. But as a more complex and
sophisticated being, humans also have functions of sense, imagination, habit,
pain, and pleasure. Following his dualistic world view, Aristotle described the
two planes of human existence. As a rational being, human beings are abstrac-
tive, symbolic, and choice-making creatures. However, a nonrational component
also exists in human nature in that the same person who is rational is also emotional and volitional. The human being's reason for being is to recognize, cultivate, develop, and use his or her rationality. The greatest source of human
happiness lies in the active cultivation of rationality, which contributes to self-
actualization or self-cultivation and self-perfection. The person who truly acts as
a human being is governed by his or her highest and defining power—reason.
Although emotions are the means to experience pleasure, and will is the instrument of obtaining ends, both the emotions and the will are governed properly by
reason. When governed by appetites, emotions, and will, the human being acts
unintelligently, is unreasoning, and debases his or her own essential humanity.
When governed by reason, human beings can develop the excellence of moral
character that is a mean between the extreme of repression and the uninhibited
expression or indulgence of passions and appetites.

In *Politics,* Aristotle argued for a general education that cultivated a reciprocal relationship between the properly educated person and the properly educated citizen.[6] The liberally educated rational person would also be the worthy
citizen of the *polis,* or society.

For Aristotle, education was to be a means of aiding human beings in their
quest for *Eudaimonia,* or happiness, which meant possessing excellence. Liberal,

or liberating, education aided human beings in perfecting their reason. As reason is perfected, so is the total human being. When directed to the perfection of rational inquiry, education is liberating in that it assists human beings to define their own future through deliberation and action.[7]

Aristotle believed that the curriculum should conform to the patterns of human growth and development. Infants were to have the opportunities for play, physical activity, and be readied for proper studies. Before adolescence, the major educative emphasis was on cultivating proper values and moral predispositions. Proper attention was to be given to physical exercises and activities. Children were to learn the fundamentals of calculating, reading, and writing that they would need for subsequent study.

For youths aged fourteen to twenty-one, Aristotle designed a curriculum that stressed intellectual subjects such as arithmetic, geometry, astronomy, music, grammar, literature, poetry, rhetoric, ethics, and politics. After age twenty-one, the more sophisticated intellectual disciplines such as physics, biology, psychology, logic, and metaphysics were introduced.

From our discussion of Aristotle's philosophical and educational doctrines, we next examine Realism as a systematic philosophy.

REALISM AS A SYSTEMATIC PHILOSOPHY

In Chapter 2, we examined Idealism in terms of its metaphysical, epistemological, and axiological components. We will use the same mode of analysis in examining Realism.

Realist Metaphysics

Realism's essential metaphysical proposition is that we live in an objective order of reality that exists independent of and external to our minds. Objects, that is, material things, exist in time and in space, and we can come to know something about them through our knowing process that involves sensation and abstraction. An object, then, is outside of us, and consists of two dimensions—matter and form. Matter, the material substratum of an object, has the potential of becoming something. To become an object, matter has to be organized according to some design or structure, By way of analogy, we might think about the carpenter using wood (matter) according to a blueprint or design (form). Wood has the potential of becoming a chair, a desk, or a house. To build one of these objects, the builder has to fashion the material (the lumber) according to the blueprint. The dualistic nature of reality should be noted. Matter and form are both necessary to an object. In our next section on Realist epistemology, we will examine the interrelationship between Realist metaphysics and epistemology.

Realist Epistemology

Realist metaphysics assumes the existence of an objective order of reality in which objects are independent of, and exist before, our experiencing of them. As we come to know this reality, we come to know the nature of things such as the structure of the universe, of human nature, of society, and of natural phenomena.

For the Realist, knowing is to have knowledge about an object. Cognition, or knowing, involves an interaction between the human mind and the world outside of the mind. Such an interaction is between the human senses and energy emanating from the object.

Sensation concerns the material component of an object, or matter. Because the material is changing, sensation varies from time to time and from place to place. It is contingent and circumstantial. While sensation is the beginning of knowing, it is not the end of knowledge. Our knowledge about an object originates with sensations such as light, sound, pressure, heat, cold, vapor, or taste that come from the object. Each of our senses has a proper object of sensation. Touch apprehends pressure or physical resistance; temperature reveals if the object is hot or cold; taste, localized in the tongue, detects flavors; smell, localized in the nasal passages, informs us of odors; the object of hearing is sound; sight, the highest and most objective sense, has color as its proper object. Sensation, then, first involves the physical action of something impinging on our sensory organs.

We first experience the immediate qualities of the object such as color, odor, taste, hardness, softness, and pitch. Needing no other senses to mediate for them, these immediate qualities are conveyed to us from the outside by the different energy patterns that activate the sensory organs. The mediate sensory qualities of size, distance, position, shape, motion, and weight are conveyed to us by the immediate sensory qualities.

As a result of sensation, we acquire sensory data, which our mind sorts out and arranges in computerlike fashion. Our common sense, the intellectual power of abstraction, sorts out our sense perceptions into the necessary conditions, those qualities that are always present in an object, and the contingent conditions, those sometimes found in the object. The necessary qualities, which are always present in the object, are its essential constituents and form the basis of our concept of the object. A concept, a meaning that applies to all things of the same class, has qualities that it shares with other objects in the same class but with no other objects.

For example, let us suppose that we are attending a dog show and see a wide variety of dogs ranging from pugs, collies, Great Danes, German shepherds to many other breeds. Although these animals differ in size, proportion, and certain characteristics, there are some essential qualities that they share as dogs. From our sense perceptions of many kinds of dogs, our mind sorts out and isolates those that they share in common. These common elements constitute our concept of what is necessary to be a dog.

For the Realist, knowing is a twofold process involving sensation and abstraction. This process corresponds to the Realist conception of a dualistic universe composed of a material and a structural, or formal, component. Whereas sensation has to do with matter, abstraction relates to form or structure. Our senses encounter objects and bring us information about the material aspects of these objects. Through the senses, data about the material components of an object are conveyed to our mind in much the same way that data are programmed into a computer. Once entered into the mind, these sensory data are sorted out, classified, and catalogued. Through the process of abstraction, our mind, or common sense, arranges the data into two broad categories: the necessary ones that are always found in an object, and those that are contingent or sometimes found in an object. Those that are always present are necessary or essential to that object and constitute its form, or structure. Form is the proper object of abstraction.

Conceptualization, or concept formation, takes place when our mind has extracted and abstracted the form of an object and recognized it as belonging to a class. Objects are classified, or put in a category, when we recognize them as possessing qualities that they share with other members of the class but not with objects belonging to different classes.

A further example helps to illustrate the Realist epistemological strategy. In our experiences, we encounter other human beings. Some of these people are of different heights and weights, speak different languages, and are of different ethnic origins. They may be Chinese, Russian, English, Nigerian, or Mexican, to name only a few of the many nationalities of people. However, underlying the variations of size, weight, height, ethnic origin, and nationality, there is something, some "whatness" or "quidity," that is common to all human beings. A common human nature identifies them as members of the class *Homo sapiens* and not of other classes of objects. A human being is different from a horse, a tree, a house, or a rock. The varieties of human beings share something that is common to them all. This commonness is what differentiates them from other objects; it is their defining quality or characteristic.

Realist epistemology has been referred to as a "spectator theory," which means that we are observers of reality. While we all commonly share the same cognitive process, our "spectating" can range from the crudely unsophisticated to highly precise data gathering. As childlike watchers of reality, we begin early to sort out objects into mineral, vegetable, and animal. Through the course of time, humankind has developed a range of sophisticated instruments—telescopes, microscopes, X-ray machines, spaceprobes, and so on—that have enhanced our knowledge and rendered it more accurate. For example, the moon, as a physical entity, exists independently of us and prior to our knowing about it. The moon has figured in many religious rituals and festivals; it has been the object of poetry and song. With the coming of the space age and interplanetary exploration, astronauts have journeyed to the moon and, with sophisticated instruments, have made our knowledge of this heavenly body more accurate. Although the process of knowing remains the same, the instruments that we develop are dynamic. Our knowledge about the moon becomes accurate when it corresponds correctly to the moon in reality.

While the "spectator theory of knowing" may appear to be passive, it has many dynamic educational implications. Education should provide the experience, training, and practice that will cultivate our potentiality to be accurate observers, discoverers of reality. It should assist us in using the instruments and technology that contribute to the accuracy of our knowledge of the universe and the world. While Realists would still agree with Aristotle that human beings intrinsically seek to know, they would also recognize the instrumental, or use, value of knowledge. Accurate knowledge about the world helps us to structure choices—to make decisions—that contribute to our continuing liberation from ignorance, superstition, disease, famine, and other human impediments.

As a systematic spectator, the Realist is concerned with discovering the essential plan or design of the universe. The philosophical and educational problem is that of extracting or abstracting the structures that explain the workings of the universe, of human beings, and of society. The discovery of structure involves extracting it from the matter that conveys it. Such organized spectating, involving the scientific method, deals with the discovery of principles and laws. Natural laws can be discovered and used to guide human conduct.

In humankind's long and continuing quest to discover the structures of reality, bodies of knowledge—learned and scientific disciplines have evolved and been added to by researchers over time. For example, linguists have worked to extract the structure of speech by analyzing various languages; the natural and physical sciences—zoology, botany, chemistry, physics, astronomy—have sought to identify the structure and patterns of natural and physical phenomena; the social sciences—sociology, economics, political science, anthropology, and psychology—have as their object of inquiry the structure of human interaction. Bodies of knowledge that are the products of this quest for structure constitute the Realist curriculum.

As a spectator searching to discover structure in reality, the Realist is a discoverer of reality that is preexistent, independent, and antecedent to his or her experience of it. Through careful observation, we can discover the structures of objects and determine how they interact with each other. We can frame generalizations based on the patterns and regularities that occur in these interactions between objects. For instance, meteorologists have observed and recorded daily temperatures. As a result of this careful observation, variations in temperature can be detected over time, and thus it is possible to generalize about temperature variations and speak about seasons. Such generalizations form basic meteorological theory that can guide such practical activities as planting crops, wearing clothes, and constructing dwellings.

The Realist theory of knowledge is also referred to as the "correspondence theory." Our ideas are true when our concepts conform to or correspond with the object in reality. Because knowledge is to conform to reality, what is taught should also conform to reality. For example, Newton's law of universal gravitation corresponds to the way the universe actually works. It is true and should be both transmitted to the young and perpetuated.

Realist Axiology

Realist value theory is an objective one that asserts that we can estimate the value nature of objects through knowledge. The value of an act lies in the object or in the relationships among objects in such a way that it can be known, judged, or estimated. In contrast to proponents of emotive theories relying on subjective feelings, Realists contend that our actions and appreciations can be estimated and judged by criteria external to us.[8]

Prizing rationality as the human being's distinguishing characteristic and defining power, Realists encourage us to shape our values in terms of the structures of reality. By knowing the structures of physical, natural, social, and human reality, we can frame realistic and viable alternatives. Through knowledge, we can rationally frame choices about life. The ability to develop such choices is at the core of a liberal, or liberating, education.

Among the leading proponents of contemporary Realism is Harry S. Broudy, a Classical Realist whose work has illuminated the value dimension of education, especially ethical and aesthetic concerns. For Broudy, the ultimate aim of education is "living the good life," which consists of cultivating human potentialities to their highest levels through processes of self-determination, self-realization, and self-integration.[9] From Broudy's perspective, the role of education and of schooling is to transform life through knowledge. The source of values lies in the relationship between the structure of objects and the structure of human nature. An object's structure makes it intrinsically as well as instrumentally valuable. Like Aristotle, Broudy asserted that our ethical decisions should be made on rational grounds. To be self-determined means that we have framed or defined our potentialities so that we can achieve worthy goals; to be self-integrated means that we have organized our values hierarchically and have resolved conflicts and inconsistencies.

Aesthetic judgment involves an interaction between a person, the perceiver, and an art object—a painting, drama, musical piece, dance, or sculpture, for example. Education enhances our aesthetic experience by cultivating our readiness to appreciate art, by providing a range of previous experience, and by providing us with some expertise in enjoying art forms.[10] Although art forms may exhibit cultural variations, Realists hold that the human desire for artistic expression and aesthetic enjoyment is universal.

THE EDUCATIONAL IMPLICATIONS
OF REALISM

In the following section, we will examine the educational implications of Realism in terms of educational goals, the role of the school, the nature of the curriculum, instructional methodology, and the teacher–learner relationship.

Realism's Educational Goals

The ultimate educational goal of Realism remains that articulated by Aristotle— namely, to aid human beings to attain happiness by cultivating their potentiality for excellence to its fullest. As such, education's goals are to

1. Cultivate human rationality, the human's highest power, through the study of organized bodies of knowledge; and
2. Encourage human beings to define themselves by framing their choices rationally, to realize themselves by exercising their potentiality for excellence to the fullest, and to integrate themselves by ordering the various roles and claims of life according to a rational and hierarchical order.

The Realist Conception of the School

Realists generally believe that each institution has a specific role and function in society. The government, the church, and the family perform definite roles. As such, the school is a special institution that has the primary mission of advancing human rationality. As a formal institution, it should be staffed by competent teachers who possess knowledge of a subject or skill and who know how to teach it to students who are immature in terms of that knowledge and are seeking to acquire it. The school has the well-defined and specific function of transmitting bodies of knowledge and inquiry skills to students. The school's task is primarily intellectual. Although the school may from time to time perform recreational, community, and social functions, these are secondary and should not interfere with the efficient performance of the primary intellectual function. In such a setting, the educational administrator's role is to ensure that teachers in a school are not distracted from their primary task or unnecessarily burdened with noneducational duties that detract from it. The administrator is especially charged with maintaining the academic freedom of the faculty to teach and of students to learn.

The Realist conception of the school clearly prescribes policies designed to protect the school from interference that detracts from its central mission. Realists reject the residual theory of schooling that asserts that schools are responsible for providing services neglected or no longer performed by other institutions.

They argue that the more schools act as medical, recreational, or employment agencies, the less time, money, and energy will be available for their primary function. To use schools as social service agencies not only confuses their purpose, but is also inefficient and costly.

The Realist Curriculum

As indicated earlier, the Realist conceives of an objective order of reality. The objects that comprise reality can be classified into categories on the basis of their structural similarities. The various learned disciplines, or subjects, of history, geography, language, mathematics, biology, botany, and chemistry, for example, consist of clusters of related concepts and of generalizations that interpret and explain interactions among the objects that these concepts represent. Each discipline as a conceptual system has a structure. *Structure* refers to a framework of related conceptual meanings and their generalizations that explain physical, natural, social, and human realities. For instance, biology consists of a number of necessary concepts appropriate to the study of plants and animals.

The role of the expert scientist and scholar is crucial in defining curricular areas. The scholar or the scientist is an expert who studies and carefully observes certain well-defined sections of reality. For example, the historian studies the past and analyzes documents explaining past events. By using the historical method, he or she re-creates events and develops generalizations or interpretations that explain and give them meaning. The historian as an expert in explaining the past has mastered a particular area of reality. He or she knows the limits of his or her expertise and is aware of what is appropriate to history and what lies in another learned discipline. The scholar or scientist is also skilled in the inquiry method, which is an efficient mode of discovery in the particular research area. Through monographs, lectures, and books, scholars make their findings available to the public and to other experts in their fields. Although scholars and scientists may disagree on interpretations, they are expected to follow the appropriate methods of investigation and conceptual framework of their disciplines.

Scientists and scholars are often, but not always, found in universities or research centers. Institutions of higher learning are expected to encourage, support, and reward research and teaching. Scholars and scientists are expected to make their findings known by publishing their research. Underlying scholarship in the Realist mode is the assumption that generalizations about reality are most accurately made by experts who have carefully investigated certain selected aspects of reality. In universities, these experts are usually organized into academic departments of history, language, chemistry, physics, English, political science, and so on. Students attend colleges and universities to study with and to obtain knowledge from these academic experts. Prospective teachers, especially secondary teachers, study academic subject matters, usually referred to as majors. They, in turn, use the descriptions, concepts, and generalizations provided by the expert to organize subject matter into instructional units for their students.

Basic to the Realist curriculum is the rationale that the most efficient and effective way to find out about reality is to study it through systematically organized subject-matter disciplines. The liberal arts and science curriculum of the undergraduate college and the departmentalized secondary school curriculum represent the subject-matter mode of curricular organization. The subject-matter curriculum consists of two basic components: (1) the body of knowledge that is the structure of a learned discipline—an organized way of viewing a certain aspect of reality, that is, historically, sociologically, biologically, chemically, psychologically, geographically, and so on; and (2) the appropriate pedagogical ordering of the subject matter according to the readiness, maturation, and previous learning of the student. In such a curricular design, teachers are expected to be knowledgeable about their subject matters and well prepared in the methods of teaching them to students.

In summary, the Realist curriculum at the primary level involves instruction in the tools of reading, writing, and computation that are needed for subsequent successful study and inquiry into the systematic subject-matter disciplines. It is equally important that early childhood and primary schooling foster predispositions and attitudes that value learning as a positive goal. Children should also gain experience with research methods, such as using the library, which aid in later learning. As indicated, the secondary and collegiate curricula consist of the bodies of knowledge that are regarded as repositories of the wisdom of the human race as determined by the most authoritative scholarship.

Realist Instructional Methods

Instruction in the Realist school involves a teacher teaching some skill or subject to a student. While this may appear to be a simple statement, it carefully defines and prescribes the instructional act. Notice that there are three elements in the act of instruction: the teacher, the skill or subject, and the student. Because each of these components is essential to the teaching or instructional act, we will comment on all three.[11]

The teacher is knowledgeable in the content of the subject; he or she is a generally educated person who knows how the subject relates to other areas of knowledge. The teacher also knows the limits of his or her competence. Thus, the goal of instruction is to provide the student with the body of knowledge possessed by the teacher.

The second element in the instructional act is some body of knowledge, such as history, or some skill, such as reading, that is to be taught to the student. In some situations, this second element is missing in schools, for example, in therapy or sensitivity sessions, or during entertainment or unfocused talking. Situations such as these, which lack the knowledge or skill element, diminish and often distort teaching. Realist teachers, like any teacher, need to know their students' backgrounds and how to motivate them. They can be entertaining as well as informative. However, they also need to be knowledge givers.

The third element in instruction is the student, the person who is present to learn the skill or knowledge. Students are expected to be ready to learn and willing to expend the effort required. While students may have many interests, they are expected to focus their attention on what is being taught.

The Realist teacher should command a variety of methods that may include lecture, discussion, or experiment. The teacher should use the method appropriate to the learner's background and situation. An ideal method, which needs to be used with great skill, would structure a learning situation that replicates the research activity of the scholar or scientist. For example, students in a history course would use the historical method to analyze and interpret primary sources.

The Realist Teacher–Learner Relationship

In our discussion of Realist philosophy, curriculum, and methodology, we have already suggested the basis of the teacher–learner relationship. The teacher, possessing subject-matter knowledge and instructional skill, is a professional educator. Teachers should be generally educated in both the liberal arts and sciences; this general knowledge is designed to assist them in being educated persons who appreciate the relationships of bodies of knowledge to each other and to the cultivation of human rationality. In addition to being generalists, teachers should be specialists in educating students.

The learner is regarded as an individual who has the essential human right to self-determination, self-realization, and self-integration. Seeking to grow in maturity in the areas of human knowledge, students have the right to have educated and professionally prepared experts as teachers. Learning, however, which requires commitment and application, is the student's primary responsibility.

CONCLUSION

Realism is a philosophy that seems to be the basis for much contemporary education. Drawing from Aristotelian origins, it argues that the primary goal of education is to contribute to the discovery, transmission, and use of knowledge. Such knowledge is essential in realizing the human potential for rationality; it is our surest guide to conduct in all the dimensions of living—personal, social, economic, political, ethical, and aesthetic.

DISCUSSION QUESTIONS

1. Identify the basic elements of Realism and compare and contrast them with Idealism.

2. Define dualism and examine its educational implications.

3. Examine the concept of change from an Aristotelian perspective. What are the educational implications of such a view of change?

4. Apply the concept of classification to bodies of knowledge. What are the implications for curricular organization?

5. From a Realist perspective, examine the relationship between theory and practice.

6. Analyze the Realist view of knowing.

7. Identify a value issue or conflict in contemporary education and examine it from a Realist perspective.

8. Analyze aesthetic education from the Realist point of view.

9. Identify several teaching situations or styles that Realists would reject. Indicate why they would react negatively to these situations or styles.

10. Define academic freedom according to the Realist philosophy of education.

INQUIRY PROJECTS

- Read the mission statements and curricular rationales that appear in several catalogues of colleges of arts and science. Compare and contrast these statements with the Realist view of knowledge and education.
- Using Realist criteria, analyze the teacher education program in your college or university in terms of the relationship between the general education and professional education components.
- Suppose you are a Realist and head a curriculum review committee in a high school. Prepare a set of guidelines based on your philosophical perspective,
- Prepare a lesson plan for teaching a subject according to the Realist rationale.
- Prepare a character sketch that describes a Realist teacher.
- Write a short essay that describes the proper relationship between the principal and teacher according to a Realist view.
- Identify some contemporary examples of the residual function of the school. Why would Realists be likely to oppose these practices?
- Following a Realist argument, prepare a policy statement that outlines the desirable relationships between university and college professors and elementary and secondary teachers.

FURTHER READINGS

Breed, Frederick, S. *Education and the New Realism*. New York: Macmillan, 1939.

Brink, David O. *Moral Realism and the Foundations of Ethics*. Cambridge: Cambridge University Press, 1989.

Broudy, Harry S. *Building a Philosophy of Education*. Englewood Cliffs, NJ: Prentice Hall, 1961.

Broudy, Harry S. "A Classical Realist View of Education," in Philip H. Phenix, ed., *Philosophies of Education*. New York: John Wiley, 1961.

Broudy, Harry S. *The Real World of the Public Schools*. New York: Harcourt Brace Jovanovich, 1972.

Brumbaugh, Robert S., and Nathaniel M. Lawrence, "Aristotle's Philosophy of Education," *Educational Theory*, 9 (January 1959): 1–15.

Brumbaugh, Robert S., and Nathaniel M. Lawrence. "Aristotle: Education as Self-Realization," *Philosophers on Education: Six Essays on the Foundations of Western Thought*. Boston: Houghton Mifflin, 1963.

Burnet, J. ed., *Aristotle on Education*. Cambridge: Cambridge University Press, 1967.

Davitt, Michael. *Realism and Truth*. Oxford, England: Basil Blackwell, 1991.

Dunkel, Harold B. *Whitehead on Education*. Columbus: Ohio State University Press, 1965.

Edel, Abraham. *Aristotle and His Philosophy*. Chapel Hill: University of North Carolina Press, 1982.

Hutchins, Robert M. *The Higher Learning in America*. New Haven: Yale University Press, 1962.

Jacobs, Jonathan A. *Being True to the World: Moral Realism and Practical Wisdom*. New York: P. Lang, 1990.

Jacobs, Jonathan A. *Practical Realism and Moral Psychology*. Washington, DC: Georgetown University Press, 1995.

Kelley, David. *The Evidence of the Senses: A Realist Theory of Perception*. Baton Rouge: Louisiana State University Press, 1986.

Layder, Derek. *The Realist Image in Social Science*. New York: St. Martin's Press, 1990.

Martin, William O. *Realism in Education*. New York: Harper and Row, 1969.

Miller, Richard W. *Fact and Method: Explanation, Confirmation and Reality in the Natural and Social Sciences*. Princeton, NJ: Princeton University Press, 1987.

Rescher, Nicholas. *Scientific Realism: A Critical Reappraisal*. Boston: D. Reidel, 1987.

Russman, Thomas A. *A Prospectus for the Triumph of Realism*. Macon, GA: Mercer University Press, 1987.

Seifert, Josef. *Back to Things in Themselves: A Phenomenological Foundation for Classical Realism*. Boston: Routledge & Kegan Paul, 1987.

Seller, Roy W. *Critical Realism: A Study of the Nature and Conditions of Knowledge*. New York: Russell & Russell, 1969.

Shi, David, E. *Facing Facts: Realism in American Thought and Culture, 1850–1920*. New York: Oxford University Press, 1995.

Tannsjo, Torbjorn. *Moral Realism*. Savage, MD: Rowman & Littlefield, 1990.

Tooley, Michael. *Causation: A Realist Approach*. New York: Oxford University Press, 1987.

Wild, John. *Introduction to Realist Philosophy*. New York: Harper and Brothers, 1948.

Wild, John. "Education and Society: A Realistic View," *Modern Philosophies and Education*. 54th Yearbook, National Society for the Study of Education. Chicago: University of Chicago Press, 1955.

ENDNOTES

1. For a discussion of the basic doctrines of Realism, see John Wild, *Introduction to Realist Philosophy* (New York: Harper & Brothers, 1948).

2. For representative works discussing the varieties of Realism, see Richard W. Miller, *Fact and Method: Explanation, Confirmation and Reality in the Natural and Social Sciences* (Princeton, NJ: Princeton University Press, 1987); Derek Layder, *The Realist Image in Social Science* (New York: St. Martin's Press, 1990); Nicholas Rescher, *Scientific Realism: A Critical Reappraisal* (Boston: D. Reidel, 1987).

3. For treatments of Aristotle, see D. J. Allan, *The Philosophy of Aristotle* (London: Oxford University Press, 1970); G. E. R. Lloyd, *Aristotle: The Growth and Structure of His Thought* (Cambridge: Cambridge University Press, 1968); J. H. Randall, Jr., *Aristotle* (New York: Columbia University Press, 1960).

4. Richard McKeon, *The Basic Works of Aristotle* (New York: Random House, 1941).

5. Robert M. Hutchins, *The Higher Learning in America* (New Haven: Yale University Press, 1962), pp. 66–67. Originally published in 1936.

6. For an insightful essay on Aristotelian education, see Robert S. Brumbaugh and Nathaniel M. Lawrence, "Aristotle: Education as Self-Realization," *Philosophers on Education: Six Essays of the Foundations of Western Thought* (Boston: Houghton Mifflin, 1963), pp. 49–75; also see J. Burnet, ed., *Aristotle on Education* (Cambridge: Cambridge University Press, 1967).

7. Adina Schwartz, "Aristotle on Education and Choice," *Educational Theory,* 29 (spring 1979): 97–107.

8. For commentaries on Realist ethics, see Jonathan A. Jacobs, *Being True to the World: Moral Realism and Practical Wisdom* (New York: Peter Lang, 1990); Torbjorn Tannsjo, *Moral Realism* (Savage, MD: Rowman & Littlefield, 1990).

9. Harry S. Broudy, *Building a Philosophy of Education* (Englewood Cliffs, NJ: Prentice Hall, 1961), pp. 3–20.

10. Ibid., pp. 202–231.

11. William Oliver Martin, *Realism in Education* (New York: Harper and Row, 1969), pp. 3–4.

▶ 4

Theistic Realism and Education

Theistic Realism, or Thomism, was formulated as a philosophy in the Middle Ages. Since the thirteenth century, it has been a major worldview that has shaped Western thought. In Chapter 3, we examined Realism as a philosophy of education and described its Aristotelian origins. Our definition of Realism as a philosophy that asserts the existence of an objective order of reality and the capability of human beings to acquire knowledge of it applies equally to Theistic Realism. In addition, we add the term *Theism,* which asserts the belief in the existence of an omnipotent, omniscient, and personal deity who created the world and all its creatures, including human beings, and keeps them in existence.

In the history of ideas, Theistic Realism represents the fusion of the ideas of Greek rationality, represented by Aristotle, and Christian theology. Although Christianity had earlier entered the Western world in the Roman period, Christian intellectuals, or scholastics, such as Thomas Aquinas, later worked to formulate a rational organization of religious doctrines in order to render them logically coherent and philosophically meaningful.

It should be pointed out at the onset of our discussion of Theistic Realism that Thomism, its dominant form, has been associated historically with Roman Catholicism; however, not all Theistic Realists, nor Thomists, are Roman Catholics. Also, not all Christians are Theistic Realists. Saint Augustine and other fathers of the Christian Church subscribed to Idealism. In addition, some philosophers associated with Christianity have been Existentialists. (Existentialism is examined in Chapter 7.)

In our discussion of Theistic Realism, we will examine

1. Thomas Aquinas's contribution to the history of Western thought and philosophy.

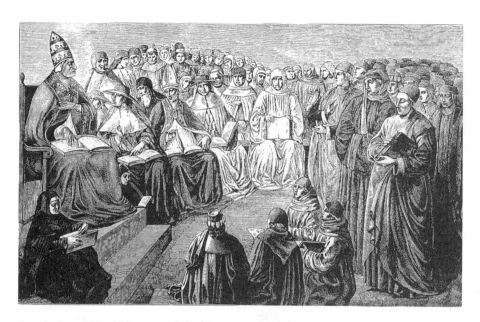

A painting, "The Triumph of St. Thomas of Aquinas," by the Renaissance artist, Benozzo Gezzoli, in which Aquinas, of whom the back only is seen, is addressing a Church Council in 1256. Aquinas (1225–1274), a Dominican scholar, developed Thomism or Theistic Realism.

2. Theistic Realism's essential philosophical doctrines.
3. The educational implications of Theistic Realism.

THOMAS AQUINAS: A FOUNDER OF THEISTIC REALISM

The development of Theistic Realism by Thomas Aquinas (1225–1274) can best be understood in the context of the scholastic movement that began in A.D. 1100 and reached its zenith in the thirteenth century. Scholasticism, the body of philosophical doctrines articulated by religious scholars, developed when many of the ancient Greek classics, including the philosophical works of Aristotle, were rediscovered and studied in the Western schools and universities, especially the University of Paris.[1] Scholastic philosophers such as Anselm of Canterbury (1033–1109), Bernard of Clairvaux (1091–1153), Peter Abelard (1079–1142), Albertus Magnus (1200–1280), and Thomas Aquinas sought to create a synthesis of Greek rationalism, especially Aristotle's philosophy, and Christian doctrines.

The philosophy developed by the scholastics should be viewed in terms of the hierarchical system of governing the Christian church and its doctrines. The

Old and New Testaments, the writings of the church fathers, the councils of the church, and the body of tradition were authoritative sources for Western Christianity. From these sources came the doctrines that were articulated, interpreted, and enforced by the church. As the primary medieval educational agency, the church, through its teachers and in its schools, transmitted the corpus of Christian doctrine to Western men and women. According to the medieval scholars, the church's divinely sanctioned teaching authority rested on sacred scripture and inspired doctrine.

From this body of theological doctrines, certain basic beliefs that characterized the Christian life can be identified. God is an omnipotent, perfect, and personal being who created all existence; human beings, possessing a spiritual soul and a corporeal body, were created to share in divine happiness. Endowed with an intellect and will, the human being has freedom of choice. Because of Adam's sin, his descendants who inherited the legacy of original sin were spiritually deprived. God sent his son, Jesus Christ, to redeem humankind through his death and resurrection. To aid human beings in achieving salvation, Christ instituted the church and charged it with administering the grace-giving sacraments. These core Christian beliefs held great importance for medieval education and continue to influence contemporary Roman Catholic education. Believers need doctrinal instruction to fortify their beliefs with knowledge. The church and its schools act to defend, transmit, and inculcate Christian doctrines.

Scholastic philosophy and education reached its high point in the writings of Saint Thomas Aquinas, a Dominican theologian.[2] Born into an Italian noble family, Aquinas was enrolled at the age of five in the Benedictine abbey of Monte Cassino, where he received his basic education. Between the ages of fourteen and eighteen, he attended the University of Naples, where he studied Aristotelian philosophy. Aquinas entered the Dominican order, studied at the monastery of the Holy Cross at Cologne from 1246 to 1252, and was ordained as a priest. In 1252, he entered the University of Paris, Western Europe's major theological center, where he taught and earned his master's degree in theology. In 1256, he became a professor of theology. From 1269 until 1272, he wrote *Summa Theologiae,* his most important philosophical work, which sought to create a synthesis of Aristotelian philosophy and Christian doctrine.

In the tradition of medieval scholasticism, Aquinas was both a theologian and a philosopher. Using both faith and reason, he sought to answer questions dealing with the Christian conception of God, the nature of the universe, and the relationship between God and humans. A philosopher-theologian, Aquinas devoted his life to reconciling the claims of faith and reason.

Following Christian doctrine, Aquinas asserted that the universe and life within it had been created by God, a supreme being who, in creating human life, had endowed it with an immaterial and deathless spiritual soul, which is the basis of human self-awareness and freedom. God had also given human beings a physical body, which on earth was temporal, that is, existing at a particular time, and spatial, existing in a particular place. Although the human being dwelt for a time on this planet, the purpose of life was that the soul should live eternally with God in heaven.

Like Aristotle, Aquinas construed human beings to be rational creatures distinguished by their intellectual powers. Again, like Aristotle, Aquinas asserted that human knowledge began with sensation and was completed through conceptualization or abstraction. However, the natural process of knowing was enhanced by the human being's cooperation with supernatural grace and acceptance of the truth of Christian doctrine.

Again, like Aristotle, Aquinas held a teleological conception of the universe. They both agreed that the universe functioned in a deliberate and purposeful way rather than by mere chance or accident. Human history—indeed, every person's life—was an expression of purposeful movement to a goal. Aristotle saw the "good life of happiness" as the human being's reason for being. While accepting the good life as the human being's purpose on earth, Aquinas argued that there was an even higher purpose—the beatific vision, or the experience of being in the presence of God.

EDUCATIONAL IMPLICATIONS OF THEISTIC REALISM

Because many of the principles of Realism discussed in Chapter 3 apply to Theistic Realism, we need not repeat them here. For a discussion of the metaphysical, epistemological, and axiological principles of Realism that are essentially shared by Theistic Realism, see Chapter 3. In this section, we will examine how Thomism adds a spiritual or religious dimension to Aristotelian Natural Realism. Further, because Thomism has long been the most influential philosophy for Roman Catholic education, we will make some special references to Catholic schooling.

Thomism's Philosophical and Theological Bases

Since the late Middle Ages, Thomism has been the dominant philosophy associated with Roman Catholicism and its institutions. In terms of philosophical classification, Thomism is a leading variety of Theistic, or religious, Realism. While accepting the basic metaphysical and epistemological tenets of Aristotelian Natural Realism, Thomism asserts Christian principles, especially as expressed in Roman Catholic theology. Thomists have also displayed a propensity to use Aristotle's logic.

In contrast with Natural Realism, Thomists embrace supernaturalism and find revelation, recorded in the Bible, to be an authoritative source of divinely inspired truth. Thomists assert that human beings have as their ultimate goal, the beatific vision of God, which is the final, highest, and most complete happiness. However, through their own actions, human beings sinned and were alienated from God, their creator. This "estrangement" or "alienation" was overcome through the redemptive act of Jesus Christ, the son of God, who instituted grace and founded a new "people of God." As a free agent, the individual can choose either to cooperate with or to oppose the work of his or her own salvation.

Because it draws from both Aristotelian Natural Realism and from Catholic Christian theology, Thomism represents the interpenetration of the two. Thomism asserts a dualistic view of reality, which has both a spiritual and a material dimension. Possessing both a body and a soul, human beings exist on both a supernatural and a natural plane. God, the first cause and creator, the source of all existence, is a personal and caring creator, not an impersonal "ground of being."

The interpenetration of Realistic philosophy and Christian theology is a consistent theme in Thomist educational philosophy. In his book, *Catholic Viewpoint on Education,* Neil McCluskey discusses both the theological, or revealed, bases of Catholic education, and the philosophical, or perennial, bases of Catholic education. According to McCluskey, the theological bases of Catholic education are the following: (1) God gave human beings a supernature that enables them to experience divine life; (2) through sin, humankind fell from grace; (3) Jesus Christ, the son of God, redeemed human beings and restored them to God's grace and to the promised supernatural life; (4) Christ, the perfect human being, is a moral exemplar for Christians who seek to live the Christlike life; and (5) the supernatural order, complementary to the natural order, in no way diminishes the value of reason and nature. It does not diminish the natural rights of the individual, the home, and society.

McCluskey also comments on the philosophical, or perennial, bases of Catholic education when he asserts that (1) there is a personal God whose existence can be demonstrated by reason; (2) human beings have a purpose for existing based on their nature; (3) each person is a free and rational agent; (4) human perfection lies in knowing and possessing truth, beauty, and goodness; and (5) the material body gives the person continuity with nature, and the spiritual soul promises a destiny that transcends the material and temporal natural order.[3]

William Cunningham, in *Pivotal Problems of Education,* has referred to this synthesis of Realism and Theism as "Supernaturalism."[4] He asserts that human beings, possessing a soul and body, are properly guided by faith and reason. For him, education has a perennial and unchanging character. For Cunningham, an educational philosophy founded on Supernaturalism can specify educational aims in terms of human origin, nature, and destiny. Humankind originated from God through the act of creation; human nature was created in God's image and likeness; the human destiny is to return to God. In asserting the value of a Supernatural philosophy of education, Cunningham claims that it can aid in identifying ultimate goals.

Thomism and Knowledge

As already indicated, Thomist epistemology follows basic Aristotelian patterns. The human being is immediately conjoined to material reality through the senses. Through sense experience, a necessary condition of knowing, we sense other objects and persons. Our minds give us the power to conceptualize from this sensory experience by abstracting and sorting the characteristics or qualities present in objects. Concepts are formed by the mind when the essential qualities are extracted from the restrictions of concrete materiality. Concepts are immaterial constructs that can be manipulated by our reasoning minds. By arranging concepts, we can generalize from experience, construct possible alternatives of action, and exercise freedom of choice.

Like Aristotle, Aquinas asserted that the highest human activity was rationality, the exercising of intellectual and speculative powers. Through conceptualization, we can overcome the restrictions of a primitive and natural determinism and transform our environment. To transform the environment, we must formulate plans and structure ends. Through the means of art, science, and technology, we can use our intelligence to humanize the material environment.

Aquinas agreed with Aristotle that humans act most humanely when reasoning. However, Aquinas qualified his agreement; while reason is the human being's highest and most satisfying earthly power, it is nevertheless an incomplete and imperfect happiness. Perfect happiness comes after the death of the body when, through the gift of divine elevation, the human being experiences an immediate cognitive and affective union with God.

Thomist educators, like most Realists, emphasize the intellectual function of the school as an agency designed to cultivate and exercise human reason. In *Pivotal Problems of Education,* Cunningham asserts that the school's function is primarily but not exclusively intellectual.[5] As an intellectual agency, the Catholic school emphasizes the transmission and the use of the liberal arts and sciences to exercise and cultivate human rationality. Although primacy is given to intellectual development, physical, social, and religious development should not be neglected.

As is true with Realism generally, formal schooling's greatest goal is to transmit subject-matter disciplines. For Thomists, a subject-matter discipline is called *scientia,* which means that it is a body of accumulated, demonstrated, and organized knowledge. For Thomists, such subject matters are organized on the basis of major premises that are either self-evident, derived from experimentation, or derived from a higher science. These bodies of knowledge are transmitted by teachers, who are expert in the disciplines which they teach, to students, who are expected to use their intellectual powers in understanding, mastering, and applying the principles contained in the subject matter.

The interpenetration of Realism and Theism in Thomistic philosophy has pronounced educational implications. Following dualistic principles, education has two complementary aims based on the human being's nature: to provide the knowledge, exercises, and activities that cultivate both human spirituality and human reason.

Moral Education

Thomist education, especially in the Roman Catholic school, is deliberately committed to supernatural values. In its goal of forming Christlike individuals, it encompasses religious and theological studies. Value formation that takes place in religious studies is also reinforced by the school milieu and activities that involve an exposure to religious practices, habits, and rituals.

Aquinas was careful to point out, however, that knowledge does not necessarily lead to morality. Although a person may know the principles of religion and may know about religious observance, knowledge cannot be equated with goodness. However, intelligent men and women can distinguish between moral right and wrong in making choices. The exercise of freedom means that every person possesses the ability to frame, recognize, and evaluate alternative courses of action.

In the Thomist context, moral education is a process of habituating the learner to a climate of virtue. Such an environment should contain models of value worthy of imitation. The Christian school milieu should provide the exercises and conditions that help to form dispositions inclined to virtue.

Curricular Implications of the Thomist Conception of Human Nature

Aquinas defined the human being as a "spirit-in-the-world," an incarnate spirit who also possesses an animated body. Unique among creatures, women and men are composed of both a corporeal and spiritual substance and live between two worlds, with their souls situated on the boundary between heaven and earth. Possessing an immortal, deathless, and immaterial soul that vitalizes each person's self-awareness and freedom, the soul's embodiment affords each person an historical time and social place, or temporal and spatial contexts, in which to know, love, and choose.

In continuity with nature, all people create their own personal biographies over the course of their lives. The human being is a social creature who is born, grows, matures, and dies within families and communities. As social beings, humans have developed communication systems, such as speaking, writing, and reading. These communication systems, needed in community life, are acquired and must be learned. As social agencies, schools contribute to human development as they encourage reasoning, communicating, and participating in community life.

Thomists recognize that people live in a particular place at a particular time. Because of historical variations and social adaptations to changing conditions, various cultures, societies, and polities exist. While recognizing these variations, the Thomist, rejecting culturally relative truth and values, asserts that the commonality of human nature and culture is more important than these variations. All people possess a common human nature, as a result of the underlying spiritual and material realities in which they participate. This assertion makes it possible to speak of universal human rights and responsibilities. Thomists contend that culturally or situationally relative theories of ethics evade the claims that universal moral and ethical standards should have on us.

The Thomist conception of human nature, or "spirit-in-the-world," provides a curriculum rationale in which the principle of the hierarchy of generality operates. Those aspects of existence that are most general, abstract, and durable are located at the summit of the hierarchy. Those aspects of life that are particular, specific, and transitory are located in a lower position. Should there be a conflict in establishing curricular priorities, it is resolved on the basis of agreement or disagreement with the more general and higher subjects of the curriculum. Because the person's soul is immortal and destined for the perfect happiness of the beatific vision of God, subjects leading to spiritual growth and formation such as theology and scriptural and religious studies receive curricular emphasis. Because the person as a rational being is a free agent, knowledge and exercises that cultivate reason, such as philosophy and logic, are emphasized so that each person will be prepared to exercise freedom of choice. And because humans live in a natural and a social environment, knowledge and skills that sustain economic well-being should be included in the curriculum.

Living in society, people need knowledge of legal, political, and economic systems that contribute to personal and social well-being. Because we are social and communal beings, the language and literary skills that contribute to communication and community are also a major foundation of formal education. The skills of reading, speaking, and writing are an important part of every person's basic education.

The following statement by Pope Pius XI, from *On the Christian Education of Youth,* clearly expresses Thomist educational principles:

> *Since education consists essentially in preparing man for what he must be and for what he must do here below, in order to attain the sublime end for which he was created, it is clear that there can be no true education which is not wholly directed to man's last end. . . . Christian edu-*

cation takes in the whole aggregate of human life, physical and spiritual, intellectual and moral, individual, domestic, and social.[6]

The Thomist Teacher–Learner Relationship

Thomist educational philosophy provides useful definitions of and distinctions between education and schooling and thinking and learning even for those who do not share its theological premises. Although recognizing that education and schooling are related concepts and processes, Thomists have carefully distinguished between education, the broader and more inclusive concept, and schooling, its more limited form. These distinctions help to define areas of competence and responsibility for teachers.

For Thomists, education—the complete formation of a person—is a lifelong process that involves many persons and agencies, such as the family, the church, and the community. Schooling, or formal education, is the responsibility of teachers who are deliberately responsible for instructing children and youth in the school, a specialized institution.

Although the Thomist distinction between education and schooling may seem obvious, it has often been ignored or neglected by educators. When it is ignored, areas of responsibility are blurred and confused. By recognizing that other agencies, such as the family, perform educational functions, Thomists argue that these agencies have responsibilities for educating children. In fact, Thomists strongly assert that parents should exercise the primary role in their children's education. This parental role is primarily informal, involving the cultivation of values that support morality, religion, and education. These values are supportive and conducive to the school's and the teacher's more specific and formal educational role. The Thomist distinctions between education and schooling also make clear that the school is not an all-powerful educational institution. Its effectiveness as an instructional agency depends on other agencies, such as the family, performing their educational responsibilities well. It is interesting to note that the Thomist distinction between education, as a general process, and schooling, as a specific but more limited form of education, anticipated the modern movement to enlarge the scope of educational history, philosophy, and sociology.[7]

For the Thomists, *educatio,* or education, is defined as a person's general formation in the broadest possible sense—spiritually, intellectually, socially, morally, politically, economically, and so forth. In the case of children, education refers to the child's total upbringing. Education, as a total process of human development, encompasses more than the formal instruction that takes place in the school's more limited environment. Because a person's total formation rests on both informal and formal educational agencies, the school's role must be considered in relationship to total human development.[8] In the school, a student is exposed to *disciplina,* or a deliberate instruction such as when a teacher teaches some knowledge or imparts some skill to the learner. The success or failure of such deliberate instruction depends at least in part on its relationship to the general formation taking place outside of the school.

In the Thomist school context, the teacher is a mature person who possesses a disciplined body of knowledge or skill and through deliberate instruction seeks to impart this to a learner. Instruction is a verbal process by which the teacher carefully selects the appropriate words and phrases to illustrate the principles or demonstrate the skill that the learner is to acquire. The teacher's language is a stimulus that serves to motivate and to explain so that the student can exercise his or her intellect. The student must be an active participant in the teacher–learner relationship, for he or she possesses the potentiality for intellectually grasping and appropriating knowledge.

The Thomist teacher should be a skilled communicator. To communicate effectively, the teacher has to select the correct words, use the proper speaking style, and cite appropriate examples, illustrations, and analogies. The teacher should be careful that instruction does not degenerate into mere verbalism or preachment in which the words used are remote from the learner's experience. Instruction should always begin with what the student already possesses and should lead to an outcome which is new. As such, teaching involves a careful structuring and organizing of lessons.

Thomas Aquinas saw teaching as a vocation, a calling to serve humanity. Because of a desire to serve others, the good teacher should be motivated by a love of truth, a love of persons, and a love of God. Unlike the emotionalism of such romantic naturalist educators as Rousseau and Pestalozzi, who also preached a doctrine of love, the Thomist teacher also prizes the cultivation of rationality. As true Aristotelians, Thomists emphasize that genuine love comes from knowing and is based on reason. Therefore, teaching is not allowed to degenerate into a merely emotional relationship. It is always about some knowledge, some truth, that is worthy of being known by a learner.

In the Thomist conception of the teacher, the art of teaching integrates the contemplative and the active life. As a contemplative, the teacher must spend time researching and planning instruction. Much of this research takes place in the serenity of a library. The teacher is to know the subject matter thoroughly, be it theology, mathematics, or science. The teacher is also an active person who is involved with students and who communicates knowledge to them.

In addition to their intellectual roles, teachers also have an important moral role. They are to serve as exemplars or models worthy of imitation by students. In the past, teachers in Catholic schools were usually members of religious communities of priests, brothers, or sisters. They followed the guidelines, the mode of religious formation, developed by a particular religious leader, usually the founder or foundress of their communities. For example, the members of the Society of Jesus, or Jesuits, followed the life and teaching style prescribed by Ignatius Loyola (1491–1556); the Dominicans followed the teachings of Dominic de Guzman (1170–1221); the Franciscans followed Francis of Assisi (1182–1226); and the Christian Brothers followed the teachings of Jean Baptiste de la Salle (1651–1719). Today, the majority of teachers in Catholic schools are laypersons who are not members of religious communities. However, these teachers are expected to be role models who possess a religious outlook and who are committed to teaching as a vocation. For example, the U.S. Catholic Conference of Bishops has urged that "spiritual and ministerial formulation" should be "an integral part of the professional preparation" of teachers in Catholic schools. Further, teacher preparation should "provide Christian formation programs for educators who are evangelizers by call and covenant and mission."[9] The preparation of Catholic school teachers emphasizes faith qualities, gospel values, and the Christian tradition. Such teachers are to share the "responsibility for establishing a community of faith within the context of the local Church and the universal Church."[10]

A significant feature of the Catholic school is that it be a "faith community" in miniature that is linked to the larger universal church. An important element of this religio-educational community is the school milieu, or educational environment. Throughout the school year, observances are linked to the church's liturgical calendar which commemorates important religious feasts and events. Also, the milieu includes religious symbols and art forms that reinforce the climate of faith.

The Second Vatican Council

In this chapter, we have examined Theistic Realism, especially Thomism, as a long-standing educational philosophy in the history of civilization. Although associated with Roman Catholicism throughout its history, Thomism also has attracted some educators who do not share Catholic doctrinal beliefs. We have, however, commented on its special relevance to Catholic schooling. We now comment on developments that resulted in Catholic education from the Second Vatican Council, which met from 1962 to 1965.[11]

The Second Vatican Council (Vatican II) emphasized themes to nurture religious renewal. Two principal themes were (1) liturgical changes in which the language used became the vernacular rather than the traditional Latin, and (2) an emphasis on the world community that stressed ecumenism, social justice, and the common human welfare.[12]

The liturgical changes of Vatican II did not alter essentials of Catholic worship but rather sought to involve the congregation in more active participation as a community of believers. For children learning to participate in the church's central mystery, the Mass, their induction into religious ritual became more active and participatory than in the traditional Latin service.

For educational theory, Vatican II encouraged changes in attitude rather than in essential doctrine. It ended the "siege mentality" in which Catholic schools were seen as citadels preparing young defenders of the faith against theological adversaries. An educational consequence of the Second Vatican Council was an ecumenical opening to the world, which, while retaining essential doctrines, encouraged Catholic teachers to develop an understanding of other religious cultures. A consequence of Vatican II was also that a true Christian education meant the study of and attempts to resolve world problems of social and racial discrimination, economic injustice, and the threat of nuclear war. For example, Catholic school teachers were encouraged to study the "contemporary social teachings of the Church" and to foster a "desire for service" that included a "commitment to action for justice, mercy, and peace."[13]

CONCLUSION

Thomist education rests on premises found in Aristotelian philosophy and Christian Scriptures. Based on its Theistic antecedents, Thomism asserts that education should aid human beings to merit supernatural life. Following Realism, it asserts that the person's distinguishing characteristic is reason and that education should contribute to an intellectually excellent life. A complete education should also facilitate every person's active participation in his or her own culture and history. Although it recommends an education that is primarily intellectual, Thomism recognizes that the human being can transform the natural environment and create culture. As a worker, the person is also a practical being who needs preparation for professional and occupational life. Ever since its formulation by medieval scholastics, Theistic Realism has sought to reconcile faith and reason, or religion and science, in a comprehensive synthesis.

DISCUSSION QUESTIONS

1. Define Theistic Realism and compare and contrast it with Aristotle's formulation of Realist philosophy.

2. Examine the impact of dualism on Thomist philosophy and education.

3. Consider the scholastic efforts to create a synthesis of Aristotelian Realism and Christian doctrine. Examine the application of the synthesis to educational theory and practice.

4. Analyze the Thomist conception of the human being as a "spirit-in-the-world." From your analysis, deduce educational goals and patterns of curricular organization.

5. Examine the concept of teleology and indicate its relationships to educational goal setting.

6. Analyze the relationships between supernaturalism and naturalism in Thomist education.

7. How do Thomists define a learned discipline or subject matter?

8. What does it mean "to write your own biography" in the Thomist perspective of human nature and purposes?

INQUIRY PROJECTS

- Examine Thomism in terms of its origins and relationships to medieval education.
- Visit a Roman Catholic school. Do you find any evidence of the supernatural and philosophical bases of education identified in the chapter?
- Examine contemporary schooling in the United States. Do you find any evidence of conflicts between faith and reason?
- Analyze the mission statements of schools and colleges that have identified themselves as operating under religious auspices. Extract the philosophical rationale from these statements.
- Prepare a lesson plan that follows the Thomist view of subject matter and method.
- Interview several teachers in Catholic schools on the changes in Catholic education that occurred as a result of Vatican II. Report your findings to the class.
- Structure a curriculum guide that follows the principle of "the hierarchy of generality."
- Visit several public and private schools. Based on your visits, determine if practices in these schools distinguish between *educatio,* education, and schooling, as differentiated in the chapter.

FURTHER READINGS

Barger, Robert N. "McGucken Revisited: A Fifty Year Retrospective on American Catholic Educational Philosophy," in *Proceedings of the Midwest Philosophy of Education Society, 1991 and 1992,* edited by David B. Owen. Ames, IA: Midwest Philosophy of Education Society, 1993, pp. 319–326.

Bleich, Russell M. *The Pre-Service Formation of Teachers for Catholic Schools.* Washington, DC: National Catholic Educational Association, 1982.

Brauer, Theodore. *Thomistic Principles in a Catholic School.* St. Louis: B. Herder, 1947.

Clarke, W. Norris. *Explorations in Metaphysics: Being–God–Person.* Notre Dame, IN: University of Notre Dame Press, 1994.

Copleston, Frederick C. *Medieval Philosophy.* New York: Harper & Row, 1961.

Cunningham, William F. *Pivotal Problems in Education.* New York: Macmillan, 1940.

Donohue, John W. *St. Thomas Aquinas and Education.* New York: Random House, 1968.

Donohue, John W. "The Scholastic: Aquinas," in *The Educated Man: Studies in the History of Educational Thought,* edited by Paul Nash, Andreas M. Kazamias, and Henry Parkinson. New York: John Wiley, 1965.

Donohue, John W. *Catholicism and Education.* New York: Harper & Row, 1973.

Filas, Francis L. "An Analysis of What the 'Faith' Element Should Be in 'Faith and Justice,'" in *Faith and Justice: The 1981 Loyola-Baumgarth Symposium on Values and Ethics,* edited by Walter P. Krolikowski. Chicago: Loyola University Press, 1982.

Gallagher, David M., ed. *Thomas Aquinas and His Legacy.* Washington, DC: Catholic University of America Press, 1994.

Gilson, Etienne. *The Christian Philosophy of St. Thomas Aquinas.* New York: Random House, 1955.

Gulley, A. D. *The Educational Philosophy of Saint Thomas Aquinas.* New York: Pageant Press, 1965.

Hudson, Deal W., and Dennis W. Moran, eds. *The Future of Thomism.* Notre

Dame, IN: University of Notre Dame Press, 1992.

Krolikowski, Walter, S. J. "Philosophy of Catholic Education Before Vatican II," in *Proceedings of the Midwest Philosophy of Education Society, 1991 and 1992,* edited by David B. Owen. Ames, IA: Midwest Philosophy of Education Society, 1993, pp. 311–317.

Little, Joyce A. *Toward a Thomist Methodology.* Lewiston, NY: E. Mellen Press, 1988.

McBride, Alfred. *The Christian Formation of Catholic Educators.* Washington, DC: National Catholic Educational Association, 1981.

McCluskey, Neil G. *Catholic Viewpoint on Education.* New York: Image Books, 1962.

McGucken, William J. *The Catholic Way in Education.* Milwaukee, WI: Bruce, 1934.

McInerny, Ralph. *St. Thomas Aquinas.* Notre Dame, IN: University of Notre Dame Press, 1981.

McInerny, Ralph M. *A First Glance at St. Thomas Aquinas: A Handbook for*

Peeping Thomists. Notre Dame, IN: University of Notre Dame Press, 1990.

O'Neill, Michael. *New Schools in a New Church: Toward a Modern Philosophy of Catholic Education.* Collegeville, MN: Saint John's University Press, 1971.

Owens, Joseph. *An Elementary Christian Metaphysics.* Notre Dame, IN: University of Notre Dame Press, 1984.

Pius XI. *Christian Education of Youth.* Washington, DC: National Catholic Welfare Conference, 1936.

Smith, Don G. "Americans First and Catholics Second: The Decline of Catholic Education Since Vatican II," in *Proceedings of the Midwest Philosophy of Education Society, 1991 and 1992,* edited by David B. Owen. Ames, IA: Midwest Philosophy of Education Society, 1993, pp. 327–334.

U.S. Catholic Conference. *Catholic Higher Education and the Pastoral Mission of the Church.* Washington, DC: U.S. Catholic Conference, 1980.

ENDNOTES

1. For treatments of scholasticism in the history of Western educational ideas, see Patrick J. McCormick and Francis P. Cassidy, *History of Education* (Washington, DC: Catholic Education Press, 1953), pp. 260–279; William T. Kane, *History of Education* (Chicago: Loyola University Press, 1954), pp. 94–129; Edward Peters, *Europe and the Middle Ages* (Englewood Cliffs, NJ: Prentice Hall, 1983), pp. 173–184, 220–237.

2. For a very readable account of the life and educational theory of Thomas Aquinas, see John W. Donohue, *St. Thomas Aquinas and Education* (New York: Random House, 1968). Also see G. K. Chesterton, *St. Thomas Aquinas* (New York: Sheed

& Ward, 1933); and Etienne Gilson, *The Christian Philosophy of St. Thomas Aquinas* (New York: Random House, 1955).

3. Neil G. McCluskey, *Catholic Viewpoint on Education* (New York: Image Books, 1962), pp. 57–79.

4. William F. Cunningham, *Pivotal Problems in Education* (New York: Macmillan, 1940).

5. Ibid.

6. Pope Pius XI, *Christian Education of Youth* (Washington, DC: National Catholic Welfare Conference, 1936), p. 36.

7. Arguments that the history of education should be broadened beyond treatments of schooling can be found in Bernard Bailyn, *Education in the Forming of Amer-*

ican Society (New York: Random House, 1960).

8. Donohue, *St. Thomas Aquinas and Education,* pp. 58–64, 82–89.

9. U.S. Catholic Conference, *Catholic Higher Education and the Pastoral Mission of the Church* (Washington, DC: U.S. Catholic Conference, 1980), p. 6.

10. Russell M. Bleich, *The Pre-Service Formation of Teachers for Catholic Schools* (Washington, DC: National Catholic Educational Association, 1982), p. 5.

11. For an historical and philosophical perspective, see Walter P. Krolikowski, S. J., "Philosophy of Catholic Education Before Vatican II," in David B. Owen, ed., *Proceedings of the Midwest Philosophy of Education Society, 1991 and 1992* (Ames, IA: Midwest Philosophy of Education Society, 1993), pp. 311–317.

12. The implications of the Second Vatican Council on Catholic educational theory are examined in John W. Donohue, *Catholicism and Education* (New York: Harper & Row, 1973).

13. Bleich, *Pre-Service Formation of Teachers,* p. 7.

► 5

Naturalism and Education

In Chapter 5, we examine Naturalism and its implications for education. As its name suggests, Naturalism assumes that nature is the ground of reality. Nature itself is a universal system that encompasses and explains existence, including human beings and human nature. In its simplest formulation, Naturalism holds that there is a single order of reality, which is matter in motion; many Naturalists, especially in ancient Greece, were materialists who denied the belief in a supernatural order of reality.

Unlike the neatly defined categories of Idealism, Realism, and Thomism, Naturalism is more ambiguous. There are also varieties of Naturalists. For example, Jean-Jacques Rousseau (1712–1778) veered back and forth from a romantic view of human nature to the rationalist perspective of the Enlightenment. Johann Heinrich Pestalozzi (1746–1827), who used Rousseau's ideas in his educational method, retained a belief in a supernatural God. Herbert Spencer (1820–1903) recast Darwinian evolutionary theory into a sociology of knowledge that stressed a highly competitive ethical system. Despite variations and ambiguities, Naturalism, particularly in education, has the following common beliefs:

1. One must look to nature and to human nature, as part of the natural order, for the purposes of education.
2. The key to understanding nature is through the senses; sensation is the basis of our knowledge of reality.
3. Because nature's processes are slow, gradual, and evolutionary, our education also should be unhurried.

In reading this chapter, note that it is located between Chapter 4, which examined Theistic Realism, and Chapter 6, which examines Pragmatism.

A sketch of Jean-Jacques Rousseau and Madame D'Epinay in which Rousseau, the author of *Émile,* discusses his theory of education. This conversation is documented as occurring in 1757. Rousseau (1712–1778) was a leading proponent of Naturalism.

Because Naturalism either rejects or diminishes the importance of the supernatural, it provides clear contrasts with Theistic Realism. Pragmatism borrowed some of the themes of Naturalism. In later chapters, we will examine Progressivism, a theory of education influenced by Naturalism, especially by Rousseau's version of it, and Pragmatism.[1]

In examining Naturalism, we will comment on Rousseau's contribution to the history of educational ideas and then examine certain of its key themes in relation to education.

ROUSSEAU: PROPONENT OF NATURALISM

In this section, we examine Jean-Jacques Rousseau as a leading proponent of Naturalism in education in the late eighteenth century. We first examine Rousseau as a contributor to the history of educational ideas and then analyze *Émile,* his didactic novel and most significant work on education.

Rousseau and the History of Educational Ideas

According to his book *Confessions,* Rousseau, who was born in Geneva, Switzerland, was a precocious, sensitive, but undisciplined child.[2] The son of a watchmaker, Rousseau's mother died when he was a week old and his father, to avoid arrest, was forced to leave him when Rousseau was ten. As a youth, Rousseau served for short periods of time as an apprentice to an engraver and to a notary but these were unsatisfactory and disappointing experiences for the young man.

Rousseau's *Confessions* show him to be a proponent of permissiveness, a theme also pursued in *Émile.* Rejecting the stern authority of the coercive teacher, Rousseau, who himself was frequently in trouble with authority figures, usually escaped from them. The character of Émile was his own authority, a person who either enjoyed or suffered the consequences of his actions, rather than subject himself to another's authority. Teachers, in Rousseau's style, were permissive individuals who learned with their students.

The year 1741 found Rousseau in Paris, not only the capital of France but also the intellectual center of the *philosophes* of the Enlightenment whose critiques of politics, society, morality, and education were challenging the old order. Attracted to and stimulated by the ferment of the Enlightenment, Rousseau joined the intellectual debates. From Rousseau's pen came a number of essays and books—*Discourse on the Arts and Sciences, Discourse on Political Economy, The Social Contract, Émile,* and *Confessions*—which earned him significant stature in the history of Western social, political, and educational ideas.[3]

In his essay *Discourse on the Sciences and Arts* published in 1750, Rousseau argued that the arts and sciences were injurious to morals insofar as they encouraged pride as a social end.[4] Rather than claiming a social position based on knowledge of the arts and sciences, the individual should follow the dictates of his or her own conscience in performing his or her duties.

Rousseau's interpretation of the educational role of the liberal arts and sciences significantly departed from the historical tradition that had originated with

Plato and Aristotle in ancient Greece and was developed by Aquinas in the Middle Ages. While Rousseau recognized the intellectual significance of the arts and sciences, he emphasized the importance of the individual's direct experience with the natural environment. Sensations and emotions, the human's own personal contact points with nature, were to be trusted and enjoyed rather than being bridled by proscriptions from theological, political, and literary authorities.

Central to Rousseau's philosophy was his belief that the development of human character should follow nature. Rousseau distinguished between two forms of self-esteem: *amour de soi,* an intrinsic love of being, and *amour propre,* or pride. *Amour de soi,* or "love of oneself," is a natural life-affirming sentiment that inclines the person to self-preservation. It is from *amour de soi* that the human being, through natural education, arrives at humane values. In contrast, *amour propre,* or selfishness, is an externally derived product of society by which individuals seek to control, dominate, and use others for their own social aggrandizement. When dominated by *amour propre,* a person sees others as either objects to be used or obstacles to be removed.

Both *The Social Contract,* Rousseau's statement of political theory, and *Émile,* his educational treatise, seek to establish conditions in which *amour de soi,* the natural inclination, will triumph over *amour propre,* the social determination of the person. In *The Social Contract,* Rousseau sought to reconcile the conflict between the person and the group.[5] The policy emerging from the "social contract" is one in which the person and his or her possessions are protected by the collective force of all the members. This meant that each person identified his or her will with the general will of the community. Quite different from the social contract theory of John Locke (1632–1704) in which policy was based on majority rule, Rousseau's contract theory saw the general will as the will of all, a unanimous expression of public sentiment. Rousseau's version of the social contract implied that as each person's will is an integral part of the general will, or the will of all, he or she is really his or her own political authority rather than a follower of the dictates of another's authority.

In *Émile,* Rousseau's didactic novel, a boy, in experiencing a natural education, forms his character in such a way that his original inclination to *amour de soi* is so developed that he can resist and overcome the social temptations and pressures that lead to *amour propre.*[6] Rousseau has Émile develop naturally, on a country estate, away from corrupting social institutions and conventions. In his novel, Rousseau developed several themes that had a pronounced effect on educational reform based on Naturalism and on progressive education: (1) childhood, as an intrinsically valuable period of human growth and development, has its own educational timetable; (2) education best occurs in a prepared environment, which, while retaining its natural features, is designed to cooperate with the child's readiness to learn by presenting situations that stimulate his or her curiosity and bring about action; (3) the child learns in a permissive atmosphere in that he or she makes the basic choices regarding one's actions but must also enjoy or suffer their consequences.

True to his belief that human beings have their own timetable for learning, Rousseau organized education according to Émile's stages of development. For each stage of development, the child, Émile, showed signs that he was ready to learn what was appropriate to that stage; his actions, or learning episodes and activities, were also appropriate to the particular developmental stage. Based on these stages, human learning could be organized sequentially with educational results that were cumulative.

Rousseau's concept of childhood sharply contrasted with the view of the child that was dominant when he wrote *Émile*. The early eighteenth-century view, still influenced heavily by John Calvin, saw childhood as a necessary evil to be gotten through as quickly as possible. Children, particularly the very young, were dirty, noisy, mischievous, and prone to evil and idleness. In the traditional view, the "good child" was as adultlike as possible. The "good child," a miniature adult, was dutiful, quiet, and obedient. The shorter the time devoted to childlike play, games, and behavior, the better. Seeing the child as a primitive innocent, Rousseau viewed childhood as the most "natural stage of human development." It was a time that was to be enjoyed and savored for as long as possible.

Like many of the educational reformers who followed him, Rousseau refused to hurry childhood. Indeed, childhood was such a valuable period of human growth and development that Rousseau wanted to extend it for as long as possible. Influenced by Rousseau, Pestalozzi argued that learning should proceed slowly, gradually, and cumulatively. Thus, twentieth-century progressive educators also emphasized direct experiences, activities, and projects rather than introduce academic subjects at an early age.

In *Émile,* Rousseau identified the following stages of human growth and development: infancy, from birth to age five; childhood, from age five to twelve; preadolescence, from twelve to fifteen; adolescence, from fifteen to eighteen; and young adulthood, from eighteen to twenty. It should be pointed out that for all his liberalism, Rousseau remained much of a male chauvinist. Sophie, who became Émile's wife, was educated to complement her husband's needs rather than to define her own educational goals.[7]

During the first stage, infancy, from birth to age five, human beings are helpless and much must be done to satisfy their needs. The major aims are to provide simple food and freedom of movement to develop a strong and healthy body. During the first stage, the human being, as a natural creature, is governed by instincts and experiences, feelings of either pleasure or pain. With memory and imagination largely inactive, human beings at this age are incapable of abstract reasoning and moral judgment. In terms of language development, the first words should be few, simple, and clear, and should refer to concrete objects.

The second stage of human development, from ages five to twelve, marked by a growing physical strength and the ability to do more for oneself, is a time when the instinct to self-preservation is strong. The boy Émile, who deals primarily with the objects of his environment, receives a negative education in which the environment is purified of social corruption, crime, and vice. The concept of negative education is important. Rousseau, who recognized the power of early childhood experiences in setting the patterns of later life, wanted these influences to be open rather than closed so that a person could fully benefit from future experience. Negative education kept out the closed, the prescribed and proscribed, patterns of social convention that limited one's openness to experience. The second stage was especially relevant to later Naturalists in education such as Pestalozzi and Francis Parker. It was a time for exercising and training the senses by measuring, counting, weighing, and comparing the objects in the environment. Rousseau also warned against the premature introduction of books and verbal lessons that developed "youthful sages" who parroted memorized bits of information.

The third stage in Émile's development occurred between ages twelve and fifteen when he began to learn about the utility of objects and the relationships among them. The observation of natural phenomena and the environment contributed to the gradual transformation of sensations and feelings into ideas. Émile reads *Robinson Crusoe,* his first book, about the survival of a shipwrecked man on an island and of the mutual relationship of Crusoe and Friday. As this stage ends, Émile has further developed the facility for acquiring knowledge.

During his adolescent stage, from age fifteen to eighteen, Émile is ready to enter into social relationships. Aware of and experiencing sexual drives, his tutor provides sex education—a direct and sensitive answering of questions devoid of coarseness and mysteriousness. Based on his nurtured sense of *amour de soi,* Émile, upon encountering poor people, has sympathy for them.

Next comes the stage of humanity, from age eighteen to twenty, when Émile, aware of moral relationships, experiences values of justice and goodness that arise from his primitive affections now enlightened by reason. Émile enters society and cultivates his aesthetic sense for literature, art, and music. He meets Sophie, a naturally educated woman, whom he marries. Together, Émile and Sophie plan to rear their children as Émile has been educated—according to nature's principles.

NATURALIST THEMES IN EDUCATION

In this section of the chapter, we examine the following educational themes based on Naturalism: (1) nature and the natural; (2) Naturalist epistemology; (3) axiology and values; (4) human growth and development from a Naturalist perspective; (5) a Naturalist view of curriculum; and (6) the teacher–learner relationship in the Naturalist context.

Nature and the Natural

For the Naturalists in education, nature and "the natural" were the key elements in their educational theory. Preferred over the artificiality and contrivance of society, the natural way in education followed nature itself in being immediate, original, free, spontaneous, and simple. In metaphysical terms, nature was the universal and beneficent order of the cosmos. Of more importance than a metaphysical rendering of nature, the Naturalists looked more to an anthropological conception of the human being in the state of nature. In this primitive and original state, human life was guided by pure motives arising from the person's unspoiled instincts. This view of human nature as being originally good, or at least unspoiled, contrasted sharply with the doctrine that human beings fell from grace because of sin.

In the previous chapter, we examined Theistic Realism, which emphasized the supernatural. Naturalism, in contrast, discounted or opposed supernaturalism and education based on it. In contrast to an abstract intellectualism or a spiritual other-worldliness, Naturalism stressed the human being's parallelism with nature. It recognized the legitimacy of sensation and feeling as well as science and reason.

In the late eighteenth and early nineteenth centuries, Naturalism in education was expressed by Jean-Jacques Rousseau and Johann Heinrich Pestalozzi. In many commentaries, the Naturalists in education are referred to as reformers who were rebelling against supernaturalism, religious indoctrination, classicalism, and verbalism in education. Rather than looking to the supernaturalism of the church or the Greek and Latin classics as authorities, the Naturalists looked to nature.

For the various Naturalists, nature was viewed in a variety of ways but always as the source of human growth and development. This perspective focused on the person, as a natural organism, who existed in a world of other natural entities that interacted with each other. Naturalists, influenced by the Enlightenment, viewed nature as a perfectly functioning world machine—a universal mechanism—of which human beings were a part. The philosophers of the Enlightenment believed that the scientific method could be used to analyze nature and to find in this analysis natural laws that governed the universe and human beings within it.[8] They further believed that these natural laws could be applied to society, economics, politics, and education. With the Enlightenment came the quest to develop a social science, or a sociology of knowledge, that described, explained, and prescribed the natural, hence correct, functioning of human social, political, economic, and educational institutions. If nature was a mechanism, then human beings could discover how it functioned. Education was to prepare people to follow their human nature and to live according to its dictates. In their desire to describe, explain, and prescribe scientifically, the Enlightenment philosophers began to look to sociological phenomena rather than metaphysics.

The Enlightenment *philosophes* and the educational Naturalists were revolutionary in their questioning of the old order. Both the American Revolution and French Revolution overthrew the inherited monarchical institutions by which kings ruled by the "grace of God." As the old political order was challenged, so was the educational order that rested on the authorities of Sacred Scripture and the ancient classics. The new order would be natural in both society and education.

With the publication of Charles Darwin's *The Origin of the Species* in 1859, Naturalism added the new dimension of evolutionary theory. Further abandoning supernaturalism, evolutionary Naturalism rejected the biblical account of creation in the Book of Genesis. According to evolutionary theory, humans, like other surviving species, were creatures who had successfully adapted to a changing natural environment.

Epistemology, Knowing, and Naturalism

In epistemology, Naturalism, especially as developed by the Enlightenment *philosophes,* was not a radical departure from Aristotelian Natural Realism. Indeed, it was instead an early form of scientific realism.

In education, however, Naturalism signaled a radical departure from verbalism as a method of instruction. Naturalism's focus was on sense experience as a means of analyzing or breaking down reality into its components. To gain an accurate and scientific impression of reality, it was necessary to reduce objects to their smallest parts. Sensationalist theorists such as Étienne de Condillac (1715–1780) and educational reformers such as Pestalozzi saw the source of error lying in both abstraction and speculation, which were not based on finely tuned or accurate sensation.

Pestalozzi referred to his great discovery as *Anschauung,* a term which meant the forming of clear concepts from sense perception.[9] While an Aristotelian could probably agree with the Swiss educator on conceptualization, Pestalozzi's object lesson was a unique rendering of instructional method. Pestalozzi's object lesson was based on the teaching of form, number, and name. Students were to extract the form or design of the object, count objects, and name them. Unlike the Thomist search for first principles, Naturalists such as Pestalozzi stressed simple beginnings, immediate experiences, and concrete cases.

For later advocates of Naturalism in education, the doctrine that we learn through our senses held pronounced implications for instruction. Francis Parker (1837–1902), a father of U.S. Progressivism, stressed nature study in which children, by means of field trips and excursions, studied nature first hand. Sensory experience as a basis for learning meant that children should have direct experience with objects in the environment. Through activities and projects, they were to be active in dealing with these objects, in conducting experiments, and in arriving at generalizations about the environment. William Heard Kilpatrick (1871–1965), a leading Progressive, devised the project method, which relied on selected aspects of Naturalism. A later-day neo-Rousseauean, John Holt, in his advocacy of child freedom, argued that children constructed their own reality as they explored their environments.[10] To shape one's own reality was a far different undertaking from coming to know and conform to the structures of reality as the Realist philosophers insisted.

Axiology, Values, and Human Nature

For the Naturalists, values arise from the human being's interaction with the environment. Instincts, drives, and impulses need to be expressed rather than repressed. This expression, however, should be based on natural self-esteem, or in Rousseau's terminology, *amour de soi,* which eliminated exploitation of others, rather than on a socially derived selfishness that gained privilege and status at other's expense.

For Rousseau, the natural person who is unspoiled by social conventions and artificialities is good. Rousseau rejected both the Calvinist view that human beings are depraved because of their inheritance of original sin and the Catholic view that they were spiritually deprived because of this inherited sinful nature. In contrast, Rousseau, finding no inherent evil in the human heart, asserted that evil came from a corrupt society. In Rousscauean terms, the child was intrinsically good at birth. Because children are good, education—if it is to cultivate moral persons—should follow children's impulses and inclinations. The curriculum and instruction should come from the child's nature.

Rousseau's ethics, as expressed in *Émile,* look to human beings' primitive state—to the state of nature—as the basis of ethical relationships. The natural person interacts and deals directly with the environment through immediate experience and not by verbal or abstract theological, philosophical, or legal formulas. A "noble savage," the natural person is direct, forthright, and unaffected. In contrast, the thoroughly social being has lost this primitive innocence. Through the processes of socialization and education in corrupt institutions, the social man or woman has learned to be a mannered but manipulative role player.

For Pestalozzi, for example, morality arose from the satisfaction of basic human needs. The satisfaction of the infant's needs for nourishment, warmth, and affection from the mother produced feelings of trust, love, and emotional security. These feelings of love and trust were then extended to other members of the family, then to members of the community, to citizens of the country, to the entire human race, and then ultimately to God.

For Rousseau, Pestalozzi, and other Naturalists, the love of self and self-esteem gradually radiated outwardly to the association with other persons. From the love of self comes a natural ethic that cultivates a sense of human equality that institutions based on rank and privilege could not impede nor deflect.

For the Naturalists, education for moral development had both positive and negative aspects. Negative education blocked out those corrupting elements that interfered with the development of a naturalistic ethic, Conventional religious education, especially in the catechistic manner of memorizing ethical prescriptions in verbal form or preachment, failed to cultivate a genuine morality because it substituted words for feelings and actions. The positive aspect of education for moral development was based on allowing the expression of the naturally valuable and elemental human instincts. Enjoying or suffering the consequences of one's own action was its own reward or punishment.

Human Growth and Development

In developing their educational theory, Naturalists looked to human beings to provide both clues and cues for education. As they go through the life span from infancy to old age, human beings exhibit stages of development. Each stage begins when the human being is ready for it—that is, is exhibiting physiological and psychological readiness, and performing the exercises and activities that develop the person. Stages of development are cumulative in that they lead to the next stage. The theory of stages of development leads to a special kind of educational "appropriateness." Instead of preparing a person for an appropriate social or economic role, Naturalists construe appropriateness as being correct for the person's readiness and development. That is, education should not be training to be either a prince or a peasant. Rather, it should be appropriate to a stage of human development.

Naturalism and the Curriculum

For the Idealists, Realists, and Thomists treated in Chapters 2, 3, and 4, the liberal arts and sciences were highly regarded as the funded wisdom of the human race and as the ideal subject matter for cultivating the human intellect. In contrast, Rousseau, disputing the value of the arts and sciences, claimed that pedantic teachers had formalized them into bodies of inert and highly verbal information that were remote from nature. They civilized human beings in the wrong way in that they detracted from the human being's primitive and pure natural virtues. For some who studied them, the arts and sciences contributed to *amour propre* in that they were used not for their intrinsic value, but to gain power and prestige.

Educators such as Pestalozzi in the early nineteenth century and William Heard Kilpatrick, a twentieth-century Progressive educator, continued to attack education that stressed the mastery of bookish information. This kind of schooling, argued the Naturalist reformers, relied on rote memorization and turned the naturally active child into a passive receptacle for information. Learning, they advised, should actively involve children in dealing with the environment, using their senses, and solving problems. The Naturalist assault on subject matter began the long series of pedagogical skirmishes on the nature of the curriculum that has occupied educators, and often public policymakers. To more traditional educators, such as Idealists, Realists, and Thomists, the Naturalist predilection for direct child experience encouraged a childish anti-intellectualism.

For Naturalists, genuine education is based on the readiness and needs of the human being. For many of the nineteenth-century Naturalist reformers and the twentieth-century Progressives, the child's nature, interests, and needs provided the basis of the curriculum. Rather than studying the hierarchically arranged subject matter of the Idealists, Realists, and Thomists, children learned what they were ready to and wanted to learn. Human experience provided a richly varied range of activities that led to growth and development. Rather than the mastery of subject matter, Naturalists and their latter-day adherents saw learning as resulting from activities, projects, and problem solving.

The Teacher and Learner

In *Émile,* Rousseau concentrates so much on developing the education of Émile that the personality, character, and qualities of the tutor can be easily overlooked. The personality of the tutor is important, however, in that it illuminates the kind of person that Rousseau had in mind as the ideal "natural" teacher. Not only is Rousseau's concept of the teacher important in fully understanding *Émile*, but it is also significant because it influenced the progressive view of the child-centered teacher.

The tutor, first of all, is a person who is completely in tune with nature. Appreciating the role of the natural environment as an educative force, the tutor does not interfere with nature but rather cooperates with the ebb and flow of natural forces. Significantly, the tutor, who is aware of human nature and its stages of growth and development, does not force Émile to learn but rather encourages learning by stimulating him to explore and to grow by his interactions with the environment.

Secondly, the tutor, an educator who is not in a hurry to have Émile learn, is patient, permissive, and nonintrusive. Émile learns when he is ready to learn. As a teacher, the tutor is congenial to the "discovery method" by which the learner discovers knowledge rather than having it given to him vicariously by the teacher. Demonstrating great patience, the tutor cannot allow himself to tell the student what the truth is but rather must stand back and encourage the learner's own self-discovery.

The tutor portrayed in *Émile* is an almost invisible guide to learning. While ever-present, he is never a taskmaster. His control is subtle in that he is shaping the learning environment and by so doing shaping the personality and character of the learner.

In many respects, Émile's tutor was prophetic of the child-centered teacher of modern Progressive education. The Progressive teacher often was depicted as a guide to learning or a manipulator of the learning environment who taught by indirect strategies rather than pouring information into the learners' minds in the traditional style. Like the Progressive teacher, Émile's tutor emphasized activity, exploration, and learning by doing. He was not a teacher who stressed books, recitations, and amassing information in literary form. Rousseau's idea of the tutor was prophetic of the version of the teacher recommended by the "romantic" critics of the school. For critics such as Jonathan Kozol and John Holt, the teacher creates an open-ended and nonprescriptive environment in which children create their own subjective realities by exploring their own worlds of learning.

An important feature of Naturalist education is informality, a relaxed and permissive teacher–student relationship. While Idealists, Realists, and Thomists defined the school as a formal institution of education, Naturalists sought to reduce its formality by transforming it into a relaxed learning environment. Rousseau's Émile was guided by a highly permissive tutor on a rural estate, a very relaxed environment. Pestalozzi's educational institutes were designed as homelike places rather than formal institutions. Naturalist educational reformers continually battled against the traditional concept of the school as a place for the formal study of academic subjects.

The child is a noble savage, a primitive unspoiled by the vices of a corrupting society. The child's needs, instincts, and impulses are to be trusted and relied on as the raw ingredients of further education. When these natural impulses are acted on, they lead to sensory experiences that provide a direct relationship with the environment. Gradually, sensation leads to clear ideas, which become the basis for reflective action. Importantly, the nobility of the noble savage is to be cultivated by a form of self-directed character development.

CONCLUSION

In Chapter 19 we will examine Progressivism as an educational theory. Naturalism was one of the theoretical strands that contributed to twentieth-century Progressive education as well as to a variety of educational reform alternatives. Some common elements derived from Naturalism are the following:

1. Children's learning should originate with direct sensory experience in their immediate environments rather than with verbalism such as lectures, preachment, and books.
2. Childhood is an appropriate, necessary, and valuable stage of human growth and development; the curriculum and instruction should flow from the child's impulses and instincts.
3. Childhood and adolescence are not of one piece but are cumulative stages of human development that have their own readiness for learning and appropriate learning exercises.

4. The school should not be regarded as separate from but rather as an extension of the child's environment.

DISCUSSION QUESTIONS

1. Define Naturalism and compare and contrast your definition with Idealism, Realism, and Thomism.

2. Refer to the concept of dualism developed in Chapters 3 and 4. Critique dualism from a Naturalist perspective.

3. Distinguish between and provide contemporary examples of *amour de soi* and *amour propre*.

4. Examine the concept of stages of human growth and development and indicate its educational implications.

5. Examine the educational implications of the Naturalist epistemology of sensation.

6. Examine the concept of the noble savage in terms of education.

7. From the Naturalist perspective, how does the curriculum come from the child?

8. Define the concept of readiness for learning from the Naturalist perspective.

9. Analyze the teacher–learner relationship from the Naturalist orientation.

10. How would Rousseau react to the views of childhood held in contemporary U.S. society?

INQUIRY PROJECTS

- Using his *Confessions* and other works, prepare a biographical sketch of Rousseau with emphasis on the forming of his educational ideas.
- Read Rousseau's *Discourse on the Arts and Sciences* and analyze his argument. Apply the argument to contemporary education.
- Review Rousseau's *Émile*.
- Prepare a paper analyzing Johann Heinrich Pestalozzi's efforts to render Rousseau's educational ideas into a method of instruction.
- Read a book by John Holt on education. Do you find any similarity or affinity to Rousseau's ideas on education? Write a criticism of Naturalism from an Idealist, Realist, or Thomist perspective.
- Prepare a teaching strategy or lesson plan according to the Naturalist perspective.
- Read Daniel Defoe's *Robinson Crusoe* and indicate the extent to which it exemplifies Naturalism.
- Identify and view several television series that feature children. After viewing these programs, apply a Rousseauean critique to them.

FURTHER READINGS

Bhaskar, Roy. *The Possibility of Naturalism: A Philosophical Critique of the Contemporary Human Sciences.* New York: Harvester Wheatsheaf, 1989.

Bloom, Allan, ed. *Jean-Jacques Rousseau, Émile or on Education.* New York: Basic Books, 1979.

Boyd, William, ed. *The Émile of Jean-Jacques Rousseau.* New York: Teachers College Press, Columbia University, 1956.

Boyd, William. *The Minor Educational Writings of Jean-Jacques Rousseau.* New York: Teachers College Press, Columbia University, 1962.

Claydon, Leslie P. *Rousseau on Education.* London: Collier-Macmillan, 1969.

Cranston, Maurice W. *Jean-Jacques: The Early Life and Work of Jean-Jacques Rousseau, 1712–1754.* Chicago: University of Chicago Press, 1991.

Cranston, Maurice W. *The Noble Savage: Jean-Jacques Rousseau, 1754–1762.* Chicago: University of Chicago Press, 1991.

Crocker, Lester G. *Rousseau's Social Contract: An Interpretative Essay.* Cleveland: Case Western Reserve University Press, 1968.

Dobinson, C. H. *Jean-Jacques Rousseau: His Thought and its Relevance Today.* London: Methuen, 1969.

Cullen, Daniel. *Freedom in Rousseau's Political Philosophy.* DeKalb, IL: Northern Illinois University Press, 1993.

Ferrara, Alessandro. *Modernity and Authenticity: A Study in the Social and Ethical Thought of Jean-Jacques Rousseau.* Albany: State University Press of New York, 1992.

French, Peter A., Theodore E. Uehling, and Howard K. Wettstein. *Philosophical Naturalism.* Notre Dame, IN: University of Notre Dame Press, 1994.

Kurtz, Paul. *Philosophical Essays in Pragmatic Naturalism.* Buffalo, NY: Prometheus Books, 1990.

Lincoln, Yvonna S., and Egon G. Guba. *Naturalistic Inquiry.* Beverly Hills, CA: Sage, 1985.

Melser, Arthur M. *The Natural Goodness of Man: On the System of Rousseau's Thought.* Chicago: University of Chicago Press, 1990.

Noble, Richard. *Language, Subjectivity, and Freedom in Rousseau's Moral Philosophy.* New York: Garland, 1991.

Roosevelt, Grace G. *Reading Rousseau in the Nuclear Age.* Philadelphia: Temple University Press, 1990.

Rousseau, Jean-Jacques. *The Confessions.* Translated by J. M. Cohen. Baltimore: Penguin Books, 1954.

Rousseau, Jean-Jacques. *Discourse on the Sciences and Arts.* Hanover, NH: University Press of New England, 1992.

Rousseau, Jean-Jacques. *Discourse on the Origin of Inequality.* Indianapolis: Hackett, 1992.

Rousseau, Jean-Jacques. *The First and Second Discourses.* Edited by Roger D. Masters. New York: St. Martin's Press, 1964.

Rousseau, Jean-Jacques. *On The Social Contract.* Edited by Roger D. Masters. New York: St. Martin's Press, 1978.

Simpson, Peter. *Goodness and Nature: A Defense of Ethical Naturalism.* Boston: M. Nijhoff, 1987.

Strong, Tracy B. *Jean-Jacques Rousseau: The Politics of the Ordinary.* Thousand Oaks, CA: Sage, 1994.

Trachtenberg, Zev M. *Making Citizens: Rousseau's Political Theory of Culture.* New York: Routledge, 1993.

Wagner, Steven J., and Richards Wagner, eds. *Naturalism: A Critical Appraisal.* Notre Dame, IN: University of Notre Dame Press, 1993.

Weiss, Penny A. *Gendered Community: Rousseau, Sex, and Politics.* New York: New York University Press, 1993.

ENDNOTES

1. For a discussion of Pragmatism and Naturalism, see Paul Kurtz, *Philosophical Essays in Pragmatic Naturalism* (Buffalo, NY: Prometheus Books, 1990).

2. William Boyd, *The Minor Educational Writings of Jean Jacques Rousseau* (New York: Teachers College, Columbia University, 1962), pp. 7–23. Also see Maurice W. Cranston, *Jean-Jacques: The Early Life and Work of Jean-Jacques Rousseau, 1712–1754* (Chicago: University of Chicago Press, 1991).

3. Recent editions of Rousseau's major works are Jean-Jacques Rousseau, *Discourse on the Sciences and Arts* (Hanover, NH: University Press of New England, 1992); and *Discourse on the Origin of Inequality* (Indianapolis: Hackett, 1992).

4. Jean-Jacques Rousseau, *The First and Second Discourses,* ed. Roger D. Masters. (New York: St. Martin's Press, 1964), pp. 34–64.

5. Jean-Jacques Rousseau, *On the Social Contract,* ed. Roger D. Masters. (New York: St. Martin's Press, 1978).

6. Editions of Rousseau's *Émile* are William Boyd, ed., *The Émile of Jean-Jacques Rousseau* (New York: Teachers College Press, Columbia University, 1956), and Allan Bloom, ed., *Jean-Jacques Rousseau, Émile or On Education* (New York: Basic Books, 1979).

7. For a comprehensive examination of Rousseau's views on gender, see Penny W. Weiss, *Gendered Community: Rousseau, Sex, and Politics* (New York: New York University Press, 1993).

8. For discussions of the Enlightenment, see Carl Becker, *The Heavenly City of the Eighteenth-Century Philosophers* (New Haven, CT: Yale University Press, 1960); Lester G. Crocker, *The Age of the Enlightenment* (New York: Walker & Co., 1969); Peter Gay, *The Enlightenment: An Interpretation* (New York: Alfred A. Knopf, 1967).

9. Gerald L. Gutek, *Pestalozzi and Education* (New York: Random House, 1968), pp. 88–93.

10. For an example of Holt's neo-Rousseauean perspective, see John Holt, *Freedom and Beyond* (New York: E. P. Dutton, 1972).

► 6

Pragmatism and Education

Thus far we have examined Idealism, Realism, Theistic Realism, and Naturalism as systematic philosophies that have significant implications for education. Whereas the origins of Idealism and Realism date back to ancient Greece, Pragmatism developed in twentieth-century America.[1] While the older traditional philosophies rested on an antecedent view of reality in which truth is *a priori,* or prior to and independent of human experience, the Pragmatists contended that truth was a tentative assertion derived from human experience. Although Naturalism, discussed in Chapter 5, may appear to be more congenial to Pragmatism, the Pragmatic philosophers were concerned with testing the consequences of our actions in a rigorously scientific manner. To the Pragmatists, Rousseau's concept of a naturally good "noble savage" expressed romantic sentimentality.

Rejecting the metaphysical speculation of the older philosophies, Pragmatists such as Charles S. Peirce (1839–1914), William James (1842–1910), George Herbert Mead (1863–1931), and John Dewey (1859–1952) believed that philosophy needed to be applied to solving human problems.[2] Ideas were to be judged by their consequences when acted on; truth was a warranted assertion, a tentative statement based on the application of hypotheses to solving problems; logic, following the scientific method, was experimental; values were experienced within the context of ethical and aesthetic problems and issues charged by the unique features of particular situations.

In many ways, Pragmatism was a philosophical expression of America's frontier experience in which westward-moving pioneers migrated through varying natural environments which they transformed but which also changed them and their society. The frontier experience caused Americans to judge success in terms of the consequences that came from transforming the environment for human purposes. Over time, the openness of an expansive frontier was translated into a wider vision of an open universe, charged by the dynamics of constant flux, change, and movement. Pragmatism appeared at a time when science and industry were creating a new technological society, the outlines of which were still emergent and flexible.[3] As the nineteenth century yielded to the twentieth, the scientific temperament was exalted as a positive force for making a better life on earth. The legacy of the old frontier of open land in the West and the new frontier of a scientifically functioning technology made the time ripe for the new, hardheaded philosophy of Pragmatism. Pragmatism proclaimed the American propensity to discard purely speculative philosophy as an empty metaphysical meandering.

The formulation of Pragmatism also coincided with that period of energetic social, political, and educational reform known as the Progressive movement, from the late 1890s to the United States' entry into World War I in 1917.[4] The pragmatic outlook, which argued that problems, if capable of definition, were also capable of solution, fitted the social reformist attitude of Progressive Americans.

Our examination of Pragmatism focuses on John Dewey's Experimentalism, or Instrumentalism. For Dewey, the method of philosophy, like the method of science, was experimental. Our ideas were instruments to be used in solving human problems. Dewey was a philosopher who concentrated much of his effort on educational problems. The consequences of his work had profound implications for education. In the sections that follow we will examine (1) John Dewey as a leader of American Pragmatism; (2) Experimentalism's philosophical bases; and (3) Experimentalism's educational implications.

JOHN DEWEY: A FOUNDER OF PRAGMATISM

While Peirce, James, Mead, and others contributed to the formulation of Pragmatism, John Dewey became the leading proponent of Pragmatism in education. Throughout the twentieth century, his ideas have shaped the philosophy of education. In this section, we will examine Dewey in terms of the history of educational ideas, and comment on his major philosophical and educational works.

Dewey in the History of Educational Ideas

John Dewey was born in Burlington, Vermont, in 1859, the year when Charles Darwin's *Origin of Species* appeared.[5] Dewey's father was a local businessman, and his family was active in the social and political life of the late nineteenth-century Vermont community, which was characterized by a spirit of democratic neighborliness. Dewey's social philosophy would stress the significance of the

A sketch of John Dewey (1859–1952), American Pragmatist philosopher and proponent of Experimentalism in education.

face-to-face community in which people shared common concerns and problems. His democratic vision was shaped by the New England town meeting, where people met to solve their mutual problems through a peaceful and shared process of discussion, debate, and decision making. When he developed his social and educational philosophy, Dewey's theory of social intelligence embraced the concepts of the participatory community and the application of the scientific method.[6]

Dewey's religious upbringing as a Congregationalist shaped his social and ethical outlook. Evangelical Protestantism was being transformed by the "social gospel," which emphasized a person's ethical responsibility of working for earthly reform and the social and economic betterment of society. Although he would later end his formal adherence to organized religion, Dewey, like many Progressives of the early twentieth century, was a social reformer who believed that people had a mission to make the earth a better place to live, by reform and education.[7]

Dewey attended the University of Vermont, where he received his bachelor's degree. He then taught school in Oil City, Pennsylvania, and later in rural Vermont. Dewey pursued doctoral studies at Johns Hopkins University, a graduate institution founded on the German research model. Also attending Johns Hopkins was the future political scientist, academic and political reformer, and U.S. President, Woodrow Wilson.

As a graduate student at Johns Hopkins, Dewey studied and accepted the Hegelian Idealism of his mentor, George Sylvester Morris, which he would later abandon for Pragmatism. Although he abandoned Idealist metaphysics, Dewey's attraction to the Hegelian theme of a unifying "great community" continued. For him, the Idealist ethic that accentuated human self-realization remained a guiding possibility but he no longer believed that it was to be achieved in a spiritual realm.[8] Rather, Dewey believed that it would be achieved in human experiences transformed by larger transactions that embraced human relationships and democratic participation in the community.[9] After receiving his doctorate, Dewey joined the philosophy department of the University of Michigan, where he taught from 1889 to 1894.

In 1894, Dewey joined the faculty of the University of Chicago, which, under the leadership of William Rainey Harper, its president, was emerging as an internationally recognized institution for graduate research and study. At Chicago, Dewey served as head of the Department of Philosophy, Psychology, and Education. These three disciplines, then jointly organized in a single academic unit, held a special interest for Dewey, who studied and wrote on each of them. All three areas focused, in Dewey's thought, on the social role of education.

Dewey's Chicago years, from 1894 to 1904, were especially significant for his philosophical development and for his educational experiment at the University Laboratory School. Dewey's association with George Herbert Mead, a colleague in his department, and his involvement in Jane Addams's Hull House helped to shape his emerging Pragmatism. Mead, sometimes called the most original of the Progressive philosophers, argued that ideas and actions ought to be fused and directed toward social reform. Among Mead's ideas shared by Dewey were that (1) democracy, as an ideal, required a public that was educated to understand the social duties and responsibilities of political life; and (2) morality should be applied to the problems of daily life—to personal, political, social, and educational behavior.[10]

Like Dewey, Mead was interested in child development, particularly in early childhood education. Mead developed a theory of play as an activity whose purposes, although not evident at the time when playing occurs, serves to create connections to later activities, including work. Mead, who saw play as a natural way to learn, argued that the child's environment provided myriad opportunities for play.[11] Teachers should arrange the learning environment, especially during early childhood, so that it stimulated the child's interest and elicited activity. Mead also advocated experimental learning in which students engaged in field studies and laboratory work. His ideas were congenial to Dewey's thought and stimulated Dewey's philosophical and educational work at the University of Chicago.

While at the University of Chicago, Dewey established and directed the Laboratory School from 1896 to 1904.[12] Dewey's Laboratory School, enrolling children from ages four through fourteen, sought to provide experiences in cooperative and mutually useful living through the "activity method," which involved play, construction, nature study, and self-expression. These activities were designed to stimulate and exercise learners' active reconstruction of their own experiences. Through such activities, the school would function as a miniature community and an embryonic society. The children's individual tendencies were to be directed toward cooperative living in the school community.

True to his Experimentalist philosophy, Dewey's Laboratory School was an experimental school in which theories about education were tested. Educational hypotheses that were effective in aiding the students to reconstruct their experiences in terms of larger social outcomes could then be disseminated to a larger professional and public audience.

In describing the Laboratory School at the University of Chicago, Dewey wrote:

The conception underlying the school is that of a laboratory. It bears the same relation to the work in pedagogy that a laboratory bears to biology, physics, or chemistry. Like any such laboratory it has two main purposes: (1) to exhibit, test, verify, and criticize theoretical statements and principles; and (2) to add to the sum of facts and principles in its special line.[13]

Dewey's experiment emphasized the social function of the school. As a "special social community," the complexity of the "social environment" was "reduced and simplified." According to Dewey:

The simplified social life should reproduce, in miniature, the activities fundamental to life as a whole, and thus enable the child, on one side, to become gradually acquainted with the structure, materials, and modes of operation of the larger community; while upon the other, it enables him individually to express himself through these lines of conduct, and thus attain control of his own powers.[14]

In 1904, Dewey left Chicago to join the philosophy department at Columbia University, where he taught until 1930. Dewey enjoyed an international reputation as a philosopher, and he lectured in Japan, China, and Mexico. He visited schools in Turkey and in the Soviet Union. A prolific author, he wrote more than 1,000 articles and books that influenced U.S. educational and social philosophy.

Dewey's Major Philosophical and Educational Works

Because Dewey was such a prolific author, we will comment only on a selected number of his books that have a special relevance for Pragmatism as an educational philosophy.[15] Drawing on his experiences at the Laboratory School, Dewey, in *The School and Society* (1899), commented on industrialism's impact on schooling and the need for schools to assume a larger social function.[16] Dewey's *The Child and the Curriculum* (1902) examined the teacher's role in relating the curriculum to the child's interest, readiness, and stage of development.[17] Emphasizing the person's experience as the basis for learning, Dewey recommended instruction that facilitated the child's immediate and personal use of knowledge.

In 1910, Dewey's *How We Think* argued that thinking is experimental in that it involves a series of problem-solving episodes that occur as we attempt to survive and grow in an environmental context.[18] Employing the scientific method, thinking occurs when we conjecture hypotheses designed to make an indeterminate situation into a determinate one. Thinking, as defined by Dewey, had implications for a method of educational inquiry based on problem solving.

Democracy and Education (1916), Dewey's most complete rendition of educational philosophy, sought to identify the foundational ideas of a democratic society and apply them to education.[19] Essentially, Dewey, who consistently rejected dualism, argued that genuine education proceeded more effectively in an open or democratic environment that was free of absolutes that blocked freedom of inquiry. In *Individualism, Old and New* (1920) he rejected the inherited notion of "rugged individualism" as an archaic historic residue.[20] In place of a competitive economy and society, Dewey urged social planning and action that would make the emergent corporate social order congenial to human growth and purposes. In *Art as Experience* (1934), Dewey elaborated an aesthetic theory that asserted that art was properly a public means of shared expression and communication between the artist and the perceiver of the art object.[21]

Although often called the father of progressive education, Dewey's identification with progressive education must be carefully considered. (In Chapter 19, Dewey's relationships to and influence on progressive education are examined.) Joe R. Burnett, in analyzing Dewey's influence, cautions that Dewey's Experimentalism should not be equated with progressive education.[22] The early roots of Progressivism can be found in Rousseau's Naturalism and Pestalozzi's efforts to create a method of instruction based on sense impressionism. Dewey's influence on Progressivism came later when he contributed to the general emphasis on social and educational reform of the early Progressive era. He agreed with many elements in progressive education and rejected others—especially the naive romanticism of the neo-Rousseaueans.

While many Progressives were influenced by Dewey's Experimentalism, others were not. The Progressive Education Association, an umbrella organization, encompassed a variety of individuals and groups ranging from neo-Rousseauean child-centered educators to neo-Freudians. The publication of many of Dewey's educational writings coincided with the Progressive education movement, and similarities existed between Dewey and the Progressive reformers who opposed a static conception of learning and schooling. Although Dewey and many Progressive educators agreed on the importance of experience, continuity, and the cultivation of the child's interests and needs, Dewey challenged the sentimental, romantic neo-Rousseauean Progressives who dogmatically asserted child-centered doctrines. Dewey's *Experience and Education* (1938) criticized Progressive educators for failing to elaborate a positive educational philosophy based on experience.[23] He cautioned educators against a simplistic categorization of educational theories and practices into "either-or" polar opposites. He also challenged Progressives to move beyond merely opposing traditional school practices and urged them to develop a positive and affirmative educational posture.

Among Dewey's other major books were *Interest and Effort in Education* (1913), *Human Nature and Conduct* (1922), and *Freedom and Culture* (1939).[24] Through his writings, lectures, and presence on the U.S. and world scene, Dewey contributed to the kind of political and social liberalism that urged social reform based on careful and pragmatic planning. His work stimulated the rise of an Experimentalist educational philosophy that profoundly influenced U.S. educational theory and practice. In the following section, we will examine the major components of his pragmatic Experimentalist, or Instrumentalist, philosophy.

EXPERIMENTALISM'S PHILOSOPHICAL BASES

Dewey's Experimentalism held a special relevance for education. Among the philosophical bases are (1) Dewey's rejection of metaphysical absolutes; (2) the organism and the environment; (3) Dewey's Experimentalist epistemology; (4) the complete act of thought; and (5) axiology as experimental valuation.

Dewey's Rejection of Metaphysical Absolutes

In earlier chapters on Idealism, Realism, and Thomism, we examined metaphysics as speculation about the nature of ultimate reality. Pragmatists, such as Dewey, rejected such speculation as being unverifiable in terms of human experience. In this section, we examine Dewey's attack on philosophical systems based on absolute metaphysical positions, dualism, and a quest for certitude.

Although *Democracy and Education* most completely stated Dewey's educational philosophy, the key to Dewey's system of thought is found in *The Quest for Certainty*.[25] Throughout his philosophical and educational writings, Dewey argued against a dualistic conception of the universe, which he claimed was merely a human contrivance designed to postulate a theoretically unchanging realm of complete and perfect certitude. The more traditional Idealist, Realist, and Thomist philosophies, based on metaphysical propositions, grounded reality in a world of unchanging ideas for the Idealist or structures for the Realist. Based on these conceptions, Western thinkers had devised a bipolar, dualistic view of reality that divided it into ideational, or conceptual, and material dimensions.

While ideas, spirit, and thought were higher in the chain of being, work and action were lower in the hierarchy. Priority was given to the immaterial and unchanging order. Thus, such classical dualisms as spirit–matter, mind–body, and soul–body came to permeate Western thought. These metaphysical dualisms had an impact on life and education in that they created distinctions between theory and practice, between liberal and vocational education, between fine and applied arts, and between thought and action.

The bifurcation between theory and practice, or thought and action, was not only a matter for speculation by philosophers, but it also had an impact on educational practice. Philosophical dualism contributed to patterns of hierarchical curricular organization in which the most theoretical subjects were given priority over practical ones. Distinguishing between theory and practice, the traditional curriculum required learners to first master symbolic and literary skills such as reading, writing, and arithmetic. Learning these tool skills prepared children to study systematically such subjects as history, geography, mathematics, and science at the secondary and higher levels. In the traditional subject-matter curriculum, disciplines were organized deductively as bodies of principles, theories, factual content, and examples. Formal education became excessively abstract and bore little relationship to the learner's own personal and social experience. Furthermore, the subject-matter curriculum aimed to prepare students for future situations after the completion of formal schooling. According to Dewey's critique, the traditional subject-matter curriculum, based on the dualism between theory and practice, created additional bifurcations that separated the child from the curriculum and the school from the society.

Dewey's social conception of education was basic to his Experimentalism, which saw thinking and doing as a unified flow of ongoing experience. Thinking and acting were not separable; thinking was incomplete until tested in experience. To understand Dewey's pragmatic philosophy, it is necessary to examine his antagonism toward the dualism that supported traditional philosophical beliefs in a higher, transcendent, and unchanging reality.

According to Dewey, human beings inhabit an uncertain world that contains threats to survival. In their minds, human beings sought to create a concept of certainty to give them a sense of permanence and security. Because actual living contains risk, traditional theorists differentiated between the uncertainty of everyday life and the security that came from an unchanging and perfect reality. Early religio-philosophical systems, such as Idealism and Thomism, created a worldview that posited reality in a perfect, unchanging, and eternal universal being. In this *Weltanschauung,* the inferior level of existence was mundane, changing, and uncertain, and the superior order was that which was beyond the scope of the empirical, experiential, and everyday existence, or, in other words, beyond the physical.

Traditional philosophies, derived from Platonism, or Aristotelianism, were occupied with speculation about permanent, eternal, and self-sufficient being.

According to the doctrines of an immutable good and fixed order of being, speculative philosophers were concerned with describing metaphysical systems of immutable and necessary truths and principles that lay beyond human experience. According to philosophical dualism, a higher realm of fixed and permanent reality existed in which truth was absolute; there was also an inferior world of changing objects and persons that was the realm of experience and practice.

Dewey emphasized a changing and evolutionary universe where the human situation was not to transcend experience but rather to use it to solve human problems. Rejecting dualistic epistemologies, Dewey emphasized a continuum of human experience that related rather than separated thinking and acting, fact and value, and intellect and emotion.[26] He argued that philosophy should recognize, reconstruct, and use experience to improve the human condition. In such a reconstruction of experience, theory and practice were fused and used in ongoing human activity. Derived from experience, theory was tested in action. Instead of a dualism between the immutable and the changing, experience was a continuum in which individuals and groups dealt with a successive sequence of problematic situations. In such a sequence, theory was derived from and was tested in practice; mind was a social process of intelligently solving problems rather than an antecedent and transcendent category; education was liberal, or liberating, as it freed human beings by giving them a methodology for dealing with all kinds of problems, including the social and vocational; and the distinction between the fine and useful arts was dissolved by integrating beauty and function. Dewey's thesis was that existence was uncertain. To exist meant to be involved in a changing world. The human quest was not for certainty but rather for a means, or a method, of controlling and directing the process of change insofar as this could be done in an imperfect world.

The Organism and the Environment

As indicated earlier, Dewey's birth in 1859 coincided with the publication of Charles Darwin's *Origin of Species*. The revolutionary implications of Darwin's biological theory reverberated throughout the late nineteenth and early twentieth centuries. Initially, Darwin's theory of evolution appeared to challenge the traditional Judeo-Christian version of creation, based on the book of Genesis, that God had created species in a fixed form. Those who accepted Genesis in a literal way found themselves in conflict with Darwinian science. For some fundamentalist Protestant Americans, the impact of Darwin's theory was a shattering experience.

According to Darwin's thesis that species evolved slowly and gradually, members of the species, or organisms, lived, adjusted, and adapted to their environments to survive. Those species that succeeded in surviving did so because they possessed favorable characteristics that enabled them to adjust satisfactorily to environmental changes. The transmission of these favorable characteristics to their offspring guaranteed the particular species' continuation. Darwin's theory emphasized the competition of individuals for survival in a frequently challenging environment.

To appreciate Darwin's impact on Dewey, it is necessary to examine briefly the initial adaptation of evolutionary theory into a sociology of knowledge by Herbert Spencer (1820–1903), who applied Darwinian principles to socioeconomic and political life.[27] Spencer viewed the human being as an individual social atom who was locked in a fiercely competitive struggle against other individuals. Through individual competition and initiative, some individuals adapted to the environment more efficiently than others. These intelligent and strong competitors climbed upward in society to positions of social, economic, and political leadership. Those who were unintelligent in their behavior, who could not compete effectively or efficiently, descended on the rungs of the social ladder to become the dregs of society. For Spencer, competition was the natural order of life with the prize going to the fittest individuals.

It is not difficult to extrapolate the social and educational implications of Social Darwinism. Spencer and his many followers in business and in academia regarded the laissez-faire economic and social order as the natural state of affairs and argued against tampering with nature's laws of competition. Society was composed of independent, autonomous, and competitive individuals, who at the most direct level struggled for economic survival. In the Social Darwinist view, schools best performed their social role by preparing individuals for a competitive society. Progress occurred as individuals invented and perfected new ways of competing against each other in exploiting the natural and social environments.

Both biological and Social Darwinism influenced Dewey's developing Experimentalist philosophy. While accepting some of Darwin's basic biological conceptions, Dewey rejected Spencer's application of competitive ethics to society. Darwin's notion of an evolutionary process was accepted by Dewey, who had rejected fixed, final, and transcendent Hegelian metaphysics. Dewey's educational philosophy, drawing on an organismic psychology, applied the terms of organism and environment to life and to education. For Dewey, the human organism was a living and natural creature, physiologically composed of living tissue and possessing life-sustaining impulses and drives. Every organism lives within an environment, or habitat, which has elements that both enhance and threaten its life.

For Dewey, the sustaining of human life required interactions with the natural environment. Rather than becoming one with nature, as Rousseau suggested, or being locked in struggle with nature, as Spencer argued, Dewey recommended that human beings instrumentally use nature to transform parts of the environment to increase life-sustaining possibilities. Through the application of scientific intelligence and through cooperative social activity, humans can use certain elements in nature to solve problems with other aspects of the natural environment.[28]

As the individual human being, or human organism, lives, he or she encounters problematic situations of an indeterminate character that interfere with the ongoing march of experience. Upon encountering such an indeterminate situation, the organism's activity is blocked or impeded until it can render the novel situation determinate and resume activity. The successful person is able to solve problems and add the elements of his or her solution to the reserves of experience. As a result of this network of interaction between the organism and its environment, the human organism acquires experience. In Dewey's Experimentalism, the key concept of experience is best thought of as the interaction of or the transaction between an organism and its environment. We know through our experiences, or environmental interactions; each experiential episode adds to our experience. When confronted by problematic situations, we examine our experience for clues, which suggest the means for resolving the present difficulty.

At this point, several basic components of Dewey's educational philosophy can be identified: (1) the learner is a living organism, a biological and sociological phenomenon, who possesses drives or impulses designed to sustain life; (2) the learner lives in an environment, or habitat, which is both natural and social; (3) the learner, moved by personal drives, is an active person engaged in constant interaction with the environment; (4) environmental interaction produces problems that occur as the individual seeks to satisfy his or her needs; and (5) learning is the process of solving problems in the environment.

From his days at the University of Chicago Laboratory School onward, Dewey emphasized the school's social function as a miniature community or embryonic society. Although holding that society was composed of separate and discrete individual human beings, he rejected Social Darwinism's competitive ethic of social atomism. For Dewey, human beings lived in both a social and a natural environment. In striving to live, human beings found that group life, or human association, most effectively contributed to their welfare and survival. Associative living, or community, enriched human experience and added to it as the group mutually engaged in problem-solving activities. Collective human experience provided the individual with a more complex set of experiences, or interactive episodes. Barriers to full human association blocked free interaction. They impeded the ability of individuals and groups to contribute to cultural growth by mutual sharing experiences.[29]

Although Dewey's model of experience arising from the interaction of the organism with the environment has often been interpreted in socio-educational terms, recent scholarship has broadened the interpretation to include an ecological-educational dimension as well. According to this view, which emphasizes Dewey's humanist Naturalism, the human organism is interacting then with "an integrated social and biophysical environment."[30]

This naturalistic element in Dewey's thought, while not romantic in the Rousseauean sense, argued against a dualism that saw human beings occupying two separate spheres of existence—one social and the other natural. It also rejects a crude Darwinism that sees human beings as combatants locked in struggle against nature. Such a broadened conception of environmental interaction encourages an ecological sensitivity to the earth as a biosphere that opens the educational process to a wide range of world problems such as pollution, conservation of natural resources, preservation of endangered species, and ultimately that of arms control.

Dewey's Experimentalist Epistemology

Rather than dealing with metaphysical issues, Dewey was concerned with epistemology. For him, as well as other Pragmatists, knowing was experimental and in a common-sense way followed the method of scientific inquiry. In the next section, we will examine Dewey's concepts of intelligence and experimental inquiry and his rendering of the scientific method into the "complete act of thought."

In breaking with the more traditional Idealism and Realism, which rested on a metaphysical conception of antecedent reality, Dewey believed that these speculative philosophies had constructed a static theory of mind that was isolated from life's personal and social realities. Dewey proposed an active social conception of human intelligence, which, while conditioned by societal institutions, could dynamically affect social change.

For Dewey, intelligence is socially built as people share their experiences in dealing with common concerns. Intelligence, the ability to define and solve problems, is acquired through the experience of persisting and working through problem-solving situations. Within the problem-solving context, intelligence results from shared activity in making and using instruments, in fashioning plans of action, and in acting on hypotheses. Human beings use their intelligence to invent and fabricate instruments or tools. The more complex and sophisticated the society, the more instruments are available to use in solving problems. Unlike Rousseau's glorification of the primitive state of nature, Dewey found the savage or primitive human being to be limited by a paucity of instruments that could be used in solving problems. In contrast, civilized society possessed the instruments that enhanced group problem-solving efforts and cultivated and enriched social intelligence.

Dewey's view of the human being as a fabricator of tools, as an instrument maker, had implications for education. Children in a civilized society needed to develop familiarity with the use of instruments. Through schooling, they could experience in a relatively short time much of the human experience that involved making and using instruments.

For Dewey, thinking began when a situation was indeterminate and a need remained unsatisfied. In the quest to satisfy needs, thinking was an instrument to secure human satisfaction. According to experimental inquiry, ideas were tentative, instrumental plans of action designed to achieve human ends. Thinking involved seeing the relationships between action and the resulting consequences.

Complete Act of Thought

According to Dewey, genuine thought occurred as the individual encountered and solved problems according to the scientific method. Although informed by the bodies of scientific knowledge accumulated by experts, Dewey's concept of the scientific method was a broadly conceived procedure of scientific intelligence that was applicable to human affairs.[31] Dewey's problem-solving method, or "complete act of thought"—the scientific method broadly conceived—consisted of five clearly defined steps or phases:

1. The *problematic situation,* in which the person was confused because he or she was involved in an incomplete situation of indeterminate character. In the problematic situation, the individual's ongoing activity was blocked by some unique situational element that deviated from past experience.
2. In *defining the problem,* the individual examined the problematic situation and identified that aspect of the situation, the deviant particular, that impeded continuing activity.
3. *Clarification of the problem* involved a careful survey, examination, inspection, exploration, and analysis of the elements involved in the problematic situation. At this third stage of inquiry, the individual systematically and reflectively researched the problem to locate the ideas, materials, and instruments that could resolve the difficulty.
4. By *constructing tentative hypotheses,* the individual established a number of generalizations, if-then statements, that were possible means of solving the problem. This process involved mentally projecting oneself into the future and seeing the possible consequences of actions. As a result of hypothesizing and conjecturing, the individual framed tentative solutions that could resolve the difficulty and that had the greatest possibilities for securing the desired consequences.
5. This crucial step involved *testing the preferred hypothesis by acting on it.* If the hypothesis resolved the problem and brought the desired consequences, then the individual resumed activity until encountering another problem. If the problem remained, then another hypothesis was needed.[32]

Dewey's experimental epistemology was used as the format for the method of problem solving in which the learner, as an individual or in association with others, used the scientific method to solve both personal and social problems. Each problem-solving episode became an experimental situation in which the learner applied the method of intelligence to real problems arising in his or her own experience. For Dewey and his followers, the problem-solving method was transferable to a variety of problematic situations.

Dewey's fifth step, the testing of the hypothesis, represented the greatest departure from the learning pattern of the traditional subject-oriented school. While teachers and students in the more conventional schools might explore problems and frame tentative solutions, rarely did they attempt to solve these problems by acting on them directly. Although they might act on problems encountered in their chemistry and mathematics lessons, the solutions to these problems had already been determined. It was most unlikely that students would be encouraged to act on the pressing social, economic, and political problems of the day. Although such problems as war, poverty, and pollution might be discussed in the conventional classroom, the student's active attempt to resolve these problems was likely to be deferred to times and situations outside the school. It might, in fact, be deferred until the student reached adulthood and became a voter.

In contrast, Dewey held that the validation of an idea occurred only as it was tested in experience. Thought was incomplete until it was acted on and the consequences of action were assessed.

Axiology As Experimental Valuation

Dewey's Experimentalism applied as well to value issues as to factual inquiry. When Dewey abandoned Idealism for Pragmatism, he began to develop a non-metaphysical value theory. He saw ethical and aesthetic sensibilities and actions as coming from human experience rather than a vision of ultimate reality.[33] Unlike the more traditional Idealist and Realist philosophers who found a hierarchy of values inherent in the universe, Dewey was a moral relativist who believed that values arose as outcomes of human responses to varying environmental situations. For Dewey, a major defect of hierarchical value systems was that humans were confronted by wide varieties of conflicting hierarchies. Each hierarchy rested on a basic assumption that was supposed to be self-evident according to some principle of "right reason."

In addition to rejecting hierarchical arrangements of values, Dewey also turned away from value theories that relied on tradition and custom as value determinants. The major weakness in the customary validation of values was that, by justifying whatever existed at a particular time and place, it became a rationale for preserving the status quo. In an interdependent modern world, a methodology of valuation was needed that could be used to adjudicate cross-cultural conflicts. In a technological society characterized by rapid social changes, customs and traditions were inadequate determinants of values.

In contrast to value systems founded on universal hierarchies of tradition and custom, Dewey argued that the method of shared scientific intelligence should be applied to axiological questions of morality, ethics, and aesthetics. He postulated a criterion of valuation based on the relationships of aims, means, and ends. The basis of Experimentalist valuation was found in human preferences, wants, wishes, desires, and needs. Evaluation arose when a conflict occurred in these raw materials of value. Because thinking occurred only within the problematic situation, valuing took place only when there was a conflict in wants, wishes, and preferences. If a person had only a single desire, then he or she would act to satisfy that desire. In the case of value conflict, it was necessary to unify the apparently conflicting desires. If the desires could not be unified, then one had to choose between conflicting alternatives. Choice was made by evaluating the possible consequences of acting on the chosen preference.

Dewey's method of valuation was designed to unify aims, means, and ends. When an end was attained, it became a means for the satisfaction of still another end. If a person desired a given end, it was necessary to ask questions about the appropriate and efficient means of attaining that end.

Although Dewey's theory of valuation followed an experimental design, it also embraced a conception of democracy that held broad implications for society and education. Democracy meant more than the particular political arrangements associated with representative, popular governments. It was both an ethical and a methodological necessity in Dewey's thought. A democratic society embraced the ideal of the widest possible human sharing, participation, and involvement in institutional life and processes. Dewey's opposition to dualism in philosophy extended to dualisms in society in which individuals or groups were segregated and left out of social participation. Societies that practiced segregation on the basis of class, race, sex, or ethnicity lost the opportunity for the growth of social intelligence and enrichment that came from a sense of community life in which all people participated. Values were to be appraised in terms of this contribution to human sharing and development.

Just as he opposed metaphysically based value criteria, Dewey challenged the strong classical liberal orientation in U.S. society that argued for values being based on individual self-interest. He opposed the trend toward a fractured polity of special interest groups. For him, human beings were communal participants who defined and tested collective goals.[34]

Democratic social arrangements were also a methodological necessity for experimental inquiry. Such arrangements were free of philosophical absolutes that blocked inquiry into what were regarded as immutable first principles. They also were free of the restrictions to inquiry imposed by totalitarian regimes that closed off public discussion and debate.

In educational situations, Dewey's value theory encourages inquiring minds in an open classroom. Such openness carries with it the risk that long-standing ideas and values may be discarded or reconstructed. Openness, however, does not mean educational anarchy or naive romanticism. Rather, openness requires social arrangements conducive to using the method of intelligence, the experimental method, to deal with human issues.

EXPERIMENTALISM'S EDUCATIONAL IMPLICATIONS

In the following section, we will examine certain aspects of Dewey's educational philosophy. These include: (1) education as conservation and reconstruction, (2) schooling and society, (3) the democratic society and education, (4) Experimentalist teaching and learning, (5) growth as the end of education, (6) the experiential curriculum, and (7) reconstructing experience and education.

Education As Conservation and Reconstruction

In *Democracy and Education,* Dewey's primary concern is the relationship between society and education. The educative process occurs informally as the person matures within the cultural milieu and acquires the language, skills, and knowledge common to group life. In the more formal sense of schooling, education is a deliberate process of bringing the immature person into cultural participation by providing the necessary symbolic and linguistic tools needed for group interaction and communication.

Dewey conceived of education as having both a conservative and a reconstructive, or renewing, dimension. Education is conservative because it provides cultural continuity by transmitting the heritage from adults to children, the immature members of the group. In both its formal and informal aspects, education is always a value-laden process that involves cultural imposition because it takes place within the context of a particular culture with its unique customs, mores, folkways, and language. Although cultural imposition is always contextual to a given time and place, it provides the communicative and expressive means by which individuals liberate themselves through group participation.

As a transmitter of the cultural heritage, education is the means by which the group reproduces the cultural type and thus perpetuates itself. In the Deweyan context, the child is socialized by acquiring and using the cultural instruments and values through association with the members of the group. Thus, education becomes the process, whereby the group transmits its cultural skills, knowledge, and values and reproduces the desired cultural type of person, who will perpetuate the heritage.

Although clearly recognizing that the conservative aspects of education provided cultural continuity, Dewey saw education in terms that were broader and more dynamic than the preservation of the status quo. Cultural conservation, for Dewey, did not mean that adults in a society used the school to reproduce currently held beliefs and values. Rather, it meant that the young were provided the cultural skills and tools by which they could improve social conditions.[35] The very cultural instrumentalities such as the language and technology that were imposed on the young carried the possibilities for altering or changing the inherited culture. Just as he conceived of the universe as undergoing constant change, Dewey believed that human culture was also changing. By using the scientific method, human beings possessed the ability to direct the course of change.

Dewey took an instrumental view of the past. Precedents were instruments in analyzing present situations rather than prescriptions to be followed implicitly in dealing with the present.[36] When reconstructed they were useful in framing new hypotheses for solving human problems.

Schooling and Society

The cultural heritage, a vast complex that included the accumulated experience of the human race and the particular experience of the group, included elements that were both worthy and unworthy of perpetuation. Formal education was one of society's means of selecting those aspects of the cultural heritage that were worthy of perpetuation.

For Dewey, the school is a specialized environment established to enculturate the young by deliberately bringing them into cultural participation. As a social institution, the school is a selective agency that, while transmitting the culture, also seeks to reconstruct it to meet contemporary needs. For Dewey, the school's threefold functions were to simplify, purify, and balance the cultural heritage.[37] Simplification meant that the school, really curriculum makers and teachers as social agents, selects elements of the heritage and reduces their complexity by designing units for learning that are appropriate to the learner's maturity and readiness. As a purifying agent, the school selects and transmits those elements of the cultural heritage that enhance human growth and eliminate unworthy aspects that limit it. Balancing the cultural heritage referred to integrating the experiences that had been selected and purified into a harmonious core of human experience. Because society is composed of many diverse groups, children need assistance in understanding individuals from other groups. The genuinely democratic society as an integrated and balanced community rests on mutually shared understanding.

Although problem solving is individualized and personalized, it is also a social process. Group experience is a cooperative enterprise in which all the participants share their experiences. The more sharing occurs, the greater are the possibilities for growth. Dewey recognized that the rise of an industrial, urban, and technological society had created a number of socioeducational problems that schools needed to address. The more complex the society becomes, the greater is the gap between the child's activities and the requirements of responsible adult life, Dewey's school society, based on mutually shared activities, was designed to be the embryo of an associative democracy. He anticipated that the school's problem-solving techniques would transfer to the larger society.

Democratic Society and Education

Dewey rejected the Perennialist assumptions, such as those expressed by Robert Hutchins, that education was everywhere the same or was intrinsically good. Rather, he reasoned that the quality of education varied as did the quality of life experienced by the group that established and supported the school. Dewey's conceptions of democratic social arrangements and democratic education were related to an experimenting society that used a process-oriented philosophy. Not particular to the U.S. form of government or to particular political institutions, Dewey's conception of democratic education was rather an epistemological and sociological one characterized by the presence of an experimental temperament. In the experimenting society, citizens were free from the impediments erected by absolutist governments or *a priori* philosophies. Because educational institutions socialized the young in group values, genuinely democratic education occurred within the milieu of the experimental or inquiry-oriented school.

In the sociological context, Dewey's democratic society was one in which its members shared the widest possible variety of interests. Any impediment or barrier to group interaction, such as racial, religious, or economic segregation, interfered with group sharing. Any form of human exploitation weakened the shared experimental temperament of a genuinely democratic society.

Dewey emphasized the cooperative nature of shared human experience. The more sharing that occurs among individuals, the greater are the possibilities for human interaction and growth. Dewey's emphasis on human association embraced three key elements: the common, communication, and community. The common, representing shared objects, instruments, values, and ideas, arises in the context of group experience. Communication occurs when people frame and express their shared experiences in symbolic patterns, in a common language. When individuals communicate, they take the perspective of the other person in developing their own understanding and behavior. Communication thus develops a commonly shared context; this context, in turn, frames the basis of community.[38] Community is the human association that results as individuals come together to discuss their common experiences and problems through shared communication. Dewey preferred the free, open, and humane arrangements of the democratic community in which the experimental processes operated without the interference of absolutist or authoritarian structures.

Although Dewey emphasized the importance of the like-minded community characterized by shared experience, such a community did not rest on conformity. A genuinely democratic community honored cultural pluralism and diversity within a shared context. For Dewey, education helped to create the sense of community.

In the current debates over multiculturalism, it is possible to extrapolate a Deweyan position. Dewey would see U.S. society and culture as being composed of smaller communities within a larger encompassing community. Each of the smaller communities—racial, ethnic, gender—has its own common communication and sense of membership. Each has a potentially enriching contribution to make to the greater community. Viewing the genuine American as an international composite, he stated that the American

> *is not American plus Pole or German. But the American is ... Pole-German-English-French-Spanish-Italian-Greek-Irish-Scandinavian-Bohemian, Jew—and so on.... the hyphen connects instead of separates. And this means ... that our public schools shall teach each factor to respect every other, and shall ... enlighten us all as to the great past contributions of every strain in our composite make-up.*[39]

For Dewey, the smaller cultural communities could be expected to differ with each other as their interests clashed. It was crucial to the larger community, the great society, and especially to its democratic sensibilities and arrangements, that this conflict be contained within a communal framework and not become noncommunal. Communal conflicts should be resolved in a procedural, nonviolent, nondestructive way. The larger community, the greater society, was one governed by commonly shared processes of conflict resolution. For Dewey, there was a communal, or communitarian, American core of beliefs and values. This core, however, rested on commonly agreed-on and shared democratic procedures.

Dewey placed crucial importance on the educative role of the human group in developing social intelligence. Dewey's school and classroom were conceived as an embryonic community in which learners worked together, in common, to solve mutually shared problems. By discussing common goals, aspirations, and projects, students transformed themselves from separate, disparate individuals into a community of mutual concerns and activities.

Dewey's democratic vista was influenced by his own formative experiences in Vermont. The vision of American life that Dewey and many of his associates shared rested on the town meeting conception of face-to-face, shared democracy. Although the directly personal social experiences of small town America had been eroded by the impersonal, industrialized, technological, and urban society, Dewey envisioned an education that would renew the sense of community. As children cooperated in group projects, he anticipated that the socialized problem-solving processes would transfer to the larger society.

In *Individualism: Old and New*, Dewey, in examining problems created by the demise of rural society and the emergence of a technological society, concluded that the era of technology would be corporate; that is, individuals would work together in large industrial-technological-managerial aggregates.[40] He criticized laissez-faire capitalism, which he believed had enabled a few rich individuals to profit by exploiting the majority of the population. A strictly laissez-faire economy made it difficult for the majority to realize their personal capacities and to effect desired social and political change. While realizing that industrial-technological change had altered social arrangements, Dewey believed that an experimentally ordered technology would benefit the entire society. A technological complex, managed by social intelligence, had the capacity of liberating human beings from a subsistence economy. If properly directed, it could free human energies to pursue qualitative aesthetic and intellectual values.

The older, competitive education was patently irrelevant to the problems of a corporate, urban, technological society. In the twentieth century, the ideologies of Fascism, Nazism, and Communism arose as totalitarian responses to the organization of the corporate state and society. Rejecting these totalitarian systems, Dewey saw Experimentalism as a social and educational philosophy that could enable people to live in and contribute to the technological but still democratic corporate society. (In later chapters, we will examine Dewey's contributions to modern Liberalism and also examine the totalitarian ideologies that he opposed.)

Dewey envisioned a "great community" or "great society" that encompassed the freest and fullest communication among persons.[41] His great community rested on an extension of local communities in which the great majority of persons had direct face-to-face experience in solving the problems of common life. In this aspect, he was true to his political roots in U.S. Progressive thought in the early twentieth century.

Experimentalist Teaching and Learning

Although his critics have often accused him of encouraging disorderly permissiveness in schools, Dewey's views of the learner, like his relationships to Progressive education, must be considered carefully. The learner's freedom was not anarchy or doing as one pleased without regard to consequences. Freedom, rather, required an open classroom environment and instructional attitude that facilitated using experimental inquiry to examine and test beliefs and values.

Dewey's group problem-solving method differed substantially from traditional classroom management in which instruction was based on the teacher's authority. Questioning externally imposed discipline, Dewey preferred an internal discipline designed to cultivate self-directing and self-disciplining persons. This kind of task, or problem-centered discipline, originated within the activity needed to solve the problem. Control came from the cooperative context of shared activity, which involved working with instruments and people. Rather than *controlling* the learning situation, the teacher, as a resource person, *guided* the situation.

In Dewey's learning situation, the starting point of any activity was the learner's felt needs. Such intrinsic interest, related to a real concern, was more effective in eliciting the effort needed to satisfy the need and to solve the problem.

Based on Dewey's conception of learning, educational aims were of two kinds: intrinsic and extrinsic. Internal to the learner's experience and interests, intrinsic aims arose from the problem or the task. In contrast, extrinsic aims were extraneous to the person's problem, task, or interest. For example, externally administered rewards or punishments, often used to motivate learning in traditional school situations, were extrinsic and often distorted genuine learning. For Dewey, intrinsic aims were always superior to extrinsic ones because they were personal, problematic, and related to the individual learner's own self-direction, self-control, and self-discipline. Intrinsic educational aims, arising within the context of the learner's own experience, were flexible, capable of alteration, and led to activity. Such an experimental aim was a tentative sketch, or plan of action, capable of being reconstructed and redirected.

In Dewey's problem-centered school, the teacher, as a resource person, guides rather than directs learning. The teacher's role is primarily that of guiding learners who need advice or assistance. Direction comes from the requirements of solving the particular problem. Educational aims belong to the learner rather than the teacher.

Teachers using the problem-solving method need to be patient with their students. Although coercion might force students to arrive at immediate results, it is likely to limit the flexibility needed for future problem solving. The teacher's control of the learning situation is ideally indirect rather than direct. Direct control, coercion, or external discipline fails to enlarge the learner's internal dispositions and does not contribute to the learner becoming a self-directed person. Teachers, motivated by a false sense of instructional efficiency, often err when their anxiety to have students arrive at the "correct answers" in the shortest possible time causes them to bypass the procedural requirements of experimental inquiry.

As resource persons, teachers need to allow students to make errors and to experience the consequences of their actions. In this way, students are more likely to become self-correcting. Dewey did not mean that childish whims should dictate the curriculum, however. The teacher, as a mature person, should exercise professional judgment and expertise so that the consequences of action do not become dangerous to the student or to his or her classmates.

Growth As the End of Education

For Dewey, the sole end of education was growth, or that reconstruction of experience that leads to the direction and control of subsequent experience. Education as a process has no end beyond growth. Particular experiences should be assessed according to the degree to which they contribute to growth, or to having more experience. Desirable experiences lead to further experience, whereas undesirable ones inhibit and reduce the possibilities for subsequent experiences. It might be recalled that intelligence involves the ability to solve problems, which, in turn, involves recognizing the connections and interrelationships among various experiences. Growth, in Dewey's context, means that the individual is gaining the ability to understand the relationships and interconnections among various experiences, between one learning episode and another. Learning by experience, through problem solving, means that education, like life, is a process of continuously reconstructing experience.

Dewey's educational goal of growth for the purpose of directing subsequent experiences rejected the traditional school's emphasis on the doctrine of preparation. According to the doctrine of preparation, students learn their lessons and master subject matter to prepare for events or situations that are to occur after the completion of school. In contrast, Dewey, who conceived of life as taking place in a changing universe and society, argued that deferring action until schooling had been completed would prepare students for a world that would be far different from the one for which they had been prepared. Instead of waiting for some remote future date, students were to act on their interests and needs to resolve present problems. By using day-to-day experiences, students would internalize a method of intelligence that was situationally applicable to the present and future.

Dewey's criticism of the doctrine of preparation was derived from his concept of the child. As was true of Naturalist reformers such as Rousseau, Pestalozzi, and Francis Parker, Dewey rejected the view of the child as a miniature or unfinished adult. He, of course, opposed the view that the child was depraved or deprived because of an inherited flaw or weakness in human nature. While rejecting the archaic concept of childhood depravity, Dewey did not subscribe to Rousseau's romanticizing of a child's nature as being completely and innately good. For Dewey, childhood was a developmental phase of human life. The child who lived well at each stage of development was likely to live an adequate and satisfying adult life.

The Experiential Curriculum

As was true of such earlier educational reformers as Rousseau, Pestalozzi, and Parker, Dewey challenged the traditional subject-matter curriculum associated with formal schooling. Critics of the subject-matter curriculum charged that the teaching of such separate bodies of information as history, geography, mathematics, science, and language had degenerated into past-centered, highly verbal bookishness and pedantry. Formal schooling had become abstract in the sense that it was separated from the child's own interests, needs, and experiences.

Dewey emphasized that methodology was intimately related to the curriculum when, in *Democracy and Education*, he recommended three levels of curricular organization: (1) making and doing; (2) history and geography; and (3) organized sciences.[42] Making and doing, the first curricular level, engaged students in activities or projects based on their direct experience and required using and manipulating raw materials. While the students were actively engaged in manipulating raw materials, these activities contained intellectual possibilities that exposed children to experience's functional aspects.

Dewey regarded history and geography, the second curricular level, as two great educational resources for enlarging the scope and significance of the child's temporal and spatial experience, from the immediate home and school environments, to that of the larger community and the world. For Dewey, history and geography should not be taught as discretely organized bodies of information but rather should begin with the child's immediate environment and then be extended so that the learner gained perspective into time and place.

Dewey recognized that all learning was particular and contextual to a given time, place, and circumstance. Although cultural particularities imposed themselves onto learning, he recognized a distinction between imposition and indoctrination. Imposition reflected the concrete contingencies of living in a particular culture and environment with its unique heritage and values, whereas indoctrination closed the mind to divergent thinking and to alternative ways of acting. Rejecting the indoctrination of the young with ideological "isms," Dewey saw social education as a means of bringing students into gradual contact with the actual realities and needs of society.

Dewey's third stage of curriculum was organized subjects, the various sciences, consisting of bodies of warranted assertions. Students gained exposure to the various bodies of scientific information as they used them in researching their problems. Knowledge from the various sciences was a necessary component in identifying problematic elements and in formulating hypotheses of action. This view of curriculum construed knowledge to be interdisciplinary and instrumental.

Reconstructing Experience and Education

For Dewey, good education was the reconstruction of experience that added to the meaning of and directed future experiences. His conception of growth as the end of education related to the intelligent and reflective direction of activity. As a broad concept, growth implied that the learner was aware of the interrelationships of experiences and the consequences that followed action. Through reflection, insight into the relationship between experience and action and its consequences was transferred into meanings through the process of symbolization. Reasoning was thus construed as a process of combining meanings, or symbols, so as to draw conclusions from their manipulation. Reasoning was validated through a process of trial and error. One could never be sure that reasoning was warranted until it was tested by acting on it. The test for thought was in its empirical verification. According to Dewey, cherished ideas and values, no matter how long they had existed, were always subjected to alteration when tested empirically.

The reconstruction of experience could be both personal and social. While each individual had private experiences, the experience of the human race was public. It was in Dewey's notion of the experiential continuum that the private and public modes of experience were blended. According to the experiential continuum, all people were what past experiences had made them; groups were also the products of their past. For both the individual and the group, the present moment reflected their personal and collective past. The future would come out of the present. To the degree that human beings controlled their destiny by applying social intelligence to their affairs, they shaped their future. Thus, past, present, and future were one flow of ongoing human experience.

In the human reconstruction of experience, it was impossible to ever reach unalterable conclusions. Rather than having absolute certitude, human knowledge consisted of warranted generalizations that had validity until a deviant particular was encountered that did not fit the rule prescribed by the generalization. Upon encountering the unique aspect in experience, it was necessary to reconstruct experience and restructure the generalization. Such a reconstruction of experience involved using those aspects of the generalization that fitted the problematic situation created by the encounter with the unique element. As a result of reconstructing experience, the deviant particular was brought into the context of the experiential continuum. Rejecting notions of absolute, unchanging, and eternal truth, Dewey held that conclusions were tentative and subject to further evaluation and reconstruction.

CONCLUSION

Pragmatism, especially John Dewey's Experimentalist version, was a philosophy that challenged existing systems of thought and education. It sought to replace absolute and immutable doctrines with experimental inquiry. It argued that the scientific method, broadly conceived, was the method of experimental and social intelligence. Dewey's work in philosophy and education emphasized the social role of the school as one of the important agencies working to generate community. From Dewey's educational philosophy came the emphasis on experience, activity, and problem solving that helped to reshape our thinking about education and schooling.

DISCUSSION QUESTIONS

1. Examine the U.S. historical experience and character. Identify and analyze the elements that are congenial to and antagonistic to Pragmatism.

2. Analyze John Dewey's life and career. Identify and analyze the elements and trends that helped shape his philosophical and educational outlook.

3. Examine Dewey's views of certainty and uncertainty in terms of their educational implications.

4. Review Chapters 3 and 4 for their discussion of dualism and then analyze Dewey's attack on philosophical dualism.

5. Compare and contrast the educational consequences that result from an educational philosophy that separates thought and action and one that fuses thought and action. Comment on the separation and the fusion of thought and action in your own educational experience.

6. Analyze Dewey's view of experience as interaction or transaction between an organism and its environment.

7. Contrast Social Darwinism with Dewey's social and educational philosophy.

8. Analyze Dewey's concept of social intelligence.

9. Compare and contrast Dewey's view of the child with that of Rousseau, which was discussed in Chapter 5.

10. Analyze the axiological and methodological implications of Dewey's concept of democracy.

11. Distinguish between education's conservative and reconstructive aspects.

12. Analyze Dewey's concept of the school.

13. Analyze Dewey's concept of the "great community" in terms of the rise of a technological society. Is his concept adequate for U.S. society?

14. Analyze Dewey's concept of discipline. Is his definition of discipline that which is usually referred to in classroom management?

INQUIRY PROJECTS

- Read an account of Dewey's Laboratory School at the University of Chicago. In a paper, examine the philosophical rationale of the school.
- Read Dewey's *The School and Society* and *The Child and the Curriculum*. In a written analysis, examine the social function of the school.
- Read Dewey's *How We Think*. In a paper, identify and examine the book's implications for instructional methodology.
- Read Dewey's *Individualism: Old and New*. Prepare a paper that analyzes the adequacy of Dewey's concept of individualism for contemporary U.S. society.
- Read Dewey's *Art As Experience* and in a paper identify and analyze the key elements in his aesthetic theory.
- Read Dewey's *Experience and Education* and use it as a source to write a critique of the basic elements of Naturalism, which were discussed in Chapter 5.
- Organize a lesson plan based on Dewey's "complete act of thought."
- From an Experimentalist perspective, write a review of several textbooks used in methods courses in teacher education.

FURTHER READINGS

Archambault, Reginald D., ed. *John Dewey on Education: Selected Writings.* New York: Modern Library, 1964.

Baker, Melvin C. *Foundations of John Dewey's Educational Theory.* New York: Atherton Press, 1966.

Baldwin, John D. *George Herbert Mead: A Unifying Theory of Sociology.* Newbury Park, CA: Sage, 1986.

Bayles, Ernest E. *Pragmatism in Education.* New York: Harper & Row, 1966.

Burnett, Joe R. "Whatever Happened to John Dewey?" in *Philosophy of Education Since Mid-Century.* Edited by Jonas F. Soltis. New York: Teachers College Press, Columbia University, 1981.

Campbell, James. *The Community Reconstructs: The Meaning of Pragmatic Social Thought.* Urbana, IL: University of Illinois Press, 1992.

Childs, John. *American Pragmatism and Education: An Interpretation and Criticism.* New York: Holt, Rinehart & Winston, 1956.

Childs, John. *Education and the Philosophy of Experimentalism.* New York: Appleton-Century-Crofts, 1950.

Colwell, Tom. "The Ecological Perspective in John Dewey's Philosophy of Education," *Educational Theory, 35,* no. 3 (summer 1985): 255–266.

Coughlain, Neil. *Young John Dewey.* Chicago: University of Chicago Press, 1975.

Cremin, Lawrence A. *The Transformation of the School: Progressivism in American Education, 1876–1957.* New York: Alfred A. Knopf, 1962.

Dennis, Lawrence J., and George W. Stickel. "Mead and Dewey: Thematic Connections on Educational Topics," *Educational Theory, 31,* nos. 3, 4 (summer/fall 1981): 319–331.

Dewey, John. *A Common Faith.* New Haven: Yale University Press, 1934.

Dewey, John. *Art As Experience.* New York: Minton, Balch, 1934.

Dewey, John. *The Child and the Curriculum.* Chicago: University of Chicago Press, 1902.

Dewey, John. *Democracy and Education.* New York: Macmillan, 1916.

Dewey, John. *The Educational Situation.* Chicago: University of Chicago Press, 1902.

Dewey, John. *Essays in Experimental Logic.* Chicago: University of Chicago Press, 1916.

Dewey, John. *Experience and Education.* New York: Macmillan, 1938.

Dewey, John. *Experience and Nature.* Chicago: Open Court, 1925.

Dewey, John. *Freedom and Culture.* New York: G. P. Putnam's Sons, 1939.

Dewey, John. *How We Think.* Boston: D. C. Heath, 1910.

Dewey, John. *Human Nature and Conduct.* New York: Holt, Rinehart & Winston, 1922.

Dewey, John. *Individualism: Old and New.* Minton, Balch, 1930.

Dewey, John. *Interest and Effort in Education.* Boston: Houghton Mifflin, 1913.

Dewey, John. *Liberalism and Social Action.* New York: G. P. Putnam's Sons, 1935.

Dewey, John. *Moral Principles in Education.* Boston: Houghton Mifflin, 1909.

Dewey, John. *Philosophy and Civilization.* New York: Minton, Balch, 1931.

Dewey, John. *Problems of Men.* New York: Philosophical Library, 1946.

Dewey, John. *The Quest for Certainty: A Study of the Relation of Knowledge and Action.* New York: Minton, Balch, 1929.

Dewey, John. *The School and Society.* Chicago: University of Chicago Press, 1899.

Dewey, John. *Schools of Tomorrow.* New York: E. P. Dutton, 1915.

Diggins, John P. *The Promise of Pragmatism: Modernism and the Crisis of Knowledge and Authority.* Chicago: University of Chicago Press, 1994.

Dykhuizen, George. *The Life and Mind of John Dewey.* Carbondale, IL: Southern Illinois University Press, 1973.

Feffer, Andrew. *The Chicago Pragmatists and American Progressivism.* Ithaca, NY: Cornell University Press, 1993.

Feinberg, Walter. "Dewey and Democracy at the Dawn of the Twenty-First Century," *Educational Theory,* 43, no. 2 (spring 1993): 195–216.

Gunn, Giles B. *Thinking across the American Grain: Ideology, Intellect, and the New Pragmatism.* Chicago: University of Chicago Press, 1992.

Hickman, Larry A. *John Dewey's Pragmatic Technology.* Bloomington, IN: Indiana University Press, 1990.

Kliebard, Herbert M. *The Struggle for the American Curriculum, 1893–1958.* London: Routledge & Kegan Paul, 1986.

Kurtz, Paul. *Philosophical Essays in Pragmatic Naturalism.* Buffalo, NY: Prometheus Books, 1990.

Mayhew, Katherine C., and Anna C. Edwards. *The Dewey School.* New York: Appleton-Century-Crofts, 1936.

Putnam, Hilary. *Pragmatism: An Open Question.* Cambridge, MA: Blackwell, 1995.

Putnam, Hilary, and Ruth A. Putnam. "Education for Democracy," *Educational Theory,* 43, no. 4 (fall 1993): 361–376.

Rochberg-Halton, Eugene. *Meaning and Modernity: Social Theory in the Pragmatic Attitude.* Chicago: University of Chicago Press, 1986.

Rosenthal, Sandra. "Democracy and Education: A Deweyan Approach," *Educational Theory,* 43, no. 4. (fall 1993): 377–389.

Ryan, Alan. *John Dewey and the High Tide of American Liberalism.* New York: W. W. Norton, 1995.

Sleeper, R. W. *The Necessity of Pragmatism: John Dewey's Conception of Philosophy.* New Haven: Yale University Press, 1986.

Smiley, Marion. *Moral Responsibility and the Boundaries of Community: Power and Accountability from a Pragmatic Point of View.* Chicago: University of Chicago Press, 1992.

Stuhr, John J., ed. *Philosophy and the Reconstruction of Culture: Pragmatic Essays After Dewey.* Albany: State University of New York Press, 1993.

Welchman, Jennifer. *Dewey's Ethical Thought.* Ithaca, NY: Cornell University Press, 1995.

Westbrook, Robert B. *John Dewey and American Democracy.* Ithaca, NY: Cornell University Press, 1991.

West, Cornel. *The American Evasion of Philosophy: A Genealogy of Pragmatism.* Madison, WI: University of Wisconsin Press, 1989.

ENDNOTES

1. Cornel West, *The American Evasion of Philosophy: A Genealogy of Pragmatism* (Madison, WI: University of Wisconsin Press, 1989).

2. A comprehensive treatment can be found in John L. Childs, *American Pragmatism and Education: An Interpretation and Criticism* (New York: Henry Holt,

1956); Ernest E. Bayles, *Pragmatism in Education* (New York: Harper & Row, 1966).

3. For a discussion of Pragmatism and technology, see Larry A. Hickman, *John Dewey's Pragmatic Technology* (Bloomington, IN: Indiana University Press, 1990).

4. Lawrence A. Cremin, *The Transformation of the School: Progressivism in American Education, 1876–1957* (New York: Alfred A. Knopf, 1962), pp. 105–126.

5. For a biographical treatment of Dewey, see George Dykhuizen, *The Life and Mind of John Dewey* (Carbondale, IL: Southern Illinois University Press, 1973); Neil Coughlain, *Young John Dewey* (Chicago: University of Chicago Press, 1975); and Robert B. Westbrook, *John Dewey and American Democracy* (Ithaca, NY: Cornell University Press, 1991).

6. Commentaries on the Pragmatist view of community can be found in James Campbell, *The Community Reconstructs: The Meaning of Pragmatic Social Thought* (Urbana, IL: University of Illinois Press, 1992); and Marion Smiley, *Moral Responsibility and the Boundaries of Community: Power and Accountability from a Pragmatic Point of View* (Chicago: University of Chicago Press, 1992).

7. Robert M. Crunden, *Ministers of Reform: The Progressives' Achievement in American Civilization, 1889–1920* (Urbana, IL: University of Illinois Press, 1984), pp. 56–57.

8. Westbrook, *John Dewey and American Democracy,* pp. 42–43.

9. Walter Feinberg, "Dewey and Democracy at the Dawn of the Twenty-First Century," *Educational Theory,* 43, no. 2 (spring 1993): 199.

10. Crunden, *Ministers of Reform,* pp. 34–38. Also see John D. Baldwin, *George Herbert Mead: A Unifying Theory for Sociology* (Newbury Park, CA: Sage, 1986).

11. Lawrence J. Dennis and George W. Stickel, "Mead and Dewey: Thematic Connections on Educational Topics," *Educational Theory,* 31 (summer/fall 1981): 320–321.

12. Dewey's Laboratory School is discussed in the following sources: John Dewey, *The School and Society* (Chicago: University of Chicago Press, 1923); John Dewey and Evelyn Dewey, *Schools of Tomorrow* (New York: E. P. Dutton, 1915); Katherine C. Mayhew and Anna C. Edwards, *The Dewey School* (New York: Appleton-Century-Crofts, 1936); Arthur G. Wirth, *John Dewey as Educator: His Design for Work in Education* (1894–1904) (New York: John Wiley & Sons, 1966); and Herbert M. Kliebard, *The Struggle for the American Curriculum, 1893–1958* (Boston and London: Routledge & Kegan Paul, 1986).

13. John Dewey, "The Laboratory School," *University Record,* 1, 32 (November 6, 1896): 417–422.

14. Ibid.

15. A useful guide to Dewey's publications is Jo Ann Boydston, ed., *Guide to the Works of John Dewey* (Carbondale, IL: Southern Illinois University Press, 1970).

16. John Dewey, *The School and Society* (Chicago: University of Chicago Press, 1899).

17. John Dewey, *The Child and the Curriculum* (Chicago: University of Chicago Press, 1902).

18. John Dewey, *How We Think* (Boston: D. C. Heath, 1910); also see John Dewey, *Logic: The Theory of Inquiry* (New York: Henry Holt, 1938).

19. John Dewey, *Democracy and Education* (New York: Macmillan, 1916).

20. John Dewey, *Individualism: Old and New* (New York: Minton, Balch, 1930).

21. John Dewey, *Art as Experience* (New York: Minton, Balch, 1934).

22. Joe R. Burnett, "Whatever Happened to John Dewey?" in *Philosophy of Education Since Mid-Century,* ed. Jonas F. Soltis. (New York: Teachers College, Columbia University, 1981), pp. 66–67.

23. John Dewey, *Experience and Education* (New York: Macmillan, 1938), pp. 25–31.

24. John Dewey, *Interest and Effort in Education* (Boston: Houghton Mifflin, 1913); *Human Nature and Conduct* (New York: Holt, Rinehart & Winston, 1922); and *Freedom and Culture* (New York: G. P. Putnam's Sons, 1939).

25. John Dewey, *The Quest for Certainty: A Study of the Relation of Knowledge and Action* (New York: Minton, Balch, 1929).

26. Hilary Putnam and Ruth Anna Putnam, "Education for Democracy," *Educational Theory,* 43, no. 4 (fall 1993): 364.

27. For a treatment of the impact of Social Darwinism and the rise of a pragmatic reformed Darwinism in American life, see Richard Hofstadter, *Social Darwinism in American Thought* (Boston: Beacon Press, 1958).

28. Feinberg, "Dewey and Democracy," pp. 204–205.

29. Putnam and Putnam, "Education for Democracy," p. 364.

30. Tom Colwell, "The Ecological Perspective in John Dewey's Philosophy of Education," *Educational Theory,* 35, no. 3 (summer 1985): 257.

31. Westbrook, *John Dewey and American Democracy,* p. 141.

32. Dewey, *Democracy and Education,* pp. 163–178.

33. Feinberg, "Dewey and Democracy," pp. 203–204. Also see Jennifer Welchman, *Dewey's Ethical Thought* (Ithaca, NY: Cornell University Press, 1995).

34. Putnam and Putnam, "Education for Democracy," p. 367.

35. Ibid., p. 365.

36. Gail P. Sorenson, "John Dewey's Philosophy of Law: A Democratic Vision," *Educational Theory,* 30, no. 1 (winter 1980): 57.

37. Dewey, *Democracy and Education,* pp. 22–26.

38. Sandra Rosenthal, "Democracy and Education: A Deweyan Approach," *Educational Theory,* 43, no. 4 (fall 1993): 377.

39. The quote is abridged from John Dewey, "Nationalizing Education," in *The Middle Works,* vol. 10, ed. Jo Ann Boydston (Carbondale, IL: Southern Illinois University Press, 1985), p. 205, as quoted in Putnam and Putnam, "Education for Democracy," p. 362.

40. Dewey, *Individualism: Old and New,* pp. 35–50.

41. Burnett, "Whatever Happened to John Dewey?" p. 73.

42. Dewey, *Democracy and Education,* pp. 228–270.

▶ 7

Existentialism and Education

Although traces of Existentialism appear in such nineteenth-century writers as Sören Kierkegaard (1813–1855), Friedrich Nietzsche (1844–1900), and Fyodor Dostoyevsky (1821–1881), it reached its greatest philosophical popularity in the twentieth century, especially during and after World War II. Among the leading Existentialist proponents of the twentieth century were the German philosophers Karl Jaspers (1883–1969) and Martin Heidegger (1889–1976), the Israeli philosopher Martin Buber (1878–1965), and the French philosophers Gabriel Marcel (1889–1973), who took a Christian perspective, and Jean-Paul Sartre (1905–1980), an atheist.[1] In addition, the eminent Protestant theologian, Paul Tillich (1886–1965) examined the relationship between Christian theology and Existentialist philosophy. Like Kierkegaard, Tillich saw the human being facing the free but awesome choice of whether or not to enter into a personal relationship with God.

The philosophical method, known as Phenomenology, developed by Edmund Husserl (1859–1938), has also been used by some Existentialists. According to Husserl, philosophy should be a method of analyzing phenomena, our conscious awareness in experience of how objects and events appear to us. This careful analysis of our awareness is to occur without limiting conditions imposed by metaphysical assumptions. Human consciousness, our awareness of phenomena, is the basis for our understanding and interpretation of our situation.

From this diverse and often conflicting array of writers of literature and philosophy, it is evident that Existentialism was and is a philosophical perspective or inclination rather than a complete system of thought. It is a convenient label that has been applied to several widely differing revolts against traditional philosophy, especially efforts to build systematic and abstract intellectual systems.[2]

By its nature, Existentialism is not a uniform body of philosophical thought. Rather, those identified as Existentialists have raised similar questions but have differed on the answers to these questions. By way of a preliminary definition, Existentialism can be defined as a kind of philosophizing that emphasizes the uniqueness and freedom of the individual person against the herd, the crowd, or the mass society. It contends, further, that all people are fully responsible for the meaning of their own existence and the creating of their own essence or self-definition.

Existentialist thinking has also influenced a development in psychology—namely, humanistic psychology—that has implications for educational psychology, learning theory, and counseling psychology. Among those who have contributed to humanist psychology are Rollo May, Viktor Frankl, Gordon Allport, and Carl Rogers.[3] Among educational philosophers, Harold Soderquist, Van Cleve Morris, and George Kneller have analyzed and elaborated on Existentialism's meaning for education.

In the sections that follow, we will: (1) consider Sören Kierkegaard's and Jean-Paul Sartre's contributions to Existentialism; (2) examine Existentialism's relationship to the crisis of modern mass society; (3) examine the Existentialist rejection of philosophical systems; (4) analyze Existentialist philosophizing; and (5) examine Existentialism's educational implications.

EXISTENTIALIST PHILOSOPHERS

In earlier chapters, we identified and commented on the contribution of a leading figure, in terms of the history of educational ideas, to the founding of the particular philosophy. In the case of Existentialism, which is characterized by great divergence in thinking, we identify two contributors—Sören Kierkegaard, a Christian Existentialist, and Jean-Paul Sartre, an atheist Existentialist.

Sören Kierkegaard

Sören Kierkegaard, a Danish intellectual, is regarded as one of the founders of Existentialism, especially of its Christian or religious perspective.[4] Criticizing religious commitment based on creedal conformity, Kierkegaard argued that the true Christian accepted God through a "leap of faith" rather than through abstract theological or philosophical arguments and proofs. For Kierkegaard, the commitment of faith was a personal and subjective choice.

Kierkegaard attacked Hegel's philosophical Idealism for its attempt to create a completely rational architectonic system of thought. He was especially critical of the Hegelian emphasis on "Absolute Reality" as the "world mind," which found fullest expression in the state. Architectonic philosophical systems, such as that of Hegelian Idealism, deceived human beings by creating a grand illusion, Kierkegaard argued, which diverts them from personal attempts to create meaning.[5]

A sketch of the Danish philosopher, Sören Kierkegaard (1813–1855), a proponent of Existentialism.

Often referred to as the first Christian Existentialist, Kierkegaard, who thought about Christianity in completely subjective terms, defined his quest as creating the way to faith. Faith did not come from abstract theology that was an external, impersonal, abstract system of thought. Rather, it came from the intrinsic, passionate, inward introspection of personal existence. Kierkegaard's paramount concern was the Christian paradox—the human being's experience of nothingness before God, which is at the same moment the complete fulfillment of human existence.[6] Although a committed Christian, he also attacked Christian conventionalism. Focusing on the human condition, Kierkegaard saw ethics not as something that mirrored eternal truths and values but as making a faith-filled decision. In making a decision, the person must be understood not as a mental or rational self but as possessing the possibility, the freedom, to choose.[7] Kierkegaard's stress on the person's absolute freedom and that human beings are totally responsible for the choices they make are recurrent Existentialist themes. It takes the free act of the human person to create values as he or she seeks to impart order and significance to the world.[8]

Kierkegaard's themes of passionate choice, absolute freedom, and total responsibility were taken up by other Existentialists. For example, Martin Buber, in his book *I and Thou,* pleaded for human relationships between free persons rather than exploitive relationships in which individuals treated other persons as objects or as means in an "I–it" relationship.[9] Martin Heidegger, like Kierkegaard and Buber, was also a religious Existentialist. In his book *Being and Time* (1927), Heidegger developed the theme of the person as a "being-in-the-world" who creates his or her meaning of life by making choices that lead to authenticity.[10]

Jean-Paul Sartre

Jean-Paul Sartre, a French novelist, dramatist, and philosopher, espoused Existentialism from an aesthetic perspective.[11] Sartre's impressions of the human predicament were shaped by the anguish experienced in Europe during World War II. After the fall of France to Nazi Germany in 1940, Sartre joined the French resistance movement. It was World War II, especially the Nazi conquest of much of Europe, that vividly portrayed, not in fictional terms but in reality, the existential situation of modern humanity. Western Europe, especially France, was regarded as the citadel of culture, civilization, and rationality. Then, the rise to power of Hitler and the Nazis brought on the world scene a fanatical and ruthless totalitarianism that, boasting of its barbaric irrationality, demanded the total subjugation of the individual to the state. With the inherited traditions of Western culture and civility rendered meaningless by the irrationality of Hitler's new barbarianism, the Europe of the 1940s became a place of human repression and of the extermination of millions of people in technologically efficient death camps. It was in the chaos of the world turned upside down that individuals faced the choice of collaborating with Nazi totalitarianism, shutting their minds to it, or actively resisting it. Even in Nazi-occupied Europe of the time, human beings still had a choice—often the ultimate choice between life and death.

Against this background, Sartre examined the predicament of the human being in an absurd world devoid of meaning, except what people create for themselves. Coining the phrase "existence precedes essence," Sartre challenged the dictum of traditional philosophies that preached that human behavior is based on an antecedent definition of human nature. Unlike Aristotle's assertion that the human being is antecedently a rational creature who inhabits a purposeful, hence meaningful, universe, Sartre countered that each person exists—comes uninvited on the world scene—and creates his or her own meaning or essence. Because no universal truths, no absolute rules, no ultimate destiny exist to guide us, each person is totally free to choose. With this total freedom comes total responsibility for our actions or choices.[12]

THE CRISIS OF MASS SOCIETY

As indicated, Existentialism's philosophical popularity coincided with the mood of disaffection against the nineteenth-century's optimistic view of science, technology, and progress. Evidence of a profound malaise in Western attitudes has existed ever since World War I. This anxiety has been aggravated by the growth of a mass society, which causes the depersonalization of the individual. Although incoherence and conflict have occurred throughout history, the rise of a mass society and technological culture has aggravated the feeling of alienation. This feeling was partially triggered by the attempt to reorder life to fit the consequences of the mass production and mass consumption generated by the industrial and technological revolutions. The industrial revolution introduced innovative mechanisms that facilitated both efficient production and massive consumption. The logic of the machine age and the efficiency of the assembly line required that machine parts be both standardized and interchangeable. When a machine part wears out, it is replaced by an identical part that fits the machine and allows it to function effectively. The logic of interchangeable machine parts was gradually extended to individuals. Those associated with the industrial-technological society acted more like functioning parts of the corporate mechanism than persons. In a massive but efficient corporate society, individuals are designated by their functions in the system. When such functioning individuals wear out or become obsolete, they are discarded and replaced by other standardized individuals who have been trained to perform the same functions. The logic of interchangeable parts and interchangeable people has profound implications for education, especially for schooling. The school, as a system, is like an assembly line that turns out products—namely, graduates trained to perform specific functions for the larger corporate system.

Although the industrial revolution and consequent rise of an industrial-technological society reduced the scarcity of quantitative goods and services, it had debilitating effects on the qualitative or humane dimension of life. While life became materially more secure, the rise of a massive industrial technology contributed to the feeling of anxiety that humans were not really necessary to the process.

The rise of mass production–consumption systems, technological society, and scientific engineering attitudes produced an urban, corporate, and mass society. At the root of the mass society is mass production, which creates mass housing, communications, media, and entertainment. The thrust of the corporate structure and its subsidiaries is to ascertain the material needs of the average person and persuade him or her to prefer certain goods. In gearing its energies to satisfying the needs of people, the corporate structure both creates and caters to the needs of a standardized human being, a composite of statistical and sampling techniques. As a consumer and as a citizen, the private person is reduced to a standardized unit whose needs, desires, and wishes can be measured and quantified.

The public life of mass society has been extended into what had once been the private preserve of human life, a person's unique lifestyle. The impersonal forces of industrialization and standardization isolate the unique elements of human life, detaching them from the realm of meaningful activity, and eventually eroding them. Uniqueness is labeled as eccentricity rather than as the means of' achieving self-definition. Success is measured quantitatively in terms of power, possessions, or control. Standardization objectifies, quantifies, and reduces human beings to objects or functional adjuncts of the corporate mechanism.

The corporate and standardized features of mass society are not restricted to economic, political, and social life; they have also been extended into education. The technology of corporate industry and advertising has encouraged an educational technology and technocracy that seek to emulate the efficiency of the corporate sector. Engines of mass production based on the factory system and the assembly line caused the demise of the entrepreneur and craftsperson. Assembly-line logic has extended into the educational complex serving the mass society as schools attempt to apply the logic and techniques of mass production to learning. Although the urban and corporate society educates larger numbers of students than ever before in human history, it does so in large buildings that resemble educational factories producing a standardized product.

Maintaining a massive corporate structure requires trained managerial and engineering elites who can apply their planning and administrative expertise to stimulating increased production and consumption. The managerial administrators in corporate industry have their counterparts in the educational administrators who staff the bureaucracies of school systems. In seeking to educate or train large numbers of students in massive educational complexes, educational administrators and curricular specialists have devised methods designed to make the learning process more efficient. Educational technology, or innovative media, has entered the school. Teaching machines, televised instruction, multimedia instructional packages, computer-assisted learning, and standardized tests are some of the tools of educational technology introduced to make instruction efficient in the vast educational complexes of the mass society. Large class sizes, impersonal bureaucracies, and little student–teacher contact have resulted from the extension of impersonality into education.

In education, Existentialists seek to reduce the impersonalization that has affected schooling and to assert an "I–Thou" relationship between the teacher and the learner. Although disagreeing on particulars, Existentialists share a common commitment to reshaping the human situation to encourage the freest and most genuine assertion of human personality.[13]

REJECTION OF SYSTEMS

Existentialism, embracing a variety of philisophical perspectives, is not a systematic philosophy in the traditional sense.[14] Rather, it encourages a philosophical examination of life that enhances personal subjectivity. Existentialist philosophizing rejects both the desirability and possibility of constructing an all-explaining architectonic or systematic philosophy. Suspicious of universal and absolute categories, Existentialists distrust philosophical systems that seek to construct an all-encompassing worldview that categorizes human experience according to conceptions of antecedent reality. Such systematic architectonic philosophical systems are based on affirmations of an antecedent reality that exists prior to the person's entry on the world scene. According to traditional views, the human being enters, is assigned a place in the world, and is expected to conform to reality. In such systems, the person is defined, catalogued, and assigned a role or place. For example, Aristotelian natural Realists assert the existence of an objective order of reality independent of human plans and purposes. The human being, a part of this reality, has an assigned place in it as a rational creature who possesses an intellect and naturally seeks to know. The descriptive assertion of human rationality also prescribes—asserts the value— that human beings ought to act or behave rationally. In countering Aristotle's premise, Existentialists contend that if reason is asserted as the primary element in defining the human being, then there is no genuine freedom in the human condition. If reason is an antecedent constituent and determinant of human nature, then humans cannot really choose reason as a value. In contrast, Existentialists contend that humans are choosing and valuing beings who can reason if they so choose. The Existentialist sees life as too varied, complex, confused, and unpredictable to be arranged in neatly structured philosophical categories.

In abandoning the metaphysical system building of Idealists, Realists, and Thomists, the Existentialist examines the most significant and persistent doubts from the perspective of the individual human person. Existentialist involvement calls for individual philosophizing about the persistent human concerns of life, love, death, and meaning. Accepting the fact that we live in a physical environment as an evident fact of life, Existentialists view this world as an indifferent phenomenon, which, while it may not be antagonistic to human purposes, is nonetheless devoid of personal meaning. In this world, each person is born, lives, chooses his or her course, and creates the meaning of his or her own existence.

Existentialism abandons not only the architectonic traditional philosophies, but it also attacks Pragmatism's reliance on the scientific method. Dewey's Experimentalism stresses both the efficacy of the scientific method and of social intelligence arising from shared human association. It stresses the individual's ability to use the empirical procedures of science as the exclusive means of establishing tentative truths. Experimentalism also asserts the individual's ability to participate in meaningful group interaction. Although Dewey believed that the individual gains freedom through group association, some Existentialists find the "like-minded" group to be a coercive agency in which the individual is subordinated to the group will. The group can overwhelm the individual who is forced to yield to its decisions and dictates.

Antiscientific Reaction

Modern technological society, which was created by applying science to industrial processes, is characterized by an emphasis on science as the means of verifying truth and of solving problems. The scientific method deliberately minimizes the subjective and the value-laden aspects of life. Personal wishes and preferences are not allowed to interfere with scientific objectivity. The demand for scientific objectivity has led to the quantification of human experience. While quantities are measurable, qualities are not. Following the physical sciences, social science, sociology, social psychology, and behaviorism also attempt to examine individuals in objective terms. The consequences of emphasizing science and de-emphasizing the humanities have been the objectification and reduction of the human being to an entity or unit that can be weighed, measured, and quantitatively analyzed. In its behavioral aspects, the use of the scientific method has contributed to a reductionism that analyzes people by breaking down the quality of human experience into measurable and quantified responses.

EXISTENTIALIST PHILOSOPHIZING

Existentialism's basic premise that existence precedes essence asserts the primacy of human subjectivity.[15] The human being first arrives on the world scene and then begins the efforts of self-definition. All philosophizing begins with an existing being who is aware of his or her own existence. This awareness of existence puts the person in a situation of being his or her own "essence-maker" through individual, personal, and subjective choice making. The Existentialist situation, however, is paradoxical. Each individual is unique, and this uniqueness is of value in the world. However, at the same time, each person lives in a universe that is indifferent to human existence. The awareness of one's own existence also implies a coordinate awareness of eventual nonexistence. The eventuality of nonexistence is a source of profound anxiety, dread, and concern. Despite the fact that existence also carries with it the ever-present threat of nonexistence, each person must work out his or her own definition in a meaningless universe.

Thus, the basic thrust of Existentialist philosophizing is to portray the human struggle to achieve self-definition through choice. Traditional philosophies, theologies, ideologies, group-centered sociology, and their educational derivatives have all looked at the world to provide the human reason for being. These views define the person as part of a system and categorize him or her as a constituent element in a structure that provides the purpose for existing. In contrast, Existentialism asserts that human purpose is not automatically prescribed in the metaphysical or theological structure of the universe or in the sociological or ideological structure of society. Each person is responsible for creating his or her own purpose.

For Existentialists, the basic philosophical issue is that of valuing and choosing. Values are not embedded in some conception of a metaphysical or sociological antecedent reality, but are created by personal choices. No external universal criterion can be used to estimate values. The person cannot escape from choice.[16]

The quest of an Existentialist education is to cultivate an authentic person who is aware of freedom and that every choice is an act of personal value creation. The authentic person knows that self-definition can never be determined by anyone or anything external. The struggle for authenticity involves being aware of the personal responsibility to make choices, to create alternatives, and to choose—without the intervention of an external moral arbiter or criteria.

A basic problem for the Existentialist is the relationship of the individual to other people and agencies. In experience, people encounter others who resemble them. This encounter between the self and another leads to anxiety that the other will limit and threaten personal freedom by using the person as a functionary to accomplish selfish purposes.

The functionalization or instrumentalizing of individuals is a particularly pernicious threat in a technological society in which mass production and consumption are organized according to the logic of interchangeable, standardized, and specialized functioning parts. When extended to social organization, the concept of standardized efficiency leads to a planned society that limits individuality. Social organization and institutionalized decision making in a mass society are beyond the control of the individual; thus, the person becomes lost in intricate systems of corporate and managerial bureaucracy. Society itself exerts a limiting influence on a person's search for authenticity. People can choose either to accept or conform to societal prescriptions or reject and revolt against them. The crucial issue for the person seeking authenticity is the free choice of either conforming or rebelling. The inner-directed, authentic person makes his or her choice as an act of value creation. The other-directed person, seeking to escape from the responsibility of self-definition, allows other persons or agencies to make the important choices.

The era of modern mass society is characterized by people who are reluctant to become personally involved with other human beings in an I–Thou relationship that is between free subjectivities. This tendency to be personally uninvolved stems from fear that the encounter with another person will lead to the objectification of the self. Although objectification always is a risk that accompanies personal encounters, it does not necessarily mean that the other person will objectify the one who is encountered. Always fragile and delicate, the I–Thou relationship is a noncoercive friendship. It means that one has encountered another person and has not used him or her as a means to an end, as a function, or as an instrument to achieve one's purposes.[17]

EXISTENTIALISM'S EDUCATIONAL IMPLICATIONS

The U.S. educational tradition, based on the common or public school conception, saw schooling as an agency to build an American national identity. As designed by Horace Mann, Henry Barnard, and its other founders, the public school was an instrument to mold varied racial, social, ethnic, religious, and economic groups into a common culture. While it served the aims of nation building, public schooling as a means of social control often disregarded linguistic, ethnic, and cultural pluralism.

It was mentioned earlier that as educational institutions in a mass society emulate the larger corporate system, they depersonalize the teaching–learning relationship. There is also another sense in which formal education systems impede personal authenticity. Various subdivisions of professional education such as educational psychology, instructional methodology, measurement, and evaluation borrow heavily from the social sciences of psychology, sociology, and political science. Emulating the physical sciences, these various social sciences and their educational derivatives seek to predict and control behavior. Instruction is structured according to behavioral objectives so that outcomes can be measured to the degree that behavior has changed. Such a conception of learning views the learner as a social object or phenomenon and elicits responses that are quantified and rendered into measurable statistical and otherwise standardized responses.

Contemporary U.S. education has become highly group-centered as a result of the progressive educator's stress on shared activity in learning situations and because of the dominance of educational psychologies that emphasize social acceptance and adjustment. The aims of socialized education are such objectives as learning to cooperate with others, functioning successfully in group situations, and working as an effective collaborative team member. According to group-centered educational theories, the individual becomes more effective and efficient by identifying with and participating in group activities.

Existentialist educators are cautious about the glorification of the group. In the midst of crowds, human beings are still lonely and anxiety ridden. Some group-centered learning situations may become so coercive of the individual that personal authenticity may be sacrificed to the pressure to achieve like-minded consensus. When a person freely chooses to join and to participate in a group, opportunities still exist for authentic choice. However, many group-centered situations in schools are not freely chosen. Learning situations organized around groups should be such that they permit and encourage opportunities for individuals to assert the unique aspects of their personalities.

An Existentialist Critique of Contemporary Education

Rather than seeking to create a systematic philosophy that explains all facets of human existence, Existentialists seek to philosophize about the human condition. Philosophizing in the Existentialist style provokes a critique of certain social and educational trends that have influenced contemporary society and schools. Among the trends that reduce personal choice and self-definition are standardization, categorization, the inculcation of socioeconomic roles, and the *tyranny of the average*. Each of these trends works against creating opportunities for authenticity.

In their desire to be scientific and efficient, modern educators have demonstrated a decided proclivity for standardization. Standardized tests, designed to measure student aptitude and achievement, are used to assign students to educational categories from which there is often little movement or escape. School records and reporting systems deal in categories that encourage little or no recognition of students' uniqueness and creativity. Mass-produced instructional materials, ranging from basal readers and textbooks to videos, are geared to categories of students in clearly defined groups. For their organization, schools rely on routinized and standardized schedules. While contributing to efficiency, the standardization of educational institutions has fostered social control that is suspicious of individual uniqueness or creativity. Whereas some teachers willingly become agents of institutional standardization, others search for opportunities to encourage their students' self-expression and self-definition.

It is not only the school's impetus toward standardized efficiency that threatens students' self-definition. Students themselves, seeking the security that comes from group identification, often become conformists who eagerly consign their peers to categories. In the typical high school, students often identify as "brains" or "grinds," students who are studious academic achievers; "jocks," those who are athletes and cheerleaders; "freaks" or "druggies," those who are on drugs; and then there are the "nobodies" who are without group identification. Once assigned to a school caste, the adolescent is identified as a member of a group, stays within that group, and often abandons the opportunities to cultivate his or her own uniqueness or to appreciate others for their own worth.

Still another tendency of contemporary society and education that limits self-definition comes from socioeconomic pressures that have shaped schooling into role playing. Schools define the role for economic success—for getting a good-paying job and moving up the economic ladder; they define what it means to be a good citizen; they define what it means to be socially successful; and so on. Students are expected to study these roles and to play them well. In so doing, the opportunities for genuine self-determined choice are fewer. Authenticity becomes too risky because it may not lead to success as others have defined it.

Among the most pervasive but most subtle of the contemporary trends that erode the possibilities of human authenticity comes from the "tyranny of the average." The tyranny of dictatorial and authoritarian rulers, regimes, and institutions is a patently obvious kind of oppression. Less obvious, the tyranny of the average appears initially to be democratic but in actuality is a symptom of mass thought and preferences. In a consumer-oriented society, products are made and marketed for the largest possible group of consumers. Mass media, art, and entertainment—television, radio, movies, newspapers, magazines, popular books— are also designed to attract the largest possible audience. Again, marketability dictates that the widest appeal will come from catering to the average. These agencies of informal education both reflect and create popular tastes. In a mass society, deviations from the average do not sell well; uniqueness either becomes so expensive that it can be enjoyed only by a privileged elite or so unpopular that it is pushed to the margins of society.

It may be argued that standardization, categorization, role playing, and the tyranny of the average are the inevitable by-products of a mass society and that contemporary schooling only mirrors these irresistible trends. An Existentialist educator would argue, however, that as society becomes more conformist, standardized, and categorized, it is the responsibility of teachers to expose these trends by having students examine and analyze them. This exposé is not merely for sociological interest; it is to raise students' consciousness so that they at least are aware of the dangers that modern technological society poses to authentic freedom.

Toward an Existentialist Pedagogy

While not specifically defining an Existentialist education, Van Cleve Morris argues that education should cultivate an "intensity of awareness" in the learner. Such an awareness means that students should recognize that as individuals they are constantly, freely, baselessly, and creatively choosing. Such an awareness carries with it the responsibility for determining how one wants to live and for creating one's own self-definition.[18]

In developing an Existentialist educational psychology, Morris identified a "pre-Existential" period of human development and the "Existential Moment."[19] During the pre-Existential period prior to puberty, the child, not really aware of his or her human condition, is not yet conscious of a personal identity and destiny. The pre-Existentialist years coincide with elementary education when children learn to read, write, do arithmetic, and acquire physical, recreational, communicative, and social skills. Children also learn some subject-matter and problem-solving skills.

For Morris, the Existential Moment arises when people become conscious of their presence as a self in the world. Although the experience of the Existential Moment varies with individuals, it generally occurs around the time of puberty and is characterized by an awareness of one's presence in the world, and an insight into one's own consciousness and the responsibility for conduct. At times, the Existential Moment is a period of great power and thrust; at other times, the person seeks to escape adult responsibilities and to return to childhood's innocence.

Existentialist education would begin in the years of the junior high school and continue onward through the senior high school and the undergraduate college. The aim of such an education would be to awaken and intensify self-awareness. Concerned with those elements of experience that are subjective, personal, and affective, an Existentialist education would encourage involvement in situations conducive to the knowledge that human choices involve personal questions of good or bad and right or wrong.

Existentialist Epistemology

Traditional philosophies such as Idealism, Realism, and Thomism emphasize the human being as a thinking and reasoning being. For example, Plato's philosopher-kings were an elite who possessed the keenest powers of speculative abstraction; Aristotle, identifying the power to reason as unique to the human being, called the human being a rational animal. Traditional educational philosophies and school practices based on the philosophies of Plato and Aristotle have stressed cognitive development as an overriding educational outcome. Unlike these philosophies, Existentialism sees the human being in more imprecise but also in more varied terms. The human person is rational but also irrational, thinking but also feeling, cognitive but also affective.

Existentialist epistemology assumes that the individual is responsible for constructing his or her own knowledge.[20] Knowledge originates in and is composed of what exists in the individual's consciousness and feelings as a result of one's experiences. Human situations are built of both rational and irrational components. The validity of knowledge is determined by its value and meaning to the individual. An Existentialist epistemology emerges from the recognition that human experience and knowledge are subjective, personal, rational, and irrational. Whereas Pragmatists emphasize using the scientific method of problem solving, Existentialists prefer to probe human aesthetic, moral, and emotional concerns as well as cognitive ones.

Humanistic Psychology

Existentialism has been influential in shaping humanistic psychology, which has implications for educational psychology and counseling.[21] Existentialists such as Sartre have criticized mechanistic and deterministic psychologies that reduce the human being to sets of instincts and impulses and neglect human freedom and choice. Arguing that human purpose is not determined, Sartre contended that it comes from personal choice arising in situations unique to each person.

Abraham Maslow, Gordon Allport, Carl Rogers, and Rollo May have been the leaders of the humanistic psychology movement in the United States.[22] Rogers, who developed the concept of client-centered counseling, emphasizes that the individual should create his or her own self-concept. This process of creating self-identity means that the person exists, or is at the center of a changing world of experience, which, while including social interaction, is ultimately private. As a result of environmental and social interaction, the structure of the self, that is, personhood, emerges but is self-formed or self-defined rather than other-directed.[23]

According to humanistic psychology, Existentialist teaching seeks to stimulate and to facilitate learning, or self-examination and definition, in the broadest sense. Maintaining the Existentialist classroom requires a delicate balance in which both teacher and students maintain their identities as persons. This means that the teacher must constantly struggle against falling into a situation in which students are defined simply by their age, academic ranking, status, or group membership. It also means that students need to be conscious that they, too, can define a teacher, not as a person, but as one who performs custodial, instructional, and supervisory functions. In other words, the delicate Existential balance breaks down when teachers reduce students to objects and students reduce teachers to functions.

An Existentialist Curriculum

From an Existentialist perspective, the curriculum includes the skills and subjects that explain physical and social reality and most importantly the humanities, which portray human choice.[24] Such subjects as history, literature, language, mathematics, science, and so forth are taken for granted as existent bodies of knowledge. The crucial learning phase is not in the structure of knowledge nor in curriculum organization but rather in the student's construction of its meaning. In the Existentialist situation, the student constructs meaning by giving the subject a personal interpretation.

The curriculum that the student interprets contains both cognitive and normative elements. The factual, descriptive, and scientific subjects of the cognitive dimension are the "givens" of the phenomenological order. The normative or attitudinal dimension contains those subjects that are value oriented. Such humanistic studies as history, the arts, literature, philosophy, and religion are especially useful in examining ethical and aesthetic values.

The arts, designed to cultivate and express aesthetic experience, include music, drama, dance, creative writing, painting, and film. The aim of aesthetic education, according to Existentialists, is not to imitate the styles of selected classical artists, although these might be studied, but rather to stimulate creative expression. In aesthetic education, the teacher is to evoke the learner's sense and desire for aesthetic expression. Although not knowing what the learner will create, the teacher provides a variety of creative media so that the learner will have the raw materials from which to create his or her own art object. The learner uses the various media to portray the world as experienced in one's own consciousness and to produce the art that comes from the center of one's private existence.

Literature and the humanities also receive emphasis in an Existentialist curriculum. Relevant for awakening the learner to the significance of choice making, literature portrays persons facing basic human issues. Through literature, drama, and film, the learner places his or her capacities for feeling at the disposal of the author or artist. The vicarious involvement of the learner in the profound human questions of love, death, suffering, guilt, and freedom are excellent means for portraying the human condition and for constructing personal meaning in an apparently indifferent world.

Like literature and the other humanities, history can be a forceful vehicle for examining how individuals in the past have faced recurrent human concerns. Historical study, as viewed by the Existentialist, is not so much a matter of establishing cause–effect relationships nor of examining the origin and development of particular civilizations. History serves to illuminate the past and to present contemporary people with alternative hypotheses for living life in the present. George Kneller dramatically states:

> *The student should therefore learn to handle his history with passion, personal thrust, and in the manner of a stage director, talently manipulating the human scene, with all its heroes, villains, and plots.*[25]

Existentialist Teaching and Learning

Although the Existentialist educator may choose to use a variety of educational methods, none of these methods should be permitted to obscure the personal I–Thou relationship that ought to exist between teacher and learner. The Socratic dialogue is an appropriate method for Existentialist teachers. The dialogue can bring questions to the learners so that they become conscious of the condition of their lives. Unlike the Idealist's use of the Socratic dialogue, the Existentialist teacher does not know the answers to the questions posed. Indeed, the best kind of question is answerable only in the student's own construction of meaning.

In an Existentialist methodology, the teacher seeks to stimulate an "intensity of awareness" in the learner, encouraging the quest for a personal truth by asking questions that concern life's meaning. It is the teacher's task to create the learning situation in which students can express their subjectivity. It is only the learner who can come face to face with his or her responsibility for self-definition. The creation of the intensity of awareness is as much the learner's own responsibility as it is the teacher's. Such an awareness involves the sense of being personally involved in the ethical and aesthetic dimensions of existence.

The Open Classroom

John Holt, an advocate of child freedom and "open education," approaches the Existentialist educational perspective in practice in school settings. Holt's educational theories grew out of his experience as an elementary school teacher. Dissatisfied with the constraints imposed by traditional school structures and bureaucracies, he argued for educational reform designed to promote the child's freedom to learn.

In *Freedom and Beyond,* Holt argued for "open learning." According to Holt, children are "smart, energetic, curious, eager to learn, and good at learning" and do not have to be tricked, enticed, or coerced into learning as is frequently done in conventional schools.[26] Continual and unnecessary constraints on children restrict the opportunities for freedom of choice necessary for intelligent and humane growth. Like the Existentialist educators, Holt wanted to bring learners to an awareness that they are responsible for their choices. He suggested the open classroom as a learning environment that creates and contains wide possibilities of choice so that children may learn by pursuing their interests without being coerced either by the school or the teacher.

Unfortunately, in Holt's view, most schools have assumed institutional functions that discourage children's freedom, choice, and personal growth. As custodial social institutions, schools sort, indoctrinate, and assign social roles to their students instead of liberating them. In its custodial role, the school segregates children and adolescents from the larger society.[27] Schools also categorize persons by sorting them into age-specific and academically arranged groups. Standardized tests and teacher preferences are the basis of the labels of competent or incompetent used to assign youngsters to academic categories. As selective agencies, schools often have far-reaching effects on a person's later life by determining the occupational and social roles that children will have as adults. Like the factory's assembly line, schooling becomes an impersonal process that reduces people to products rather than persons. An equally pernicious consequence of the school's selective function is that education is made into a competitive race that has many losers and only a few winners.

Holt also charged that schools deny their humane function when they act as agencies of indoctrination to inculcate the moral, economic, political, and sexual values that create unthinking and unfeeling conformists.[28]

The open classroom is a learning situation that encourages the widest possible range of alternatives so that children can choose what they will learn. Holt argues for self-initiated and self-directed learning carried on by the students themselves. Teachers in open classrooms are to create and encourage opportunities for self-directed learning.

Holt's concept of structure can be illuminated by examining it in relationship to both the traditional and open classrooms. It should be noted that, while both traditional and open classrooms have structures, they have differing ones. Also, the open classroom is not a structureless learning situation. Holt contended that the conventional classroom is often "inflexible, rigid, and static" in that students, despite their individual differences, are required to perform the same tasks. Instruction in traditional classrooms is extrinsic to student's interests and needs because it has been imposed by institutional authorities who function outside of the classroom and through a bureaucratic chain of command. In traditional classroom settings, teachers are expected to follow the curriculum guide, to give commands and transmit information, which students can either passively receive, accept, or reject. Of course, acceptance is rewarded and rejection is punished.

Rewards become grades, grades become the academic record, and the academic record becomes the occupational and social determinant that often follows individuals throughout adult life.

In contrast to the constraints of the traditional classroom, the open classroom is rich in its varied opportunities for learning. It has as many opportunities for learning as there are teachers and students within it. Because the different interests of students are recognized and their personal choices are encouraged and respected, learning in the open classroom must be flexible and dynamic. Growing out of the interests, needs, and problems of its members, the open classroom has to be flexible and free in the relationships of students to each other and of the teacher to students.[29]

Holt, concerned with enhancing the opportunities for choice making in the open classroom, encouraged choice within limits. A person's choice, he contended, is limited by prescriptions indicating what one *must* do and proscriptions signifying what one *must not* do. Coercive social, political, and educational situations have many vague, ill-defined prescriptions and proscriptions that bring "authoritarian others" into a person's life. A free society, in or out of school, has clearly and specifically defined limits. In a free society, and in the open classroom, its educational counterpart, rules are reduced to a necessary minimum and are intended to protect a person's freedom from arbitrary infringement by others. Because they are clearly stated and minimal, the rules of the open society and open classroom require little interpretation; students do not have to guess about the degree of authority that will be exercised over them. In such a society and in such a classroom, the rights of persons are protected by limiting the power of others over them.

Holt examined the question of what must be done to create open classrooms and to give greater freedom to persons. Although it is impossible for one to give freedom to another, it is possible to create opportunities for choice by removing unnecessary restraints. Like the Existentialists, Holt argued that choosing involves tension and risk. When a person is free to choose, then that person is responsible for his or her choice and its consequences.

In *Freedom and Beyond,* Holt sought to answer critics who charged that open education would produce undisciplined people and social anarchy. Holt, analyzing the conventional view of discipline, found it divided human experience into tightly defined categories of work or play, the easy or the difficult, and the agreeable or the disagreeable. In contrast, Holt, arguing against dividing learning or any other human activity into parts, contended that all activity is an unbroken flow of human experience. For Holt, the person's interest in freely chosen projects will elicit the efforts necessary for their completion. Only when a project is imposed by others, without the consent of the person who must perform the task, is external pressure needed to see that it is completed. Holt condemned the conventional conception of discipline that calls for giving unquestioning obedience to an authority, because it rests on the following assumptions: (1) Obedience is necessary for character formation, (2) following orders leads to efficient performance of duty, (3) assigned rules should be accepted wihout complaint, and (4) punishment is needed to remediate disobedient individuals.[30] Although these assumptions have long been associated with traditional school discipline, Holt argued that such discipline is more appropriate to despotic regimes than to democratic and free societies. In contrast to the assumptions that support despotic discipline, he identified legitimate discipline as coming from (1) nature, (2) culture or society, and (3) superior force.

As a given that exists prior to our existence, nature limits our choices because we must conform to it. For example, if children choose to establish a terrarium with growing plants and then neglect to water them, the plants will die. The consequences of neglecting such a natural requirement are clear and indicate what must be done if the plants are to grow. Whenever a learner tries to do or make something—be it the simple planting of a flower or executing a complicated chemical experiment—nature's discipline is present.

Holt identifies culture or society as exerting a disciplining force on children. Sensing the intricate network of social relations, customs, and manners around them, children want to understand, be involved in, and participate in their culture. Wanting to share in society, they observe and try to emulate the social amenities of their culture. In so doing, they participate in the cultural heritage.

The discipline of superior force comes into play when a superior commands a subordinate. Although adults too often exercise this kind of discipline over children, Holt contended that it is used legitimately to protect the children's safety. However, its exercise should be restricted to those situations in which it is necessary to protect children from dangers they do not fully understand. Adults legitimately administer this discipline to children because they have greater experience and understanding and not merely because they are older and bigger. Holt warned that the discipline of superior force should be used cautiously and as seldom as possible; otherwise, children whose lives are "full of the threat and fear of punishment" will be locked into childishness because they are deprived of the need and opportunity to learn responsibility.[31]

Open and Nonformal Education

Schools, like other institutions, are rule oriented and bureaucratic; while serving individuals, the norms by which institutions function are geared to the group. Essentially age-specific in organization, schools, despite some deviations, move classes of children or adolescents through the institution in age-determined categories. Becase of these institutional and organizational patterns, it is difficult but not impossible to create Existentialist learning possibilities in the school situation.

Because of the constraints in formal educational institutions, some educators have turned their attention to informal and nonformal kinds of education outside of the school. Ivan Illich, for example, has defined schooling as an institutionalized process that (1) segregates children and adolescents in special institutions; (2) requires their compulsory, full-time attendance in these institutions; (3) places them under the custodial jurisdiction of teachers; and (4) mandates that they complete a prescribed and mandatory curriculum.[32]

Illich's concept of "learning webs" or educational networks resembles the freely chosen involvement and participation that Existentialists advocate. Learning webs or networks are of four types: (1) reference services of educational tools, objects, and resources; (2) educational exchanges designed to provide the opportunity and training to learn particular skills; (3) peer-matching, which facilitates finding persons who want to engage in a similar learning activity; and (4) "educators-at-large," experts who can be consulted on particular educational problems.[33] These webs or networks exist outside of institutions and are used by persons for periods of time that they define, rather than having these matters defined by others.

CONCLUSION

Unlike the systematic worldviews presented by the more traditional philosophies, Existentialism seeks to free people from the constraints of a categorized universe. Emphasizing human subjectivity, personal freedom, and individual responsibility, Existentialism boldly portrays the human being as a person who exists in a world in which he or she alone is responsible for his or her self-definition. In the quest for authenticity, individuals must become aware that they make their own values and create their own essence without recourse to an external criterion.

Existentialist education holds human freedom as its paramount concern. Stressing individual subjectivity, the Existentialist educator seeks to cultivate a sense of self-awareness and responsibility in students. By making significant personal choices, the student alone can create his or her own self-definition. The goals of such an education cannot be specified in advance nor can they be imposed by the teacher or the school system. Each person has the responsibility for his or her own education. To summarize, Existentialist education seeks to

1. Create a conscious awareness of the institutions, forces, and trends that limit freedom.
2. Create an intensity of awareness regarding the meaning of the freedom to choose.

3. Cultivate a sense that each human being is responsible for his or her own self-definition and for acting to fulfill that emerging self.
4. Distinguish between trivial and meaningful choices.

DISCUSSION QUESTIONS

1. Compare and contrast Existentialism with the traditional philosophies of Idealism, Realism, and Thomism.

2. How did the political and cultural anguish of World War II stimulate the rise of Existentialism?

3. Identify the constraints that a mass society poses on individual freedom and choice.

4. Why does Existentialism reject philosophical systems that define the person?

5. Examine group-centered instruction from an Existentialist perspective.

6. What is the Existentialist meaning of choice?

7. Do the major trends in modern education encourage or discourage personal authenticity?

8. Describe and give an example of the Existentialist epistemology of "appropriation."

9. How has humanistic psychology helped to reshape the concept of the learner along Existentialist lines?

10. What is the role of the humanities in an Existentialist curriculum?

11. Distinguish between an open and a closed classroom situation.

INQUIRY PROJECTS

- Read and locate the existentialist themes in a book by one of the following authors: Sören Kierkegaard, Friedrich Nietzsche, Fydor Dostoyevsky, Karl Jaspers, Martin Buber, Gabriel Marcel, Jean-Paul Sartre.
- Read and locate the Existentialist themes in a book by one of the following humanistic psychologists: Rollo May, Abraham Maslow, Gordon Allport, Carl Rogers.
- In a paper, identify and analyze practices in education that are antagonistic to Existentialism.
- Write a sketch that describes the character of an Existentialist teacher.
- Identify a novel or a motion picture that portrays an Existentialist situation. In a review, indicate how it portrays Existentialist themes.
- Read *Freedom and Beyond* or another book by John Holt. Write a review that identifies and analyzes Existentialist themes.
- Read Ivan lllich's *Deschooling Society*. In a review essay, assess the possibilities of nonformal education as a means of self-definition.

• Review several books on instructional methods or school administration. Do these books advocate procedures that are antagonistic to an Existentialist educational perspective?

FURTHER READINGS

Barrett, William. *Irrational Man: A Study in Existentialist Philosophy.* New York: Anchor Books, 1990.

Billington, Ray. *East of Existentialism: The Tao of the West.* London and Boston: Unwin Hyman, 1990.

Buber, Martin. *I and Thou.* New York: Charles Scribner's Sons, 1958.

Catalano, Joseph. *A Commentary on Jean-Paul Sartre's Critique of Dialectical Reason.* Chicago: University of Chicago Press, 1986.

Dobson, Andrew. *Jean-Paul Sartre and the Politics of Reason: A Theory of History.* New York: Cambridge University Press, 1993.

Gould, William B. *Viktor E. Frankl: Life with Meaning.* Pacific Grove, CA: Brooks/Cole, 1993.

Green, Maxine. *Existential Encounters for Teachers.* New York: Random House, 1967.

Green, Norman. *Jean-Paul Sartre: The Existentialist Ethics.* Ann Arbor: University of Michigan Press, 1966.

Grene, Marjorie. *Introduction to Existentialism.* Chicago: University of Chicago Press, 1959.

Heidegger, Martin. *Being and Time.* New York: Harper & Row, 1962.

Hendley, Steve. *Reason and Relativism: A Sartrean Investigation.* Albany: State University of New York Press, 1991.

Kneller, George F. *Existentialism and Education.* New York: John Wiley, 1966.

Kruks, Sonia. *Situation and Human Existence: Freedom, Subjectivity, and Society.* London and Boston: Unwin Hyman, 1990.

Lowrie, Walter. *A Short Life of Kierkegaard.* Princeton, NJ: Princeton University Press, 1942.

Macquarrie, John. *Existentialism.* Baltimore: Penguin Books, 1973.

Marcel, Gabriel. *The Existential Background of Human Dignity.* Cambridge, MA: Harvard University Press, 1963.

Marcel, Gabriel. *Homo Viator.* Translated by Emma Crawford. New York: Harper & Row, 1962.

Marcel, Gabriel. *The Philosophy of Existentialism.* Translated by Manya Harari. New York: Citadel Press, 1956.

May, Rollo. *Existential Psychology.* New York: Random House, 1960.

May, Rollo. *Psychology and the Human Dilemma.* Princeton, NJ: D. Van Nostrand, 1966.

McCulloch, Gregory. *Using Sartre: An Analytical Introduction to Early Sartrean Themes.* London and New York: Routledge, 1994.

Mihollan, Frank, and Bill E. Forisha. *From Skinner to Rogers: Contrasting Approaches to Education.* Lincoln, NE: Professional Educators Publications, 1972.

Morrison, Harriet B. *The Seven Gifts: A New View of Teaching Inspired by the Philosophy of Maurice Merleau-Ponty.* Chicago: Educational Studies Press, 1988.

Morris, Van Cleve. *Existentialism in Education: What It Means.* New York: Harper & Row, 1966.

Peters, Helene. *The Existential Woman.* New York: Peter Lang, 1991.

Rogers, Carl R. *Freedom to Learn.* Columbus, OH: Charles E. Merrill, 1969.

Sartre, Jean-Paul. *Being and Nothingness.* Translated by Hazel E. Barnes. New York: Washington Square Press, 1966.

Sartre, Jean-Paul. *Existentialism and Human Emotions.* New York: Citadel Press, 1957.

Scudder, John R., and Algis Mickunas. *Meaning, Dialogue, and Encultura- tion: Phenomenological Philosophy of Education.* Lanham, MD: University Press of America and The Center for Advanced Research in Phenomenol- ogy, 1985.

Soderquist, Harold O. *The Person and Ed- ucation.* Columbus, OH: Charles E. Merrill, 1964.

Swenson, David. *Something About Ki- erkegaard.* Minneapolis, MN: Augs- burg Publishing House, 1941.

Tillich, Paul. *The Courage to Be.* New Ha- ven: Yale University Press, 1952.

Vandenberg, Donald. *Being and Education: An Essay in Existential Phenomenol- ogy.* Englewood Cliffs, NJ: Prentice Hall, 1971.

Vandenberg, Donald. *Human Rights in Ed- ucation.* New York: Philosophical Li- brary, 1983.

Wilson, Colin. *An Essay on the "New" Existentialism.* Nottingham, England: Pauper's Press, 1986.

Wolin, Richard. *The Politics of Being: The Political Thought of Martin Heidegger.* New York: Columbia University Press, 1990.

ENDNOTES

1. For Marcel, see Gabriel Marcel, *The Existential Background of Human Dig- nity* (Cambridge, MA: Harvard University Press, 1963); for Heidegger, see Richard Wolin, *The Politics of Being: The Political Thought of Martin Heidegger* (New York: Columbia University Press, 1990).

2. Walter Kaufmann, *Existentialism From Dostoyevski to Sartre* (New York: World Publishing, 1956), pp. 11–12.

3. For example, see William B. Gould, *Viktor E. Frankl: Life with Meaning* (Pacific Grove, CA: Brooks/Cole, 1993).

4. For biographical treatments of Kierkegaard, see Walter Lowrie, *A Short Life of Kierkegaard* (Princeton, NJ: Princeton University Press, 1942); David Swenson, *Something About Kierkegaard* (Minneapo- lis, MN: Augsburg, 1941).

5. Marjorie Grene, *Introduction to Existentialism* (Chicago: University of Chi- cago Press, 1959), pp. 19–20.

6. Ibid., p. 6.

7. Kaufmann, *Existentialism,* p. 17.

8. Grene, *Introduction to Existential- ism,* p. 11.

9. Martin Buber, *I and Thou,* trans. Ronald G. Smith (New York: Charles Scrib- ner's Sons, 1958).

10. Martin Heidegger, *Being and Time* (New York: Harper & Row, 1962).

11. Sartre's expression of Existential- ism is found in Jean-Paul Sartre, *Existen- tialism and Human Emotions* (New York: Citadel Press, 1957), and Jean-Paul Sartre, *Being and Nothingness* (New York: Wash- ington Square Press, 1966).

12. For commentaries on Sartre, see Joseph B. Catalano, *A Commentary on Jean-Paul Sartre's Critique of Dialectical Reason* (Chicago: University of Chicago Press, 1986); Andrew Dobson, *Jean-Paul Sartre and the Politics of Reason: A Theory of History* (New York: Cambridge Univer- sity Press, 1993); Steve Hendley, *Reason and Relativism: A Sartrean Investigation*

(Albany: State University of New York Press, 1991).

13. For an analysis of situational meaning, see Sonia Kruks, *Situation and Human Existence: Freedom, Subjectivity, and Society* (London and Boston: Unwin Hyman, 1990).

14. George F. Kneller, *Existentialism and Education* (New York: John Wiley & Sons, 1966), p. 19.

15. For a clear and very readable treatment of Existentialism's educational implications, see Van Cleve Morris, *Existentialism in Education* (New York: Harper & Row, 1966).

16. Ibid., pp. 31–53.

17. Ibid., pp. 69–78.

18. Ibid., p. 110.

19. Ibid., pp. 111–116.

20. Ibid., pp. 120–122.

21. For example, see Gerald J. Pine, "The Existential School Counselor," *Clearing House,* XL–III (February 1969): 351–354.

22. See, for example, Rollo May, *Psychology and the Human Dilemma* (Princeton, NJ: D. Van Nostrand, 1966); Rollo May, ed., *Existential Psychology* (New York: Random House, 1960); Carl Rogers, *Freedom to Learn* (Columbus, OH: Charles E. Merrill, 1969).

23. Frank Milhollan and Bill E. Forisha, *From Skinner to Rogers: Contrasting Approaches to Education* (Lincoln, NE: Professional Educators Publications, 1972), pp. 98–113.

24. Morris, *Existentialism in Education,* pp. 124–125.

25. Kneller, *Existentialism in Education,* pp. 129–130.

26. John Holt, *Freedom and Beyond* (New York: E. P. Dutton, 1972), p. 2.

27. Ibid., pp. 244–245.

28. Ibid., pp. 251–256.

29. Ibid., p. 11.

30. Ibid., pp. 100–101.

31. Ibid., p. 104.

32. Ivan Illich, *Deschooling Society* (New York: Harper & Row, 1971), pp. 25–33.

33. Ibid., pp. 77–104.

▶ 8

Philosophical
Analysis and
Education

Philosophical Analysis, or Analytical Philosophy, a contemporary movement in educational philosophy, conceives its function to be the examination and classification of the language of both common discourse and scientific expression. Philosophical Analysts who are concerned with educational philosophy seek to examine critically the language associated with teaching and learning and with the formulation of educational goals and policies.[1]

Philosophical Analysis differs in its intent and method from the older systematic Idealist, Realist, and Thomist philosophies, which are grounded in metaphysical conceptions of an antecedent reality. The more traditional speculative philosophers attempted to construct worldviews that systematized all human experience and knowledge into a unitary and systematic philosophy. They sought to discover an ultimate principle or first cause that was the source of all existence. Philosophical Analysts reject the system building of the speculative philosophers, which they claim has produced only philosophical chaos and confusion. They contend that the so-called systematic philosophies that were supposed to unify merely succeeded in dividing the intellectual world into a bewildering array of conflicting "isms."

As they work to examine, classify, and verify ordinary and scientific language, the Analytical Philosophers seek to establish meaning rather than to create new philosophical or ideological systems. As a means of resolving controversy, the Analysts seek to identify and to clarify the fundamental assumptions of contending points of view. They do this by asking for operational definitions of the terms used. Unlike the speculative philosophers, the Analytical Philosophers are concerned primarily with the problems of clarification of language. They do not consider it their function as philosophers to advise others on life's prescriptive or normative issues. However, they believe that their philosophy will clarify policy issues and aid in the formulation of clearly stated policies. The function of Analytical Philosophy may be examined more clearly by turning to the origins, development, and educational implications of this method of philosophical inquiry. In the sections that follow, we examine the origins of Analytical Philosophy, the classification of propositions, and the search for order and clarity.

ORIGINS OF ANALYTICAL PHILOSOPHY

Rather than identifying a particular philosopher of education who is representative of the philosophical position, this section traces the origins of Philosophical Analysis or Analytical Philosophy in terms of a group of individuals who collectively developed this approach or "method of doing philosophy."

G. E. Moore (1873–1958) and Bertrand Russell (1872–1970) are often identified as the founders of the Analytical movement in Anglo-American philosophy. Although both Russell and Moore were interested in analyzing the language of both common and scientific discourse, Russell sought to discover and analyze the logical structure that he believed was present within any given language. For Russell, the task of philosophy was to find and formulate the logical rules underlying language usage. In seeking to develop an analytical system of symbolic, or mathematical, logic, Russell sought to understand the nature and meaning of discourse. Russell, in effect, proposed a set of mathematical symbols that represented words, concepts, and propositions, which, when processed mathematically, would render solutions unaffected by the subjectivism of personal preferences and emotions.[2]

George E. Moore, whose work is often associated with Russell's, was a philosopher at England's Cambridge University. Moore raised many of the issues that have since concerned Analytical Philosophers. Moore, the author of *Refutation of Idealism in Mind* (1903) and *Principia Ethica* (1903), was identified with the New Realism. His questions, however, stimulated the use of language analysis as a method among English-speaking philosophers. Moore questioned metaphysical attempts to derive values from existing objects or their relationships. Values, for Moore, were emotive and signified approval or disapproval. Moore's approach was to isolate issues and to analyze them thoroughly. Rather than seeking conclusions, this approach often generated new issues and further questioning.

In addition to Russell's and Moore's contributions to the origins of language analysis, other British philosophers, following their lead, sought to divest philosophy from speculative metaphysics. Notable leaders in the Analytic effort were Percy Nunn, D. J. O'Connor, Louis A. Reid, and R. S. Peters. Associated with the London Institute of Education, Reid and Peters and their "London line" moved British educational philosophy from an approach based on a history of educational ideas—that is, the thoughts of great theorists—to the analysis of educational discourse as a means of building "a fundamental educational language."[3]

On the European continent, a group of philosophers had also rejected the attempts of the more traditional and speculative philosophers to create complete philosophical systems. The most famous of these were a group of like-minded philosophers known as the Vienna Circle. A leader of this group was Moritz Schlick (1882–1936), whose approach to analysis is called Logical Empiricism. Schlick sought to apply rigorously the scientific method to philosophical issues. Primarily, he concentrated on philosophers who had defined problems and analyzed their errors of definition and formulation. When problems were defined incorrectly, the solutions that were developed were also incorrect. In his efforts to clarify, Schlick focused on analyzing the concepts and symbols used to express ideas about knowledge.

Ludwig Wittgenstein (1889–1951) was a philosopher who was a link between the Vienna Circle and Moore and Russell, the British philosophers. Wittgenstein was G. E. Moore's successor at Cambridge University. Wittgenstein's *Tractatus Logico-philosophicus* (1922) was a germinal work that stimulated the development of Logical Positivism or Logical Empiricism.[4] Logical Empiricism is based on the language through which scientific propositions are expressed. They are either logical, as in the case of mathematics, or empirical, based on sensory observation and experience. Logical Empiricism examines and analyzes the relationships between mathematical language and empirical propositions.

In his *Tractatus,* Wittgenstein examined the logical structure of language with the aim of clarifying it and establishing meaning. Analytical Philosophers, following Wittgenstein's method of clarification, reject philosophy as a system of metaphysical or axiological doctrines. Regarding philosophy as an activity of clarifying and classifying language, they contend that they are engaged in "doing philosophy."[5]

For Wittgenstein, a language presents a picture theory of reality that we portray in meaningful statements. Such statements are conveyed through our language. The method of philosophy, so conceived, examines the logical structure of language. It could be determined that our sentences were either analytically true or synthetically true. If they were not classifiable into these categories, then they were merely emotive statements affirming personal preferences.

CLASSIFICATION OF PROPOSITIONS

In this section, we examine the classification of language propositions into analytical statements or synthetic statements. The nature of pseudopropositions, to which Philosophical Analysts assign metaphysical propositions, is also examined. From the Analytical perspective, this classification of language can also be applied to the ideologies and theories that are presented in later sections of the book.

An analytical statement is true by virtue of the terms that it contains. The truth of the statement comes from the terms internal to the statement. An example of such a statement is $1 + 1 = 2$; the terms in this statement can be reversed: $2 = 1 + 1$. It is tautological in that it tells nothing beyond what is already implicit in the meaning of the terms.

Synthetic statements are either true or false because they can be verified empirically. The truth of such statements is not *a priori,* or implicit, but is *a posteriori,* discovered afterwards. An example of a synthetic statement is, "John weighs 170 pounds." John can be placed on a scale and the assertion that he weighs a given number of pounds can be tested. A synthetic statement is meaningful only when it can be tested empirically through the means of some empirical data or by observation.

The language analyst's assertion that meaningful statements are either analytical or synthetic eliminates a number of statements that do not meet the requirements of either category. Such statements as "The world is mind" or "God is love" are not analytical tautologies but bear a superficial grammatical resemblance to synthetic statements. The difficulty with these statements is that no evidence could possibly be gathered to determine their truth or falsity. They are not true by definition. Such statements are neither true nor false; they are literally senseless or nonsense because no empirical data can be found to determine their validity. The meaning of a statement is found in its method of verification. If there is no method of verification, it has no meaning.

If the Philosophical Analyst's principle of verification is adopted, then most traditional philosophy is nonsense. Idealism, Realism, Thomism, and Existentialism all rest on what the Analyst would call pseudopropositions. When an Idealist states that "reality is mind," or when a Realist asserts that "nature contains a moral law," or when an Existentialist claims that "existence precedes essence," they are all talking nonsense. They are making claims that cannot be verified by sense or empirical tests. For Analysts, the metaphysical disputes that comprise so much of the history of philosophy are without meaning. Philosophy should not spin castles in the air, nor build worldviews, nor construct metaphysical grand designs. It should deal with the consequences of human language.

The statements found in much of metaphysics, theology, and even the social sciences merely express opinions or personal preferences. When one says that "democracy is the best political system" or that "there are three persons in God" or that "humans are rational," one is merely voicing one's preference that this is the way things should be. Of course, individuals have the freedom to make such statements about politics, religion, and philosophy if they wish to do so. But such statements are not genuinely meaningful for anyone else for they will not have the same meaning for another person. They are emotive statements, personal preferences, or poetical statements rather than factual statements. Although teachers are certainly free to use such language, they should make certain that they do not confuse poetry, preference, or prejudice with fact.

The relevance of Philosophical Analysis as a method of working with language can best be examined by an examination of the conditions of modern life and education that make such an approach a useful one. It should be remembered that Analysts do not wish to create a new philosophical system. They are concerned with eliciting the meaning of our language. The following section of this chapter deals with the impact that a broadly conceived approach to language analysis can have in humankind's search for order and clarity. Such a quest is at base an educational one.

SEARCH FOR ORDER AND CLARITY

Modern people, living in a highly specialized technological society, find themselves beset by problems of understanding and communication. Specialization has resulted in the rise of specialized occupation and professional groups, each of which has developed its own language, vocabulary, and jargon. While they are able to communicate with each other in the language of their specialties, specialists are often unable to communicate with those outside of their areas of expertise. Analytical philosophers see their role as aiding in communication across specialties.

Modern humans also live in an era in which the channels of communication have been multiplied through the refinement and sophistication of various media: the press, radio, television, the Internet, and so on. Indeed, people today are bombarded by a steady flow of information, communication, or just plain noise. Although the proliferation of communication systems has quickened the pace of national and global communication, one can seriously question if people today are any better connected to each other through meaningful communication than they were in the past.

The problems of understanding and communication are not only those of sorting out messages sent out by the various media. They are also problems of deciphering and of separating image from reality. The political, social, and economic life of people in a mass society is highly determined by those who seek to shape opinions and influence decisions. In the United States, candidates for public office have frequently molded their images so that they have an appeal on the television screen. Television commercials that appeal to the emotions rather than to critical intelligence convey their messages through the mouthing of slogans. Political and consumer campaigns become a matter of selling a product rather than conveying the information that would appeal to sensible people. When it is broadly conceived rather than pedantically structured, the task of the

Analytical philosopher can be one of helping to defuse the propaganda and to examine the substance of the many slogans that beset modern society.

Professional education is a discipline that has borrowed heavily from the various social sciences—anthropology, economics, psychology, sociology, political science, and so forth. Likewise, the language used in educational writing is frequently an uncritical blending of the descriptive, or factual, elements and prescriptive ones. Thus, the Analytical philosopher can perform a service by clarifying the language used in teaching and learning situations. He or she can examine educational policy statements and make their meaning clear to educators. Analytical philosophers can do this if they dispel the jargon that frequently besets writing in education and in the other social sciences.

Education is related to broad personal, social, national, and international purposes. In the United States, education has always been in the public domain and subject to public scrutiny. The school is a major societal agency that has social and political consequences. In the United States, educators and educational institutions—from elementary schools to universities—are subjected to social, economic, and political pressures. School administrators and teachers find themselves in situations that are no longer solely pedagogical but that have social, political, and economic implications. Contemporary educators not only have to deal with questions of curriculum and methodology—with alternative approaches to the teaching of reading, mathematics, and social science—but they also must be concerned with issues of community control of schools, racial integration, foreign policy, and kindred other crucial sociopolitical issues. Educational issues frequently become framed in slogans that lend themselves to propagandizing rather than to learning. Among the terms that the popular media have used to portray educational controversies are "quality education," "meaningful education," "relevant and irrelevant education," "confrontation," and so on. Analytical philosophers, who conceive of their function in broad terms, can do much to examine such terminologies so that they can help in understanding educational controversy rather than in confusing it.

Professional educators, too, need to clarify their language so that their own terminology becomes meaningful rather than pedantic jargon. If one surveys educational literature for the past decade, the following phrases can be found in hundreds of articles: "learning by doing," "creative expression," "culturally different," "urban child," "meaningful life experience," "life adjustment," "equality of educational opportunity," "quality education," "education for international understanding," "education for freedom," "effective schools," and other catchy phrases. Again, Analytical philosophers can perform a service by either reducing such phrases to terms that are sensible or exposing them as nonsense.

Further, a great deal of the lecturing and writing about education has been homiletic and has taken the form of preachment in which the speaker or writer seeks to inspire younger teachers. Such discourse, which is often merely the statement of a person's educational preferences, is often presented as a descriptive and factual account of the actual conditions of schooling. Examples of such preachment often take quite different forms. For example, lectures by superintendents and principals on such subjects as "the duty of the teacher," "professionalism and teachers," and "educators and change" are often notorious examples of preachment in the guise of description. Perhaps a more serious source of uncritical language and ideas is the deluge of books that are anecdotal in character and portray the success of a beleagured individual teacher who succeeds in winning the hearts and then the minds of students in a difficult teaching situation, usually an inner-city school attended by disadvantaged youth. The key to success is usually found in the narrator's concern for the students and in his or her use of creative methods. The villains of such pieces are usually members of a pedantic and unsympathetic faculty and a bureaucratic school administration. While such anecdotal accounts may make interesting reading, they, too, need cool and critical examination.

Simply stated, then, Analytical philosophers can serve education by encouraging the critical examination of its language and terminology. They can aid by exploring the verbal interactions that go on in teaching–learning situations. They can help to clarify the goals and policies that direct the course of education.

CONCLUSION

Philosophical Analysis is a method of analyzing language to clarify and establish its meaning. It does not attempt to create new philosophical systems or worldviews that embrace all of humanity's experiences. Through the methodology of empirical verification, Analytical philosophers seek to classify our language statements. They dispassionately seek to disentangle description from prescription. Their service to education has been that of examining the concepts, language, and strategies that deal with the formulation of policies and the elaboration of teaching–learning strategies.

As indicated in this chapter, Philosophical Analysis in its various forms differs from the speculative philosophies that attempt to create comprehensive systems. It finds metaphysical propositions important for their significance to the history of philosophy, but meaningless in terms of clarifying policy. Philosophy's function is to clear up the confusion of our language, to clarify rather than to create propositions.

DISCUSSION QUESTIONS

1. How does Philosophical Analysis differ from Idealism, Realism, and Thomism?

2. Identify the problems that Philosophical Analysts would have with such philosophies as Naturalism, Existentialism, and Pragmatism.

3. Give an example of a statement that is neither analytical nor synthetic.

4. Identify and examine some currently used phrases and attempt to establish their meanings. For example, consider the following: "Have a nice day," "disinformation," "the excellence movement in education," and "effective schooling."

5. Give some examples of specialized terminologies.

6. Explore the ways in which Philosophical Analysis could be applied to classroom instruction.

7. Identify and analyze some examples of educational jargon.

INQUIRY PROJECTS

- Read a chapter in a textbook used in an education or social science course. Identify the analytical or synthetic statements used in the chapter.
- Using the Analytical method, read and analyze a book by an Existentialist philosopher.
- Identify an educational topic such as equality of educational opportunity, effective schools, or excellence in education. Lead a class discussion on that topic and record the discussion. Using an Analytical approach, analyze the discussion in terms of the categories of propositions used and their meaningfulness.
- Collect several statements of philosophy from local school districts. Examine these statements in terms of the Analytical approach.
- Collect several examples from the media (newspapers, radio, or television) of advertising that promotes a product or a political candidate and examine them according to the Analytical method.
- Using the Analytical method, analyze several national reports on education.

FURTHER READINGS

Archambault, Reginald D., ed. *Philosophical Analysis and Education.* New York: Humanities Press, 1965.

Austin, David F., ed. *Philosophical Analysis: A Defense by Example.* Boston: Kluwer Academic Publishers, 1988.

Charlton, William. *The Analytic Ambition: An Introduction to Philosophy.* Cambridge, MA: B. Blackwell, 1991.

Cohen, L. Jonathan. *The Dialogue of Reason: An Analysis of Analytical Philosophy.* New York: Oxford University Press, 1986.

Dummett, Michael A. E. *Origins of Analytical Philosophy.* Cambridge, MA: Harvard University Press, 1994.

Fann, K. T., ed. *Ludwig Wittgenstein: The Man and His Philosophy.* New York: Dell Publishing, 1967.

Harris, Ron, and Roy Harris. *Linguistics and Philosophy: The Controversial Interface.* New York: Pergamon Press, 1993.

Hospers, John. *An Introduction to Philosophical Analysis.* Englewood Cliffs, NJ: Prentice Hall, 1988.

Hylton, Peter. *Russell, Idealism, and the Emergence of Analytic Philosophy.* New York: Oxford University Press, 1990.

Irvine, A. D., and G. A. Wedeking, eds. *Russell and Analytical Philosophy.* Toronto: University of Toronto Press, 1993.

Kaminsky, James S. *A New History of Educational Philosophy.* Westport, CT: Greenwood Press, 1993.

Kneller, George F. *Logic and Language of Education.* New York: John Wiley, 1966.

Malcolm, Norman. *Ludwig Wittgenstein: A Memoir.* London: Oxford University Press, 1958.

Norman, W. J. *Taking Freedom Too Seriously: An Essay on Analytic and Post-Analytic Political Philosophy.* New York: Garland, 1991.

O'Connor, D. J. *An Introduction to the Philosophy of Education.* London: Routledge & Kegan Paul, 1957.

Peters, Richard S. *Education and the Education of Teachers.* London: Routledge & Kegan Paul, 1977.

Peters, Richard S. *Ethics and Education.* London: George Allen & Unwin, 1966.

Russell, Bertrand. *The Autobiography of Bertrand Russell.* Boston: Little, Brown, 1951.

Scheffler, Israel. *Conditions of Knowledge.* Chicago: Scott, Foresman, 1965.

Schilpp, Paul A., ed. *The Philosophy of G. E. Moore.* La Salle, IL: Open Court Publishing, 1968.

Soltis, Jonas F. *An Introduction to the Analysis of Educational Concepts.* Reading, MA: Addison-Wesley, 1968.

Sorenson, Roy A. *Pesudo-Problems: How Analytical Philosophy Gets Done.* New York: Routledge, 1993.

Wang, Hao. *Beyond Analytic Philosophy: Doing Justice to What We Know.* Cambridge, MA: MIT Press, 1986.

Wittgenstein, Ludwig. *Tractatus Logico-Philosophicus.* New York: Humanities Press, 1955.

Wittgenstein, Ludwig. *Philosophical Investigations.* New York: Macmillan, 1953.

ENDNOTES

1. For commentaries on language analysis, see Ron Harris and Roy Harris, eds., *Linguistics and Philosophy: The Controversial Interface* (New York: Pergamon Press, 1993); and Charlton William, *The Analytic Ambition: An Introduction to Philosophy* (Cambridge, MA: B. Blackwell, 1991).

2. For a discussion of the origins of the movement, see Michael A. E. Dummett, *Origins of Analytical Philosophy* (Cambridge, MA: Harvard University Press, 1994). Also see Peter Hylton, *Russell, Idealism, and the Emergence of Analytic Philosophy* (New York: Oxford University Press, 1990).

3. James S. Kaminsky, *A New History of Educational Philosophy* (Westport, CT: Greenwood Press, 1993), p. 172.

4. Ludwig Wittgenstein, *Tractatus Logico-philosophicus* (New York: Humanities Press, 1955).

5. For example, see Roy A. Sorenson, *Pseudo-Problems: How Analytical Philosophy Gets Done* (New York: Routledge, 1993).

▶ 9

Ideology and Education

In Chapter 9, we examine ideology and its impact on education as an introduction for the later chapters in which we discuss particular ideologies, their general significance for policy formulation, and their impact on education. Ever since the eighteenth-century Enlightenment, ideologies have been and remain potent forces for shaping and expressing social, political, economic, and educational ideas. The great series of revolutions—the American Revolution in 1776, the French Revolution in 1789, the Bolshevik Revolution in 1917, and the Chinese Communist Revolution in 1949—were, in large part, manifestations of ideology. Ideology has also had significant consequences for education in both the formal and informal sense. A particular ideology, for example, Liberalism, Conservatism, Socialism, or Fascism, carries with it a model of citizenship—an ideological portrait of the preferred person. In painting this portrait with an ideological brush, the ideologist uses strokes that are historical, sociological, political, and economic. In reproducing or formulating the preferred person, the ideologist relies heavily on education. Informal educational agencies, especially the media—the press, motion pictures, radio, and television—are used, as well as the formal educational agency, namely the school, which recreates the prototype through the milieu (hidden curriculum) and the curriculum, the official and explicit program.

Since the rise of the modern nation-state, ideology has influenced policy making and policy execution in many areas such as economics, science, technology, and education. Educational policies, and the programs and practices that they engender, have a direct impact on schooling.

Although we will propose a stipulated definition (from the author's perspective) later in the chapter, we begin with an initial definition of the term *ideology* to guide our preliminary discussion. Ideology is often defined as the belief system of a group, usually based on a rendition of its past, which carries prescriptions for policy.[1] Group beliefs arise primarily in an historical, social, political, and economic context, however, rather than in a metaphysical system that seeks to transcend such cultural particularities. The ideological interpretation of the past also suggests how this past has created and shaped the individual's and the group's present situation; from this interpretation comes a theory of social change that seeks to predict the course of future social developments. Ideologies are prescriptive in that they recommend policy guidelines for programs to move society in the desired direction.[2]

Although some ideologists have sought to create a worldview that appears to transcend a particular cultural context, their abstractions are generally historically derived and represent the desire to give worldwide validity to a particular interpretation of the past. Indeed, the particular cultural heritage of the group holding the ideology often brings about a significant reshaping of the ideology. For example, the Chinese version of Marxism and the resulting policies reflect the Chinese cultural heritage and environmental conditions (geographical, political, social, and economic).

Action-oriented, rather than merely theoretical, ideology is used to guide political, social, economic, and educational policies. Insofar as institutionalized education, especially schooling, is used as an instrument of achieving these policies, education follows an ideological direction.

Ideology serves to give theoretical legitimacy to a group's outlook, aspirations, program, and action. Rather than appearing to be based on personal or group special interests, ideological justification or legitimacy appeals to a higher and seemingly more generalizable, hence more applicable, authority. Often the appeal to myth or history is used to legitimize policies and actions.

Ideology is also used to justify and determine the power relationships between contending groups. For example, contemporary educational policy in the United States has tended toward inclusiveness rather than exclusiveness; that is, it has worked to make educational opportunities more available to groups, such as African Americans, Native Americans, Hispanics, women, and people with disabilities, who were excluded in the past. In contrast, educational policy in Nazi Germany from 1933 to 1945, based on the official ideology of National Socialism, deliberately excluded groups such as Jews, Social Democrats, and liberal and religious opponents of the Hitler regime.

The impact of ideology on modern education is as profound as that of the traditional foundational disciplines of philosophy, psychology, and sociology. Since the eighteenth-century Enlightenment, individuals and societies have inhabited an ideological world. After the sociopolitical theorists of the Enlightenment and the revolutionaries in the American colonies and in France shattered the absolutist status quo, people first in Western nations and then throughout the world experienced a time during which ideologies originated and then competed for the loyalty of individuals, groups, and nations. With the emergence of nationalism and the rise of modern nation-states, schools were organized to function as constituent parts of national systems of organized education. Further, the rise of social-class consciousness, stimulated by industrialization, also engendered competition between socioeconomic and political groups over the control of nation-states and their governmental and educational systems. As a result, much institutionalized education, or schooling, has been shaped by ideological outlooks and programs.

HISTORICAL ORIGINS AND DEVELOPMENT OF THE CONCEPT OF IDEOLOGY

In this section, we will examine the historical origin of the concept of ideology in the eighteenth-century Enlightenment and the rise of contending ideologies in the nineteenth century. The section concludes with an analysis of Karl Marx's critique of ideology.

The Origins of Ideology in the Enlightenment

In the eighteenth century, the *philosophes* of the French Enlightenment originally used the term "ideology" in an epistemological sense to explain how groups generated and used ideas. In contrast to the traditional intellectual authorities of theology and metaphysics, the *philosophes* hoped to create a science of ideas. For example, the French *philosophe,* Étienne Bonnot de Condillac (1715–1780), denying that ideas were innately present in the mind as asserted by Plato, claimed that sensation was the source of all human ideas. In relationship to the development of ideology, Condillac and other *philosophes* asserted that human ideas did not originate in a metaphysical realm that was prior to human experience but rather resulted from the human being's sensory experience with the environment. As they fashioned a nontheological and nonmetaphysical explanation of the origins of human knowledge, the *philosophes* attempted to develop a social science that imitated the scientific investigation of physical phenomena.

In the case of the Enlightenment ideologues, ideas about society eventually led to action that altered social and political institutional arrangements. If the *ancien regime* of the French Bourbon monarchy rested on scientifically untenable propositions such as the divine right of kings or the theory of absolute monarchy, then the *philosophes* reasoned that these obsolete and erroneous political and social residues should be discarded and replaced by ones that were accurate scientifically. Enlightened persons could use the scientific method to investigate social phenomena in the same way that Isaac Newton and others had investigated physical phenomena. A genuine social science could uncover the natural order of society. Once the natural laws of social, political, and economic life were discovered, they could be used to create a new and scientifically legitimate social and political order. In eighteenth-century America and France, the Enlightenment ideology stimulated two major revolutions that shook the foundations of the Western political order and ushered in republican governments, which, supporters claimed, conformed to natural laws. The theory of natural law applied to government was proposed by the Enlightenment ideologues and had general educational implications. In the past, individuals had been indoctrinated by archaic structures of religious or classical education to accept a static view of society. A new education had to be developed to educate a rising generation of republican citizens who could establish representative institutions and govern themselves by the methods of science and reason.

The Rise of Contending Ideologies in the Nineteenth Century

In the late eighteenth and early nineteenth centuries, those who sought to design the ideal social and political order did not reach a single conclusion for creating the "heavenly city" on earth. Social theorists and practicing politicians devised a variety of alternative models for creating the good society, the ideal *polis*. In England, John Locke's notion of the natural rights of life, liberty, and property for all people became the influential doctrine that guided the politics of the United Kingdom. In the United States, Jefferson used a republican adaptation of Lockean principles as the ideological guide for the new republic. In France, in the years following the revolution that dethroned the Bourbons, a plethora of political plans were proposed by moderate monarchists, republicans, socialists, and communists. Each of these formulations of the "good political order" had its corresponding educational equivalent.

The late eighteenth and early nineteenth centuries experienced not only political revolution but also the economic and social transformation produced by the industrial revolution and then a pervasive technological modernization. The use of mechanical power, the development of the factory system of mass production, and the greater availability of inexpensively manufactured products dramatically transformed economic life in Western Europe and North America. The well-known recital of the growth of large industrial cities, the development of transportation networks, and the urbanization of society has been recounted in many historical works. The industrialization of society had a profound impact on the concept of ideology. The industrial revolution nurtured socioeconomic class antagonisms. In the nineteenth century, the middle class, consisting of factory owners, professionals, merchants, and business people, became the emergent class that challenged the social and political supremacy of the older landed gentry and traditional aristocracy of birth and blood. Those who worked in the factories, mills, and mines—the working class, the future industrial proletariat—would eventually challenge the middle class in the twentieth century.

To the older conceptions of political ideology that arose from political theorizing were added economic class conceptions of ideology. The middle class—

the bourgeois—found a congenial and supportive political ideology in the Liberalism of Locke and other proponents of individualism. To the formation of Lockean individualism was added the laissez-faire theories of Adam Smith, David Ricardo, and Thomas Malthus. A body of social, political, economic, and educational ideas emerged under the aegis of liberal ideology.

In the early nineteenth century, a counterideology emerged to challenge Liberalism. Saint-Simon, Fourier, Owen, Cabet, and others believed that liberal ideology was an erroneous interpretation of socioeconomic realities. Lumped together under the vague term of "Communitarian Socialism," the visionary reformers condemned what they regarded as the dismal theories of classical Liberalism that justified working-class repression and exploitation. Communitarian Socialism argued that the emergent forces of urbanization and technology could be planned and patterned in a rational way to alleviate human misery and suffering.

Whereas classical liberal ideology sought to explain, to justify, and to rationalize middle class supremacy, and whereas Communitarian Socialists challenged these assumptions, the defenders of the old order—the landed gentry, the wealthy establishment, and the traditional aristocracy—developed a counterrevolutionary ideology. This was a conservative ideology, ably stated by Edmund Burke, which sought to preserve an older and more settled way of life.

Marx's Critique of Ideology

By the mid-nineteenth century, the Western nations witnessed a proliferation of ideologies that sought to explain, justify, rationalize, and enlist adherents. Karl Marx, the genius of what would be termed "Scientific Socialism," hurled his theoretical invective against all of these ideologies and denounced them as theoretical smoke screens designed to cloud the vision of the exploited working class. According to Marx, the various ideologies of Liberalism, Conservatism, and even of Communitarian Socialism merely served to preserve the power of the exploiting classes. In Marx's analysis, such ideological formulations produced a false rather than a genuine consciousness in the minds of people, especially in the outlook of the working class proletariat.[3]

According to Marx, all social and political phenomena and institutions arose from the economic base of productive means and modes. Roughly defined as raw materials, techniques, and human and mechanical energy, the means and modes of production were the economic bedrock of society. Throughout history, Marx reasoned, the means and modes of production had been controlled by a specific economic class. For instance, in the Roman Empire, the wealthy estate owner had controlled the agricultural base of society and had exploited the slaves who tilled the soil. During the Middle Ages, the manorial feudal lords had replaced the old Roman magnate as the exploiting class, and the victims of exploitation then were the serfs. At the time of Marx's writing of the *Communist*

Manifesto and *Das Kapital,* the exploiters were the middle class—the bourgeois capitalists—who owned the factories, the mills, the mines, the railroads, and the banks. The victims of exploitation were the workers. Using a dialectical conception of history, Marx predicted that the working class would eventually arise in armed revolution to displace the capitalists and initiate a new classless society.

In Marx's analysis, then, the foundations of reality are material and are lodged in the economic means and modes of production. Convinced of the scientific accuracy of his historical interpretation, Marx attacked the Liberals, Conservatives, and Communitarian Socialists for creating false ideologies. While the Liberals had deliberately distorted history, the visionary Communitarians had created confused theories that Marx labeled "utopian."

Although the Marxist formulation will be examined in greater detail in Chapter 14, a brief examination of what he regarded as false consciousness illustrates Marx's view of ideology. Although middle-class capitalists exploited their workers, they used ideology to rationalize their action and to confound their opponents. Claiming to be the proponents of representative institutions and popular education, Liberals pretended to defend freedom of speech, press, assembly, and religion. For Marx, these Liberal gestures created an ideological smoke screen to camouflage their true designs. According to Marx, those who controlled the economy ruled society's institutions. The bourgeois slogan of "freedom of the press" disguised the capitalist control of information, which defended the special interests of the capitalists and ignored the system's critics. The exercise of freedom of speech, if it challenged the capitalist system, meant the loss of employment. Schools in a capitalist-controlled society did not educate but indoctrinated students to believe that they lived in the best of all possible worlds. According to Marx, the false ideologies had to be demolished so that the proletariat could become conscious of its destined social and political role.

This brief examination of Marx's conception of ideology is useful in explaining how *ideology* came to take on a negative connotation. In terms of historical development, the Marxist conception of history and of the good society became another ideology that competed for people's hearts and minds.

A STIPULATED DEFINITION OF IDEOLOGY

As indicated, the term *ideology* has acquired a variety of meanings and uses since it was coined by the *philosophes* who sought to create a science of ideas. The definition used in this text, stipulated as a working definition of ideology, will be used to refer to the set of related ideas held by a group that explains its past, examines its present, and points to its future. This definition suggests the following elements: (1) an ideology provides an orientation for a group in time and space by interpreting its history; (2) the ideology explains the group's present social, economic, political, and educational circumstances; (3) the examination of the past contributes to a conception of social change; that is, it attempts to predict that what can be expected to happen in the future is likely to follow patterns that occurred in the past; and (4) the ideology is also policy generating in that it presents a blueprint for the future that indicates to the group what policies are needed to attain certain desired ends or goals; in this way, an ideology becomes programmatic or action-oriented. To attain the group's goals, the ideologue recommends political or educational action.

Ideology As an Interpretation of the Past

First of all, an ideology examines a group's past. The group may be the citizens of a nation, such as the German people or the Russian people; or the group may refer to the members of a socioeconomic class such as the working class or the middle class. The group may consist of a professional or an occupational group such as teachers, clergy, or physicians. The ideologue examines the group's past to develop an historical interpretation that orients the group in time and place and gives meaning to group membership. That is, it creates a sense of group identification and solidarity.

The interpretational component, which interprets the past as well as assesses the present situation with the intent of shaping the future, is an important element in an ideology.[4] It influences the shaping of beliefs as well as their application to policy formulation and programmatic action. According to the interpretational component, a correct interpretation of the belief system guides the programmatic implementation.

The ideological interpretation of the past may or may not be historically accurate. The ideologist examines a group's past for a particular interpretation or justification. Such a highly selective search for meaning often leads to a tortured view of history, which frequently confuses myth with history, fiction with fact. Using what historians condemn as "presentism," the ideologist uses the past to create a version of how the group's present came to be. If necessary, past events may be shaped to fit a preconceived thesis that justifies a present or future program. For example, in the Classical Liberal formulation, John Locke referred to the state of nature in which the individual possesses natural rights to life, liberty, and property. Although it is impossible to locate such a state of nature in a definite historical time frame, the mythical state of nature is used as the point of origin and of departure for social, political, and economic doctrines that assert the individual's priority over society.

Another example is that of Marx, who used history to find evidence of one economic class's exploitation of another. Operating from a preconception that asserted that economic factors determined historical events, Marx argued that intellectual, artistic, religious, political, and educational events were secondary to the economic factors that caused them. Through a selective past, Marx explained the existence of two antagonistic economic classes—the bourgeois capitalists and the proletarian workers. By such a highly selective historical interpretation, Marx used the past to orient the proletariat to class consciousness and a sense of meaning and destiny.

Adolph Hitler's National Socialist ideology (Nazism) represents a conception of German history that rested on the mythology of Aryan (German) racial superiority. Stressing the instinctive nature of "blood and soil," Hitler developed the theme of the folkish people. His conception of Germanic racial superiority was used to explain Germany's history and to create a sense of mission in which the German people were to establish a new racial order in Europe.[5]

The Present Situation and Ideological Interpretation

Once the ideologist has used the past to create a sense of group solidarity and identity, then it is possible to assess the group's contemporary social, political, economic, and educational condition. For example, the liberal middle class value orientation that emphasizes individualism, competition, property rights, and representative. government can be explained and justified in terms of the history of the middle class in its struggle with oppressive aristocratic and monarchial governments that interfered with these values.

Another example of the use of the past to explain a present situation can be seen in the conceptions that certain "oppressed people" have developed. For example, the Basques of Spain reckon themselves to be a people who once had a great and noble history. Historic events have caused this once great culture to be submerged by the Hispanic culture that surrounds it. Thus, part of the movement for Basque freedom, or autonomy, derives from their view of the past. The historically or mythically derived idea that a particular racial or ethnic group has been repressed in the past and is now seeking to secure its lost freedom is an important driving force in the contemporary reassertion of ethnonationalism. An important part of the ideology of ethnonationalism is that the sense of a "lost greatness or grandeur" be nurtured and kept alive in the young until the moment comes for liberation from the oppressors.

In many of the former colonial nations of Africa and Asia, a tendency exists to point to a time when theirs was a great nation conquered by European imperialists who suppressed a rich cultural heritage. Ideologies in such nations emphasize a slumbering greatness that needs to be rekindled and used to stimulate a new sense of national awakening and development.

In this linking of the past with the present, educational processes acquire a significant importance. Informal sources of education, such as the mass media, become the means for forging the links between what was and what is and what ought to be. Institutionalized education, in the schools, functions to create a sense of group identification in the minds of the children, the immature members of the group, that connects them to the past. In such a linkage, myths, stories, and heroic portrayals are particularly useful. In India, for example, the story of Gandhi's struggle for Indian independence provides a figure of heroic dimension that in a dramatic way links the young Indian with both his or her past and present. Additionally, the figure of Martin Luther King, Jr., becomes an heroic figure who exemplifies values that are worthy of imitation by the young African American. In a more advanced school situation, at either the upper grades of the elementary school or in secondary education, the selection of both historical and literary works cultivates a means of linking the individual with the past in such a way that the present situation acquires an added significance that is meaningful to group identity.

Social Change and Ideology

Ideologists are rarely content to have their interpretation of the past and assessment of the contemporary situation remain at the level of academic explanation. The conception of the past and the assessment of the present often imply a desire to fashion values and to shape behavior. In other words, ideologies possess elements that are both descriptive and prescriptive. The descriptive phase of an ideology arises from the explanation of the past and the examination of the present. The view of the past, especially when portrayed by heroic models, is used to reinforce the concept of what constitutes proper behavior in the present. Such behavior is also designed to guide future action. Depending on the particular ideology, the prescriptive element may be a set of simple behaviors that characterize the good member of the group. Or it may become an elaborate social, political, and educational code. A particular approved behavior in ideological terms can be illustrated by a brief examination of Classical Liberal attitudes. The child who is being raised in the milieu of Classical Liberalism learns that he or she is an individual who has certain rights and certain responsibilities. For example, he or she learns that it is important and desirable to compete against peers and to win. Competition and winning are defined in personal and individualistic terms. If there are winners, then there are also losers. Winning the spelling bee, the track meet, an essay contest, or the musical competition requires that effort be expended to discipline oneself and to acquire the skills needed to win. It is important to be a winner.

Further, the value of competition is presented as being socially useful as well as personally fulfilling. Competition leads to discovery, invention, and human progress. In fact, the liberal tradition of progress by means of individual effort is a linking device that connects past, present, and future. It becomes a crude linear theory of social change. The progress of humanity depends on individual initiative within a social, political, economic, and educational milieu that emphasizes competition.

The Marxist historical interpretation and assessment of the present offers a very different theory of social change from that of Classical Liberalism. For Marx, the economic class rather than the individual is important. Personal values are determined by one's relationship to the means and modes of production. In a prerevolutionary situation, members of the working class need to identify with their class and to struggle for its liberation. In a postrevolutionary situation, members of the society are to work to realize Communist (Marxist) goals by cooperating for the good of the state. Beyond this, Marx developed a theory of social change based on history's dialectical pattern. Throughout history, Marx argued, economic classes struggled to control the means and modes of production. In the course of historical evolution, the proletariat will come to control both the economic base of society and the political, social, and educational superstructure that has been erected on it. The proletariat's coming victory is historically destined and irreversible, Marx and his followers preached.

Ideology As Policy Generating and Programmatic

Although ideologues may use academic devices, they rarely expend their energies in the pursuit of knowledge because of its intrinsic value. Ideologies, embracing as they do theories of social change, become instruments for achieving a desired social goal or even a new social order. The programmatic element in ideology stems from the prescription that arises regarding the contours of the desired social order.

Ideologies are prescriptive in that they make social, political, economic, and educational assessments or judgments. These assessments, identifying what is good or bad, lead to prescriptive policies. If the assessment is favorable to the status quo, then the ideological policy is conservative in that it seeks to preserve it. If unfavorable, then it seeks to bring about change in ways that may range from the evolutionary to the revolutionary. Indeed, ideologies are action oriented or programmatic. The revolutions of the nineteenth and twentieth centuries were inspired and guided largely by ideologies. For example, both American and French revolutionaries used the doctrine of individual rights to destroy the old monarchical order. Lenin's study of Marxism was not intended to be an academic examination of the philosophy of dialectical materialism. Rather, it was designed to provide the theory needed to bring about the revolution that eventually toppled the Tsarist regime in Russia.

The Ideological Continuum and Educational Policy

To illustrate the functioning of ideology and its impact on education, we can use the concept of the ideological continuum. Ideology operates as a continuum that encompasses the following: (1) the origins of the belief system usually based on a view of the past that may be mythic or historical or a combination of both; (2) an instrumental interpretation of the past that is intended to make certain aspects of it operational in the present; this attempt to operationalize an ideology results in policy formulation—the design of a plan to bring about some action in the present that will shape the future; and (3) action, based on the policy guidelines, that will bring about the desired results.

The ideological continuum suggested here contains both descriptive and prescriptive elements. For example, we might consider the formulation of educational policy in the United States to illustrate the functioning of the ideological continuum.

A Nation at Risk, Action for Excellence, and many of the national reports on education were based on an interpretation of the U.S. educational present.[6] This perspective expressed beliefs such as the following: (1) the U.S. preeminence as a leading technological, economic, and military power had been established, at least in part, by the nation's educational system; (2) other nations, especially Japan and Germany, were threatening to overtake the United States and surpass it as a preeminent technological and economic power; and (3) the U.S. educational system, especially the public schools, was in a state of crisis because of poorly defined goals; a soft, nonacademic curriculum; declining scholastic standards; permissiveness; inadequately prepared teachers; and myriad other causes of educational malaise. Although some educators, including philosophers and historians of education, questioned the accuracy of the analysis, it nevertheless was accepted as accurate by large segments of the public and by policymakers in both the national administration and Congress, and by state governors, legislators, and many local school boards.[7]

The interpretation that came from the analysis of the condition of U.S. education led to a generalized policy that stated: U.S. education was in a state of crisis that could be resolved by strengthening the academic components of schooling, especially mathematics and science, and by restoring discipline to the schools. Various states and local boards developed a wide range of specific policies to resolve the crisis. Among them were the following proposals: increase the length of the school day and school year; require competency examinations to guarantee that students master basic skills; establish teacher competency examinations to ensure that teachers possess adequate skills and knowledge; reduce expenditures for nonacademic and vocational components of schooling.

The policy proposals were designated as educational reforms by their proponents, who anticipated improvement in mathematics and science teaching and competencies in particular, and higher standards of achievement in other academic subjects. Some proponents of "reform" believed that the restoration of discipline would lead to a decrease in juvenile delinquency, drug abuse, and an affirmation of political and moral values. Ultimately, the proponents of reform believed that schooling, conceived of as the rigorous study of academic subjects, would substantially aid the efforts of the United States to regain its economic and military preeminence as a world power.

Our purpose in using the example of the national reports is not to debate the accuracy of their analyses, describe the policies, or assess the results. Rather, it is to illustrate how ideology leads to policies, which, in turn, leads to programs.[8]

THE USE OF IDEOLOGY
TO CREATE CONSENSUS

Ideology, which gives identity to a group, is used to create a sense of shared ideas, goals, and commitments. It functions to form group identity and to sustain group cohesion by generating a "we-feeling" or sense of group solidarity.[9] Assumptions about the world and the society that are embraced by the particular ideology are publicly expressed and used to develop togetherness, solidarity, and agreement among group members.

As a molder of consensus, ideology functions in the society as a whole and also in its informal and formal educational agencies. Informal educational agencies, especially the media, express and reinforce ideological commitments. Formal agencies, such as schools, likewise build a sense of group identification, or a "we-feeling" in the young through the school milieu—the hidden curriculum—and through certain components of the formal or explicit curriculum, such as literature and history. All school systems work to cultivate a sense of national identity and loyalty in the young; they also function to cultivate a sense of social consensus, an adherence to the group's dominant values.

Ideology and Outlook

As part of the process of forming social consensus, ideology also serves to shape a person's outlook on self and society. The use of *outlook* is deliberately imprecise. It refers to the way in which we intellectually organize or "put together" our ideas about social, political, economic, and educational concepts, events, and trends. It creates a view of the world in which we live and seeks to answer the following questions: Who am I? What are my origins? What is the role of society and my place in the social order? What are the requirements and responsibilities of citizenship? How should I function in the economic system? *Outlook,* broadly defined, is shaped by formal and informal educational agencies. A major part of the schooling process is devoted to shaping a person's social, political, and economic perspective and to developing skills and knowledge for functioning in the society, in the economy, and in the political process.

Shaped by ideology, a person's outlook not only affects external relationships to social, political, economic, and educational systems, but it also shapes a person's interior sense of being or self-identity and esteem. How one ultimately relates to these systems determines a person's attitude about his or her identity, role, function, aspirations, and destiny. Ideology, through both the hidden curriculum of the educational milieu and the formal curricular components of schooling, serves to organize the various role personalities and role functions of persons both in school and in future social, political, and economic (employment) situations.

The Functional Flexibility of Ideology

In building consensus and commitment, ideologies vary in their functional flexibility.[10] The efficacy of an ideology in building consensus ranges between those ideologies that encourage or tolerate pluralism and those that are monolithic. Throughout its history, there has been continuous debate in the United States about how new immigrant groups were to function in U.S. society. Antagonists in the debate were divided between those who argued for Americanization of immigrants and those who argued for cultural pluralism.

According to the ideological orientation of the "Americanists," the American past was largely the history of the contributions and achievements of white, English Protestants. The development of institutions of representative government, judicial practices based on the common law, and the nation's rise to an industrial world power were interpreted as achievements of the dominant English-speaking Protestants of the older stock of Americans. The study of history and social studies reinforced the ethos of the dominant group by portraying historic heroic models from the dominant group.

Anticipated results of the Americanization policy were to enculturate immigrants—the great majority of whom were neither English nor Protestant after 1880—into a monolithic national character. For Americanists, this policy would preserve the national character and institutions.

Educational policy conceived according to such a monolithic ideological interpretation shaped both the school's milieu—the hidden curriculum—and the formal or explicit curriculum. The school's milieu—namely the rules, regulations, etiquette, and student–teacher relationships—emphasized the values associated with the Protestant ethic: punctuality, orderliness, frugality, industriousness, and respect for private property. These values were also congenial to training a disciplined work force for an emerging industrial society.

The educational policy of the Americanization ideology used certain components of the formal curriculum to create a monolithic society. The language of instruction, reading, and literature was English. Non-English-speaking children were to learn English and abandon their own languages in order to become like the dominant group.

In contrast to a monolithic conception of the American character, those who subscribed to the ideology of cultural pluralism saw the American past in a broader and more varied perspective. Many groups and peoples contributed to the still emerging and evolving American character—Native Americans, African Americans, Hispanics, Asians, and Europeans from both southern and eastern Europe as well as the British Isles and northern Europe. Such a culturally pluralistic interpretation of the American past was multilingual, multisocial, and multiethnic. The consensus-generating power of cultural pluralism, though less specific than the Americanist version, possessed a vitality that had the capacity to unite various groups into a larger American identity that respected and did not jeopardize other group identifications. In other words, the core beliefs of cultural pluralism could be shared without eradicating distinctive characteristics of ethnic or language groups. For example, a policy designed to encourage bilingual education rests on the assumption that the use of English as well as another language enhances a student's development in both the linguistic-ethnic subgroup and the larger society.

Just as a monolithic ideology has implications for the school milieu and the curriculum, so does a cultural pluralistic ideology. In terms of the school milieu, language, ethnic, and racial differences would be valued. The school's value orientation would emphasize multicultural understanding. The formal curricular components, especially literature, history, and civic education, would include the contributions of various ethnic and racial groups to the common heritage. It should be noted, however, that the dominant contemporary U.S. public school ideology, while culturally pluralistic, continues to emphasize commonalities related to government, law, and property. The delicate balance in a culturally pluralistic ideology and society is that of maintaining a commonly shared framework of experience and belief in which cultural differences can exist and flourish.

IDEOLOGY, EDUCATION, AND SCHOOLING

Ideology, particularly that of the dominant group, or the official ideology, has a direct impact on education, especially on schooling, in the following areas:

1. It works to shape educational policies, expectations, outcomes, and goals.
2. Through the school milieu or environment, it conveys and reinforces attitudes and values.
3. It emphasizes selected and approved skills and knowledge through the curriculum, which is the formal and explicit program of the school.

Educational Policies, Expectations, Outcomes, and Goals

In any given society, a range of ideologies is likely to exist. If we use the United States as an example, we can identify a variety of ideological perspectives. The two major U.S. political parties—the Democrats and Republicans—operate from ideological bases that include views of the past with their own heroes. Traditionally, these heroes have been Abraham Lincoln for the Republicans and Thomas Jefferson and Andrew Jackson for the Democrats. Every four years, the national convention of each political party approves a platform that identifies its policies. Like the national political parties, other groups—the American Federation of Teachers, the National Education Association, the American Medical Association, the National Farmers Union, the National Association of Manufacturers, and countless others, for example—present an array of ideological shadings. Despite this spectrum of ideologies, the dominant ideology in the United States appears to be based on middle-class conceptions of knowledge, values, and standards of behavior that influence educational policies, attitudes toward schooling, and measures of educational success. This ideology, really the ideology of the dominant class or group, influences education, schools, and the curriculum.

Values Conveyed by the School Milieu

The school milieu or environment—the atmosphere in which teaching and learning take place—helps to shape student social and intellectual attitudes and values. In terming the school milieu the "hidden curriculum," Michael Apple refers to the inculcation of "norms, values, and dispositions" that occurs as students experience the school's institutional expectations, incentives, routines, rewards, and punishments.[11] The milieu reflects ideological factors arising both in and out of the school. Power, prestige, and status, as determined by the dominant or official ideology's criterion of success, shape not only educational goals but also teacher and student behavior.

Ideology and Curriculum

In terms of the formal curriculum, ideology seeks to answer the question, What knowledge is of most worth? Most worth to whom? To national policies and priorities? To personal goals and expectations? For participation in the society and the group? For preferred social and economic positions? Does the policy emphasize the mathematical and scientific knowledge needed for technological development? Or does the curriculum reflect the literary and artistic styles and tastes of a leadership elite? As these questions are answered, often in terms of an ideological perspective, the curriculum takes shape.

IDEOLOGY AND PHILOSOPHY

Although it may appear difficult to distinguish between philosophy and ideology, we will attempt to do so. The traditional philosophies discussed earlier, namely Idealism, Realism, and Thomism, were based on a metaphysical view of reality. These philosophies, which explained reality in terms of universal being or essence, are therefore abstract in the sense that they answered the question What is real? in general, abstract, and universal terms. In contrast, ideologies are contextual and concrete. By contextual we mean that they are heavily related to time, their historical point of origin, and to place, a geographical, economic, political, sociological situation. While most philosophies, especially the traditional systematic ones, seek to transcend time and place, ideologies are essentially contextual. For example, Liberalism, which arose in the late eighteenth and early nineteenth centuries, found political expression in the American Revolution of 1776 and in the French Revolution of 1789. As an expression of middle-class aspirations, it flourished as an ideology in North America and Western Europe.

Operating at a high level of generality, philosophies are explanatory; they seek to explain what is real, how we think, and how we value. In terms of valuing, in the area of ethics and aesthetics, philosophies are also prescriptive. All philosophies, in attempting to explain the most general human concerns, seek to establish meaning. For example, the Experimentalist's analysis of the interaction of a human organism with the environment seeks to explain and make meaningful to us the nature of experience. The Existentialist is more concerned with the private and subjective meaning that we give to ourselves by choosing to act in the most significant situations that we encounter. Philosophical Analysts seek to establish meaning in our language.

Ideologies, while also a quest for meaning, look more to economics, politics, and society for meaning. Meaning in these contexts comes from an interpretation of the past, which is either historical or mythological, or a combination of the two, and from an interpretation of policies and programs. In contrast to the speculative detachment or analytical reflection of philosophy, ideology is oriented to action. It is often a rationale for explaining action.

In contrast to philosophy's speculative or analytical quest for meaning, ideology functions to create loyalty to the vision of the group's past and sense of historic destiny and to mobilize resources to achieve desired programmatic goals. In creating loyalty and commitment, ideologists use a variety of persuasive techniques that range from the rational to the emotional. Ideologies also possess a rhetorical or journalistic element, a persuasive means for fostering commitment and bringing about mobilization, that is generally absent from philosophy.

Although there are contrasts between philosophy and ideology, there are also comparisons. Some ideologies make use of certain philosophical concepts and seek to use these in formulating policy and action.[12]

CONCLUSION

Ideology, as the belief system of a group, is a potent force in shaping social consciousness, attitudes, and values. Although operative within the total society, ideology has a particular impact on education and schooling. It functions in informal educational agencies to shape social outlooks and expectations. In schools, ideological factors shape the school milieu and the "hidden curriculum" as well as the formal curriculum. Although similarities exist between philosophies and ideologies, the latter are distinguished by their contextual and action-oriented nature. In the chapters that follow, we will explore the basic ideological foundations of education by examining the relationships of such classic ideologies as

Nationalism, Liberalism, Conservatism, Communitarian Socialism, Marxism, and Totalitarianism to educational policies and schooling.

DISCUSSION QUESTIONS

1. Examine the relationship between ideology and policy formulation and execution.

2. Analyze the functions of an ideology.

3. Analyze the origins and development of the concept of ideology.

4. Analyze how the interpretation of the past functions in an ideology.

5. Using the concept of the ideological continuum, analyze a contemporary educational policy.

6. Analyze the role of ideology in shaping group identity and consensus.

7. Compare and contrast the efficacy of Americanization and cultural pluralism in generating consensus.

8. How does the school milieu shape social, economic, and political outlooks?

9. Analyze and identify examples of the "hidden curriculum."

10. How does the explicit, or formal, curriculum reflect ideological perspectives?

INQUIRY PROJECTS

- Examine books used in courses in political science, sociology, and education. In a paper, isolate and analyze the definitions of ideology that appear in these disciplines.
- Read a history of the American, French, or Russian revolution. In a paper, assess the role of ideology in this revolutionary movement.
- Examine your own education. How has an interpretation of the past—either historical or mythical—shaped your outlook? Analyze your insights in an autobiographical paper.
- Identify an heroic model whose life is used as an example for children. Read a biography of that person that is appropriate to elementary or secondary school students. Analyze in a paper how the model may be used to support an ideological frame of reference.
- Read an historical or contemporary statement of educational policy, such as *A Nation at Risk* or *Action for Excellence*. In a paper, describe any ideological overtones you may detect.
- Visit a school and identify the means used to create a sense of group identity. Write a paper that describes your findings.
- In an autobiographical self-analysis, write a paper that examines how schooling contributed to your political, social, and economic outlook.
- Visit an elementary or secondary school classroom. Identify elements that relate to the "hidden curriculum." Describe your impressions in a paper.

FURTHER READINGS

Apple, Michael W. *Ideology and Curriculum.* London: Routledge & Kegan Paul, 1979.

Bailey, Leon. *Critical Theory and the Sociology of Knowledge: A Comparative Study in the Theory of Ideology.* New York: Peter Lang, 1994.

Balaban, Oded. *Politics and Ideology: A Philosophical Approach.* London: Avebury, 1995.

Ballinger, Stanley E. *The Nature and Function of Educational Policy.* Bloomington, IN: Center for the Study of Educational Policy, Department of History and Philosophy of Education, Indiana University, 1965.

Ball, Terence, and Richard Dagger. *Political Ideologies and the Democratic Ideal.* New York: HarperCollins College Publishers, 1995.

Berliner, David C., and Bruce J. Biddle. *The Manufactured Crisis: Myths, Fraud, and the Attack on America's Public Schools.* Reading, MA: Addison-Wesley, 1995.

Bernier, Normand R., and Jack Williams. *Beyond Beliefs: Ideological Foundations of American Education.* Englewood Cliffs, NJ: Prentice Hall, 1973.

Boudon, Raymond. *The Analysis of Ideology.* Translated by Malcolm Slater. Chicago: University of Chicago Press, 1989.

Bowen, Robert. *Universal Ice: Science and Ideology in the Nazi State.* London: Belhaven Press, 1993.

Eagleton, Terry. *Ideology: An Introduction.* London: Verso, 1991.

Edel, Abraham. *Interpreting Education: Science, Ideology and Value.* New Brunswick, NJ: Transaction Books, 1985.

Ellsworth, Elizabeth A., and Marianne H. Whatley, eds. *The Ideology of Images in Educational Media: Hidden Curriculums in the Classroom.* New York: Teachers College Press, Columbia University, 1990.

Funderburk, Charles. *Political Ideologies: Left, Center, Right.* New York: HarperCollins College Publishers, 1994.

Guillaumin, Colette. *Racism, Sexism, Power, and Ideology.* London and New York: Routledge, 1995.

Hagopian, Mark N. *Regimes, Movements, and Ideologies: A Comparative Introduction to Political Science.* New York: Longman, 1978.

Hoover, Kenneth R. *Ideology and Political Life.* Belmont, CA: Wadsworth, 1994.

Ladd, Everett Carl. *The American Ideology: An Exploration of the Origins, Meaning, and Role of American Political Ideas.* Storrs, CT: Roper Center for Public Opinion Research, 1994.

Larrain, Jorge. *Ideology and Cultural Identity: Modernity and the Third World Presence.* Cambridge, MA: Polity Press, 1994.

Lichtheim, George. *The Concept of Ideology and Other Essays.* New York: Vintage Books, 1967.

Mannheim, Karl. *Ideology and Utopia.* New York: Harcourt, Brace, 1936.

Paris, David C. *Ideology and Educational Reform: Themes and Theories in Public Education.* Boulder, CO: Westview Press, 1995.

Pratte, Richard. *Ideology and Education.* New York: David McKay, 1977.

O'Toole, James. *Leading Change: Overcoming the Ideology of Comfort and the Tyranny of Custom.* San Francisco: Jossey-Bass, 1995.

Rothstein, Stanley W. *Identity and Ideology: Sociocultural Theories of Schooling.* New York: Greenwood Press, 1991.

Susser, Bernard. *Political Ideology in the Modern World.* Boston: Allyn and Bacon, 1995.

Torrance, John. *Karl Marx's Theory of Ideas.* Cambridge and New York: Cambridge University Press, 1995.

Ward, Irene. *Literacy, Ideology, and Dialogue: Toward a Dialogic Pedagogy.* Albany: State University of New York Press, 1994.

Zizek, Slavoj. *Mapping Ideology.* London: Verso, 1994.

Watt, John. *Ideology, Objectivity, and Education.* New York: Teachers College Press, Columbia University, 1994.

ENDNOTES

1. The pioneering sociological analysis of ideology can be found in Karl Mannheim, *Ideology and Utopia* (New York: Harcourt, Brace, 1936). For an analysis of the concept of ideology in relationship to education, see Richard Pratte, *Ideology and Education* (New York: David McKay, 1977), pp. 15–67.

2. For definitions of ideology, see Chaim I. Waxman, ed., *The End of Ideology Debate* (New York: Simon & Schuster, 1969), pp. 186, 283, 320.

3. For a commentary on Marx and ideology, see John Torrance, *Karl Marx's Theory of Ideas* (New York: Cambridge University Press, 1995).

4. For an analysis of the "interpretational component," see Stanley E. Ballinger, *The Nature and Function of Educational Policy* (Bloomington, IN: Center for the Study of Educational Policy, Department of History and Philosophy of Education, Indiana University, 1965); Richard Pratte, "Structural Analysis of Ideology," in *Ideology and Education* (New York: David McKay, 1977), pp. 49–51.

5. For ideology in the Nazi state, see Robert Bowen, *Universal Ice: Science and Ideology in the Nazi State* (London: Belhaven Press, 1993).

6. Among the national reports recommending educational reform are: National Commission on Excellence in Education, *A Nation at Risk: The Imperative for Educational Reform* (Washington, DC: Government Printing Office, 1983); and Task Force on Education for Economic Growth, *Action for Excellence* (Denver, CO: Education Commission of the States, 1983).

7. Gerald L. Gutek, *Education in the United States: An Historical Perspective* (Englewood Cliffs, NJ: Prentice Hall, 1986), pp. 334–350.

8. An important book that critiques the authenticity of the evidence of the educational situation is David C. Berliner and Bruce J. Biddle, *The Manufactured Crisis: Myths, Fraud, and the Attack on America's Public Schools* (Reading, MA: Addison-Wesley, 1995).

9. Normand R. Bernier and Jack E. Williams, *Beyond Beliefs: Ideological Foundations of American Education* (Englewood Cliffs, NJ: Prentice Hall, 1973), p. 25.

10. Ibid., p. 38.

11. Michael W. Apple, *Ideology and Curriculum* (London: Routledge & Kegan Paul, 1979), p. 14.

12. Mark N. Hagopian, *Regimes, Movements, and Ideologies: A Comparative Introduction to Political Science* (New York: Longman, 1978), p. 392.

▶ 10

Nationalism, Ethnonationalism, and Education

In this chapter, we examine the phenomenon of nationalism, devotion to one's nation and its interests, and the recent revival of ethnonationalism, the identification of one's ethnic group as the primary source of identity, and focus of loyalty and commitment. Both of these ideologies, nationalism and ethnonationalism, though related, have somewhat different educational implications. Nationalism, centered on nation-states historically, has worked to shape larger national loyalties in people than ethnonationalism, which is focused on one's particular racial or ethnic group.[1] Nationalism, as an historical force, has sought to move people from very local and provincial kinds of identification to the larger identification with the nation-state. Ethnonationalism, which focuses personal identity and loyalty on the ethnic or racial group, may break down larger commitments and replace them with a more local identification. The joining of ethnicity with nationalism in the concept of ethnonationalism often means that ethnic groups desire their own separate nation-states.[2] As we reach the end of the twentieth century, the phenomenal revival of ethnonationalism appears to be setting in motion trends that will have profound educational implications. In Chapter 10, we examine some of these implications.

In later chapters, we will examine ideologies such as Liberalism, Conservatism, Utopianism, Marxism, and Totalitarianism. The inclusion of nationalism and ethnonationalism makes our study of ideology more complex in that these forces can penetrate the other ideologies and reconceptualize them in ethnic, racial, and even linguistic terms. For example, historically, Conservatives and Liberals and even Marxists, who claim that economically based classes are the primary forces in history, have embraced nationalism. The Totalitarians, such as Hitler and Mussolini, have made extreme nationalism the cornerstone of their ideologies.

While we can analyze nationalism and ethnonationalism rationally, they rest on highly mythic and emotional bases. Most national and ethnic groups have very powerful myths regarding their origins. These myths, often having some remote historical base, give the members of the national or ethnic group a sense of unique identity. Both informally as an oral and written tradition and in schools, national and ethnic groups have used education to transmit the sense of identity. Educational issues become even more complicated in that some ethnic groups may dominate a given society and subordinate others. Often, the class-based analysis provided by Social Reconstructionists and Critical Theorists is inadequate to explain the phenomenon of racial and ethnic political and educational struggles.

A PRELIMINARY DISCUSSION

Historically, the term *nationalism* has been broadly used to mean an identification with and a loyalty to one's nation-state or country, as in being loyal to Germany, France, China, or the United States. The conventional definition of a nation-state is a polity that is recognized as independent and sovereign, that is, it has its own government, makes its own laws, and controls its own territory. Education, in the informal sense, and schooling, as organized institutionalized learning, have been used to promote deliberate identification with nation-states. Public or government-sponsored school systems have been identified with nation-states. It is possible to talk about the German, Russian, Chinese, and French school systems, for example. The role of schooling in nation-state contexts is to transform the nationally neutral child into a German, a Russian, or a Chinese. Schools, in national contexts, accomplish this transformation through the curriculum, especially through the national language, literature, and history.[3] They do it informally by building identification in the young with national heroic figures, commemorative days, anthems, and symbols such as the national flag.

Although the United States constitutionally has fifty state systems of education rather than a unified national system, these state and local schools make for national homogeneity or Americanization. For example, the use of the English language, the selection of a particular version of American history and literature, and the cultivation of democratic processes of citizenship all contribute to forming the American character type. Equally, and perhaps even more powerful in the national character formation process, are the informal educational agencies—the family, media, and community—that likewise contribute to instill a national character.

Not new, the identification of schools with nation-states occurred in Western countries throughout the late eighteenth and nineteenth centuries. For example, the American common school, the public school's mid-nineteenth century prototype, had as one of its goals the Americanization, or the forming of American character, of its students. The process of assimilation of immigrants through the imposition of the English language, a selected history and literature, and standards of behavior was the public school's contribution to forming and imposing a particular version of American cultural identity. The current debates over multiculturalism show tensions between those who want to maintain a particular version of American character that has been traditionally defined and those who want to either enlarge or totally revise that version.[4] The same phenomenon of creating national identity through schooling was also occurring in other countries, such as Germany, France, and Italy. However, in nation-states that were more racially, ethnically, or linguistically homogeneous, such as Denmark, Japan, and Germany, in contrast to multicultural societies such as the United States, the process of closely identifying nation-states and schooling proceeded more definitely and efficiently.

For everyone who has attended a public school, it is easy to recall how the school curriculum built a sense of national identity through songs and stories, literature and history, and especially through language. The same was true of people around the world who attended schools in their own nation-states. National flags symbolized the nation. Certain heroic figures emerged as models from the nation's past: Washington, Jefferson, and Lincoln in the United States, and Gandhi and Nehru in India, for example. The very books used to teach reading carried national values and preferred ways of behaving. The idea of citizenship was reinforced not only by the formal curriculum but also by the way in which school organizations and clubs conducted their affairs.

While schools have been used to build nationalism in the young by identifying them with the nation's heroes, history, language, and literatures, the degree to which nationalism should impact schooling has been much debated. A lyric from an Irish patriotic song goes, "The love of one's country is a terrible thing." While constructive patriotism has been much lauded by educators, destructive chauvinism has been much condemned. The pedagogical question that nationalism raises for educators is where to find the balance between a force that can be constructive or destructive.

The history of the nineteenth and twentieth centuries can be viewed as the history of wars: the Napoleonic Wars from 1800 to 1815, the Crimean War of the 1850s, the Franco-Prussian War of 1870, World War I from 1914 to 1918, and World War II from 1939 to 1945. The history of the modern world also tells the tragic story of genocide: the Turkish atrocities against Armenians and the massive extermination of Jews by Hitler's Nazi regime. Reports of genocide in the contemporary world include tribal atrocities in Rwanda and Burundi in Africa and "ethnic cleansing" in the former Yugoslavia in the conflict between Serbs, Croats, and Slavic Muslims. War and atrocities have often been stimulated by nationalistic excesses—when one racial or ethnic group regards itself as superior to others and even puts them into a subhuman caste.

A crucial challenge for education is that of developing a properly balanced sense of national identity that unites the person with the nation as a political and cultural community but does not exaggerate national identity in such an exclusive way that it creates the irrational sense of superiority that has had such tragic consequences for humanity.

The Origins of Nationalism in Educational Theory

The classic studies of the impact of nationalism on education were by Isaac Kandel and Edward Reisner. Their studies focused on nationalism's development within the political context of particular nation-states such as France, Germany, Italy, and Russia. They examined nationalism as a force in creating identity with the nation-state and its use in mobilizing the populace of these nation-states for politically based agendas such as imperialism and modernization. Nationalism was generally identified with modernization and treated as a force that eroded residues of feudalism, localism, and provincialism. In these studies (1) nationalism was examined as a mobilizing force for creating national identities; (2) modern state school systems were seen as agencies for deliberately instilling a sense of national identity and building a nationally based consensus; (3) the modern curriculum, dating from the early nineteenth century, also was seen as a medium for instilling national sentiments, loyalties, and values through language, national history and literature, and civic studies.

In educational literature, a serious theoretical ambiguity developed around the issue of the nature and impact of nationalism on education and schooling. It was seen as a necessary element in the modern nation-state and in organized education, or schooling, for the nation-state. However, too much nationalism, especially when it became chauvinistic, was condemned as dangerous to world peace and security. The pioneering studies, while seminal in developing the importance of nationalism and national identity, tended to take the large picture or global approach and did not assess the related subject of ethnonationalism, especially in the multiethnic or multinational nation-states. The current debates over multiculturalism in the United States, Germany, the United Kingdom, and other countries reflect the problem of relating cultural, racial, or ethnic diversity to a larger and more encompassing sense of national identification. The early studies were highly useful, however, in establishing the definitions of nationalism, its power in mobilizing nation-state energies, and in identifying the nonrational elements lodged in the concept. While nationalism has been portrayed as a force for creating national identities, its full complexity and power was not adequately analyzed in a way useful in interpreting the rise of contemporary ethnonationalism.

In the works of the scholars on nationalism in education, particularly the comparativist, Isaac Kandel, and the historian, Reisner, nationalism was a major theme in illustrating how organized education, or schools, were agencies in creating national identity, fostering a national curriculum, and building national character. Although at birth infants are not culturally French, English, or Russian, schooling helps to make them such.

Nation-States, Nationalism, and Schools

The modern nation-state can be defined as an independent and sovereign polity that is the central focus of its citizens' cultural, social, political, and economic life. Nation-states range in size from such large countries as the United States, the People's Republic of China, and the Russian Federal Republic, to much smaller but still equally sovereign nation-states such as Singapore, Costa Rica, and Nepal.

Historically, modern nation-states developed in the eighteenth century in Europe, North America, and South America. Of interest to educators is the fact that state or public schools arose, often as national education systems, in the nineteenth century. This development saw a convergence between the nation-state and its school systems, especially as they educated the young to become citizens with a dedication and loyalty to the nation-state. An important task of the school curriculum, especially in the areas of language, literature, and history, has been to build identification in the young with the nation-state. By creating a national identity, these particular subjects contribute to a sense of nationalism.

Nationalism, Nation Building, Modernization, and Education

After World War II, the newly independent former colonial nations of Africa and Asia emphasized education as a means of nation building. The concept of nation building was allied with modernization theory, which saw education, particularly schooling and training, as agencies for transforming traditional societies, often former colonial and now newly independent nations, into modern nation-states. To create the necessary infrastructures for modernity, organized education, or schooling, was used to foster national loyalties, commitments, and identities that focused on the nation rather than on particular local or regional areas.

Educators promoting nation building and modernization seemed to believe that nation building, while advancing modernization by reducing localism and tribalism, would not necessarily rekindle peace-threatening nationalist antagonisms. Rather, they argued that nation building would lead to a constructive nationalism conducive to modernization but not threatening to international stability. This constructive nationalism would be unlike the chauvinistic nationalism that developed in Nazi Germany, Fascist Italy, and Imperial Japan in the 1930s, which led to World War II. According to Walker Connor, "Scholars associated with...'nation building'...tended to ignore the question of ethnic diversity," or to treat it superficially as a "minor impediment to effective state-integration."[5]

A leading theorist who developed key concepts linking modernization and nation building was Karl Deutsch, author of *Nationalism and Social Communi-*

cation.[6] According to Deutsch, as modernization transformed traditional societies, especially those of the newly independent nations, the development of industrial, urban, communication, transportation, and educational infrastructures would lead to greater assimilation in the nation-state. Using a functionalist argument, Deutsch reasoned that modernization would reduce ethnonationalism, which would be replaced by self-interest rather than ethnic group loyalties. Political and economic processes, supported by an educational infrastructure, would move societies from being collections of tribes and separatist ethnic and language groups to being politically and economically assimilated nation-states with common languages, cultures, and institutions.

Leading U.S. international educators enthusiastically affirmed that organized education could effectively promote modernization through nation building.[7] Indeed, nation building was often identified as one of the "most pressing" challenges of the less technologically developed nations. Further, national integration meant that, psychologically, citizenship education would include "identification with the nation-state and with national symbols."[8]

The concept of nation building obscured the reality of ethnonationalism which was submerged by the overarching monolithic ideology of Communism in the former Soviet Union and eastern Europe, and by tribalism in Sub-Saharan Africa. Many educators underestimated the force of ethnonationalism in the newly independent nations of Asia and Africa, where it took the form of tribalism and communalism. These educators overestimated the impact of economic development in arresting and limiting the ethnonationalist impulse. Indeed, infrastructure developments in transportation, communication, and schooling may make ethnic groups more aware rather than less aware of cultural differences. It appears that a high degree of technological, economic, and educational integration does not guarantee that ethnonationalism will not surface in a particular nation-state.

THE REVIVAL OF ETHNONATIONALISM

Ethnonationalism, an old but revived ideology, refers to a belief that an individual is a member of a unique group because of descent from a common ancestor and a blood relationship shared with others descended from this common ancestor, as is the case of Serbs, Croats, Québecois, Ibos, and Basques, for example.[9] Those sharing a perceived common ancestry may address each other as brothers or sisters. The belief in common ancestry does not depend on biological or DNA verification but is mythic and highly psychological, emotional, or nonrational. Myth, as used here, means a highly powerful form of meaning that may be partially historical or pseudohistorical but nonetheless is the reference point for belief in a common ancestral identity. The various ethnonational myths often have their own creation stories and narratives about the particular group's origins and heritage. The passing of ethnonational myth, history, and traditions between the generations is an informal but highly powerful means of education. Although the nonrational belief system supporting ethnonationalism is emotional and subconscious, it nonetheless creates a self-view of membership in the particular ethnic group. For ethnonationalist identity, what is paramount is not the scientifically correct description of the group, but what the group believes it was and is as it answers the questions, Who am I and who are we? What was our origin and what is our destiny?

Although ethnonationalism often has been a force in arousing ideological identification, loyalty, and commitments, it has had a pronounced revival as the twentieth century draws to a close. Since the end of the Cold War and the political disintegration of the Soviet Union and its satellite Communist regimes in eastern Europe, the power of broad architectonic ideologies such as Marxist Communism to shape political and educational structures and goals has eroded and virtually disappeared. In the former Soviet Union, eastern Europe, and other nations as well, ethnonationalism has resurfaced as a politico-cultural force that has powerful educational implications. For example, in 1990, the Union of Soviet Socialist Republics, the USSR, disintegrated as a multinational nation-state and was replaced by a number of newly independent nation-states—Russia, Ukraine, Belorussia, Uzbekistan, Armenia, and so forth. The former Yugoslavia also broke apart into new ethnically based nation-states of Croatia, Slovenia, Bosnia, and Serbia. However, in these new nation-states, ethnic groups' locations did not neatly correspond to national boundaries. The result has been ethnic conflict within the new nations between ethnic majorities and minorities.

Although ethnonationalist conflicts have been most dramatic in eastern Europe, particularly in the former Yugoslavia with the crisis in Bosnia, they have occurred with increasing violence throughout the world. In Africa, it manifests itself as tribalism. In Nigeria, for example, the political and educational situation has been tortured by attempts of one tribe to gain hegemony over others. Western nations such as Canada have experienced ethnic and language tensions between English and French speakers.

Education creates a cultural identity both informally through socialization in a given ethnocultural milieu, and formally through schooling. In education, the conflicts between multiethnic state identity and subgroup ethnonational identity have occurred over control of schools, curriculum, and the language of instruction. Cases of such conflict have occurred in Canada where the Québecois have resisted Anglicization, in Belgium where the Flemish have resisted the imposition of French, and in India where non-Hindi speakers have opposed the imposition of Hindi. While ethnonationalism creates a resistance to cultural and educational imposition by other groups, it also uses education positively to preserve and extend the tangible ethnic characteristics of the group. These tangible characteristics are preserved through the following rights: (1) the right to use the ethnic mother tongue as the medium of instruction rather than another official national language; (2) the right to include the ethnic group's literature, history, and traditions in the curriculum to create a sense of group identity; and (3) the right to use the hidden curriculum to reinforce a sense of "we-feeling" by cultivating a group response to ethnonational symbols.

U.S. Multiculturalism and Ethnonationalism

Education, in its organized form as schooling, has traditionally transmitted the cultural heritage from the adult members of the particular society to the children. Since the late eighteenth century, education has been a force for creating national identity through the teaching of a national language, literature, and history in the school curriculum. While involving some degree of imposition, these two large goals have shaped educational programs in the modern nation-state. U.S. educators have debated the degree to which the school and the curriculum should transmit and cultivate a common cultural identity, and also encourage the recognition and cultivation of more particular racial, ethnic, and language identities. Multiculturalism has been an educational response in the United States to cultural, racial, ethnic, and language diversities. However, there are many features of the U.S. situation that differ from the ethnonational resurgence taking place throughout the world. The U.S. educational experience, with its manifestations of assimilation and multiculturalism, fails to adequately correspond to the international phenomenon. Unlike many ethnonational groups throughout the world, immigrant and racial groups in the United States tend not to be located in particular regions which they consider to be their traditional ancestral cultural preserves and homelands.

Although the themes of ethnicity, race, and multiculturalism have been thoroughly examined and are firmly embedded in U.S. education's recent history, the concept of multiculturalism, while useful in interpreting ethnic and other kinds of cultural diversity, appears to be conceptually limited in explaining the power of ethnonationalism as a resurfacing global force. Although the United States has been described as a nation of immigrants, its multiethnic and multiracial composition has not prepared U.S. educators to understand the vehemence often found in the resurgence of ethnonationalism worldwide.

Historically, the United States has embraced the principle of self-determination of peoples, as enunciated by Woodrow Wilson during World War I and at the Versailles Peace Conference. While U.S. international educators have generally endorsed people's right to self-determination, they have also argued for the social, political, and economic integration of nations in the modern world. The dilemma becomes acute when ethnonationalism becomes the driving force for the disintegration of nation-states that are multiethnic in composition.

CONCLUSION

Nationalism has been an important historical and ideological force since the late eighteenth century. As indicated, national school systems arose as nation-states consolidated themselves politically. As the twentieth century ends, ethnonationalism is a powerful reemergent ideology. It is a highly consequential force in nation-states that range from technologically developed countries such as Canada and Belgium, to former Soviet-bloc countries in eastern Europe such as the constituent republics of the former USSR and the former Yugoslavia, to less technologically developed countries such as Nigeria and Sri Lanka.

Ethnonationalism is a worldwide reality since the majority of nation-states are multiethnic and ethnic consciousness has been rising rather than diminishing. Today, scholars are beginning to examine ethnonationalism but there is little consensus on how it can be accommodated in a nonviolent or noncoercive way. In order to understand the current international scene, U.S. international educators must understand the concept of ethnonationalism and its dynamics. Ethnonationalism, as a newly resurrected concept, is a significant international force, and international educators, having the goal of advancing international and intercultural understanding, need to be aware of the unsettling nature of ethnonationalism, particularly in multiethnic or multinational nations. These educators must develop tools of conceptual analysis, in order to identify and accentuate the constructive aspects of ethnonationalism.

Although ethnonationalism has long been a force throughout the world, it has had a marked and often violent resurgence in the 1990s. Throughout the world, there are signs of ethnonationalist conflict and a recognition that political and ethnic boundaries rarely coincide. Among the peoples experiencing ethnonationalist resurfacing and conflict are: Tibetans in the People's Republic of China, Ebo and Yoruba tribespeople in Nigeria, Mayan Indians in Mexico, and Tamils in Sri Lanka. In addition, ethnonationalism has been a force for political mobilization and separatism among the Québecois in Canada, the Flemish in Belgium, and Welsh and Scottish nationalists in the United Kingdom. Indeed, the visible signs of ethnonationalism are apparent throughout the world, in Russia and the other republics of the former Soviet Union; in Northern Ireland; in the successor states of the former Yugoslavia; in tribal conflict in Nigeria, Burundi, Uganda, Somalia; in ethnic and racial conflict in Tibet and other border regions of the People's Republic of China; in communal strife in India, especially among Muslims, Hindus, and Sikhs; in language conflict in Belgium among Flemings and Walloons; in ethnic and language conflict in Canada between English- and French-speaking groups, particularly in Québec; and in Mexico between mestizos and Indians. Ethnonationalism is the root cause in these and many other conflict areas.

DISCUSSION QUESTIONS

1. How can self-differentiating and self-determining ethnonational cultural groups coexist peacefully within a single nation-state's political and educational structure and system?

2. Is it possible to transmit cultural heritage in plural form within the nation-state framework?

3. Do you believe that the larger nation-state concept will reassert itself and absorb smaller conflicting ethnonational groups?

4. Are we witnessing the emergence of a new global reality in which ministates based on ethnicity will replace the larger nation-state?

5. How can ethnonationalism become part of the curriculum for international education in the United States?

6. How can educational theory be reconnected with the earlier theories of nationalism so that it more adequately incorporates an examination of ethnonationalism?

7. What are the implications of ethnonationalism for educational goals and curriculum throughout the world?

8. How well does the concept of multiculturalism relate to the phenomenon of ethnonationalism?

INQUIRY PROJECTS

- Reflect on your own nationalist and ethnonationalist formation and experiences. In an autobiographical account, comment on these experiences.
- Begin a clippings file of newspaper and magazine articles that deal with ethnonationalist conflicts. After you have amassed a number of articles, analyze them for educational implications.
- Organize a panel of international students from various countries who are studying at your college or university. Invite them to discuss education, schooling, and the forming of national character from their own perspectives.
- If you are engaged in field work in a school setting, identify how that school, both informally and formally, builds a sense of American identity.
- If you are engaged in field work in a school setting, identify how that school, both informally and formally, builds a sense of multicultural identity.
- Examine the commemorative days, or holidays, celebrated by schools in the United States. Discuss the role of these events in shaping national character.

FURTHER READINGS

Alter, Peter. *Nationalism.* New York: Edward Arnold, 1994.

Beer, James E., and James E. Jacob, eds. *Language Policy and National Unity.* Totowa, NJ: Rowman and Allanheld, 1985.

Brass, Paul R. *Ethnicity and Nationalism: Theory and Comparison.* Newbury Park, CA: Sage, 1991.

Connor, Walker. *Ethnonationalism: The Quest for Understanding.* Princeton, NJ: Princeton University Press, 1994.

Diamond, Larry, and Marc F., Plattner. *Nationalism, Ethnic Conflict, and Democracy.* Baltimore: Johns Hopkins University Press, 1994.

Edwards, John R. *Language, Society, and Identity.* New York: B. Blackwell, 1985.

Eriksen, Thomas H. *Ethnicity and Nationalism: Anthropological Perspectives.* London and Boulder, CO: Pluto Press, 1993.

Farnen, Russell F., ed. *Nationalism, Ethnicity, and Identity: Cross National and Comparative Perspectives.* New Brunswick, NJ: Transaction Publishers, 1994.

Gates, Henry L., Jr. *Loose Canons: Notes on the Culture Wars.* New York: Oxford University Press, 1992.

Gellner, Ernest. *Encounters with Nationalism.* Oxford, England, and Cambridge, MA: Blackwell Publishers, 1994.

Gillis, John R., ed. *Commemorations: The Politics of National Identity.* Princeton, NJ: Princeton University Press, 1993.

Gutek, Gerald L. *American Education in a Global Society: Internationalizing Teacher Education.* New York: Longman, 1993.

Hunter, James D. *Culture Wars: The Struggle to Define America.* New York: Basic Books, 1991.

Hutchinson, John, and Anthony D. Smith, eds. *Nationalism.* New York: Oxford University Press, 1994.

Ignatieff, Michael. *Blood and Belonging: Journeys into the New Nationalism.* New York: Farrar, Straus, and Giroux, 1994.

Kammen, Michael. *Contested Values: Democracy and Diversity in American Culture.* New York: St. Martin's Press, 1995.

Kellas, James G. *The Politics of Nationalism and Ethnicity.* New York: St. Martin's Press, 1991.

Nieto, Sonia. *Affirming Diversity: The Sociopolitical Context of Multicultural Education.* New York: Longman, 1992.

Smith, Anthony D. *National Identity.* Reno, NV: University of Nevada Press, 1991.

Synder, Louis L. *Global Mini-Nationalisms: Autonomy or Independence.* Westport, CT: Greenwood Press, 1982.

Takaki, Ronald. *A Different Mirror: A History of Multicultural America.* Boston: Little, Brown, 1993.

Watson, Michael, ed. *Contemporary Minority Nationalism.* New York: Routledge, 1990.

Williams, Colin H., and Eleonore Kofman, eds. *Community Conflict, Partition and Nationalism.* New York: Routledge, 1989.

ENDNOTES

1. For treatments of nationalism, see Michael Ignatieff, *Blood and Belonging: Journeys into the New Nationalism* (New York: Farrar, Straus, and Giroux, 1994); Ernest Bellner, *Encounters with Nationalism* (Oxford, England, and Cambridge, MA: Blackwell, 1994).

2. For commentaries on ethnonationalism, see Thomas H. Eriksen, *Ethnicity and Nationalism: Anthropological Perspectives* (London and Boulder, CO: Pluto Press, 1993); Paul R. Brass, *Ethnicity and Nationalism: Theory and Comparison* (Newbury Park, CA: Sage, 1991).

3. For the congruence of the nation-state and national systems of education, see Gerald L. Gutek, *American Education in a Global Society: Internationalizing Teacher Education* (New York: Longman, 1993), pp. 30–35.

4. For examples of the debate over multiculturalism and interpretations of the American character, see James D. Hunter, *Culture Wars: The Struggle to Define America* (New York: Basic Books, 1991); Ronald Takaki, *A Different Mirror: A History of Multicultural America* (Boston: Little, Brown, 1993).

5. Walker Connor, *Ethnonationalism: The Quest for Understanding* (Princeton, NJ: Princeton University, Press, 1994), p. 29.

6. Karl Deutsch, *Nationalism and Social Communication: An Inquiry into the Foundations of Nationality* (Cambridge, MA: Harvard University Press, 1966).

7. Harold G. Shane, ed., *The United States and International Education: The Sixty-Eighth Yearbook of the National Society for the Study of Education,* Part I (Chicago: University of Chicago Press, 1969).

8. Donald Adams, "Development Education and Social Progress," Chap. 2 in *United States and International Education,* ed. Shane, p. 55.

9. Although I have stipulated definitions for nationalism and ethnonationalism, my stipulated definition for the latter term relies on Walker Connor, *Ethnonationalism: The Quest for Understanding* (Princeton, NJ: Princeton University Press, 1994), p. xi.

▶ 11

Liberalism and Education

Liberalism originated in the late sixteenth and early seventeenth centuries when medieval feudalism was disintegrating and the middle class, composed of professionals, bankers, and businesspeople, was beginning to challenge the old landed aristocracy for social and political supremacy. These emergent middle classes sought to throw off the shackles imposed on them by the old political, social, and economic establishment.

By the second half of the eighteenth century, Liberalism had become a well-developed ideological challenge to the aristocratic old order. Liberal impulses accompanied the intellectual currents of the eighteenth-century Age of Reason, or Enlightenment, which exerted a profound impact on Western thought. The French *philosophes,* who initially articulated the concept of ideology, attacked absolute monarchy and the dogmas of the church, which they believed impeded human progress.

In attacking traditional institutions, the intellectuals of the French Enlightenment condemned what they construed to be ignorance and superstition. They also criticized existing educational institutions for keeping students in intellectual bondage. Dominated by catechetical religious instruction at the primary level and scholasticism at the higher levels, schooling reflected the old order's intellectual stagnation rather than a progressive scientific outlook.

The *philosophes* believed it was possible to examine human and social conduct in a way that approximated scientific inquiry into the physical realm. Once the natural laws of human growth and social development could be ascertained, they reasoned, a natural society modeled on nature's own order could be created.

The *philosophes'* ideas were not simply speculative; they were implemented by the American revolutionaries of 1776 and the French revolutionaries of 1789.

For the American and French revolutionaries, the natural social order envisioned by the *philosophes* would be a republican government.

Shortly after these momentous political changes had occurred, the industrial revolution transformed the world economically. Using new processes of production that generated surplus wealth, the industrial revolution also triggered the rise of the capitalist class that soon dominated commerce. The general principles of Liberal ideology can be examined against this background of economic and political change.

In the following sections we will examine the life of John Locke, a founder of Liberalism, identify the key elements of Liberal ideology, and analyze Liberalism's educational impact.

JOHN LOCKE: A FOUNDER OF LIBERALISM

In this section of the chapter, we will examine the contribution of the English philosopher John Locke (1632–1704) to Liberal ideology. Our treatment of Locke is divided into three parts: (1) a short biographical sketch, (2) a discussion of his work on epistemology and education, and (3) an analysis of his *Two Treatises on Civil Government* (1690), which established Liberalism's essential tenets.

Locke's Biographical Sketch

Locke was the son of John Locke, an attorney and small landowner. Locke's family were Puritans who dissented from the Church of England. For the first fourteen years of his life, Locke was tutored by his father.[1]

From 1646 to 1651, John Locke attended Westminster School. At this famous preparatory institution, he studied traditional Latin and Greek classics to prepare for entry into Oxford University. In 1652, at the age of twenty, Locke received a junior studentship at Christ Church College in Oxford. He was awarded the bachelor of arts degree in 1656 and earned his master's degree in 1658. In 1660, he became a lecturer in Greek, rhetoric, and moral philosophy. He then studied medicine. Although he did not complete a medical degree, he became a respected physician.

Locke's great attraction was to political philosophy rather than medicine. An appointment as secretary and personal physician to Lord Ashley, Earl of Shaftesbury, in 1667 brought Locke into contact with the world of politics. Among his duties, Locke served as the tutor of Ashley's son.

While Ashley was Lord Chancellor, from 1672 to 1674, Locke was close to political power and enjoyed several government appointments. When Shaftesbury fell from power during the Stuart restoration, Locke went into exile as an expatriate in Holland. While in exile, Locke completed his *Treatises on Civil Government,* published in 1690. With the Glorious Revolution of 1688 and

John Locke (1632–1704), an English philosopher, who was a founding theorist of Liberalism.

William and Mary's accession to the English throne, Locke returned to England where he was appointed Commissioner of Appeals. In ailing health, Locke retired from government service in 1700 and died four years later.

Locke on Epistemology and Education

Locke's greatest philosophical effort, *An Essay Concerning Human Understanding,*[2] published in 1690, became a classic statement of empiricist epistemology. Locke began his analysis by attacking the Platonic theory of innate ideas, which asserted that knowledge originated in fundamental concepts that were present in the mind at birth and prior to sensory experience. In attacking Platonic assumptions, Locke sought to establish the empiricist view that all human knowledge originates in sense perception. At birth the mind is a *tabula rasa,* a clean slate, a white paper, on which the data of experience are impressed. These ideas are either simple or complex. If complex, they are relational and arise from mental faculties that enable us to compare, contrast, abstract, and remember them.

Locke's theory denied the exclusive reliance on tradition, custom, and authority based on immutable first principles. His empiricism emphasized the use of the scientific method. Locke's rejection of innate ideas and his *tabula rasa* concept of mind suggest that human character is shaped by experience. However, while there are no innate ideas in the mind, different people have different mental potentialities.

Some Thoughts Concerning Education, which Locke published in 1693, was not a philosophical treatise but rather a practical guide to an English gentleman's education.[3] In it, Locke identified four major educational aims. The first is virtue, consisting of the practice of self-denial, which inhibits impulsive behavior and resists temptation. The cultivation of virtuous habits facilitates leading a life governed by reason. Education's second aim is wisdom, the shrewd and practical wit that enables a person to manage affairs and property successfully and to be prudent in human affairs. The third aim, good breeding, guides one in fulfilling life's social obligations. Learning, the fourth aim, is most properly concerned with morality and politics and deals with civil society, government, law, and history.

Locke on Government

Locke's *Two Treatises of Government* had the greatest significance for Liberal ideology. His concepts of representative government and the inalienable rights of the person expressed Liberalism's germinal concepts. In this section, we will examine these concepts and their educational implications.

Locke's social contract theory contributed to a new conception of the polity—a commonwealth of self-governing individuals. While both Rousseau and Locke wrote about the social contract, Locke's natural rights theory and contract form of government had the greatest impact on the American Liberal theorists, especially Thomas Jefferson and the framers of the Declaration of Independence.

Locke and Human Rights

In 1690, Locke's *Two Treatises of Government* not only justified Britain's Glorious Revolution of 1688 but also elaborated a new ideological perspective. Finding the general principles governing human association in the original state of nature, Locke claimed that "no one ought to harm another in his life, health, liberty or possession." Each person, like every other individual, equally possessed inherent natural rights to life, liberty, and property. When these natural rights were in jeopardy, individuals in common association formed a social contract in mutual defense against those who transgressed these natural rights. Individuals entered into political society and formed a government to protect these natural rights. According to Locke, individuals who unite in one civil body have agreed to "a common established law" and can appeal to a judiciary to which they have given "authority" to settle "controversies between them" and to punish offenders.[4]

For Locke, individuals are free, equal, and independent and no one can deprive them of property or subject them to another's political power without their consent. Arising from the mutual agreement of those who form the civil society, government relies on majority rule, the fairest way of formulating policy and making political decisions. According to Locke, every person, by agreeing to form a government, enters "an obligation to everyone of that society to submit to majority rule."[5] While all the members of the society agree to the general processes of the social contract, some will agree and others will disagree on specific legislation. Majorities and minorities that arise over specifics are temporary and shifting. Based on the mutual respect of the individuals who comprise the civil society, the rights of both the majority and the minority are to be respected.

In Locke's version of civil society, the three branches of government—legislative, judicial, and executive—are calculated to achieve a balance of power. This threefold division of powers is clearly apparent in U.S. political institutions. In Locke's social compact, a known common law arises from common consent through elected representatives in the legislature. The executive of the commonwealth enforces the common law; the judiciary renders objective decisions based on its interpretation of the common law.

The legislature is created by the individuals who enter into the social contract; its power to enact laws is given to it by the members of society. The elected members of the legislature are subject, as are other individuals, to the laws they enact. Whereas the enacted legislation grows into a cumulative body of law that is subject to revision, the composition of the legislature itself is temporary, its members serving fixed terms. When its work is done in a particular session, the members of the legislature return to their various constituencies.

For Locke, and for Liberals in general, the legislature was the basis of representative government. Members of the legislature, coming from the ranks of the people who have joined in the social contract, represent these people. Crucial to the principle of a representative government was the process of election by which citizens elect their representatives to the legislature.

In addition to its political prescriptions, Locke's Liberalism held significant implications for education. First of all, Locke's prescription of representative institutions directly challenged the doctrine of the "divine right of kings," which held that authority descended from God to the king, then downward to an hereditary aristocracy, and then further downward until it reached the masses of the population. In the theory of the divine right of kings, no check existed on the sovereign except that which came from God.

In the class structure based on the divine right of kings theory of government, three political castes existed: (1) the reigning monarch and aristocracy of birth, (2) the clergy, and (3) the so-called third estate, which included all other people. Members of all three classes were educated according to the doctrine of social class appropriateness. Because the social roles of both the members of the aristocracy and the masses were ascribed at birth, the type of education that they were to receive depended on, or was appropriate to, their membership in an hereditary social class. Each hereditary socioeconomic class had political and economic duties that were also ascribed on the basis of birth. For the prince who was expected to succeed his father to the throne, there were instructions in statecraft, diplomacy, and royal etiquette. The prince's education was to prepare him to rule and to exercise authority. The aristocracy received the appropriate education to serve as the monarch's subordinates, magistrates, and officers. They were prepared to be generals in the army, administrators, or diplomats. The hereditary aristocrats were educated in the rubrics of court ceremony. Conversely, the masses of the population were trained as toilers, workers, and soldiers. Their civic duties were to hear and obey the commands of hereditary superiors.

The education of the hereditary aristocracy was based on ascribed political and economic roles. Leaders were born to rule and then prepared to exercise their authority. Likewise, followers were born to follow and then conditioned by their training to follow with docile obedience. Because a person's political role was ascribed, civic education was based on performing a specifically defined role rather than participating in the general political process.

In contrast to the theory of the divine right of kings, Locke's contract theory of government and the resultant Liberal ideology created a change in politics and education. To be sure, the political implications were evident much earlier than were the educational ones. Representative government meant that any citizen could be elected to serve in the commonwealth's legislature. The flow of political authority was no longer downward through an hierarchical pattern as in the model of the divine right of kings; rather, it arose from the people—from the governed—who, in forming the social contract, created the government. Because service in the legislature was not hereditary and was temporary, civic education was no longer appropriate to membership in a particular class. Instead, education was necessary for all citizens of the commonwealth so that they might participate in elections and serve in one of the three branches of Liberal government: the legislature, executive, or judiciary.

Of greatest significance in Lockean ideology was the need for members of society to be political generalists rather than specialists. An individual's civic destiny was not specifically defined at birth but was influenced by many factors, one of which might be election to office. The elective process also meant that every citizen would be a voter and a decision maker. Because Locke's ideology called for civic generalists, it also implied that a person's civic education should be general and include the following: (1) the theory of contract government based on the recognition of fundamental human rights, (2) knowledge about the organization and functions of government based on the divisions of power, (3) knowledge of the procedures of representative institutions, and (4) cultivation of civic attitudes and values that sustain representative institutions and processes. The educational implications of Locke's political theory were of immense significance in the United Kingdom and the United States. What was required was a new conception of civic education.

Locke and the Right of Revolution

In his *Two Treatises of Government,* Locke argued that the purpose of government was to protect the rights of its citizens. Whenever a government violates that trust, the people may replace it with a new one. Locke's treatise sought to justify the revolt of 1688 against the Stuart monarchy and the establishment of William and Mary as constitutional monarchs, subject to parliamentary rule, on the English throne. When a government—such as that of the Stuarts—sought to subvert basic human freedoms, then the people had the right to revolt to regain their original liberty and to establish a new government, thus renewing the social contract.

Thomas Jefferson, in writing the Declaration of Independence, used Locke's arguments to justify the American Revolution against King George III and English rule. Accusing the British monarch of violating the social contract and of depriving the American colonists of their natural rights, the Americans, Jefferson argued, had a right to overthrow and replace English monarchical rule with a new republican government. In appealing to the theory of natural rights, Jefferson proclaimed the self-evident truths that, "all men are created equal, that they are endowed by their Creator with certain unalienable rights, that among these are life, liberty, and the pursuit of happiness."

By ignoring these self-evident truths, George III had violated the contract between the governed and the government. Jefferson affirmed the colonists' right to revolt and to establish a new government to fulfill the social contract and to secure the people's unalienable rights:

> *Whenever any form of government becomes destructive to these ends, it is the right of the people to deter or abolish it, and to institute a new government, allying its foundation on such principles, and organizing its powers in such form as to them shall seem most likely to effect their safety and happiness.*

Both Locke and Jefferson identified liberty as one of the three unalienable human rights. Liberty meant freedom to frame alternatives, to choose between them, and to fulfill them through political, social, economic, religious, intellectual, and educational action.

KEY ELEMENTS IN LIBERAL IDEOLOGY

In the following section, we will identify and examine certain key elements in Liberal ideology. Among them are the Liberal conception of property and the economy, the Liberal view of human nature and reason, secular orientation, the emphasis on the individual, the propensity for progress, the reliance on representative institutions, the programmatic nature of Liberalism, and the view of social change. In the general ideological sense, these concepts provide the framework for Liberal views of schooling.

The Liberal Conception of Property and the Economy

In its historical origins, Liberalism appealed to the property-owning professional and business middle classes. Note that Locke asserted that the possession of property was an inherent personal right. Liberal policy and legislation have sought to safeguard the individual's economic freedom to compete and acquire property.[6] Economic initiative and competition are believed to be an effective means of satisfying needs arising from self-interest as well as bringing about general economic prosperity.

Although agreeing on the basic core right of individuals to hold private property, Liberals disagree on the extent to which the economy should be regulated. Laissez-faire classical Liberals, insisting that government should keep its hands off the economy as much as possible, would restrict the role of government to guaranteeing a free enterprise climate and a competitive marketplace, governed only by the laws of supply and demand. Conversely, reformist Liberals, such as U.S. progressives, see the government functioning as a regulating agency to prevent restraint of trade, to ensure the health and safety of workers and consumers, to protect the environment, and to regulate the hours and conditions of work. Progressive reformist Liberals initiated legislation to restrict child labor and to make schooling compulsory for certain age groups. Their argument is that such actions improve the quality of people's lives and also enhance economic well-being in the long run.

The Liberal economic perspective has an impact on educational policy making and on schooling. In the broad sense of policy making, education relates to the economic needs of the society, its employment requirements, and to its determinants of economic success. Liberal societies tend to develop policies that encourage educational freedom of choice in terms of choosing a career. At the same time that choice is encouraged, however, the vagaries of supply and demand, with their alternating effects on the academic marketplace, add an element of insecurity in terms of employability to these educational decisions.

It is an interesting and somewhat confusing ideological twist that contemporary U.S. Neo-Conservatives have made key economic principles of Classical Liberalism part of their agenda. They seek to deregulate the economy by removing or reducing Reformist Liberal regulatory controls over business and the corporate sector. They also seek to eliminate affirmative action guidelines designed to provide reserved proportionate educational places and jobs for underrepresented members of minority groups, on the grounds that it unfairly circumscribes individual initiative and merit. Some Neo-Conservatives would privatize schooling by issuing vouchers that parents could use to select educational alternatives to public schooling. (For a further discussion of the Neo-Conservative appropriation of Classical Liberal economic theory, see Chapter 12, Conservatism and Education.)

Educational materialism arising from Liberalism's economic context is often stimulated by future financial rewards. School attendance and completion of one's education are encouraged by pointing to the higher salaries and income earned by graduates and by those who continue their education. Many recent educational initiatives, such as those stimulated by *A Nation at Risk,* were based on economic arguments designed to enhance U.S. competitiveness in the global economy. Although originating with Neo-Conservative policymakers, these initiatives incorporated the Classical Liberal ideological premise that schooling contributes to increased economic productivity and growth.

View of Human Nature and Reason

When Liberalism emerged in the eighteenth century, it was the ideology of what was then a suppressed class. Although the industrial revolution gave economic power to the middle class, these people found themselves deprived of the political, social, and educational rights they felt should be theirs. As indicated earlier, absolute monarchy and the privileged sociopolitical position of the landed aristocracy denied the middle class a role in political decision making. The discontented middle class felt that its taxes supported governments in which people had little or no voice.

Not only did the Liberal middle class find itself coerced politically, but it also found that it had to support established churches, such as the Anglican Church in England and the Roman Catholic Church in France, to which many of them did not belong. Furthermore, the middle classes also felt that they were denied social status by the older aristocrats who held commerce in contempt. Educational institutions that were sponsored by the established churches were often unresponsive to the kind of education the middle classes desired.

As a suppressed group, the Liberal middle classes wanted to remove the political, religious, and educational obstacles that blocked their progress. Freeing human beings from arbitrary restriction and coercion became a paramount Liberal theme.

For some French *philosophes,* such as Rousseau, human nature was intrinsically good—not deprived or depraved. French Liberals found the source of evil to lie in corrupt social, political, and educational institutions rather than in human nature. For example, an absolute monarchy resting on unquestioned traditions caused political evil; the superstition encouraged by the established churches interfered with rational inquiry and corrupted the morality of the natural order. Liberals in England and America considered human beings to be either good or morally neutral at birth, but certainly not depraved. Once humanity was seen to be benevolent, then Liberals could argue that the irrational restrictions of arbitrary governments and religions ought to be eliminated. They argued for a social and political order that recognized every person's fundamental rights to life, liberty, and property. They believed that human beings should be free from arbitrary restraints and allowed to express themselves freely on all matters in print, in speech, and in teaching.

Liberals take an optimistic view of human nature, which sees human beings acting according to reasoned self-interest. With enlightenment and education, Liberals believe people will act to achieve their goals but also maintain the social order that encourages them to satisfy their needs. Government in such a society is to respect the autonomy of its individual members to form associations and to exercise the freedom of inquiry, speech, press, and assembly that promote personal and social growth.

Liberal assumptions about the human potential for benevolence have important educational implications. Liberals contend that children should be freed from arbitrary restrictions imposed by coercive teachers, the memorization of the catechism, and rote learning that stifled individual creativity. Liberal reformers in education saw in the child's nature the hope of personal and social growth and reformation.

Efficacy of Human Reason

Reflecting its Enlightenment origins, Liberalism asserted the power of human reason to solve problems, to create remedies, and to improve life and society. Powers of reasoning gave human beings a formidable instrument for transforming and reconstructing the old order. Liberals such as John Dewey argued that the scientific method could be applied to life's myriad social, political, economic, and educational problems. What interfered with human reason were the residues of superstition and ignorance. Once the obstacles to inquiry were removed, human intelligence could be freed. James Mill, a convinced Liberal, argued that reasonable persons could "weigh evidence" and be guided by it in their decisions. Stressing the power of the majority, he argued that the greatest number of such reasonable persons would "judge right."[7]

Liberalism's stress on reason and the efficacy of the scientific method have obvious educational consequences. In informal education, there must be freedom of access to information. Freedom of speech and assembly would allow individuals to express opinions without fear of punishment. Remove censorship of the press, Liberals urged, so that ideas could be printed and freely circulated. As John Stuart Mill argued, freedom of speech, press, and assembly would allow for competition in the marketplace of ideas.[8]

In formal education, that is, in schools, the impact of Liberalism's emphasis on human rationality is equally obvious. Liberal educational theorists of the nineteenth century, such as Herbert Spencer, argued against the domination of the curriculum by the ancient Latin and Greek languages and urged that the curriculum be revised to emphasize scientific knowledge and the scientific method.[9]

Secularism

Although they might be religious in their personal lives and be members of churches, Liberals generally opposed state efforts to enforce religious conformity and support officially established churches. In France and Mexico, Liberals worked to disestablish the Roman Catholic Church as the official religion. In England, Liberals, often members of dissenting or nonconformist churches, wanted to free both political and educational life from domination by the official

Anglican Church. In the United States, the Constitution prohibited the establishment of religion by the government.

Regarding themselves as agents of freedom of thought, Liberals viewed established churches and church schools as agencies of intellectual repression. Established churches meant officially sanctioned unscientific dogmatism. Upon gaining political power, Liberals sought to separate church from state and church from school. Public or state schools were to be free of religious control. For Liberals, a person's religious beliefs were private and not a state matter.

In schooling, the Liberal attitude varied from that of benign neglect of all religions to outright anticlericalism. In their efforts to negate church influence on the schools, Liberals sought to remove religious conformity as a requirement for either entry into teaching or for admission to educational institutions. They also worked to remove religious doctrines from the school curriculum.

As mentioned earlier, current U.S. Neo-Conservativism has incorporated basic Classical Liberal economic ideas on free trade, increased competition, and the deregulation of business and environmental protection. However, on matters of religion, Neo-Conservatives part company with Liberals. The Neo-Conservative position is much closer to traditional Conservativism (which is discussed in Chapter 12). While embracing Classical Liberal and even Social Darwinist economic theories and values, the "religious right" in the United States wants a more public testimony to religious beliefs, symbols, and values than Liberals. Based on religious fundamentalism, Neo-Conservatives want the recognition that U.S. cultural, political, and legal principles originated in and are grounded in the Judeo-Christian tradition. They want opportunities for religious expression, such as prayer in the public schools, parity between the theories of creationism and evolution in the curriculum, and freedom to organize and maintain religiously based organizations and clubs in schools. Liberals, convinced of the need to protect the wall of separation between church and state, have opposed these initiatives that are part of the Neo-Conservative political and educational agendas.

Individualism

Foremost among Liberalism's propositions was that the individual person is prior to society. As indicated, Locke asserted that the individual person possessed unalienable natural rights to "life, liberty, and property" that government was created to protect. Liberal movements were committed to the equality of individuals as expressed by the French "Declaration of the Rights of Man and the Citizen" that affirmed that "all men are born and remain free and equal in rights."

In the Lockean and Jeffersonian conceptions of individualism, the person was prior to the society and possessed rights of the particular sociopolitical order in which he or she happened to reside. In the best political society, the activities of the individual were to be as private and as free from governmental regulation and interference as possible.

By the early nineteenth century, the British economists of the Manchester school interpreted the priority of the individual as the person's right to unrestricted economic competition. The Social Darwinist Herbert Spencer asserted that individual competition was nature's means of selecting the fittest for survival.[10] Even in the reformed Darwinism of John Dewey, the individual was still prior to the group. While social intelligence came from group interaction and participation, the group, composed of separate individuals, depended for its existence on its individual members.[11]

Clearly, the Liberal impulse sought to advance the freedom and development of the individual person. In education, Liberals, concerned with the individual student and his or her progress, did not sacrifice individual needs to group or social needs. Some Liberals, such as Herbert Spencer, saw education as preparing individuals for a competitive world; others, such as John Dewey, stressed cooperative group participation. What was common to educational Liberals was their emphasis on individuals, their needs and development.[12]

Once it had evolved from its revolutionary origins in the early nineteenth century, Liberalism came to emphasize a cautious, moderate, and balanced approach to solving social, economic, and political problems. Liberal methodology was one of limited objectives in which problems were solved one by one. Liberals avoided developing utopian grand designs that promised to solve all social problems in one broad sweep. Liberals, including modern Social Welfare Liberals such as John Dewey, were suspicious of large-scale hypotheses for social transformation.[13] Large transformative agendas broke the continuity of testable experience by making often utopian leaps into untested, uncharted, and remote waters.

Although they shared some basic common assumptions, Liberals eventually divided into two camps. Classical Liberals, such as Herbert Spencer, continued to believe that government was best which governed least. Classical Liberals, who preferred that government maintain its role of passive watchdog and avoid entering into social reform, regarded any such ameliorative legislation as social tampering that would only confuse and worsen the condition that it sought to remedy.

On the other hand, modern Liberalism—originating with the British Utilitarians and continuing down to the reformist progressives—believed that government should exercise regulatory and ameliorative functions. Where social abuses or injustices existed, the government should correct them. Furthermore, only government could provide needed social services in such areas as sanitation, factory regulation, water supply, and education, among others. In approaching problems, however, modern Liberals usually deal with specific issues rather than general social reconstruction.

Theories such as Social Reconstructionism and Critical Theory, discussed in later chapters, have attacked Liberal incremental reforms as being piecemeal and lacking the power to transform society. Liberals would counter that sweeping transformative agendas, generally more polemical than substantive, fail to arise from existing conditions and neglect the necessity to constantly relate means and ends. They would contend that supposedly transformative, good-intentioned proposals have often had tragic consequences, unanticipated by utopian reformers, such as the reign of terror in Robespierre's revolutionary France or the massive purges of Stalin in the Soviet Union.

Liberalism encouraged an intellectual outlook that recognized change as part of an evolutionary process. Change could be encouraged by nonrevolutionary and gradual legislative reforms. The traditional Liberal process of legislating change was to investigate a problem; collect statistics, data, and evidence; and then recommend reform legislation.

Gradualism, moderation, balance, and the absence of a sweeping grand design all characterized the Liberal temperament. Liberals were process oriented in their devotion to the scientific method or the method of legislative reform. The efficacy of the process required that its users respect it. It was not the end result that was important in the long run; it was, rather, a willingness to use process and to implement its results.

In school curriculum and instruction, Liberal educators, especially in the United States, emphasized process-centered education. Both John Dewey and William Kilpatrick exalted democratic processes in education. Kilpatrick's "project method" was designed so that children would work in groups to solve specific problems. Learners would not only solve the specific problems, but also concomitantly acquire experience in using group-centered democratic procedures. Collaborative learning, a contemporary revival of the project method, sees learning enriched by the sharing of information and the participatory use of skills. Collaborative learning, in some respects, is a pedagogical counterpart to Reformist Liberal participatory democracy.

Liberals emphasized process and opposed ideologies in which the ends justified the means. As life, society, politics, and education changed, the processes of the scientific method or of democratic procedures gave individuals some control over their destinies. Human intelligence could chart the course of the future. Not bound by long-standing traditions nor mired in abstract theoretical dogmas, Liberals could deal with present problems in an unencumbered and relativistic way.

Progress

Since the French Enlightenment, Liberals have believed that the liberation of human intelligence would lead to progress. Although not defining progress specifically, Liberals were committed to the possibility of improving the human condition. Because Liberalism arose in the context of the rapidly changing society and economy of the industrial revolution, Liberals saw science and technology as instruments to improve the conditions of life. Unlike traditionalists or conservatives, followers of Liberalism did not look backward to a "golden age" in the past.

Utilitarian Liberals such as Jeremy Bentham and James Mill believed it possible to calculate and to achieve good for the greatest number of people. U.S. Progressives believed it possible to create a "Great Society" in which all Americans could share in the good things of life. Woodrow Wilson could design plans for the ending of World War I by means of an international parliamentary body such as the League of Nations. In general, Liberals believed that society was dynamically changing for the better and human intelligence could create a good society by means of reform.

Running throughout Liberalism—from its view of the past to its present policies, programs, and projects—is the concept of progress—the belief that the future can be better than the past through liberating human energy and creativity, using the methods of science, and exercising freedom to inquire and to act. The Liberal outlook has been progressive and directed to the present and future rather than to the past. Liberals eschew utopianism and do not envision the establishment of a perfect society. Rather, their view of social reform is limited and relative in that if a social or institutional imbalance or strain appears, then reform is needed to apply the necessary remediation or regulation so that the institution will function more effectively and efficiently.[14]

Representative Institutions

Liberalism's emphasis on process, gradual reform, and change contributed to a conception of political order that functions by means of elected legislative bodies. The interests of the people are identified with the power of the state through a representative government in which elected representatives are responsible to the electorate. Liberalism's political approach, especially in England and in the United States, emphasized the power of numbers and the roles of majorities and minorities in the process. With the creation of parliamentary government, revolution left the street and entered the legislative chamber where it became institutionalized in peaceful parliamentary processes. In such a system, the majority is not to abuse its power; the minority has the right to work for change through legislative processes. Further, majorities and minorities are temporary and will change as their members shift their positions on specific issues.

Further, within the Liberal state, constitutional guarantees of civil rights protect the individual against arbitrary action by the government. The U.S. Constitution, adopted in 1788, illustrates the constitutional process. According to the U.S. Constitution, the state machinery is based on the principle of popular sovereignty; the Bill of Rights protects and guarantees civil liberties, and the Constitution may be amended peacefully.

Constitutional Literacy

Similar to the Liberal emphasis on constitutional processes, Toni Marie Massaro recommends constructing a core curriculum around the theme of the U.S. Constitution and cases related to its interpretation, especially those concerned with rights and due process. Massaro argues that (1) there is an "American paideia," a concept of formative education, that brings persons into cultural understanding and participation; (2) schooling has been and is a powerful force of cultural transmission and formation; (3) a curricular core that emphasizes constitutional literacy can revitalize schooling's cultural mission in U.S. society; and (4) such a constitutional curricular core can develop a consensus to accommodate both political and procedural commonalities and cultural conflicts.[15] Massaro's emphasis on constitutional literacy reiterates Liberal arguments that in order to maintain and renew itself in a continuous fashion, a society needs agreed-on processes that can keep conflict within a communal framework. When the framework does not exist or has eroded to the degree that it is ineffective, disagreements may become noncommunal to the extent that the society can no longer maintain and renew itself in a peaceful, nonviolent way. Necessary to agreed-on processes is the building and creation of a consensus—a shared commitment to accept and to use the processes. Liberals, historically, have been consensus builders. They seek to create a middle, moderate, or centrist position in politics, society, and education that can accommodate pluralisms within a shared framework of processes or procedures.

Massaro's argument for constitutional literacy seeks to develop a middle position to the current debates over multiculturalism and the need for a cultural core. Proponents of a national core curriculum, such as E. D. Hirsch, Jr., Allan Bloom, Arthur M. Schlesinger, Jr., and others, have argued that the U.S. cultural commonality, its consensual core, is seriously disintegrating and needs restoration. Proponents of a national core curriculum attribute this cultural disintegration to both a declining historical and political public literacy and to a deliberate disuniting of the strands of U.S. cultural identity by extremist multiculturalists. Critics of a national core curriculum, preferring cultural diversity and multicultural pluralism, counter that the public school curriculum should no longer transmit a monocultural version of U.S. cultural identity as it did in its assimilationist past. Rather, it should encourage racial, religious, gender, and ethnic pluralism.[16]

Arguing for constitutional literacy, Massaro offers a theoretical synthesis that unites contentious factions in a procedural framework. She argues that (1) a national core curriculum is needed; (2) such a curriculum can embrace both the commonality which unites Americans as well as the diversity and pluralism that enriches their society; and (3) the U.S. Constitution, its rights and processes, provides the context for constructing both the curricular core and for cultivating a sense of constitutional processes. Massaro contends that the Constitution and its legal interpretation offer a coherent framework for a core curriculum that can be used to educate a constitutionally literate populace that is sensitive to the issues of freedom of religion and expression, and equal protection of the law. Her analysis confronts what she regards as Liberal democracy's essential educational paradox—promoting "neutrality among competing versions of the good life while trying to instill . . . the principles of the liberal democratic state, among them the nonneutral preference for critical deliberation."[17]

Meaningful conversation, informed by constitutional literacy and undertaken within a consensual framework of shared processes, will encourage productive explorations about religious, racial, ethnic, gender, class, and other differences. With a constitutional core in place, teachers and students then can critically examine the U.S. continuing multicultural issues—its racial, religious, ethnic, gender, and class conflicts.

For Liberals, a balanced state and society are best maintained by a division of powers that prevents an excessive accumulation of power in any one person or group. In the United States, for example, power at the national level of government is divided among the executive, legislative, and judicial branches. A further division of power in the U.S. system is among the federal, state, and local governments. This division of power, or system of checks and balances, contrasts sharply with ideological orientations in which power is held monolithically by a single person, party, or group.

Among Liberals, an elected representative government is the ideal political order. Necessary educational corollaries to such a political order are (1) the existence of a generally educated public, (2) the cultivation of a particular kind of civic education that stresses participation, and (3) the acceptance of a sense of civic accountability that stresses the responsibility of officials to the public.

The Programmatic Nature of Liberalism

Liberalism's most general programmatic orientation seeks to (1) protect the rights and corresponding liberties of individuals according to clearly defined relationships, (2) advance the welfare of individuals in the society, and (3) maintain the sociopolitical balance that allows the free interaction of persons. It is on the second point, advancing the welfare of individuals, that Liberals disagree among themselves. Classical Liberals generally believe that balance can best be achieved by maintaining competition among individuals with little or no government interference. Social Reformist Liberals, like the U.S. Progressives, believe that regulation is often required to keep the processes of change and interaction open. Social Welfare Liberals believe that definite social and educational programs may be needed to advance the welfare of individuals for their personal as well as social betterment.

Social Change

For Liberals, the good society is a balanced one in which representatives of diverse interests interact within an agreed-on social, political, and economic institutional framework. The various interests use a common method to adjudicate disputes and to resolve conflicts. The balanced society is not static, however, but is continually changing as interests shift, coalesce, and form new constellations at the center of the social order. This concept of the "vital center" is important; it is the moderate, nonextremist perspective that is crucial in maintaining balance and preventing the society from being pulled off center.

Adversaries of Liberalism

Liberals challenged what they regarded as the coerciveness and repression of absolute monarchy and dogmatic churches. However, the adversaries of Liberalism have been the overtly totalitarian ideologies and regimes such as Nazism, Fascism, and Communism that condemn Liberalism as a rationale for economic selfishness, political indecisiveness, or moral relativeness. These ideologies offer a new absolutism based on the cult of the leader or on unquestioned doctrines.

While totalitarianism is an obvious threat to Liberalism, a more complicated issue is raised by the rise of a mass society, with mass media and a mass system of education. John Stuart Mill warned of the tendency of modern society to create homogeneous styles of life and standards of behavior that were intolerant of those who dissented from them. The industrial revolution, with its system of mass manufacturing, created a standardized material culture with products made for a mass market. Manufacturers wishing to sell to the largest market designed products for the tastes of the so-called average person. But appealing to what is "average" results in a leveling that pulls the extremes to the middle with the result that uniqueness is diminished. These same averaging or leveling trends similarly emerged in the social, intellectual, political, and educational spheres of society. The media—newspapers, the popular press, motion pictures, radio, and television—try to appeal to the largest possible audience. The result was not John Stuart Mill's competition in the marketplace of ideas but the creation of homogeneous persons inhabiting an homogeneous society.

In a mass society, institutionalized education, or schooling, also tended to diminish individualism and to create homogeneity. Liberal societies faced an educational dilemma of profound social and educational complexity—that of simultaneously cultivating excellence and equity. If progress resulted from open inquiry, invention, the testing of ideas, and innovation, then individual talent and potential needed to be encouraged and developed. At the same time, the individual in society needed access to education on a nondiscriminatory basis. Because of the tension between excellence and equity, educational policies in Liberal societies have alternated between these poles.

EDUCATIONAL IMPLICATIONS OF LIBERALISM

In this section, we will examine how the ideological concepts of Liberalism influence and shape education. The discussion focuses on such topics as popular education, educational policy, the need for a generally educated public, the nature of civic education, freedom in a Liberal society, and procedures in the school milieu.

Popular Education

In nations governed by Liberal political parties such as the United Kingdom, the United States, France, and Mexico, popular systems of education were established in the nineteenth century. These school systems turned the basic Liberal values into a set of pedagogical requirements and values. Liberals tended to value literacy, order, process, and utility, and the schools that they established emphasized these same values. Liberals such as Horace Mann believed that a representative government required literate citizens who knew and respected the laws and processes of the commonwealth. When schools were established under Liberal auspices, civic attitudes, values, and loyalties often replaced the older religious values that had dominated schools in earlier times. British, American, and French Liberals came to advocate publicly supported and controlled school systems as a necessary buttress of parliamentary institutions.

For Liberals such as Horace Mann and Henry Barnard in the United States, popular education was a necessary corollary of republican institutions. It was a means of social insurance against the ever-present danger that representative republican institutions could be subverted by demagogues and irresponsible mobs. French Liberals such as Guizot saw the extension of popular education—at least at the elementary level—as a means of preserving the status quo against socialism and anarchy.

In addition to the arguments that were cited by Liberals on the relationship of universal education to government, business interests saw organized education to be a means of training future generations to be industrious workers and efficient managers. Industrial intelligence could be diffused throughout the population through the schools. Thus, Liberals in Western Europe and in the United States could be counted among the friends of organized systems of education. While some Liberals were altruistic, others saw schools to be instruments of social control of unruly elements in society.

Educational Policy in a Liberal System

In a Liberal ideological system, especially one such as that of the United States, policy development and implementation are often slow and uneven. This is especially true if one considers two prescriptions of Liberalism, namely, (1) that power should be diffused through a system of checks and balances; and (2) the need to maintain a vital center, or sense of balance. Although U.S. education is constitutionally a state responsibility, educational policymaking is also done by the federal government and local school boards. In particular, the U.S. historical tradition supports locally controlled school policies. The process of making educational policies, then, is slow and uneven, depending on a variety of policy-making authorities. This diffusion of power protects schools from monolithically imposed policies and also from rapid reform.

In public education, various individuals, groups, and associations have agendas for policy formulation. These organizations include such diverse groups as the National Education Association, the American Federation of Teachers, parent–teacher associations, the National Association of Manufacturers, the American Legion, and many others. The result of these often conflicting educational agendas has been that policy tends to be centrist, not moving in radically different directions, as least in the public sector.

Development Policy and Liberalism

Holding an optimistic and progressive view of human nature, Liberals see human beings as possessing a capacity for rational and scientific inquiry. Liberals believe that societies—if at the necessary stage of development—can establish and maintain representative institutions. Indeed, such noteworthy Liberals as William Gladstone in the United Kingdom and Woodrow Wilson in the United States believed the establishment of representative institutions throughout the world was possible and desirable for human progress.

An important concept in the Liberal ideology is that of the stage of development of a particular society. Societies that have reached a stage of political, economic, and educational development are more likely to be successful in establishing representative institutions than those that are underdeveloped in these crucial areas. Extreme poverty, large-scale unemployment, illiteracy, inadequate health and sanitation services, and rigid class divisions are some of the symptoms of underdevelopment. The Liberal challenge is twofold: (1) to ensure that policies are designed and programs implemented that prevent developed societies from slipping backward into underdevelopment, and (2) to aid underdeveloped societies in becoming sufficiently developed so that they can establish representative institutions and parliamentary processes.[18]

In the areas of both internal (domestic) and external (international) development, education exercises a crucial role in providing the skills and knowledge that contribute to political and civic competency, social responsibility, and economic growth. Domestically, educational development is necessary to ensure that certain groups, because of race, ethnicity, or economic conditions, do not become underclasses alienated from mainstream institutional life.

In the Western perspective, programs of international education have emphasized development as well as the promotion of international understanding. Education is designed to increase literacy, introduce methods to increase agricultural productivity, and improve health and sanitation services. The anticipated result is a higher stage of development that will include representative institutions and political and social stability or balance.

The Existence of a Generally Educated Public

Liberal societies and governments have established systems of popular education designed to cultivate a generally educated public. While particular career, occupational, and professional training are also provided, schools at the primary level cultivate basic education, especially literacy, in the belief that the performance of responsibilities, such as voting in elections, requires a literate and generally educated citizenry. Secondary education continues the process and provides background into a range of subjects such as literature, history, mathematics, and the sciences. The assumption underlying general educational policies and programs is that citizens will be called on to make decisions in areas other than the specialties related to their occupations or professions. General education provides the knowledge base needed to make such decisions intelligently.

A portrait of John Stuart Mill (1806–1873), an English Liberal and Utilitarian, who advocated individual freedom and expression.

Still another argument for general education arises from the need to have educated persons who can be disinterested decision makers. John Stuart Mill believed that disinterested decision making was needed to maintain the sense of objectivity that Liberals see arising from the application of reason to the political, social, economic, or educational situation.

Liberals believe that an educated citizenry should have a general interest in the problems and issues of the society and also have a methodological commitment to the representative and parliamentary processes designed to resolve these issues. In addition to this general interest, individuals and groups have special interests. For example, teachers may have a special interest in the support given to schools but a general interest in trade or energy policies. In dealing with general interests, individuals can be disinterested (not having a special interest) in resolving them. On any given issue, a body of disinterested citizens can be expected to deal with the issue objectively.

Civic Education

In addition to general education, Liberalism emphasizes a particular kind of civic education that is specific to both the cognitive and affective development of future citizens. In the cognitive dimension, civic education seeks to develop knowledge of the institutions and structures related to government. This would include an historical perspective on the organization and development of these institutions and an analysis of their functions in contemporary society. For example, the civic education of a U.S. student would involve an examination of federal, state, and local government and of the executive, legislative, and judicial branches of government. Civic education also seeks to cultivate values that encourage a commitment to participate in the political process.

The affective dimension of civic education, according to Liberalism, is public accountability. All those who hold public office are expected not only to fulfill the requirements of the position but also to maintain the integrity of the process. Public service, though renewable, is temporary in that elected officials come from the public and return to it on completing their terms of office.

An important cognitive and attitudinal blending is found in the Liberal notion of civility. As indicated, Liberals tend to stress process or procedures both in politics and in education. They assume that individuals need to know what the process is, how it came to be, and how it works. Raising issues, then defining, discussing, and resolving them are to take place in a reasonable, nonviolent, procedural fashion in which the participants agree to the process, follow it, and exercise civility. For Liberals, civility means to have a respect for but not necessarily an agreement with the opinions of others and to follow the rules of orderly decision making. Obviously, Liberals in education would stress learning and playing by the rules.

View of the Past as "Freedom From"

In the Classical Liberal view of the past, liberty is defined as freedom from coercive restraint. For Locke, "life, liberty, and property" were individual rights that were to be protected from an arbitrary government. For Utilitarian Liberals such as John Stuart Mill, freedom meant the free and open exchange of ideas. The freedom of speech, press, and assembly meant the absence of restraint by institutional authorities whether in the government or the church.

Educational policies derived from Liberalism give a special emphasis to academic freedom, or the freedom to teach and to learn. Teachers, at least in Liberal theory, are expected to exercise this freedom within the area of their particular competency and specialization. We will examine the impact of academic freedom in three areas: (1) as an expression of the negative freedom from institutional coercion, (2) as an expression of institutional freedom, and (3) as a component of methodological efficacy.

Freedom from Institutional Coercion

As a general principle of Liberalism, originating with Classical Liberal doctrines but also carried into Reformist Liberalism, academic freedom is intended to protect the freedom of teachers and students from coercive and repressive agents of government, churches, or special interests. Academic freedom, as an extension of the right to free speech or freedom of information, seeks to keep education free of censorship, which may limit inquiry. Within an educational institution or school, academic freedom is also protection against school boards, trustees, or administrators who may attempt to interfere with freedom of expression and inquiry.

The Liberal guarantees of academic freedom exist within a framework that defines its exercise. Teachers are free to teach in the areas of their competencies. For example, a teacher of biology has the right to teach that subject matter. The privileges of academic freedom, however, do not extend to that teacher's right to make pronouncements, as an authority, on other subjects. To fail to recognize the limits of one's competency is to infringe on the rights of other teachers.

Students have the right to learn. Teachers violate that right when they fail to maintain a classroom environment conducive to learning. Students who are disruptive equally interfere with the right of teachers to teach and students to learn.

Academic Freedom As an Expression
of Institutional Freedom

Within the Liberal context, schools as institutions are to be free of overt politicization. They are not to function as ideological voices of particular political parties, platforms, or programs. The rationale for this separation from explicit politicization is that such identification interferes with freedom of inquiry.

The distinction between schools as separate from explicit political ideology and yet reflective of and encouraging of attitudes, values, and methods supportive of a Liberal civic outlook is a difficult and delicate one. In the Liberal orientation, the methodology associated with decision making in the broader society is also compatible with academic freedom within the school. Critics, however, allege that the school in a liberal democracy is a servant of the reigning political ideology.

Academic Freedom As a Component of Methodological Efficacy

Academic freedom, as freedom of inquiry and expression, has a range of educational implications. It means that students can investigate controversial issues. Such investigation is regarded as a necessary condition in problem solving and the application of inquiry methods to instruction. It is also freedom to do research and to use the results of that research in teaching. Freedom of inquiry in teaching, learning, and research requires that there are no preconceptions that cannot be altered nor are there areas not open to investigation.

Procedures in the School Milieu

The Liberal conception that life should be lived, especially socially and politically, according to well-defined and mutually accepted procedures has a particular relevance for the school milieu, or the hidden curriculum. Both early childhood education and primary education are likely to establish and reinforce procedural habits such as respecting other children's property and of taking turns and waiting to use certain items or playthings.

The concept that the group should establish its own rules of governance and conduct is also a Liberal derivation found in some classrooms. The assumption underlying this kind of discipline is that such rules will be more readily accepted and adhered to by members of the group if they arise out of common consent and consensus. In U.S. secondary schools, a wide variety of student organizations, clubs, and associations exist, each having its own elected officers who conduct meetings according to parliamentary processes.

It is anticipated that these procedural behaviors, learned by participating in the school milieu, will become habitualized standards of behavior that will be transferred to the larger out-of-school society. Membership in school clubs or associations provides experience and may lead to the skill of working well with others, which can contribute to success in business. Participation in school activities is expected to reinforce a civic outlook that sees voting in elections, running for office, and serving on juries as an ethical responsibility. These predispositions arising in the school milieu are also designed to create an attitude that disputes and conflicts should be settled according to nonviolent and fair procedures.

In all of these examples of student self-government and of discipline arising from the consent of the governed, there is an implicit understanding that the school is an essential social institution. Although some school procedures may be altered or reformed, the school's essential functioning role in a balanced society remains and continues.

CONCLUSION

Liberalism is an ideology that has had a pronounced impact on Western thought and institutions. It has carried into the modern era its emphasis on human rationality, progress, and science. These concepts have been infused into the U.S. school system as has the stress on individualism and private property.

DISCUSSION QUESTIONS

1. How did John Locke's concepts of unalienable rights and the contract theory of government shape Liberal ideology?

2. How did Locke's theory challenge the sociopolitical position of hereditary classes, and how did it require a change in the processes of civic education?

3. How would a Liberal justify taxation for the support of public schools?

4. What are the educational implications of the Liberal concepts of rationality, science, and progress?

5. Why is a moderate point of view, based on maintaining the vital center, important to the Liberal concept of society? How should the school function in such a social order?

6. Analyze the role of the disinterested person in formulating public policy and in decision making.

7. Analyze academic freedom within the context of Liberal ideology.

8. Analyze how the school milieu can reinforce certain ideological attitudes and values.

9. Examine the tensions that exist between excellence and equity in the Liberal social and educational context.

10. Why do Liberals place such an emphasis on building consensus and following procedures?

11. Identify and analyze the ideological tensions that exist in Liberalism.

12. How would Liberals react to the debates regarding multiculturalism?

INQUIRY PROJECTS

- Read Locke's *Essay Concerning Human Understanding* and write a review that comments on its educational implications.
- Read the Declaration of Independence. In a paper, identify the Lockean elements used by Jefferson and extrapolate the implications for civic education.
- In a survey of the members of the class, determine their motivations in seeking higher education. To what extent do these motives reflect Liberal economic concepts?
- Examine and analyze the textbooks and other materials used in the professional education courses at your college or university. Do you find evidence of a Liberal orientation in these books and materials?
- Create a clippings file of articles from newspapers and magazines that deals with issues in schools such as prayer, creationism, evolutionism, dress codes, and freedom of speech. Identify the Liberal position in these arguments.
- Read John Stuart Mill's *Autobiography* and in a paper identify the influence that shaped his Liberalism.
- Read and then prepare an analysis of Herbert Spencer's essay "What Knowledge Is of Most Worth?" in terms of the essential concepts of Liberalism.
- Prepare a research paper that analyzes Horace Mann's conception of representative government and common schools. Try to determine the relationship that Mann believed existed between these political and educational institutions.
- Examine recent reports and policy statements on educational reform and prepare an analysis of their treatments of equity and excellence.

FURTHER READINGS

Aaron, Richard I. *John Locke.* London: Clarendon Press, 1963.

Ackerman, Bruce. *Social Justice in the Liberal State.* New Haven: Yale University Press, 1980.

Donner, Wendy. *The Liberal Self: John Stuart Mill's Moral and Political Philosophy.* Ithaca, NY: Cornell University Press, 1991.

Garforth, Francis W., ed. *John Locke's Of the Conduct of the Understanding.* New York: Teachers College Press, Columbia University, 1966.

Garforth, Francis W., ed. *John Stuart Mill on Education.* New York: Teachers College Press, Columbia University, 1971.

Gay, Peter, ed. *John Locke on Education.* New York: Teachers College Press, Columbia University, 1964.

Gouinlock, James. *Excellence in Public Discourse: John Stuart Mill, John Dewey, and Social Intelligence.* New York: Teachers College Press, Columbia University, 1986.

Gutek, Gerald L. *American Education in a Global Society: Internationalizing Teacher Education.* New York: Longman, 1993.

Jackson, Julius. *A Guided Tour of John Stuart Mill's Utilitarianism.* Mountain View, CA: Mayfield, 1993.

Kahan, Alan S. *Aristocratic Liberalism: The Social and Political Thought of Jacob Burckhardt, John Stuart Mill, and Alexis de Tocqueville.* New York: Oxford University Press, 1992.

Kazamias, Andreas M., ed. *Herbert Spencer on Education.* New York: Teachers

College Press, Columbia University, 1966.

Kreml, William P. *Losing Balance: The De-Democratization of America.* Armonk, NY: M. E. Sharpe, 1991.

Kurer, Oskar. *John Stuart Mill: The Politics of Progress.* New York: Garland, 1991.

Massaro, Toni Marie. *Constitutional Literacy: A Core Curriculum for a Multicultural Nation.* Durham, NC: Duke University Press, 1993.

Mill, John Stuart. *Autobiography of John Stuart Mill.* New York: Columbia University Press, 1960.

Paringer, William A. *John Dewey and the Paradox of Liberal Reform.* Albany: State University of New York Press, 1990.

Paxton, Nancy L. *George Eliot and Herbert Spencer: Feminism, Evolutionism, and the Reconstruction of Gender.* Princeton, NJ: Princeton University Press, 1991.

Rawls, John. *A Theory of Justice.* Cambridge, MA: Harvard University Press, 1971.

Rawls, John. *Political Liberalism.* New York: Columbia University Press, 1993.

Strasser, Mark P. *The Moral Philosophy of John Stuart Mill: Toward Modifications of Contemporary Utilitarianism.* Wakefield, NH: Longwood Academic Press, 1991.

Taylor, Michael W. *Men Versus the State: Herbert Spencer and Late Victorian Individualism.* New York: Clarendon Press, 1992.

Yolton, John W. *John Locke and Education.* New York: Random House, 1971.

Zerilli, Linda M. G. *Signifying Women: Culture and Chaos in Rousseau, Burke, and Mill.* Ithaca, NY: Cornell University Press, 1994.

ENDNOTES

1. Richard I. Aaron, *John Locke* (London: Clarendon Press, 1963), p. 2; M. V. C. Jeffreys, *John Locke: Prophet of Common Sense* (London: Methuen, 1967), p. 21.

2. John Locke, *An Essay Concerning Human Understanding,* ed. Raymond Wilbur (New York: E. P. Dutton, 1947), pp. 8, 65, 106, 145, 253; also see Francis W. Garforth, ed. *John Locke's Of the Conduct of the Understanding* (New York: Teachers College Press, Columbia University, 1966).

3. John Locke, *Some Thoughts Concerning Education* (Cambridge: University Press, 1902), p. 419; for an analysis of Locke's educational ideas, see John W. Yolton, *John Locke and Education* (New York: Random House, 1971).

4. John Locke. *Two Treatises on Government,* 1690, from the 1823 edition of Locke's works published in London by Thomas Tegg and others; in *Communism, Fascism, and Democracy: The Theoretical Foundations,* ed. Carl Cohen (New York: Random House, 1972), p. 399.

5. Ibid., p. 402.

6. The essential economic elements in Liberalism are treated in J. Salwyn Shapiro, *Liberalism: Its Meaning and History* (New York: D. Van Nostrand, 1958), pp. 21–26, 32–38, 42–43.

7. James Mill, "Liberty of the Press," *Essays,* 22, as quoted in J. Salwyn Shapiro, *Liberalism and the Challenge of Fascism: Social Forces in England and France, 1815–1870* (New York: McGraw-Hill, 1949), p. 5.

8. For Mill's views on education, see Francis W. Garforth, ed., *John Stuart Mill on Education* (New York: Teachers College Press, Columbia University, 1971).

9. Andreas M. Kazamias, ed., *Herbert Spencer on Education* (New York: Teachers College Press, Columbia University, 1966), pp. 121–159.

10. For an analysis of Spencer's philosophy of science, see Valerie A. Haines, "Spencer's Philosophy of Science," *The British Journal of Sociology,* 43 (June 1992); 155–172.

11. A still useful interpretation of the impact of Darwinism on social theory is found in Richard Hofstadter, *Social Darwinism in American Thought* (Boston: Beacon Press, 1955).

12. R. S. Dreyer, "Take a Tip From Herbert Spencer," *Supervision,* 54 (May 1993): 22–23.

13. Walter Feinberg, "Dewey and Democracy at the Dawn of the Twenty-First Century," *Educational Theory,* 43 (spring 1993); 200–201.

14. D. J. Manning, *Liberalism* (New York: St. Martin's Press, 1976), pp. 20–23.

15. Toni Marie Massaro, *Constitutional Literacy: A Core Curriculum for a Multicultural Nation* (Durham, NC: Duke University Press, 1993).

16. For examples of the debate, see M. K. Asante, *The Afrocentric Idea* (Philadelphia: Temple University Press, 1987); Henry L. Gates. *Loose Canons: Notes on the Culture Wars* (New York: Oxford University Press, 1992); Dinesh D'Souza, *Illiberal Education: The Politics of Race and Sex on Campus* (New York: The Free Press, 1991); Arthur M. Schlesinger, Jr., *The Disuniting of America: Reflections on a Multicultural Society* (Knoxville, TN: Whittle Direct Books, 1991); James A. Banks, *Multiethnic Education: Theory and Practice* (Boston: Allyn and Bacon, 1994).

17. Massaro, *Constitutional Literacy,* p. 73.

18. Gerald L. Gutek, *American Education in a Global Society: Internationalizing Teacher Education* (New York: Longman, 1993), pp. 61–79.

▶ 12

Conservatism and Education

Chapter 12 examines the Conservative ideology and its educational implications. Conservatism is distinguished by its tendency to preserve established institutions and conditions. It emphasizes tradition as an integrating authority, advocates a hierarchical conception of society, and relies on the past as a source of guidance. It encourages a suspicion of social, political, economic, and educational change and innovation. In the sections that follow we will (1) examine the ideas of Edmund Burke as a source of Conservative principles, (2) analyze Conservativism's basic themes, (3) describe the features of the contemporary U.S. Neo-Conservative revival, and (4) consider the educational implications of Conservative ideology.

EDMUND BURKE: PROPONENT OF CULTURAL CIVILITY

Edmund Burke (1729–1797), a graduate of Trinity College in Dublin, was a distinguished British statesman and writer on political philosophy. Elected to the House of Commons in 1765, Burke became a leader of the Whig party. Opposing the royal policies that he believed were forcing the thirteen American colonies into rebellion, Burke urged conciliation. Although he supported moderate reform policies, Burke believed that traditional political, social, and religious institutions manifested the evolved wisdom of the human race.

In addition to his political career, Burke wrote on philosophical and political themes. His *Vindication of Natural Society* (1756) was a satire against political rationalism and religious skepticism. Burke's *Philosophical Enquiry into the Origin of Our Ideas of the Sublime and Beautiful* (1756) examined aesthetics

A portrait of Edmund Burke (1729–1797), English Conservative ideologist and statesman.

from a romanticist perspective. His antagonism toward the violence and excesses of the French Revolution was expressed in his *Reflections on the Revolution in France* (1790), which became a classic statement of Conservative ideology.

Burke, in *Reflections on the Revolution in France,* reacted against revolutionary change. Distrusting Locke's philosophical empiricism and revolutionary justification, Burke exalted the power of cultural tradition, the accumulated wisdom of the human race, as a force for social stability. Although he did not write on educational themes, Burke, by implication, saw education as an agency to transmit the cultural heritage to the young and hence preserve it through the generations.

For Burke, the cultural heritage or tradition was a repository of the time-tested achievements of humankind. He saw the social, political, religious, and educational institutions—the family, state, church, and school—as cultural products that had evolved over the centuries of human experience. Standards of civility and discourse, of ethics and values, were not the results of majority rule.[1] For Burke, these represented the conventional wisdom of the human race. An educational ideology derived from Burke would stress the need to cultivate in the young a sense of awe and respect for institutions. Education would involve the inculcation of traditional standards of behavior and civility in the young. Such an ideological orientation would be suspicious of change, seeing it as a threat to both civilization and civility.

The following tenets constitute Burke's major contributions to Conservative ideology: (1) institutions form a complex framework of customary practices and historically evolved rights and duties; (2) human behavior evolves within the conditioning influence of the institutional system, and it is a cultural inheritance to be transmitted from one generation to the next; (3) human culture and institutions represent a continuum of tested experience that should not be broken by untested innovation or revolutionary action; and (4) tradition is the repository of a collective social intelligence. To be educated according to these Burkean principles meant that the young were to be enculturated in the traditions of their parents, who in turn had been nurtured in the traditions of their parents. Thus, the heritage was passed on and kept alive.

Burke, who distrusted Locke's reliance on government by majorities, believed in decision making by an elite of well-educated persons, an aristocracy of culture and civility. He did not believe that the genuine interests of a nation and a people could be determined by taking polls or adding up numbers. Further, he feared that Liberalism would lead to a society of selfishness where decision making would fall to narrow special-interest groups. Burke believed that Conservative leadership and decision making should come from a public-spirited elite, who, steeped in tradition, would represent the enduring interests of the entire nation.

The assumption that every society should be governed by the elite is an important Conservative principle that has serious educational implications. Throughout history, the belief in rule by an elite has had many proponents, the most prominent of whom was Plato, who argued that the philosopher-kings, an aristocracy of intellectuals, should rule. Difference in human potentiality results from the social milieus into which people are born and reared; as a result, being a member of a "good family" and having a proper upbringing become important social credentials. A contemporary example of an elite governing class is that of the graduates of England's famous public schools (really private preparatory schools) such as Eton, Rugby, Winchester, and Harrow, who, after completing university studies at either Oxford or Cambridge, become the nation's ruling class. This British elite, generally deriving from the gentry, was, by birth and breeding, destined to rule. Their education in the classics, languages, and history, in addition to learning sportsmanship, was designed to make them the bearers of traditional outlooks and values.

Elitism in the Burkean sense rejected both Locke's and Rousseau's ideas of equality in the state of nature as fiction. If attempts were made to implement equality in society, the results would be a disastrous leveling or mob rule. The good society, in Burkean terms, recognized and prized uniqueness or differences. The better-educated, the more prudent, the more expert were to protect and guide the less-educated, the weaker, and the inexpert. Educationally, the Conservative society would prepare the culturally gifted to rule and prepare those of lesser ability to respect and follow their rule.

Burke's vision of society, like Plato's, was not one in which the ruled were suspicious of or tending to rebel against the rulers. Manifesting a great deal of paternalism, the society governed by Conservative ideological principles was like a family, where love and loyalty emanated from a respect for the past and engulfed all in a single community. This community was deeply rooted in a sense of identity, membership, and duty. Burke's expression of Conservatism moved the Conservative attitude from a sentiment or feeling to the level of a consciously articulated ideology.

CONSERVATISM'S BASIC THEMES

In the following section, we examine some of the basic Conservative themes and indicate their educational implications. Among these themes are the impact of the past, the role of tradition, the organic society, the hierarchical principle, social change, human nature, and the fear of alienation.

Conservatism and the Past

For Conservatives, the past is the source of the traditions that shape social institutions and human relationships. From the past, people acquire a sense of cultural identity and belonging as members of a distinct community, a nation, that is rooted in a given place at a particular time in history. A moment in human history, a person's present, is not transitory but rather is part of a continuum that binds the past and the future. From the past, a people, a particular society, inherits a collective wisdom based on lessons learned over time.

The Conservative reverence for the past and the historic sense is to be cultivated through education. Today, the incessant mobility and social change associated with modern life has produced a sense of rootlessness in which people find themselves without a sense of place or belonging. Conservatives argue that education should create a sense of cultural identity in the young by emphasizing a literature and a history that build connections with a great and vital past. Language, literature, and history should celebrate the achievements of the past, the major events in the collective life of the group, and the heroes and heroines who best exemplify the group's values and aspirations. Indeed, when such a heritage and its values are reinforced by religious observance and ritual, they are encased in dramatic form in the psyches of the young.

The Role of Tradition

Closely related to the Conservative interpretation of the past is the importance of tradition in maintaining social stability and continuity from one generation to the next. Tradition represents the funded and collective experience of the human group, especially within a particular cultural context. Through enculturation, reinforced by schooling, the individual becomes identified with and part of the group. Traditional values, representing the collective experience of the group, are a means of containing the selfishness, egotism, and irrationality of the individual.

The Organic Society

For Conservatives, society is an organism in which social classes and members function for the good of the whole. An organic society is held together by the common cultural threads of language, nationality, tradition, and custom.

An example of an organic society is provided by Plato, who, in *The Republic*, described a perfectly balanced society that functioned like a living organism. The ruling intellectual elite, the philosopher-kings, functioned as the head or mind of the society; the military defenders, a caste of soldiers, defended the society much like the arms and legs defend the body; the workers who provided the food and services needed to maintain the society were like the bodily organs that ingest food and provide nutrition. Each of the social castes—philosopher-kings, defenders, and workers—functions for the good of the entire society. Within this organic society, the community welfare is the paramount goal rather than special interests specific to each class. Like Plato's ideal republic, the organic society is structured hierarchically.

The Hierarchical Principle

The principle of the hierarchy operates throughout the Conservative ideology. Society, when properly functioning, is organized hierarchically, with members arranged in a graded or ranked order, with appropriate superordination and subordination. While they may agree that the principle of social rationality is an hierarchical arrangement, Conservatives may disagree as to the basis of determining ranking. For example, according to monarchical principles, society was properly organized in a flow of authority downward from God, to the king, to the aristocracy of birth, to the mass of population, the commoners. In Plato's republic, society is still organized hierarchically but the principle of identifying and ranking social classes is that of intellectual ability. The hierarchical principle rests on the assumption that human beings are unequal in some way—in capacity, in abilities, or in breeding. According to their character or characteristics, people are assigned to different classes, categories, or even castes.

The principle of the hierarchy leads to the educational corollary of appropriate education according to capacity or social rank. In a monarchical society, where social ranks and positions are ascribed, what constitutes an appropriate education can be clearly described and prescribed. For example, the education appropriate to a prince is that which prepares him to be a king; the education appropriate to an aristocrat is that which contributes to governance of estates, military skill, and court etiquette.

In Plato's republic, the ruling philosopher-kings receive an extended education that cultivates their capacity for intellectual abstraction through the study of logic, mathematics, and philosophy. The auxiliaries, the military protectors of the society, those who exhibit will and courage as their outstanding characteristics, receive training in military strategy, gymnastics, and the heroic ethic. The workers, tradespeople, and farmers who satisfy the republic's economic needs are given training appropriate to their abilities and career destinations. In Plato's model of society, and its more modern variations, society is regarded as a social organism in which each part or member functions for the good of the whole. In the hierarchical society, with its appropriate form of education, the individual acquires social significance and meaning through position in a rank or grade.

Conservatism and Change

The Conservative outlook emphasizes a preference for maintaining historically evolved institutions, for relying on tradition as a source of authority, and, if not a resistance to change, then a cautious and moderate disposition toward it.[2] The tendency to preserve the status quo and social stasis rests on the view that society, a product of long historical evolution, embodies the accumulated wisdom of the past. Such an inheritance should not be jeopardized by rapid or untested innovation. Such change is likely to bring about confusion and disequilibrium rather than true progress.[3] While suspicious of innovation, Conservatives are willing to accommodate to those changes that can be integrated into the cultural heritage. Leadership and policy in the Conservative perspective are designed to integrate the new element into existing patterns without jeopardizing the integrity of traditional institutions and behavior. Conservatives prefer change that is incremental—based on a small element that can be added gradually to the larger, ongoing tradition and to the community. They reject utopian schemes to reconstruct totally the life and structure of an entire society as well as revolutionary actions that would violently overturn the status quo. Utopian social engineering and revolutionary action do violence to the principle of historical continuity, which is orderly, gradual, and peaceful. Conservatives argue that, rather than bringing about a better life, the French Revolution brought about the despotism of Napoleon and that the Bolshevik Revolution brought about the totalitarianism of Lenin and Stalin.

It is obvious that schools that function according to a Conservative ideology would not be centers of social change or cultural reconstruction. Rather, their foremost goal would be to cultivate a social stasis and continuity. Conservative educators seek to preserve the traditional curriculum and would be suspicious of educational innovations. They would use the history of education to illustrate the fleeting insignificance of many highly publicized educational innovations such as team-teaching, competency-based learning, the discovery method, the "new mathematics," collaborative learning, and whole language reading. What persists over time, they would argue, are the essential skills and subjects, especially those that exemplify cultural roots, such as literature and history.

Despite their reservations about educational innovations, Conservatives recognize that from time to time certain mechanical or technological changes occur that have an impact on culture and society. When such an innovation occurs, it is important that it is linked to and connected with the heritage so that it is not socially or culturally disruptive. An example of such a technological innovation is the computer. Conservatives would see computers as an instrument to make instruction in the traditional subjects efficient rather than to transform or radically alter the curriculum.

The Conservative View of Human Nature

Conservatives assume that human beings are sinful creatures possessed of egotistical and selfish instincts. Unless curbed by long-standing traditions and social institutions, these instincts will lead to violence, anarchy, or exploitation. By following the custom and tradition of a stable institutional order, human impulses can be given order and balance.

Conservatives would find the open classroom and Rousseauean child permissiveness to be occasions that invite educational disorder. Schools are to be places of institutionalized order and discipline. Like other social institutions, schools are to provide checks on human beings' tendencies to disorder.

The Conservative Fear of Alienation

Conservatives regard community as coming from historically evolved institutions and the integration of individuals in such institutions as the family, church, and school. The church, especially established churches that are intertwined in the culture, promote interpretive moral and ethical values in a religiously charged context. The family is the setting in which traditional values are transmitted in an intimate and personal way from the old to the young. The school, as a social agency, builds on and extends familial and religious values. These primary institutions—family, church, and school—are encouraged by the state to transmit the traditional core of knowledge and value so that the society and its institutions can be perpetuated and protected against change that would weaken or jeopardize cultural and social stability.

Conservatives contend that the Liberal emphasis on individualism will lead to an atomistic society in which people will act on their self-interests without regard to historically evolved cultural traditions. Just as undesirable to the Conservative is the mass society with its mass culture and mass-produced tastes that result in social leveling rather than in a hierarchy which recognizes quality, good taste, and talent.

CONSERVATISM AND SCHOOLING

In the next section, we will examine Conservatism and schooling in terms of the role of the school, the nature of the curriculum, and the role of the teacher.

The School

The school, in the Conservative ideology, is a repository of cultural values. It is an agency for transmitting the cultural heritage and values from the mature to the culturally immature, thus preserving them for future generations. The school's role is to unite the individual with the heritage and to instill a sense of belonging to the group whose traditions are manifested in the institution.

In addition to its general role as an agency for transmitting and perpetuating the cultural heritage, the school also aids other institutions by identifying the future elite and providing the education appropriate to its destiny as a leadership group. The education of a leadership elite can take place either through special schools established solely for the task, or by tracking or streaming, which places those who display leadership potential in special classes within a comprehensive setting. Whatever the mode, there is an appropriate preparation for the elite. It should be noted that this leadership elite is to exhibit both character and intellectual acumen.

The Curriculum

For Conservatives, the curriculum transmits the general culture to all and also provides appropriate education to the various strata of the society. It includes the generally accepted basic skills found in most school programs—reading, writing, and arithmetic. In addition, loyalty to and membership in the community, often the nation-state, is developed by a selective use of the literature to exemplify significant cultural themes. History, too, is a core subject for providing a perspective into the evolution of the culture and its heritage. Fine arts, music, and dance are also used to expose students to the cultural heritage. Defined and prescribed cultural values are used to shape behavior or character to conform to traditional norms or to national character. Wherever possible, Conservatives prefer to integrate character formation or development within a religious context.

Secondary and higher education continues to cultivate intellectual discipline through the study of subjects such as the native language, classical and foreign languages, mathematics, history, literature, and science. Often, Conservative educators identify a core of prescribed studies designed for all students to ensure the uniform transmittal of the cultural heritage.

The Conservative Teacher

The teacher in the Conservative educational setting is an agent of transmitting the cultural heritage to children and youth so that they can incorporate it into their intellectual outlooks and characters. Such teachers should be people who cherish the cultural heritage, who know it well, and who reflect in their personalities and behavior the culture's traditional values. Like the Idealist teacher, they are character models that students can imitate. While they may use educational technology to transmit the tradition more effectively, Conservative teachers are not agents seeking to change or reconstruct society. Nor do such teachers encourage cultural alternatives and diversity. In a world that has grown increasingly unstable because of social and technological change, incessant mobility, and moral relativism, Conservative teachers use the school as a stabilizing agency. Their task is to maintain the cultural heritage as a repository of the enduring achievements of the human race by introducing it to the young so that they can absorb it and perpetuate it.

CONTEMPORARY NEO-CONSERVATIVE REVIVAL

Since the 1980s, the contemporary United States has experienced a strong revival of Neo-Conservatism in politics, economics, and education. The U.S. Neo-Conservative movement is complex since it brings together some rather diverse strands that while related are not truly interwoven into one ideological fabric. In the following section, we analyze the following strands: (1) a need to reconnect with a particular version of the cultural heritage; (2) Classical Liberal economic theory; (3) religious fundamentalism; and (4) Essentialist and Perennialist educational themes.

A Version of the Cultural Heritage

In the discussion of general Conservative principles, it was asserted that Conservatives find authority in the past, in the traditions of the cultural heritage. U.S. Neo-Conservatives are no exception. They tend to view the past as the glorious creation of a special and exceptional American identity. For them, the American heritage represents the creating of a special people who conquered a wilderness and established a republic governed by law and civility. It should be noted that the tendency to create a particular version of the past is not unique to Conservatives but is true of other ideologies.

Although Neo-Conservatives are likely to recognize the historical realities of cultural pluralism associated with an immigrant nation such as the United States, they tend to see a distinct U.S. culture formed by a special past. For them, government arose from covenant, represented by the Constitution, which they insist rested on essential Judeo-Christian principles. For them, the common law, based on the Anglo-American juridical heritage, guarantees order, stability, freedom, and the right to hold property.

Neo-Conservatives hold that a profound need exists, especially in a dynamic technological society, to maintain a stable cultural core. They locate the U.S. cultural core in the tradition of Western civilization, particularly in its Anglo-Saxon, English-language, common-law precedents that were transferred to the new world. The essential educational core is to be transmitted by the schools.

Classical Liberal Economics

Although identifying themselves as Conservatives, many U.S. Neo-Conservatives are deeply committed to Classical Liberal economic theories of an open market, free trade, supply and demand, competitiveness, and the privatization of social and educational services. Some subscribe to a revived Social Darwinist ethic which asserts that competition in an unfettered marketplace will encourage the most industrious and able individuals to achieve and produce without having to carry the less productive on their economic shoulders.

U.S. Neo-Conservatism has little of the European sense of paternalism about it. For U.S. Neo-Conservatives, paternalism keeps one group in childlike dependence on another. Let all compete and ensure that competition is not interfered with by well-meaning but misguided Liberal reformers whose social welfare schemes limit the free play of competition.

For Neo-Conservatives, modern welfare state Liberals have interfered with the natural economic processes. Bureaucratic regulations have slowed the engines of U.S. industry, making them unproductive in the face of foreign competition. A sluggish school system that has downgraded basic skills and essential subject matter has replaced hard work and discipline with permissiveness and educational fadism. Rather than preparing an innovative and productive work force, the public school system, often in the hands of misguided Liberals and bureaucratic educationists, has miseducated students. In place of the virtually monopolistic public school system, educational freedom of choice, through a voucher plan, will permit parents and students to choose the kinds of schools that serve their needs. In a competitive educational arena, the most effective and efficient schools could be identified from those that are mediocre. These effective schools would attract academically inclined and motivated students. The voucher system, a form of educational privatization, would make schooling an arena of challenging competition.

Religious Fundamentalism

Following the general tendency historically true of Conservatism, U.S. Neo-Conservatives see supernatural and religious principles undergirding social and educational institutions. For them, many issues, such as the abortion debate over the "right to life" versus "freedom of choice," are essentially religiously grounded moral issues. Family values and women's role in society are also defined in strongly religious terms that define the family as a nuclear unit in which husband and wife have a continuous monogamous relationship. Women tend to be defined as homemakers, child rearers, and caregivers; men as the primary breadwinner, the chief wage earner. Despite the separation of church and state, Neo-Conservatives see themselves struggling to restore a past vitalized by religious principles and meanings.

Neo-Essentialism and Neo-Perennialism

For many Neo-Conservatives, U.S. public schooling has been moving in the wrong direction. They believe that Dewey's Pragmatism, Progressive education, and secular humanism are philosophies and theories that have contributed to the schools' miseducative problems. These philosophies and theories have brought about a decline of academic standards, an increase of indiscipline and incivility in both schools and society, an erosion of traditional ethical values, and a decline in U.S. economic productivity. To remedy these perceived defects, Neo-Conservatives have called for educational reforms. Although the theories of Perennialism and Essentialism are discussed in Chapters 17 and 18, we will treat them briefly here in relationship to the Neo-Conservative educational agenda.

Many of the reforms of the 1980s that were stimulated by *A Nation at Risk* were designed to correct what Neo-Conservatives regarded as declining academic skills and subjects. Similar to Idealists and Realists, they argue that schools have a primary function: to foster basic skills and competency in traditional academic subjects, namely, mathematics, science, language, and history. To return to fundamental skills and subjects, the curricular residues of Liberalism and Progressivism need to be removed. For example, they challenge the Liberal concept that the school is a multifunctional community service institution. Multifunctionalism, Neo-Conservatives assert, weakens the schools' primary role.

Neo-Conservatives, especially those inclined toward Perennialism, see the schools as transmitting a knowledge and value core derived from the Western cultural experience. They see the classical Greco-Roman, Medieval, Renaissance, Reformation, and Enlightenment eras as presenting a needed cultural frame of reference that orients the young to the cultural heritage. Within this framework are the languages, literatures, history, and arts that were developed in Western civilization. Encased within the larger Western heritage is the American experience in which European settlement is highlighted. Neo-Conservatives resist the more extensive multicultural interpretation which would also include the cultural contributions of Asians and Africans. Also, for many Neo-Conservatives, the issue of the language of instruction in the schools is highly significant. Some would end bilingual and bicultural programs, claiming they erode an English-language-based cultural core.

Neo-Conservatives, similar to Essentialists, also argue that schools are tied to the country's economic growth and productivity. Using studies that compare the academic achievements of U.S. students in mathematics and science with those of other countries, Neo-Conservatives claim that U.S. productivity has been declining in the face of foreign competition. Japan is usually identified as the chief competitor; it is claimed that Japanese students are superior to U.S. students in the key subjects of mathematics and science. Neo-Conservatives have engineered reforms in the state legislatures to mandate increased requirements in mathematics and science.

It is interesting to note that the Neo-Conservative agenda in education has included both Perennialist and Essentialist arguments. From Perennialism it takes the position that schools must identify and transmit a stable cultural core that links generations in an inherited tradition. From the Essentialist position, it argues that the efficient and effective teaching of key skills and subjects has a positive impact on economic productivity.

Neo-Conservatives decry what they perceive to be declining standards of morality and civility in society. The failure of schools to impart a stable cultural core and universal ethical standards to the young has resulted in violence, immorality, and mediocrity which are all symptomatic of cultural rootlessness. Further, the failure of schools to hold up worthy personal models that young people can emulate further compounds the moral malaise besetting a relativist society. Some Neo-Conservatives, especially those who identify with religious orthodoxy and fundamentalism, look to a revival of traditional religious values to remedy what they see as moral slippage. They advocate prayer in the schools, religious observances, and religious education. Other Neo-Conservatives see moral and ethical decline to be the result of cultural relativism and situational ethics in education. For them, the remedy is to turn to the Western heritage, especially those aspects of it which assert universal, eternal truths and values.

CONCLUSION

Arising as a reaction to revolutionary social change, Conservatism moved from an attitude or outlook to a fully articulated ideology. Stressing continuity rather than change, it emphasizes the power of the cultural tradition to shape knowledge, character, and values. Seeing human beings as unequal in abilities and capacity, Conservatism views the good society as one that is organized hierarchically. Education, based on the Conservative ideology, is primarily a process of cultural transmission and preservation. Indeed, it is part of the cultural continuum that exists between the generations. Neo-Conservatives in the United States endorse these cultural principles in their educational agenda.

DISCUSSION QUESTIONS

1. Identify the Conservative principles endorsed by Edmund Burke and examine the kind of society and school that would result from their implementation.

2. Are Burke's principles relevant to modern U.S. society?

3. Identify and analyze examples of elitism that you have observed in your educational experience.

4. What are the educational implications of the Conservative view of the past?

5. How does tradition function as a means of controlling individual egotism and self-ishness?

6. Describe the functions of a hierarchy. Can you identify contemporary institutions that function hierarchically? What education is appropriate for their members?

7. What is the Conservative view of change? According to this perspective, what is the proper relationship between technological innovation and society?

8. Describe the sense of alienation that is often ascribed to modern mass society. Is Conservatism a practical alternative?

9. Using the Conservative ideological perspective, analyze the role of the school, the curriculum, and the teacher.

10. Analyze the revival of contemporary Neo-Conservativism in the United States. What groups are likely to embrace the Neo-Conservative educational agenda?

11. What are the key elements used by Neo-Conservatives to critique U.S. public schools?

INQUIRY PROJECTS

- Write a review of Edmund Burke's *Reflections on the Revolution in France*. Include a section that discusses the work's educational implications.
- Begin and maintain a clippings file of newspaper and magazine articles that uses the Neo-Conservative critique of education and schooling. Analyze the general arguments used in these articles.
- Prepare a rescarch paper that examines the education of an elite such as the graduates of the British "public school" or prestigious preparatory schools in the United States.
- Write a short story or play that describes the roles of people living in a fictional organic society.
- Organize a debate in which members of the class argue for either the Liberal or Conservative ideology.
- Develop a character sketch of a person who would be inclined to Conservatism.
- Prepare a sketch of the Conservative teacher as a role model. Also, include a section on the method of instruction that this teacher would use.
- Prepare a paper that analyzes the ideas of U.S. Conservatives such as Russell Kirk, William F. Buckley, Jr., or T. S. Eliot, with special emphasis on education.

FURTHER READINGS

Abbott, Pamela, and Claire Wallace. *The Family and the New Right*. London and Boulder, CO: Pluto Press, 1992.

Barry, Norman. *The New Right*. London and New York: Croom Helm in association with Methuen, 1987.

Boston, Thomas D. *Race, Class, and Conservativism*. London: Unwin Hyman, 1988.

Burke, Edmund. *Reflections on the Revolution in France*. New York: Liberal Arts Press, 1955.

Bredvold, Louis I., and Ralph G. Ross. *The Philosophy of Edmund Burke: A Selection from His Speeches and Writings.* Ann Arbor: University of Michigan Press, 1960.

Buckley, William F., Jr., ed. *American Conservative Thought in the Twentieth Century.* Indianapolis: Bobbs-Merrill, 1970.

Chapman, Gerald W. *Edmund Burke: The Practical Imagination.* Cambridge, MA: Harvard University Press, 1967.

Cooper, Barry, Allan Kornberg, and William Mishler, eds. *The Resurgence of Conservatism in Anglo-American Democracies.* Durham, NC: Duke University Press, 1988.

DeMuth, Christopher, and William Kristol, eds. *The Neoconservative Imagination: Essays in Honor of Irving Kristol.* Washington, DC: AEI Press, 1995.

Devigne, Robert. *Recasting Conservatism: Oakeshott, Strauss, and the Response to Postmodernism.* New Haven: Yale University Press, 1994.

Eliot, T. S. *Notes Towards the Definition of Culture.* New York: Harcourt, Brace, 1949.

Eliot, T. S. *The Idea of a Christian Society.* New York: Harcourt, Brace, 1940.

Frohnen, Bruce. *Virtue and the Promise of Conservatism: The Legacy of Burke and Tocqueville.* Lawrence, KA: University Press of Kansas, 1993.

Gottfried, Paul. *The Conservative Movement.* New York: Twayne Publishers, 1993.

Honderich, Ted. *Conservatism.* Boulder, CO: Westview Press, 1991.

King, Desmond S. *The New Right: Politics, Markets and Citizenship.* Chicago: Dorsey Press, 1987.

Kirk, Russell. *Academic Freedom.* Chicago: Henry Regnery Co., 1995.

Kirk, Russell. *The Conservative Mind: From Burke to Santayana.* Chigago: Henry Regnery, 1953.

Kirk, Russell. *Edmund Burke: A Genius Reconsidered.* New York: Arlington House, 1967.

Kirk, Russell. *Prospects for Conservatives.* Washington, DC: Regnery, Gateway, 1989.

Kirk, Russell. *A Program for Conservatives.* Chicago: Henry Regnery Co., 1955.

Levitas, Ruth. *The Ideology of the New Right.* New York: Basil Blackwell, 1986.

Nisbet, Robert A. *Conservatism: Dream and Reality.* Minneapolis: University of Minnesota Press, 1986.

O'Sullivan, Noel. *Conservatism.* New York: St. Martin's Press, 1976.

Rossiter, Clinton. *Conservatism in America: The Thankless Persuasion.* New York: Random House, 1962.

Tannsjo, Torbjorn. *Conservatism for Our Time.* New York: Routledge, 1990.

Wilson, Glenn D. ed. *The Psychology of Conservatism.* New York: Academic Press, 1973.

ENDNOTES

1. Edmund Burke, *Writings and Speeches,* vol. VII (London: Bickers & Sons, 1865), pp. 93–95. Also see Edmund Burke, *Reflections on the Revolution in France* (New York: Liberal Arts Press, 1955).

2. Glenn D. Wilson, ed., *The Psychology of Conservatism* (New York: Academic Press, 1973), p. 13.

3. John J. Ray, "Conservatism, Authoritarianism, and Related Variables: A Review and Empirical Study," in Wilson, *Psychology of Conservatism,* p. 22.

► 13

Utopianism and Education

Throughout human history, individuals, ranging from mystics to social scientists, have speculated about creating the perfect society, or utopia, on earth. At times, attempts to establish the perfect society were made by religious groups who sought to create a "New Zion" or a "New Jerusalem." At other times, the quest for perfection was a complex communitarian design of interwoven social, political, economic, and educational strands. This was true of the plans of Robert Owen (1771–1858), Charles Fourier (1772–1837), and Étienne Cabet (1778–1856). In still other cases, utopia was described in instructional novels, as was done by Sir Thomas More in *Utopia* (1516), Edward Bellamy in *Looking Backward* (1888), and B. F. Skinner in *Walden Two* (1948).[1] Because the literature of Utopianism is so vast, we will concentrate on Utopian Socialism, sometimes called Communitarian Socialism.

In this chapter, we examine the utopian educator Robert Owen; the general framework of Utopian principles; the Utopian critique of Liberalism; human nature and Utopian Socialism; Utopianism and work; the family and women in utopia; and Utopians and education.

ROBERT OWEN: UTOPIAN EDUCATOR

Robert Owen, a British industrialist, turned to Utopian theorizing after a successful career as a self-made businessman. In both England and the United States, he tried to establish communities of perfect harmony and equality. Owen believed he could create these perfectly balanced and integrated communities through education rather than political organization or violent revolution. Because education was a powerful instrument in Owen's communitarian theory, we will analyze his views on it.

Robert Owen: Biographical Sketch

Robert Owen was born in 1771 in the Welsh town of Newtown in the United Kingdom.[2] Never restrained about his achievements, Owen reminisced that he was a precocious student who was popular with both peers and adults. The village schoolmaster, who recognized Owen's intellectual acumen, relied on him to tutor his slower classmates. From childhood onward, Owen exuded an uncritical and optimistic confidence in his ability to accomplish his goals. In 1781, Owen, aged ten, left Newtown to make his fortune in the industrial city of Manchester, where his first job was as an assistant in a drapery shop. In 1791, Owen established his own cotton-spinning mill and began his climb to prominence in Manchester's business community.

In 1799, Owen purchased David Dale's cotton mills in New Lanark, married Dale's daughter, Ann Caroline, and settled in New Lanark where he planned to create a model factory community that, while earning profits, would also be a humane place for its workers. When he arrived in New Lanark, Owen found a typical early nineteenth-century factory town with cotton mills dominating the bleak landscape. The mills employed entire families and a large number of under-nourished pauper and orphan children. Owen was especially depressed by the condition of the six-, seven-, and eight-year-old child laborers who worked from six in the morning until seven at night. New Lanark's social life was poverty ridden and depressing. Undaunted, the optimistic Owen planned to create a harmonious and happy society. It was his experience at New Lanark that would lead to his utopian vision of a better world.

Through social reform and education, Owen inaugurated his plan of community regeneration. Basing his reform on the environmentalist principle that he could shape human character, Owen stated:

> Any general character, from the best to the worst, from the most ignorant to the most enlightened, may be given to any community, even to the world at large, by the application of proper means; which means are to a great extent at the command and under the control of those who have influence in the affairs of men.[3]

From this theory of character formation, Owen developed his design of communitarian control. If the proper community is established and guided by the correct social science principles, then human character can be shaped in specific directions.

Owen began his community reform by winning the confidence of his employees, who were also New Lanark's citizens. He prohibited the sale of gin to reduce alcoholism. He improved the homes, streets, and sanitary conditions in the town. Fuel and clothing were sold from the company stores at reasonable prices. But Owen's most striking innovations were educational. Ending the practice of employing young children in the mills, Owen established a school where children between the ages of five and ten were taught without expense to their parents.

A portrait of Robert Owen (1771–1858), a Utopian or Communitarian Socialist, who sought to create a new world society based on communities of mutual cooperation and equality.

Education at New Lanark

An account of Owen's school at New Lanark was written by his eldest son, Robert Dale Owen, in *An Outline of the System of Education at New Lanark*.[4] Like Rousseau, Pestalozzi, and other naturalistic educators, Owen abolished external rewards and punishments, believing that they assumed children's responsibility for their actions. Owen, who claimed that a person's character was formed by environmental forces, denied that human beings were responsible for their behavior. External rewards and punishments, being of an artificial nature, created attitudes of superiority and inferiority in the children that stimulated mutual antagonism and egotistical competition. The only kinds of rewards and punishments that Owen recognized as educationally valuable came from the direct consequences of actions immediately experienced by the person.

Owen's basic instructional method used objects and involved simple, direct conversations about these objects. Like Rousseau, Owen believed that reading was begun too early and that children were taught to read materials that they did not understand. In teaching reading, his general principle was that children should read only what they could understand and explain in their own words. Writing should begin as soon as the student could copy a text. Arithmetic was taught by counting, adding, and subtracting concrete objects.

Under one heading, Owen integrated natural science, geography, and ancient and modern history. It was important, Owen observed, that the generalizations that explained natural, historical, and cultural phenomena be clear to students.

Owen, who was antagonistic to organized religion, believed that the churches supported traditionalism and impeded human progress. Denominational education, he argued, interjected bias, dogmatism, and contention into children's minds. Opposing the view that human beings are either innately evil or deprived at birth because of the effects of original sin, Owen argued that a person's inherently good characteristics need only the correct environment to come to perfection.

True to his belief that a genuine education was multidimensional, Owen also sought to cultivate the aesthetic side of a child's nature. Children, above age five, were taught singing and dancing.

Owen's experiment in social and educational reform at New Lanark made him famous, and a stream of visitors, many of them notables, visited his model community. Soon he was acclaimed the "benevolent Mr. Owen."

Owen's Social Theory

As his fame spread, Owen sought a larger location to play out his utopian drama. He believed he was specially destined to create a "New Moral World." In 1813, his *A New View of Society* proclaimed his social theories.

Growing increasingly critical of the individualistic, laissez-faire, competitive, capitalistic system, Owen envisioned a new world of self-governing communities in which all property would be owned in common by residents who lived in complete equality.

Although condemning early industrialism's exploitation, Owen saw economic growth and productivity as beneficial to humankind. A modernizer who believed that much of early industrialism's hardships were unnecessary, Owen argued that economic growth and abundance could be achieved without human suffering.

Believing that the "New Moral World" could be created by nonviolent means, Owen used education to disseminate information about his social system in order to stimulate the desire to live in the cooperative commonwealth. His communities of cooperation were to be educative environments that would shape the new society by forming new moral citizens.

Owen's theory of social change was based on a secular millennialism that convinced him that the "New Moral World" would be a product of historical inevitability. He believed that society could be changed by knowledge, education, and example. His conviction that the coming new society was inevitable caused him to neglect political organization and revolutionary tactics.

Holding that social reform could be achieved without violence of any kind, Owen believed that when people were educated to recognize the injustice of the old system, they would rush to replace it with his vision of the humane society. Because individuals were not responsible for their character and behavior, class hatred was irrational and irrelevant to achieving the new society.[5] Owen's rejection of class conflict and revolutionary violence led Marx and Engels to condemn Owenism as Utopian Socialism—a soft-headed approach to class struggle that deluded the working classes and detoured them from their true revolutionary role.

Owen believed that he had created a new social science that conformed to the laws governing the universe. Basically, Owen's social science statements derived from his central thesis that human character was based on social engineering and control. It was possible, therefore, to design a society that would be most conducive to human growth and development. Using the premise that the controlled environment would produce the desired kind of person, Owen was a thoroughgoing social engineer. He believed that the social scientist, armed with the laws of social organization and human development, could construct a planned environment in which its residents would be developed according to a societal blueprint or design. Because social engineering was a way of creating the new person who would inhabit the new moral order, Owen saw himself as the chief engineer who would create the "New Moral World."

Owen's educational theory rested on his central thesis that human character resulted from the experiences that people had as members of a social group, living within a particular societal mode. The reconstructing of the social environment would lead to a fundamental reshaping of human character. By living in a properly constituted community and by being educated in the laws of society, the new person would be a moral person who would end the chaos of the old, irrational, disintegrative social order. For Owen, education was broadly construed as the total process of enculturation, which included schooling. In the new society, schooling based on social science would aid in the creation of a new community.

Owen's theory of social science and social engineering was characterized by its originator's comprehensive goal of changing the entire social order. Owen had a view of the community, marriage, family life, education, schooling, international relations, economics, religion, law, and government. Owen's theory was, then, a multifaceted and comprehensive plan for reconstructing society that branched out into economic, social, political, and educational arenas.

Human Nature and Education

After examining Owen as a social and educational reformer, it is possible to consider three questions that illustrate his educational theory and suggest its relevance for contemporary educators. What was Owen's conception of human nature? What was his conception of education? What curriculum and methods were appropriate to Owenite education?

Owen believed that the social environment was crucial in forming human character. Human beings, he argued, could be given any kind of character. If the environment was competitive and based on private property, then those who were reared in it would be selfish and egotistical. If the community was one of cooperative sharing, then those who grew up in it would be communitarian in outlook and values.

Because he stressed the plasticity of human nature, education was a key instrument in Owen's theory of society. First of all, he saw education in its broadest terms as a form of enculturation by which humans were totally formed by community life. Such education was a form of upbringing according to prescribed communitarian standards. The lectures, concerts, living arrangements, newspapers, libraries, and working conditions of the community all worked to form human character.

Within the community, the school was to cultivate a communitarian commitment in the young. Here, children began their communitarian career as infants in community nurseries. Every child was the ward of the entire community, which was construed to be a large extended family. The child's first inclinations were to be molded into predispositions for sharing and cooperating with others. Once such communitarian predispositions or habits had been formed in early childhood, they were to be nurtured throughout adolescence, youth, and adulthood.

Opposing what he regarded as word-centered, artificial, or ornamental knowledge, Owen, like Rousseau, believed that instruction should begin with sensation of objects. Unlike the Naturalist educators, Owen believed that children were capable of amassing scientific and historical data about the world. His curriculum was full of varied subjects and skills that ranged from the natural sciences, to regional geography, to modern and ancient history. Owen also argued for practical vocational education, occupational training, and the learning of crafts and trades. The young inhabitants of his projected communities were to be educated, skillful producers and consumers. In many ways, Owen was an early advocate of career and consumer education.

In terms of curriculum and method, Owen was an iconoclast who sought to break down the old educational forms based on the learning of the catechism, rote memorization, and the study of classical languages. He also regarded aesthetic and social development to be as significant as cognitive development. Children should paint, sing, and dance. They should socialize as well as learn to read, write, and compute.

Significance and Relevance

To assess Owen's significance for modern education, he must be viewed as a theorist who saw that education was inextricably related to society. Not content to theorize, he wanted to use education to create a new society. Developing the very modern argument that model cities will create model men and women, Owen's designs for planned communities anticipated the strategies of contemporary urbanologists and community planners. Corrupt, degenerative, and polluted environments, Owen said, would create selfish, sick, and sluggish human beings. Clean, productive, and integrated social environments would, conversely, create harmoniously functioning members of society.

While Owen was a humanitarian, he was also a benevolent paternalist who invaded an individual's right of privacy. A pedagogical and social busybody, Owen's theory of the planned society interfered with the individual's freedom to choose his or her own lines of self-development and self-cultivation. He was a self-appointed prophet and social engineer who sought to shape people according to what he believed was in their best interests. In many respects, he was a forerunner of the mind shapers, the molders of public opinion, and even of the totalitarians who regarded humans as bits of clay to be molded as they saw fit. Although Owen could claim benevolence to be his guiding principle, there was also a deterministic denial of human freedom present in his theory.

As a visionary, Owen believed it possible to create a better world and better inhabitants within it. As a social and educational critic, his diagnosis pointed to needed reforms. Unfortunately, he also was a presumptuous man who believed that he could manage people by manipulating their environments.

UTOPIAN PRINCIPLES

Of the various ideologies, Utopianism relies most heavily on education. While the educational implications of Liberalism and Conservatism must be deduced from ideological doctrines, Utopians rely on education as the chief means to initiate peaceful social change.

Since the days of Plato's *Republic*, theorists have devised designs for the perfect society. Sir Thomas More's *Utopia* and Tommaso Campanella's *City of the Sun* were significant contributions to Utopian literature. Generally, Utopian theorizing has flourished during periods of profound social change. During such times, Utopian thinkers sought new social and community structures to replace those that were disintegrating.

Utopian theorists, especially the Utopian and Communitarian Socialists, were influenced by the ideas of the eighteenth-century Enlightenment. Foremost among these rationalistic concepts was the notion of progress, which promised a future that would be better than the past. Many Utopians believed in the existence of natural laws that could be extended to create a perfect life on earth. Indeed, the "heavenly city" need not remain a speculative vision, but could become a reality.

Like the religious millennialists, the Utopians often had a sense of missionary zeal that compelled them to convert others to the new and better society that was inevitably destined by history. Although imbued with a sense of historical inevitability, Utopians believed that the human race had to be prepared and educated for the new era. Human progress to perfection would not result from evolutionary accidents; it had to be planned by human intelligence and directed by social engineering into particular social models and modes.

While Liberals also believed in progress, they, unlike the Utopians, rejected the necessity of comprehensive social planning. According to Liberal ideology, progress would come as individuals competed with each other for economic and social gain. To the Utopians, the Liberal prescription of competition was wasteful, harmful, and exploitative, The Utopian view of human perfection directly opposed the Conservative attitude that saw human history as a great continuum in which the truly important elements of the cultural heritage remained constant.

For Utopians, the key to creating the perfect society was primarily educational. The leading Utopian theorists—Robert Owen and Charles Fourier—used education as an instrument of social reform and societal reconstruction. Eschewing political strategy and organization to accomplish their objectives, they relied on peaceful persuasion and education. Once the public had been informed of the beauties of Utopianism, they reasoned, all people would willingly embrace the design of the future.

The industrial revolution transformed much of the Western world from an agricultural to an industrial society and had a profound impact on the Utopian ideologists. This theme would later be used by the social and cultural reconstructionists as part of their educational theories.

The forces of industrialization and urbanization fundamentally altered the conditions of life in Western society during the nineteenth century. Industrialism's mass-production techniques, the factory system, and the assembly line brought long hours of repetitious work. The use of children and women as cheap laborers eroded the role of the family from a semiautonomous economic unit to one that depended almost entirely on a livelihood external to the home.

In many industrializing nations, the population of cities tripled and quadrupled, and the growth of these urban centers was unplanned and haphazard. Little or no provisions were made for meeting the sanitary, medical, and educational needs of the growing urban populations. Among the working classes, the premature death rate was high. The inherited values of traditional rural society had been torn asunder as people moved from farms to cities and experienced intense pyschological and sociological changes. The impact of these changes was often pervasive enough to produce personal, social, and psychological disintegration. To overcome personal and social alienation, the Utopians sought to design a community that achieved a perfect balance between agriculture and industry. Often invoking the metaphor of "the machine in a garden," Utopian ideologists saw human perfection arising from perfectly integrated communities.

Psychological alienation, a byproduct of unplanned urbanization and industrialization, was also induced by the pervasive economic changes that occurred because of alterations in production and consumption. The sense of craftsmanship, resulting from the artisan's handicraft production, had been severely eroded by the mass-production techniques that reduced the worker to an appendage of the machine. Although Marx later charged that an exploitative capitalism had alienated workers from their work, the Utopians earlier had condemned the human depersonalization that accompanied early industrialization.

The early formulation of the Utopian Socialist ideology came as a reaction to the conditions of early nineteenth-century life and work. Whereas the working conditions in the factory were burdensome, economic activities in the projected Utopian communities were to be pleasant, easy, and efficient. In place of the inchoate urban society, the Utopians emphasized the planned community where sanitary, educational, and recreational facilities were a part of the planning process.

Utopian theorists such as Owen, Fourier, and Cabet believed that the key to personal and social integration was the restoration of a sense of community. When translated into social policies, their ideology became a kind of Communitarian Socialism. Unlike the rural villages, in the city people lived lives that were disconnected and disjointed. Unlike the Conservatives who looked to the past and to tradition to provide a sense of community, the Utopian Socialists were not backward-looking antimodernists. Rather, the Utopian Socialists saw the genesis of a new community in the future. Owen, Fourier, and Cabet saw themselves as creating a new social science that would provide the ideological strategies to restore a sense of community. The Utopian critique required them to search for and identify the cause of human alienation. Once they knew the cause of alienation, they could remedy that deficiency. One obvious source of alienation came from the occupational changes that resulted from the industrial revolution. In the pre-industrial handicraft society, the artisan was closely connected to the tools and to the products that he or she created. Conversely, the productive conditions of an industrial society made workers distant from their finished products. Because of an exploitative capitalism, workers were not compensated fairly for their labor. Not only were workers alienated from their products but they were also isolated from the companionship of coworkers.

Based on their analysis of the causes of alienation, Utopians devised remedies that went far beyond reformist legislation. For them, the world had to be socially re-created. The proper remedy was to devise plans for organically integrated communities in which agricultural and industrial activities were balanced as were work and play.

THE UTOPIAN CRITIQUE OF LIBERALISM

Utopian Socialism essentially originated as a critique of the social, economic, and political institutions and conditions of the early nineteenth century. While the Utopian critics used various expressive forms, they commonly shared a distaste for the status quo and a desire to bring about change through communitarian and educational means. Some Utopians, such as Edward Bellamy, used the didactic novel to analyze the existing social order. Bellamy's *Looking Backward* criticized the existing society and outlined a plan for a new social order.[6] For others, the road to Utopianism involved a series of stages in which the theorist was first a social critic, then a social reformer on a limited scale, and finally a comprehensive social engineer, as was true of Robert Owen.

Utopian Socialists attacked Liberal ideology, capitalism, and individual ownership of private property. They sought to expose the weaknesses of the system of individual ownership of property and to devise plans to create a new society of common property and social equality.

Utopian Socialists rejected the Liberal ideological assertion that the individual was the basis of society. John Locke, a Liberal precursor, had asserted that individuals had rights prior to their membership in society. Locke also claimed that one of the most important human rights was private property. Liberals had asserted that progress resulted from competition in which fit individuals would rise to the summit of the social hierarchy.

In attacking the individualism of Liberalism, the Utopians offered an organic communitarian society in its place. Examples of such organic communitarian societies were Fourier's phalansteries and Owen's community of equality. In place of the Liberal idealization of the individual, Utopian Socialists stressed the group. Instead of competition, they stressed communal cooperation. Rather than seeing progress as a product of competitive individualism, Utopian Socialists saw perfection resulting from collaboration.

Utopian Socialists also attacked the Liberal support of capitalism. Under capitalism, they argued, wealth was unequally distributed. Modern industrialism produced greater wealth but concentrated it into fewer hands. Utopian Socialists argued that the Liberal reliance on supply and demand and on the free market system had produced alternating cycles of boom and bust, inflation and recession, employment and unemployment. Further, capitalism had created a bipolar, two-class society in which the rich and poor were pitted against each other in an inexorable struggle.[7]

What was weakest about the Liberal economic order, according to the Utopians, was the absence of social and economic planning. In a planned and egalitarian society, the regulated economy would be without alternating cycles of prosperity and depression. In such a society, integration would replace polarization and class hatred.

In educational terms, several strong implications for education can be found in the Utopian critique of Liberal ideology and of capitalist society. First, the Utopian critics regarded their writings on society as educational documents. Their broadsides, pamphlets, and books were designed to educate the general public by providing a critique of society. In the schools that they designed for their communities, the Utopian Socialists stressed the communal nature of society. Children would be reared from infancy onward to live in mutual association with each other. Competitive inclinations, which the Utopians believed were socially acquired by the old system of family life and schooling, would be discouraged.

While Liberals saw individuals locked in competition and classes locked in antagonism, the Utopian Socialists did not stress conflict. They believed, instead, that human beings had no real antagonism toward each other and that they could live in mutual association and friendship. Education, both informally and formally in the sense of schooling, would provide the needed mortar that would cement social relationships.

One of the major Utopian contributions to educational theory was that of developing a sense of social planning or social engineering. While many Liberals decried social engineering as jeopardizing freedom, the Utopian Socialists believed that planned communities were needed to integrate life. The Social Reconstructionist educators would borrow from Utopian social planning. For both the Utopian and social engineers, education was to develop an attitude of planning and foster a mentality that encouraged a planned society. Such a planned society was to have no class antagonism, no unemployed, no ill-housed people, and no underclass of undereducated persons. At root in the Utopian critique was a desire to re-create a holistic community.

HUMAN NATURE AND UTOPIAN SOCIALISM

The Utopian concept of human nature was inspired by the Enlightenment view of human beings as benevolent creatures. If people were not innately good in the Rousseauean sense, then they were at least neutral beings whose characters could be shaped. The Utopian view of human nature sharply contrasted with the Conservative view that saw humankind as perpetually weak, innately flawed, and tending to disorder.

It was crucial that the human being be socialized in the correct kind of social environment, reasoned the Utopians. Character formation in the new society could not be left to chance, according to Utopians such as Robert Owen. The community would be a perpetual school. Because human nature was malleable, it needed to be shaped by the correct environment, correct education, and correct pattern of social organization. What lurked in the Utopian desire to bring about the correct patterns for character formation was the possibility that "correctness" so construed would lead to total control of one's life and learning.

UTOPIANISM AND WORK

The Utopians, especially the Utopian Socialists and Communitarians, believed that new forms of production were needed to end the alienation associated with industrialization. Ideologically, the Utopians were challenging the Conservative and Liberal conception of work.

Conservatives often saw work as a consequence of a fallen and weak human nature. Using the old cliché "idleness is the devil's workshop," Conservatives believed that the human propensity to disorder and vice was checked partially by industriousness. In addition, the Conservatives believed in hierarchical social and occupational arrangements. Plato, in his ideal republic, followed a hierarchical pattern in which categories of work were assigned to classes that ranged from philosopher-kings at the top, to soldiers at the middle, down to workers at the bottom. In the Conservative ideological framework, some occupations and professions had a higher rank than others. Usually, the top rungs of the social hierarchy were occupied by professions that required little or no manual or physical work. The lowest rungs were occupied by manual or menial laborers.

Although Liberals recognized the existence of a class structure and of occupational rankings, they did not see such positions as a result of birth. Rather, Liberals saw socioeconomic rankings resulting from competition in which the most able secured merited positions over those who were less competent. In industrial society, the professional and business classes secured a higher rank through industry rather than birth.

The Utopians critiqued the ideological positions of both Conservatives and Liberals, and offered a conception of work based on their view of human nature. In the communitarian social design, work had a positive value that related to the community's well-being. To reduce the alienation of workers from both the products they create and their peers, the Utopians wanted to design productive forms that integrated individual efforts and products with the needs of the community. Indeed, education—including vocational training—was to emphasize both the positive and the liberating nature of work.

The machine was often related to the Utopian concept of work. Utopians generally did not see the machine as a threat to the worker; neither did they see the worker as an appendage in an assembly line of machines. Rather, Utopians such as Saint-Simon and Owen believed that machines could reduce the hours of labor, increase leisure, and produce abundance. It was necessary, however, that the role of the machine be regulated and planned so that human burdens were reduced rather than increased.

Generally, Utopians rejected the concepts of occupational hierarchy and social class structure. In the egalitarian society, individuals would choose the work that interested and suited them best. Their intrinsic interest in the kind of work that they were doing would blur the distinctions between work and play and create new productive forms that would unleash liberating and productive activity. Work in the Utopian community would be integrated with the good of the entire community and the needs of those who lived in that community. It would be for the welfare of the entire community rather than an individual's self-interest. Thus, Utopians believed that the onerous conditions of the factory system and its debilitating effects on individuals were unnecessary and harmful.

From the conception of meaningful work, the Utopian planned community took its vision. Stressing balance and abundance, the Utopian occupational vision integrated agricultural and industrial work and leisure and recreation in the metaphor of the "machine in the garden."[8]

Educationally, the younger as well as the older generation needed to be reeducated from the old conception of work as burdensome and isolated from the rest of life. Rather than a burden or a means by which dominant persons exploited subservient persons, work was to be a means of creative expression and cultivation. Once the creative impulses of work were liberated, the social and occupational distinctions would come tumbling down.

In the old social order, certain kinds of work were ascribed to certain people on the basis of their birth or their social class. In a Utopian community, children were to be exposed to the variety of work and occupations that were possible and needed. Each child would be introduced to a number of occupations so that his or her interests and aptitudes could be matched to the needs of the society. To avoid routine, a variety of work and play situations would be created so that each person might pursue many interests.

THE FAMILY AND WOMEN IN UTOPIA

The Utopian Socialist view of the role of the family was related to its conception of the community. Utopian Socialists believed that the nuclear family was socially divisive. Either they opposed the nuclear family arrangement, as did Owen, or believed that industrialization had weakened the nuclear family to the extent that a substitute had to be found for it. For some Utopians, the community itself became a family in which its members were united by sociality rather than by blood.

In the older society, the nuclear family encouraged economic and social competition and perpetuated the inequality of women. Because the family would no longer be the primary economic unit, the general Utopian strategy was to turn loyalty away from the family and toward the community.

Utopians generally believed that a change in family relationships would liberate women and children. Traditional marriage relationships and contracts, such as dowries and property requirements, based on economic considerations, placed women in an inferior and subservient relationship. In Utopia, marriage would be based on love, not on property.

Parental authority over children was also downplayed in many of the Utopian plans. Authority over children was located in the community rather than in the family. There were to be more opportunities for freer and open relationships between boys and girls in the schools of Utopia. Childhood would be a time for education and play and not for factory labor.[9]

Utopians generally advocated women's rights and equality that would end sexual or gender discrimination. The equal educational opportunity provided to women would encourage them to advance as far as they were able in the community. Because the nuclear family relationships would be altered by the provision of community services such as communal kitchens, dining rooms, and laundries, women would be freed from the burdens of child care, cooking, and housekeeping, which were gender specific in the old society.

Utopian theorists such as Fourier and Owen challenged the traditional conception of gender-specific education, which was based on the assumption that certain studies were appropriate to the role women played in society. In traditional society, women were destined to exercise the conventional roles of wife and mother. Education appropriate to such conventional sexual stereotyping included sewing, embroidery, domestic tasks, managing a household, cooking, and child care. For girls of the upper classes, it might also include subjects such as music, dancing, singing, and foreign languages. Utopians rebelled against gender-specific forms of education and viewed women's education in a broader communitarian context in which they were to be full participants in the community's life.

UTOPIANS AND EDUCATION

As indicated, Utopians relied on education rather than political organization or revolutionary activity to bring about the ideal society. Education, in the Utopian context, can be analyzed in three dimensions: (1) as persuasive propaganda; (2) as part of the process of communalization; and (3) as schooling, designed to bring the young into communal life.

Education as Persuasion

Utopians, such as Owen, Fourier, and others, tended to be true believers in their own social creed. Convinced that they possessed the truth, they often exhibited a sense of mission by which they sought to convince the unbeliever to accept the truth of their visions. Nonviolent but persuasive, Utopians relied heavily on providing unbelievers with information to convert them to the Utopian vision so that they joined the cause. For propagandizing, Utopians relied on informal education to make their messages known to an ever-widening audience. Owen and Fourier, for example, were tireless writers who produced volumes of essays, tracts, and polemics. In particular, Owen was a frequent lecturer and organizer of committees designed to advance his Utopian schemes.

As persuasion, education was designed to create a popular movement for joining the Utopian cause. In this journalist or lecture stage, Utopian education consisted of two elements. First, it provided a critique of the ills of society and how they might be remedied. Second, it presented a picture of life, often minutely detailed, in the new society.

Education as Communalization

As indicated, the Utopian analysis of modern industrial society identified alienation as a cause of personal and social disorganization. To overcome this sense of alienation, Utopians sought to create perfectly integrated communities. Like the ancient Greek *polis,* the new community would be a totally educative milieu. Work, leisure, art, and social and economic relationships would reinforce the sense of community and cultivate communitarian values. The total lifestyle would work to bring about the communalization of the inhabitants of the new Utopias.

Fourier's form of communal organization, the phalanstery, consisting of two thousand members, was organized into flexible groups that provided for production, education, and recreation. As well as having communal workshops, kitchens, and laundries, the phalanstery would also provide libraries, concert halls, and study rooms for its members.

As a means of communalization, education was broadly construed. There were to be many opportunities for adult and continuing education that would prepare the communitarians as producers and consumers of the community's goods and services. Education was a form of enculturation by which a person became a Utopian Socialist or communitarian.

Education as Schooling

Utopian theorists, especially Owen, emphasized the education of the young in institutes and schools. The child, they reasoned, held the key to the perpetuation of the new society. Rejecting older concepts of child depravity and inherited human weakness, Utopians believed that human nature is malleable. Owen and other Utopians advocated beginning children's education as early as possible. Young children, they reasoned, were free of the prejudices and biases of the old social order. If they were educated in community nurseries, they would be free from the contaminating ideas of those who had not yet been purged of the vices of the unreconstructed, older society. They could be shaped into the desired type of communitarian human being. Community nurseries and infant schools also performed a second function. They freed women from the burdens of childrearing and allowed them to have full equality with the male residents of Utopia.

According to Fourier, the family and the school in the old order were agencies used to criticize and correct children. Fourier intended to replace them with associative or group-centered education in which peer friends would correct negative behavior in the spirit of frank friendship.[10] Fourier's associative form of education involved mutual self-criticism and group correction, which was a form of character molding that brought about community social control and conformity.

Fourier believed that children, like adults, had many instincts and interests that should be encouraged rather than repressed. He envisioned a system of miniature workshops in which children could follow, test, and develop their instincts of industriousness. Fourier's associative education was also intended to further the children's complete development. First, the body and its senses were exercised and developed. Second, cooking, gardening, and other productive activities would cultivate the skills of making and managing products. Third, mental, moral, and spiritual development would incline the child to truth and justice.

Schooling in the Utopian designs of Owen, Fourier, and others rejected highly verbal learning, catechetical instruction, and the domination of the classical languages. Because of its concern for forming character, it often led to pioneering insights in early childhood education. It was intended, however, to bring about a communitarian like-mindedness, a pervading sense of conformity to group norms and rules. While immersion in the group diminished the personal fragmentation and alienation of industrial society, it also restricted the opportunities for individual initiative, divergence, and creativity.

CONCLUSION

The search for Utopia remains an elusive but fascinating one. Although it is nowhere to be found, an examination of the concept of Utopia and of Utopian literature raises many questions for educators. Among them are the following:

1. What are the ills of our society?
2. What remedies can we devise to correct social injustices and malfunctions?
3. Would the total implementation of our solutions create a Utopia?

The Utopian aversion to conflict distinguished them from Marxists and others who rooted their theories in economically based class antagonism, and caused them to articulate theories that stressed human mutuality and collaboration. While their critique of Liberal capitalism in some ways resembles those of Marxism and Critical Theory, conflict theory is absent in many Utopian arguments.

To the Marxists, who will be examined in the next chapter, Utopians often had the correct analysis of social problems but unrealistic and muddled solutions. For the Social Reconstructionist educators of the twentieth century, the Utopians developed an ideological critique that was a useful stage on the way to creating a reconstructed or new social order that promised humankind a better life on earth.

DISCUSSION QUESTIONS

1. Trace the evolution of Robert Owen's ideas on society and education.

2. Arrange a debate in which the contending sides argue Owen's proposition, "Any general character, from the best to the worst, from the most ignorant to the most enlightened, may be given to any community, even to the world at large, by the application of proper means; which means are to a great extent at the command and under the control of those who have influence in the affairs of men."

3. Identify and examine the major principles of Utopianism.

4. Examine the concept of alienation. Is the Utopian recommendation of community involvement an adequate solution?

5. Does Utopian theorizing contain the seeds of human liberation or human enslavement?

6. Compare and contrast the views of human nature held by Liberals, Conservatives, and Utopians.

7. What is the role of work in the Utopian context? What are the implications of this concept for education?

8. Analyze the concept and educational consequences of gender-specific education from the Utopian ideological perspective.

9. Why did many Utopian theorists emphasize early childhood education?

INQUIRY PROJECTS

- Read and review a book by a Utopian author.
- Using a Utopian frame of reference, identify the major problems of modern society and their solutions.
- Write a critique of Utopianism from either a Conservative or Liberal ideological perspective.
- In an essay, present a plan for organizing a Utopian community, with a special emphasis on education.
- In a comparative analysis, examine the educational ideas of several Utopian thinkers.
- Read George Orwell's *1984* and write an analysis that examines the theme of *dystopia*—what can go wrong with a planned society.

FURTHER READINGS

Donawerth, Jane L., and Carol A. Kolmerten, eds. *Utopian and Science Fiction by Women: World of Difference.* Syracuse, NY: Syracuse University Press, 1994.

Fogarty, Robert S. *American Utopianism.* Itasca, IL: F. E. Peacock, 1972.

Fox, Alistair. *Utopia: An Elusive Vision.* New York: Twayne Publishers, 1993.

Geoghegan, Vincent. *Utopianism and Marxism.* London: Methuen, 1987.

Gide, Charles, ed. *Design for Utopia: Selected Writings of Charles Fourier.* New York: Schocken Books, 1971.

Harrison, John F. C. *Quest for the New Moral World: Robert Owen and the Owenites in Britain and America.* New York: Charles Scribner's Sons, 1969.

Harrison, John F. C. *Utopianism and Education: Robert Owen and the Owenites.* New York: Teachers College Press, Columbia University, 1968.

Iggers, Georg G. *The Doctrine of Saint-Simon: An Exposition.* New York: Schocken Books, 1972.

Kesten, Seymour R. *Utopian Episodes: Daily Life in Experimental Colonies Dedicated to Changing the World.*

Syracuse, NY: Syracuse University Press, 1993.

Kumar, Krishan. *Utopianism.* Minneapolis: University of Minnesota Press, 1991.

Kumar, Krishan, and Stephen Bann, eds. *Utopias and the Millennium.* London: Reaktion Books, 1993.

Loubere, Leo. *Utopian Socialism: Its History Since 1800.* Cambridge, MA: Schenkmen, 1974.

Mumford, Lewis. *The Story of Utopias.* New York: The Viking Press, 1962.

Orwell, George. *1984.* New York: Harcourt, Brace, 1949.

Owen, Robert. *The Life of Robert Owen.* London: Effingham Wilson, 1857. (Reprinted by Augustus M. Kelley, New York, 1967.)

Ozmon, Howard. *Utopias and Education.* Minneapolis, MN: Burgess, 1969.

Pollard, Sidney, and John Salt, eds. *Robert Owen: Prophet of the Poor.* Lewisburg, PA: Bucknell University Press, 1971.

Poster, Mark, ed. *Harmonian Man: Selected Writings of Charles Fourier.* New York: Doubleday, 1971.

Richter, Peyton E. *Social Ideals and Communal Experiments.* Boston: Holbrook Press, 1971.

Russell, Raymond. *Utopia in Zion: The Israeli Experience with Worker Cooperatives.* Albany: State University of New York Press, 1995.

Silver, Harold, ed. *Robert Owen on Education.* Cambridge: Cambridge University Press, 1969.

Skinner, B. F. *Walden Two.* New York: Macmillan, 1948.

TeSelle, Sallie, ed. *The Family, Communes, and Utopian Societies.* New York: Harper & Row, 1972.

Tod, Ian, and Michael Wheeler. *Utopia.* New York: Harmony Books, 1978.

Zeldin, David. *The Educational Ideas of Charles Fourier.* New York: Augustus M. Kelley, 1971.

ENDNOTES

1. For a survey of the educational designs of various utopian theorists and writers, see Howard Ozmon, *Utopias and Education* (Minneapolis, MN: Burgess, 1969).

2. Robert Owen, *The Life of Robert Owen* (London: Effingham Wilson, 1857; reprinted by Augustus M. Kelley Publishers, New York, 1967).

3. Owen, "Essays on the Formation of Character," in *The Life of Robert Owen,* p. 265.

4. Robert Dale Owen, *An Outline of the System of Education at New Lanark* (Cincinnati: Deming and Wood, 1825).

5. John F. C. Harrison, *Quest for the New Moral World* (New York: Charles Scribner's Sons, 1969), p. 81.

6. Edward Bellamy, *Looking Backward* (New York: Harper and Brothers, 1959; originally published in 1888).

7. Leo Loubere, *Utopian Socialism: Its History Since 1800* (Cambridge, MA: Schenkman, 1974), pp. 21–22.

8. Ibid., pp. 43–45.

9. Ibid., pp. 46–47.

10. Charles Gide, ed., *Design for Utopia: Selected Writings of Charles Fourier* (New York: Schocken Books, 1971), pp. 67–75.

► 14

Marxism and Education

In this chapter, we examine Marxism and education. Although Marx used the term *ideology* to refer to the false consciousness created by the dominant class to "brainwash" the subordinate class, we will consider Marxism to be another ideological perspective with its particular view of history, explanation of social change, and program for the future. The following sections include discussions of Karl Marx as a revolutionary educator, Marxist ideology, Marxist educational theory, and Neo-Marxism's educational implications.

KARL MARX: REVOLUTIONARY EDUCATOR

Karl Marx, the son of a prominent lawyer, was born in 1818 in Trier, Germany, into a middle-class family of Jewish ancestry. Marx, who was educated at home until age twelve, was heavily influenced by his father, who believed in the ideas of the Enlightenment philosophers.[1] The young Marx was also influenced by Baron von Westphalen, his future father-in-law. Young Karl was encouraged to read the history, philosophy, and literature that filled the shelves of von Westphalen's library.

Marx's formal schooling began in Trier, where he attended the local *gymnasium,* or academic secondary school. He received a classical humanistic education, studying Latin, Greek, French, religion, mathematics, and history.

Intending to become a lawyer like his father, Marx entered the university at Bonn in 1835, where he studied philosophy and literature as well as law. After spending a year at Bonn, he transferred to the more prestigious University of Berlin. There Marx studied Hegelian Idealism, the philosophy that dominated German intellectual life at the time. Although he would reject Hegelianism's non-

Karl Marx (1818–1883), a philosopher, who developed the ideology of Marxism.

materialism and spiritualism, Marx did retain Hegel's dialectical process, which he incorporated into his philosophy of dialectical materialism.

For Hegel, the dialectic meant that each idea contained its opposite. From the conflict of ideas, a newer and higher-order synthesis would result.[2] The Hegelian dialectical process was an ongoing one that reached its conclusion only in the absolute world spirit. From Hegel, Marx took the principle that history is based on tension and conflict. When Marx formulated his own dialectical materialism, the dialectic became an analytical tool that pointed to the eventual conflict between the proletariat and the bourgeoisie.

In addition to Hegel, Marx was also influenced by Ludwig Feuerbach, author of *Theses on the Hegelian Philosophy*. Like other nineteenth-century German intellectuals, Feuerbach was reacting to Hegelian Idealism. Rejecting the Hegelian concept that historical events were caused by the unfolding of a spiritual force, the Absolute Idea, Feuerbach asserted that human history was a product of material conditions, the economic factors that existed at a particular time. Nonmaterial products such as art, literature, and other cultural forms were not independent entities but reflected the underlying economic reality. Impressed by Feuerbach's arguments, Marx later united the concept of materialism to the Hegelian dialectical process. The resulting synthesis was Marx's dialectical materialism.

Marx later studied at the University of Jena, where he completed his doctorate in philosophy in 1841. Unable to find a position in higher education, he accepted a job as editor of a liberal Rhineland newspaper, the *Rheinische Zeitung.*

Marx's evolving ideology was influenced by Moses Hess, the publisher of the *Rheinische Zeitung,* who combined traditional Judaism and humanitarianism with an overlay of Hegelian Idealism. From Hess, Marx came to see private property as the source of all human ills. As a humanitarian, Hess wanted to organize an international society based on a collective economy. As a result of his association with Hess, Marx came to emphasize economic influences in shaping historical and social forces. He also stressed the need for an international revolutionary organization.

As editor of the *Rheinische Zeitung,* Marx attacked the conservative policies of the Prussian government. In 1843, the government suppressed the journal's publication. Now unemployed, Marx, who had married Jenny von Westphalen in 1843, decided to emigrate to France. He went to Paris with his young wife to write for the German-language periodical, *Deutsch-Französische Jahrbuchër.* He had already formulated some basic ideas which would be expressed in his synthesis of scientific socialism, such as the premise of a material universe, dialectical processes of social change, and the coming class struggle.

As an exile in France from 1843 to 1845, Marx completed his ideological transformation and became a convinced socialist. During his French exile, Marx encountered the writings of Saint-Simon and other Utopian Socialist theorists. He agreed with Saint-Simon that economic relationships determined the course of history, which was largely the record of the conflict of competing economic classes. Saint-Simon's belief that the government should be in the hands of a small group of expert scientists and technicians contributed to Marx's emphasis that the coming revolutions should be led by an elite vanguard of the proletariat. However, he rejected what he regarded as the naive view of Fourier, Owen, and other Utopians that social and political change could be attained without revolutionary violence.

While in Paris, Marx became a lifelong collaborator with the wealthy German radical Friedrich Engels. Devoting himself to theory and writing, Marx and his family lived in near poverty. It was Engels who provided the economic support that enabled Marx to do his work.

The years between 1847 and 1848 found Marx still in exile from his native Germany, living in Brussels, Belgium. He now developed his basic ideological themes, especially on economic determinism and historical inevitability. Marx believed that economic forces, the means and modes of production, were at the base of society. Historical processes and events were the products of history's inevitable and inexorable course. These economically directed historical forces would lead to the inevitable triumph of the proletariat, the working class.

Marx's theorizing was broken by the momentous revolutions that swept Europe in 1848. It was this revolutionary situation that stimulated Marx and Engels to write their famous *Communist Manifesto,* which begins: "A specter is haunting Europe—the specter of Communism," and concludes:

> *The Communists disdain to conceal their views and aims. They openly declare that their ends can be attained only by the forcible overthrow of all existing social conditions. Let the ruling classes tremble at a Communist revolution. The proletarians have nothing to lose but their chains. They have a world to win. Workingmen of all countries, unite!*[3]

When the uprisings of 1848 failed to overthrow the reactionary Prussian government, Marx spent the rest of his life in London, researching and writing his monumental work, *Das Kapital,* an extensive treatment of economics.

MARXIST IDEOLOGY

The basic dynamic of social change in Marx's theory was "matter in dialectical motion." Marx's dialectical materialism incorporated Hegel's concept of dialectical change with Feuerbach's emphasis on materialism. For Hegel, change resulted from a ceaseless succession of ideational conflicts. Every idea embodied both a partial truth and also its contradiction. From the conflict of thesis and antithesis emerged a newer and higher idea that generated a new conflict. Through the dialectical forms of thesis, antithesis, and synthesis, Hegel saw human history as the unfolding of the Absolute Idea. Whereas Hegel's metaphysics was nonmaterial, Marx transferred the dialectical process to the physical or material realm. Instead of a conflict of ideas, Marx saw human history as a ceaseless struggle between conflicting economic classes.

Thus, for Marx, historical change is economically caused by the struggle to control production. The origins of classes and the resulting class conflict were economically determined. Marxist economic determinism rested on the premise that the production and the exchange of products formed the basis of the social order. Social class divisions were determined by the means, modes, and ownership of production. The ideological rationales used to legitimize class domination rested on an economic base.[4]

Over the course of time, developments in economic production had destroyed the feudal system. Like the feudal system, modern capitalism also contained its own antithesis, namely the proletariat. The exploitative methods of capitalism brought into existence—and increased the numbers of—exploited, propertyless laborers.[5]

In the early stages of economic development, the proletariat joined the capitalists to destroy the remnants of feudal society in the French Revolution and the revolutions of 1848. In these struggles, the whole historical movement concentrated on capitalist ascendancy. The proletariat, dependent for livelihood on selling their labor, were forced to resign any claim to the product of their labor. As factory workers, the proletariat were denied ownership of the means of production. However, they created wealth by laboring on the machines and using the materials owned by their exploiters, the capitalists.[6]

Control of wealth is power; wealth in capitalistic society is an immense accumulation of commodities, external objects that satisfy human needs and which may be exchanged for other products. Because it satisfies human need, a commodity has a "use value." The amount of the value is determined by the amount of necessary labor needed to produce the commodity. Labor power is also a commodity. In exchange for their labor, workers receive a wage that sustains them for further production. Because labor creates more exchange value than it is itself worth, "surplus value," a price higher than the cost of production, provides the capitalist with profit.

Marx, in the *Communist Manifesto,* predicted that the final struggle to control the means of production would result in a class war, or the proletarian revolution.

Marx saw modern society arrayed into two great opposing camps: capitalist and proletariat. The capitalists were defined as the owners of the productive resources on which the proletariat was employed to work.[7] The capitalist lived on the receipt of surplus value, which Marx conceived of as a fund, arising out of the exploitation of labor, from which rent, interests, and profits were paid.

In this last struggle, the bourgeoisie would face the proletariat, their economically determined successors. Although it was the unalterable course of history that the proletariat would gain control of the means of production, it was also inevitable that the capitalists would resist historical inevitability by vainly trying to keep their power. As a result of proletarian revolution, the capitalist system would be violently overthrown. In Marx's analysis, only capitalists and the proletariat were significant classes. Subgroups that could not be classified within either of the two major conflicting classes were really satellites of the major contenders for power.

However, a significant role was to be played by the small group of bourgeois ideologists who detached themselves from their class to join the proletariat. This "vanguard of the proletariat," able to comprehend the course of history, was to lead the proletarian revolution. Because they were far removed from the actual means of production, this group of intellectuals could escape their economically determined class position. This ideological detachment enabled them to comprehend the path they must follow. It is interesting to note that Marx and Engels saw themselves as part of this group.

The lower middle class of small manufacturers, shopkeepers, artisans, and peasants would join the proletariat to save themselves from extinction by the industrial bourgeoisie. This lower strata of the middle class was destined to sink gradually into the proletariat because their puny capital was insufficient for the scale required by modern industry. Marx also identified a group of dregs, criminals, and socially parasitic individuals from the lowest levels of society. Although this "scum" might be swept into proletariat ranks by the revolutionary impetus, it was more likely to be enlisted as paid agents of bourgeois reaction.

Although the other subgroups might engage in revolutionary activity, only the proletariat was a fully revolutionary class. The inevitable social revolution could be made only by the workers who alone had the strength and will to accomplish it. Therefore, any permanent compromise between the proletariat and other classes was impossible.

Arising out of the economic base, the modern national state was the political agency of the sociocultural superstructure. The nation-state was a reflection of the interest of the dominant economic class, the capitalists. As an arm of capitalism, it repressed the exploited proletariat. Although the church and school also reflected the dominant economic class, the state—with its army, police, courts, and prisons—was the most evident agency of repression.

The modern industrial nation was fashioned by the industrial revolution. Large metropolitan centers of population were created as workers came to cities from rural areas. As old loyalties disintegrated, the capitalists created a subterfuge, namely, nationalism, which was used to divert the proletariat from their real interests. Thus, misguided workers gave their loyalty to national states. They thought of themselves as French, English, or German rather than as workers united behind the single cause of proletarian revolution. As subsidiary institutions of the national state, the school and the church are also instruments of the dominant capitalist exploiting class. Systems of mass education were created to inculcate loyalty to the nation in working-class children. The Communist Party, as the most advanced and resolute section of the working class, had the responsibility of educating the proletariat by making them aware of their historic destiny. Because the Communists clearly understood the course of history and the conditions of the proletarian movement, they were to educate the working class to their real interests and the best means of attaining these interests.

For Marx, political and social change occurred when the exploited class revolted against their exploiters. Such radical change occurred when the need for change had accumulated sufficiently to break the old system and to supersede it by a new system embodying a different set of class ideas and claims. Because any form of the political state merely reflected class struggle, the capitalist state was such an instrument of exploitation used by the dominant class in enforcing its interests. The entrenched class of exploiters could be overthrown only by force. Any policy of conciliating the class struggle was an illusion.

The capitalist system of production sowed the seeds of its own destruction by spirals of overproduction, which would lead to economic crises, recessions, and the social chaos of economic depression. Under capitalism, productivity would reach a point beyond which it could not be coordinated. The capitalists

A classroom scene from a ten-year school in the former Soviet Union during the period when Marxist-Leninism was the official ideology.

would be compelled to reinvest profits to increase production without being able to guarantee the consumption of the commodities produced.[8] Crisis would ensue. Imperialist wars would result between the capitalist nations that sought mastery over colonial sources of raw materials and markets. Meanwhile the proletariat would grow more and more oppressed and miserable. Unemployment, once periodic, would become chronic, and conditions would grow ripe for revolution.

Inevitably, the proletariat would revolt and wrest all power from the capitalists. All the instruments of production would be centralized in the proletarian state. The "dictatorship of the proletariat" would be established to enact the reforms needed to bring about a classless society. Until the classless society is reached, the proletariat would have to act as a dictatorship, using the state to destroy the remnants of the old system. When these remnants were destroyed, a classless society would emerge. The state, an instrument of class oppression, would disappear as it would no longer be needed. Its successor, the proletarian state, would lead to the classless society. In these classless societies, requiring no repression, the state would wither away.

The State

According to orthodox Marxism—with its juridical, military, police, and educational powers—in a capitalist society, the dominant classes use the state as an instrument for the social control of subordinate classes. In Marxist-Leninist theory, the state apparatus taken over by the proletariat would be used to ensure the working classes consolidation of power and control. Eventually, when all classes had disappeared and the society was classless, the state, as an instrument of the domination of one class over another, would wither away. However, in the historical reality of the Soviet system, the state, especially under Stalin, became an instrument of totalitarian repression. Schools, as agencies of the Soviet state, transmitted an academically rigid Communist Party line.

Some theorists who continue to subscribe to Marx's basic theories have revised them. These revisionist Marxists are called Neo-Marxists. In contemporary Neo-Marxism, the role of the state in a capitalist society is more complex. While generally reinforcing the hegemony of the dominant class, the state, especially its legislative and judicial branches, acts as an arena of class conflict. Under Neo-Conservatives, the state would encourage and sponsor market-driven educational programs. It would frame its educational agenda in terms of increasing economic productivity, as occurred in the wake of the publication of *A Nation at Risk* in 1983 with the Reagan administration. However, Liberals also view the state as an arena in which social movements and forces seek to implement their agendas.

MARXIST EDUCATIONAL THEORY

Karl Marx was primarily a social, economic, and political, rather than an educational, theorist. His general ideology has had a significant impact on modern history.

Marx believed that the task of a genuine education, based on the principles of scientific socialism that he developed, required the exposure and eradication of "false consciousness" from the minds of the proletariat. False consciousness was the product of a dominant class ideology, which was imposed on and accepted by the subordinate class. For example, the ruling class will claim that its political and economic principles are universally true; schools should transmit these general universal truths and values to the young.[9] For Marx, these dominant class principles were a form of ideological brainwashing in capitalist schooling.

Contemporary Neo-Marxists, taking a broader perspective than orthodox Marxists, see capitalism as a cultural as well as an economic system.[10] Capitalist culture, reflected in schools and other social institutions, becomes hegemonic as the dominant group imposes its ideology on subordinate groups. In addition to analyzing economic conditions, they examine how schools have reproduced ideological, social, and political relationships that reflect dominant group interests.

Speculative philosophies such as Idealism and Thomism, like religion, contributed to the false consciousness of the proletariat, according to Marx. Realism, especially its scientific variety, could be used to gain an accurate picture of reality when incorporated with Marxist dialectical materialism. Ideologies such as Liberalism and Conservatism were also part of the defensive armor of dominant groups to control subordinate ones. Certain aspects of Utopian Socialism, Marx believed, provided a useful analysis but a muddle-headed strategy for social change. Thus, Marx saw part of his task as consigning the philosophies and ideologies that contributed to false consciousness to the trash heap of history.

In a world that was purged of false philosophies, Marx's ideology, which he called "scientific socialism" or Communism, could be used to establish a revolutionary consciousness in the working class. The vanguard of the proletariat, a revolutionary elite, could educate the working class to their true interests. The purpose of education, for Marx, was to put revolutionary theory into practice. Theory, arising from an analysis of concrete historical events and movements, was to be the basis for the strategy of the revolution and the coming classless society. By adhering to these revolutionary guidelines, the proletariat would be victorious.

Marxist educational theory arises from a conception of the human being as a natural person whose social nature is based on the means and modes of economic production. Human beings, particularly the proletariat, need to be imbued with the materialist concept of consciousness.

Marx envisioned schooling, or formal instruction, as consisting of both intellectual and physical development, as well as technological, or polytechnical, training, which was to introduce the young to productive processes.

Industrial, or polytechnical, education was to be more than the occupational specialization of the capitalist system. It was to be a means of reducing the alienation of workers from their labor and its product. Polytechnical education was to be a generalized industrial preparation that, by combining theory and practice, prepared a person to perform a variety of work and to understand the meaning of economically produced social change.

NEO-MARXISM'S EDUCATIONAL IMPLICATIONS

In addition to theorists who adhere to orthodox Marxism, there are those who have modernized Marxism for use as an analytical instrument. These Neo-Marxists, who have modified and revised classical Marxist theory, have examined the process of schooling in capitalist society. Like most educational ideologies and theories, Neo-Marxism contains a general frame of reference derived from Marxism. It also contains, however, differing reinterpretations of Marxist ideology.[11]

In the section that follows, we will examine selected concepts from the Neo-Marxist critique.

Like their orthodox Marxist kindred, Neo-Marxists are conflict theorists in that they see society and its institutions as the scene of struggle between contending groups for power, prestige, and social dominance.[12] For them, cultural conflict involves (1) class and class culture, (2) the distribution of power between classes, (3) the social control of one class by another, and (4) the use of schools by the dominant class to control subordinate classes. For the Neo-Marxists, schools, like other institutions, are designed to serve and advance the interests of the dominant class.

Neo-Marxist educational theorists have analyzed the role of schools in culturally reproducing the dominant capitalist culture. They see the curriculum, both overt and hidden, methodology, and testing as representing the dominance of one group over another. Neo-Marxists see a deliberate connection between the curriculum and instruction and the larger society. They believe that the symbols and meanings filtered into the capitalist schools' curricula shape, confirm, and maintain the dominant class ideology. In a capitalist society such as the United States, the very location of the school, whether it is in an affluent suburb or in the economically depressed inner city, reflects and reproduces the attitudes and values of the surrounding locality. Within a school setting, the grouping and instructing of students reproduce the social, political, and economic status quo. The school mirrors the essential class divisions of the larger society, and rather than changing them, hardens these divisions by perpetuating them in the young.

Neo-Marxists are also concerned with identifying and analyzing class consciousness, which is the perception of reality, the social outlook, and the values held by a given group or class.[13]

Because Marxists define class on the basis of people's relationships to the means and modes of economic production, class is an economically derived social phenomenon. Schooling in a capitalist society, argue the Marxists, reflects the outlook and values of the dominant or privileged class. Again, it perpetuates these dominant class values by transmitting and inculcating them in the young.

The interests and values of the dominant class will be framed in a context of the common good. For example, the values of respect for private property, the sanctity of contracts, and respect for law and order have long been traditional public school values. According to the Neo-Marxist critique, these traditional values are designed to protect the property of the dominant monied class. By encasing these class-centered values in a framework that extols the common good, the school is bending the minds of the young to accept their society as being the best of all possible worlds.

When a privileged and dominant class has managed to establish its thought-ways and values among subordinate or suppressed classes, it has established ideological control over them.[14] Rather than being a place where ideas contend in an open market, as Liberal apologists assert, the school in a capitalist society is closed to alternative viewpoints that may threaten the hegemony that the dominant class enjoys over the lower class, argue the Neo-Marxists. Such hegemony is truly established when members of the lower or subordinate class begin to express the views and to share the values of the dominant class.

Contemporary Neo-Marxists, such as Michael Apple, have revised the bipolar model of class conflict of the more orthodox Marxists who see class conflict as historically destined to occur between two incompatible classes—the capitalists and the proletariat. Apple contends that the class structure within capitalism is more complex than that suggested by orthodox Marxists in the nineteenth century.

Class structure refers to "the organization of social relations" based on class interests. Class formation, which refers to the "organized collectivities" within the structure, is related to economic forces and also to cultural, political, and social patterns and trends.[15] The formation of class cultures is further complicated in racially and ethnically diverse nations such as the United States. In addition to economic conditions, class cultures also reflect racial, ethnic, and gender histories, relationships, and conflicts.[16]

For Neo-Marxists, such as Apple, class, especially in the United States, is conditioned by gender and race as well as economics. Apple argues that seventy percent of working class occupational positions are filled by women and members of minority groups. Thus, an analysis of class formation needs to consider patriarchal and racial dominance themes.[17]

The middle class, with its interest in acquiring technical and managerial information and skills, holds an important place in an advanced capitalist society.[18] The middle class situation rests more on control of cultural reproduction than on economic exploitation. In educational policy, the middle class has its own general ideological orientation but it tends to be fractionalized into those who favor subject-matter competency and economic efficiency, such as the Essentialists, and those who are more progressively inclined to child-centered schooling.

Through their formal curricula and instructional programs, schools prepare the members of the future work force.[19] In establishing and maintaining these programs, a determining element is exercised by those who hold economic power. The economic function of the school is to identify and select those who will occupy the various rungs in the corporate ladder of the capitalist society. It trains people for the specialties that make the division of labor possible. It prepares people to be consumers of the products of a capitalist economy. Based on premises of economic inequality, such schooling is a determinant, albeit a partial one, of the rewards and penalties that its graduates will receive. In effect, it perpetuates the economic inequalities of the society and maintains the status quo.

In a capitalist society, schools reproduce the educational sorting that precedes and accompanies the functional division of labor. Further, they condition the dominated group to accept as legitimate the testing, grouping, and selecting processes that will make them into subordinate cogs in the corporate–industrial machinery. For example, homogeneous grouping in a capitalist society reproduces socioeconomic phenomena. The reproduction of social strata in the school, allegedly based on academic ability, implies that membership in a particular group or track is determined by an objective and competitive meritocratic system. In reality, Marxists would argue that the identification of a student with a particular track is economically based. Schools reproduce the existing socioeconomic structure and condition students to accept the legitimacy of that structure.

In addition to the overt economic programming done by schools, Neo-Marxist interpreters of education often refer to the hidden curriculum, or the concomitant learning that goes on in a school. According to Michael Apple, the hidden curriculum "reinforces basic rules" regarding conflict and its uses. It establishes a "network of assumptions" that reinforces legitimacy and authority.[20] The hidden curriculum underscores the norms and values of the dominant group in such a pervasive way that challenges to it are rendered illegitimate.

For example, the emphasis on the sanctity of private property can be reinforced as a value by assigning certain school spaces to particular individuals. Punctuality and the efficient use of time are also values reinforced by the school process. These attitudes and values, which are held to be characteristics of the effective school, are also conducive to the functioning of a capitalist economy.

CONCLUSION

After the Bolshevik Revolution in 1917, Marxism became the official ideology in the Soviet Union. Reinterpreted by Lenin, dialectical materialism was the regnant theory in Soviet schools until the collapse of the Soviet Union in 1990. In the People's Republic of China, Marxism as reinterpreted by Mao ZeDong has been the official ideology. In the Soviet Union, Marxist Leninism was supposed to create the new proletarian Soviet man and woman. Marxist Leninism, the Soviet Communist ideology, has been repudiated in contemporary Russia and the other successor states to the former Union of Soviet Socialist Republics. Also, Marxism, while still the official state ideology in Communist China, has grown theoretically inadequate to explain the course of modernization in that country.

Liberal and Conservative critics of Marxism refer to it as a fallen and failed system. They contend that when Marx's ideas were actually put into practice in the Soviet Union and China, they resulted in an immensely bureaucratic and repressive totalitarian state system, a society imprisoned in a gulag in which human freedom was shackled.

Despite the failure of the Soviet system, Marxism continues to have a pronounced theoretical attraction, especially among some academics. Neo-Marxist educational theorists would contend that neither the Soviet nor the Chinese Communist systems genuinely represented Marx's ideology. Rather, they are likely to say that the Soviet system, especially under Stalin, was a totalitarian state rather than a proletarian society. For Neo-Marxist theorists, Marxism continues to be a highly potent theory which carries with it a high level of analytical power, especially for schools.

Marxism interprets educational goals and schooling, curriculum, and instruction within a primarily economic context. Neo-Marxism, while stressing the economic base of society, politics, and education, moves the analysis into the cultural and political arena.

Regardless of one's ideological position, Karl Marx has to be recognized as formulating a powerful intellectual synthesis of Western thought. Marxist doctrine presents one perspective of analyzing historical, social, and educational forces and trends. Neo-Marxism, a recent theoretical development derived from Marx's theory, is an instrument for analyzing social and educational institutions.

DISCUSSION QUESTIONS

1. Examine the influences that shaped Karl Marx's ideological perspective.

2. Is Marxism a philosophy or an ideology?

3. Review Chapter 2 on Idealism. Compare and contrast Marxism and Idealism.

4. Review Chapter 13 on Utopianism. Compare and contrast Marxism and Utopianism.

5. Review the Pragmatist view of social change discussed in Chapter 6. Compare and contrast it with the Marxist view.

6. Analyze and provide examples of the Marxist concepts of "false consciousness," "alienation," and "hegemony."

7. Do you consider the Neo-Marxist educational critique to be a useful instrument in analyzing contemporary U.S. schools? Provide a rationale for your answer.

8. Is the collapse of the Soviet Union relevant or irrelevant to discussions of Marxism and Neo-Marxism?

INQUIRY PROJECTS

- Based on your reading of the chapter, prepare written critiques from a Marxist perspective of Liberalism, Conservatism, and Utopianism.
- Prepare a paper that analyzes the social and educational ideas of a Communist or Marxist leader such as Lenin, Stalin, or Mao ZeDong.
- From a Neo-Marxist perspective, prepare a paper that analyzes U.S. schooling.
- Review the book by Samuel Bowles and Herbert Gintis, *Schooling in Capitalist America.*

- In a paper, define the "hidden curriculum" and discuss examples that you have encountered in your own education.
- Research recent articles on educational theory appear in journals such as *Educational Theory* or *Educational Studies*. Identify and analyze those articles written from a Marxist or Neo-Marxist perspective.
- Analyze the textbooks that are being used in the teacher education program at your college or university. Do you find a Neo-Marxist perspective?

FURTHER READINGS

Apple, Michael W. *Ideology and Curriculum.* London: Routledge, 1990.

Berlin, Isaiah. *Karl Marx: His Life and Environment.* New York: Oxford University Press, 1959.

Bowles, Samuel, and Herbert Gintis. *Schooling in Capitalist America.* New York: Basic Books, 1975.

Brosio, Richard M. *A Radical Democratic Critique of Capitalist Education.* New York: Peter Lang, 1994.

Carnoy, Martin., ed. *Schooling in a Corporate Society.* New York: David McKay, 1972.

Churchich, Nicholas. *Marxism and Alienation.* Rutherford, NJ: Fairleigh Dickinson University Press, 1990.

Churchich, Nicholas. *Marxism and Morality: A Critical Examination of Marxist Ethics.* Cambridge: James Clarke, 1994.

Femia, Joseph V. *Marxism and Democracy.* New York: Oxford University Press, 1993.

Gottlieb, Roger S. *Marxism, 1844–1990: Origins, Betrayal, Rebirth.* New York: Routledge, 1992.

Hudelson, Richard. *Marxism and Philosophy in the Twentieth Century: A Defense of Vulgar Marxism.* New York: Praeger, 1990.

Larrain, Jorge. *Marxism and Ideology.* Atlantic Highlands, NJ: Humanities Press, 1983.

Levi, Margaret, ed. *Marxism.* Brookfield, VT: E. Elgar, 1991.

Lichtheim, George. *Marxism: An Historical and Critical Study.* New York: Praeger, 1965.

Liss, Sheldon B. *Fidel: Castro's Political and Social Thought.* Boulder, CO: Westview Press, 1994.

McLellan, David. *Karl Marx: His Life and Thought.* New York: Harper and Row, 1973.

Miller, Richard. *Analyzing Marx: Morality, Power and History.* Princeton, NJ: Princeton University Press, 1984.

Ollman, Bertell. *Alienation: Marx's Conception of Man in Capitalist Society.* New York: Cambridge University Press, 1971.

Pike, Shirley R. *Marxism and Phenomenology.* London: Croom Helm, 1986.

Strike, Kenneth. *Liberal Justice and the Marxist Critique of Education: A Study of Conflicting Research Programs.* (New York: Routledge and Kegan Paul, 1988.

Torrance, John. *Karl Marx's Theory of Ideas.* New York: Cambridge University Press, 1995.

Van Parijs, Philippe. *Marxism Recycled.* New York: Cambridge University Press, 1993.

Wood, Ellen M. *Democracy Against Capitalism: Renewing Historical Materialism.* New York: Cambridge University Press, 1995.

ENDNOTES

1. David McLellan, *Karl Marx: His Life and Thought* (New York: Harper & Row, 1973), pp. 2–6.

2. A recent treatment of Hegelianism can be found in Michael O. Hardimon, *Hegel's Social Philosophy: The Project of Reconciliation* (New York: Cambridge University Press, 1994).

3. Karl Marx and Friedrich Engels, "Manifesto of the Communist Party," in Carl Cohen, ed., *Communism, Fascism and Democracy: The Theoretical Foundations* (New York: Random House, 1972), pp. 80, 98.

4. Kenneth Strike, *Liberal Justice and the Marxist Critique of Education: A Study of Conflicting Research Programs* (New York: Routledge and Kegan Paul, 1988), p. 23.

5. E. A. Burns, *A Handbook of Marxism* (New York: International Publishers, 1935), p. 30.

6. G. D. H. Cole, *What Marx Really Meant* (New York: Alfred A. Knopf, 1937), p. 102.

7. Ibid., p. 102.

8. Sidney Hook, *Toward the Understanding of Karl Marx* (London: Victor Gallancz, 1933), p. 127.

9. Michael W. Apple, "Education, Culture, and Class Power: Basil Bernstein and the Neo-Marxist Sociology of Education," *Educational Theory,* 42, no. 2 (spring 1992): 127.

10. Ibid., p. 128.

11. Frank Margonis, "Marxism, Liberalism, and Educational Theory," *Educational Theory,* 43, no. 4 (fall 1993): 449.

12. Walter Feinberg and Jonas Soltis, *School and Society* (New York: Teachers College Press, 1985), pp. 43–44.

13. Ibid., p. 49.

14. Feinberg and Soltis, *School and Society,* pp. 50–52.

15. Michael W. Apple, "Education, Culture, and Class Power," p. 137.

16. Ibid., p. 139.

17. Ibid., p. 143.

18. Ibid., p. 134–135.

19. Samuel Bowles and Herbert Gintis, *Schooling in Capitalist America* (New York: Basic Books, 1975).

20. Michael W. Apple, *Ideology and Curriculum* (London: Routledge & Kegan Paul, 1979), p. 87.

▶ 15

Totalitarianism and Education

In Chapter 15 we examine totalitarianism and its educational implications. As a form of social, political, economic, and educational organization, totalitarianism has taken a variety of ideological forms such as Fascism in Mussolini's Italy from 1923 to 1944, Nazism in Hitler's Germany from 1933 to 1945, and Stalinism in the Soviet Union from 1928 to 1953. Totalitarianism continues to be a form of total organization in the contemporary world in countries ruled by personal dictatorships or one-party monolithic political systems. In examining totalitarianism as an ideology, we describe its theoretical features using Adolf Hitler as an example of a totalitarian leader. We also indicate the educational consequences and controls exercised in a totalitarian society and state. Often associated with totalitarianism is racism, which asserts the supremacy of one race or ethnic group over another.

TOTALITARIANISM'S THEORETICAL FEATURES

Like democracy, despotism has its origins in antiquity. The ancient empires of Egypt and Persia were ruled by emperors and kings who claimed to be divine and expected the unquestioning obedience of their subjects. Genghis Khan and the Mongol leaders ruled with iron fists.

Europe had its petty despots and absolute monarchs. While totalitarianism retains many features of the despotism of the past, it is a modern form of social and political organization that was made possible by the emergence of mass technology, mass society, and mass media. Whereas despots of the past lacked the means of establishing complete control over their subjects, modern dictators have used technology to establish systems of total control.

Totalitarianism can be defined as a system, headed by a single person or party, that seeks complete or total control over all aspects of life—social, cultural, economic, and educational. It uses agencies such as courts, schools, the media, churches, youth organizations, and art to carry out the policies of the leader or party. In the following sections, we will examine the role of the leader, the role of the persuasive ideology, the nature of totalitarian morality, and the police state.

The Leader

One of the key elements in totalitarianism is the leader, a supreme head of the total system, who is often regarded as having powers and abilities that surpass those of ordinary persons.[1] Examples of such totalitarian leaders are Benito Mussolini, called *Il Duce* by the Italian Fascists, and Adolf Hitler, the Führer, of Nazi Germany. Leaders are elevated to such prominence at mass meetings or by the mass media, where they are seen to possess personal powers that give them authority over the masses of people who become obedient and pliant followers.

While Mussolini and Hitler were charismatic leaders who did gain control of mass followings, their support, although appearing to be spontaneous, was also the result of preparatory psychological manipulation in which opponents were purged, eliminated, or silenced. In addition to the terror that could be exerted to produce unanimity, the media—press, radio, and motion picture—presented only the officially approved party line so that divergent views were eliminated. Once the totalitarian machinery is in full operation, the leader not only requires that opponents be silent but that subordinates and the mass of people affirm the leader's policies. For example, Hitler claimed that his power came from the German people and that he was an instrument of their united will.

In both the totalitarian society and state, the leader principle is established and reinforced by informal educational means—the manipulation of the media and use of propaganda—as well as by the coercion of the police state. For example, Joseph Goebbels headed the Nazi Ministry of Public Enlightenment and Propaganda, which controlled all agencies of information and opinion for the indoctrination of the German masses and the glorification of the leader, Hitler.

In the Soviet Union during the Stalinist period, teachers were instructed to influence the political and moral development of their students by stressing the qualities of the leader. A Soviet education journal advised teachers, "Everyone knows the irresistible, shattering power of Stalin's logic, the crystal clearness of his intellect, his iron will, his devotion to the Party, his hot faith in the people and his love for the people."[2] Ironically, the Soviet dictator was praised for his modesty and solicitude.

The preeminence given to the totalitarian leader bears a resemblance to that of a cult figure who is a source of truth and an object of devotion. The charismatic powers attributed to the totalitarian leader, like the cult leader, are not dependent on reason. They are irrational and require the follower to accept and obey instinctively and emotionally.

In addition to reinforcing the propaganda agencies of the state, the school and curriculum also build loyalty to the leader in the young. The newspaper of the Hitler Youth organization, for example, stated, "We desire at the head a leader, a true leader, into whose hands the people willingly and gladly place power and of whom it knows that he will not abuse it but will apply it to the benefit and advantage of the people as a whole."[3]

A Single and Persuasive Ideology

Whether it took the particular political form of Fascism, Nazism, or Stalinism, totalitarian societies were and still are characterized by a single, pervasive, all-encompassing ideology. Often intertwined with nationalism and racism, totalitarian ideology seeks to appeal to the deep instincts, fears, hatreds, and emotions of the masses and to use these emotional elements to effect the total mobilization of the society to implement policies.[4]

In totalitarian societies, the single ideology monopolizes the channels of information, opinion, and education. Because the expression of alternative or divergent viewpoints is prohibited, spokespersons for the officially approved ideology can disseminate propaganda in a vacuum.

While censorship and the control of information is not a new phenomenon in human history, totalitarian mind control with its techniques of mass indoctrination is a modern development that was made possible by mass communications and mass media. The media—radio, television, and the press—can be centrally controlled and can reach into every household. In his book *1984*, George Orwell portrayed a totalitarian society that was propagandized by programs shown on massive television screens.[5]

Moreover, each person's living space contained a small television monitor so that the person was continually subject to the flow of propaganda. Through the media, the subjects in the totalitarian society, such as that depicted in Orwell's *1984*, are kept in a state of continual mobilization.

The mass media are important agents of informal education in modern society. In totalitarian societies, however, the media play a powerful role in indoctrinating the citizenry to conform to the ideological line. As the word *totalitarian* suggests, this control is *total*. The process of indoctrination is completed in formal educational agencies, where the young are shaped in the prepared and controlled environment.

In totalitarian societies, the official ideology is ritualized in behavioral codes. In both Fascist Italy and Nazi Germany, distinctive uniforms were worn by party elite. Youth groups, such as the Hitler Youth, also wore a distinctive uniform. Mass rallies involving carefully staged pageantry were organized to produce massive demonstrations of popular support for the leader, regime, and official ideology. For example, the Hitler salute of "Heil, Hitler" was made mandatory as the official greeting in German schools.

Totalitarian Morality

In totalitarian societies, moral issues and ethical decision making become a matter of state regulation. Individuals are to obey the dictates of the leader, the party, or regime without question. Complete submission to the totalitarian dictatorship is justified in the official propaganda on the grounds that the leader (and the regime) is pursuing a great and noble aim. This great purpose, however, is being frustrated by internal or external enemies. Only through disciplined obedience will the loyal members of the society be able to overcome these enemies. Thus, repressive statutes, purges, concentration camps, and coercive actions are justified by the totalitarian leader and regime on the grounds that the end justifies the means.

The Police State

The totalitarian state and society is a police state where individuals who oppose the regime, or who are suspected of opposing it, are hunted down, exiled, imprisoned, or executed. The concentration camp in which suspected persons are confined, brutalized, and reeducated to conform to the ideological strictures of the regime is an invention of the modern totalitarian state. For reasons that are often irrational, as in the case of Hitler's persecution and extermination of over six million Jews of Europe, groups are identified for persecution. The police state

Adolph Hitler (1889–1945), totalitarian leader of Germany from 1933–1945. Hitler's ideology incorporated totalitarianism and racism.

further completes the circle of coercive controls employed by the modern totalitarian state.

HITLER AND TOTALITARIAN EDUCATION

Although some people naively believe that organized education is intrinsically good, this is not always the case. The goals of formal education are often determined by the ideology of those who hold power in a society. When power is held by inhumane individuals, then the educational program that such people shape will be dehumanizing, coercive, and debasing of human freedom. Adolf Hitler (1889–1945) gained control in Germany by forcefully using a racist ideology, by coercing his opposition, and by developing the instruments of the terroristic totalitarian police state. The career of the Nazi dictator represents the life of a man who attempted to and almost succeeded in destroying the humanistic values of Western civilization. An examination of Hitler's educational ideas reveals the modern totalitarian leader who sought to mold a nation of puppetlike supermen.

Hitler: A Biographical Sketch

Hitler's birth, childhood, and formative years gave little evidence of his later career. In many ways, the upbringing of the young Hitler was commonplace and mundane. Adolf Hitler was born on April 20, 1889, in the small Austrian town of Braunau am Inn, the son of Alois Hitler, a petty customs official in the Austrian civil service, and Klara Hitler, nee Pölzl, the daughter of a farmer.

Hitler began his formal education in 1895 at the primary school at Fischlam. The next year he transferred to the church school at Lamback conducted by the Benedictines. His teachers generally liked young Hitler, who sang in the choir and was reported to be a good student. When his family moved, Adolf was transferred to his third primary school at Leonding, which he attended until 1900.[6] Hitler's favorite subjects were history, geography, and drawing. When he became the Nazi dictator of Germany, he considered himself to be an expert on history and what he termed geopolitics. As he ended his elementary education, however, Hitler decided that he wanted to be an artist. His father, however, wanted him to have a career in the civil service.

Although Hitler wanted to pursue humanistic studies in the *gymnasium,* his father enrolled him in the *realschule* in Linz, the state secondary school that prepared boys for practical careers. During adolescence, Hitler revealed an unevenness of personality and temperament. Pointing to deficiencies in mathematics and natural sciences, his secondary teachers described his work as academically uneven. Hitler later commented that he studied what he enjoyed and ignored what he disliked, saying, "What gave me pleasure, I learned.... What seemed to me unimportant...or was otherwise unattractive to me, I sabotaged completely."[7]

Upon completing secondary school, Hitler sought admission to the School of Painting at the Academy of Fine Arts in Vienna. When he failed to meet the rigorous admission requirements, he unsuccessfully applied to the Architectural School. After being rejected a second time, the despondent Hitler drifted around the Austrian capital, took some art classes, and visited the art galleries. When he ran out of money, he supported himself by selling sketches. During this time, he grew increasingly anti-Semitic, believing that his career in the fine arts had been thwarted by Jewish interests.

When World War I erupted, Hitler enlisted in a German infantry regiment. The war excited him, and he threw himself into military life with zeal. He carried messages at the front, rose to the rank of corporal, was wounded, and received the Iron Cross. When the civilian government that had replaced the Kaiser accepted the armistice that ended the war, Hitler felt that the army had been betrayed. He dedicated himself to working for the overthrow of the Weimar Republic. Germany's defeat in World War I had an important formative effect on Hitler's ideology. As a politician, he spoke unceasingly about the humiliation of Germany. If given power, he vowed to avenge those who had fought and died for Germany and to punish those who had contributed to her defeat.

Hitler joined and later became the leader of the small National Socialist German Workers Party, or Nazi Party. The anti-Semitic Nazis called for the deportation of Jews from Germany. Extreme nationalists, the Nazis urged the union of all Germans into a great German empire, or *Reich*. In 1923, Hitler failed in an attempt to seize power, was arrested, and spent a rather comfortable year's confinement dictating his ideology, which he titled *Mein Kampf* (My Struggle).

Upon his release from jail, Hitler forged the Nazi Party into a powerful organization with its own paramilitary army of street fighters, the S.A., which coerced political opponents and broke up opposition meetings. He developed into a forceful orator who mastered crowd manipulation. Believing that he possessed unusual public-speaking abilities, he was convinced that the spoken word was far more persuasive than the written word.

Hitler's oratorical style was highly effective in arousing his own emotions as well as the passions of his audience. For him, speech was an emotional release. Using a few simple slogans and basic themes, he would repeat them over and over until they were drilled into his audience. He would begin his speeches by condemning those whom he claimed had wronged the German people. He would proclaim that he and the German people had borne these injustices with patient resignation but that his patience had now ended. He was ready to revenge the misdeeds perpetrated on an innocent people. In a harangue that had an hysteria-like effect on him and his audience, he would threaten his enemies.

By the early 1930s, a worldwide economic depression had catastrophic consequences on the German economy and political situation. Massive unemployment and chronic political unrest set the stage for Hitler's coming to power. Finally, the aged president von Hindenburg made Hitler the German chancellor in January 1933. Three months later, the Nazi leader assumed dictatorial power and established totalitarian rule.

Upon taking power, Hitler and his Nazis molded Germany into a totalitarian police state where opponents were terrorized, imprisoned in concentration camps, and often murdered. The Nazi regime mobilized all the forces of formal and informal education to create a nation that thought as Hitler wanted it to think. The school, press, radio, and motion picture industry became propaganda tools for Hitler's Nazi regime. Massive patriotic rallies were organized in carefully orchestrated rituals of speeches, songs, marching formations, banners, and flags. A single-party state was created in which the Führer's will replaced the law. In commenting on the Nazi use of psychological manipulation, the British historian Allan Bullock wrote, that as a "master of mass emotion," Hitler paid "careful attention to psychological factors in politics." To heighten "the emotional intensity" of the mass rallies, "every trick of the theatre was used."[8]

Under the Nazis, Germany became a nation ruled by the will of one man—Adolph Hitler. Hitler had developed the *Führerprinzip*, or leadership principle, originally to control the Nazi Party. But as Germany's dictator, he used it for total state control. Hitler's will became law. In addressing the Hitler Youth at Nuremberg in 1933, the Nazi Führer proclaimed,

> *One will must dominate us, we must form a single unity; one discipline must weld us together; one obedience, one subordination must fill us all, for above us stands the nation.*[9]

Under Hitler, Germany became a totally mobilized garrison state bent on conquering Europe. The course of events that led to World War II is well known. When the German army invaded Poland in 1939, World War II began. The conflict did not end until Hitler committed suicide in his underground bunker in the ruined city of Berlin in 1945. By that time, millions had perished in the slaughter of the war that Hitler had caused or in the extermination camps that he had directed.

In creating his totalitarian nation, Hitler obviously relied on brute force and raw power. He believed that he was training German youth to be a race of supermen who would be obedient to his will. In the following sections, we will examine Hitler's ideology and its impact on the education of Nazis.

Hitler's Ideology

In 1924, Hitler wrote *Mein Kampf* (My Struggle), an autobiographical work that revealed his psychology as well as his ideology.[10] An ideological diatribe, *Mein Kampf* conveyed the Nazi dictator's views on racial purity, the folkish state, anti-Semitism, and Germanic destiny. These concepts formed the ideological basis of National Socialism.

Hitler's Nazi ideology was permeated by a crude racism that asserted that the racially strong were biologically and historically destined to rule the weak, inferior peoples. The strongest and most racially fit group Hitler called the Aryans, an elite even among the Germans. In the past, Hitler asserted, the Aryans had founded a superior culture by conquering and mastering their biological inferiors. Now, he claimed that the Nazi Party was leading a new racial revolution that would bring a new order to Europe and to the world. As the elite among the peoples of the earth, the racially superior Germans would rise to world dominance.

In *Mein Kampf,* Hitler venomously attacked the Jewish people. The Jews, he wrote, were racially impure intruders on Germany's sacred soil and the cause of all the world's ills. Hitler's anti-Semitic diatribes became the basis for a policy of extermination that caused six million Jews to perish in Nazi death camps. Not only were Jews subjected to the Führer's hatred but also the Slavic peoples of Eastern Europe, whom he regarded as subhumans. Hitler planned to create an Aryan empire in central Europe by depopulating the Slavic peoples and replacing it with Aryan colonists.

Rejecting the basic ethical standards of Western civilization, Hitler claimed that might makes right and that the strong have the right to rule the weak. Drawing on a crude Darwinism, he viewed nature as an unceasing struggle between the strong and the weak. In the struggle between nations, the battle would be won by those nations that had a stronger drive for self-preservation.

Not concerned with rationality, Hitler regarded the primal force in human nature to be an instinctive racism. The educational task was to train the will of young Germans to obey with an unquestioned discipline. Arguing that nothing would be possible until all obeyed the will of the leader, Hitler ordered that youth be ingrained with the concept of obedience to the Führer. Hitler claimed he was introducing "a new type of education" that would stress "the duty of everyone to serve" the nation.[11]

In *Mein Kampf,* Hitler identified three basic objectives for education in National Socialist Germany: physical training, character building, and mastery of practical skills. First, a concerted emphasis on physical training was needed to produce sound, healthy, and racially pure men and women. Because the boy was destined to be a soldier and the girl a mother of soldiers, physical and military training took foremost priority in the Nazi curriculum. Second, character training was to discipline the will of young Germans to follow the orders of those in authority. Third, useful and practical instructions should be given as a matter of routine in schools rather than useless intellectual lessons. Hitler summed up his educational objectives:

> *The folkish state must not adjust its entire educational work primarily to the inoculation of mere knowledge, but to the breeding of absolutely healthy bodies. The training of mental abilities is only secondary. And here again, first place must be taken by the development of character, especially the promotion of will-power and determination, combined with the training of joy in responsibility, and only in last place comes scientific schooling.*[12]

Hitler also had some specific curricular changes in mind. History, for example, should stress the national pride of being a German and should inculcate an all-consuming patriotism. Racism would also be emphasized in the schools of the New Germany. From Hitler's educational beliefs, a more generalized Nazi ideology emerged. In the following section, we examine the Nazi process of thought control.

A rally during the Nazi period in Germany that illustrates the use of symbols and crowd psychology for totalitarian mobilization.

Totalitarian Education

Nazi educational theory and practice were used as instruments by Hitler and his followers to mold a totalitarian society in which there was only one leader, one party, one people. Conceptually, Nazi education was based on the ideology that emanated from Hitler and those in the elite of the National Socialist Party. It was political theory and practice transferred to the school rather than a system of education that originated in pedagogical thought and practice.[13]

According to Nazi educators, a *Weltanschauung,* or worldview, was the ideological base for education in Hitler's Germany. This *Weltanschauung* rested on the premise that the Aryan race had a folk spirit, a mentality, and feelings that stimulated German progress and development. The *Weltanschauung* arose from a combination of blood and soil.

To Hitler, National Socialist education had the objective of creating a homogeneous racial community whose members would be physically and mentally alike. Such an education would create the total society in which there would be no divergent attitudes or alternative lifestyles. Such an education would discipline the will, mold the proper ideological attitude, and create a collective folkish community. The Nazi teacher was to combine the roles of soldier, disciplinarian, party worker, and educator, and was to imbue young Germans with the concept that their race was unconditionally superior to all others.

While the folkish nation was to be trained to obey the Führer's will, Nazi education was also to identify and to train a selected leadership elite, who would be controlled by rigorous discipline. Adolf Hitler schools were established to train selected boys, between the ages of twelve and eighteen, to be the future leaders of Germany.

In the totalitarian state, education was a total process in which informal educational agencies were also controlled by those who ruled the state. Party-directed youth organizations were established to complete the total formation of German young people in the Nazi ideological mold. The *Hitlerjugend,* or Hitler Youth, was to complete the work of the school by "hardening the character through an exacting self-discipline and physical training." Headed by Baldur von Schirach, the Nazi youth leader, the Hitler Youth was to unite all German young people in an educational totality that stressed the values of toughness, endurance, self-confidence, fighting spirit, and willpower.[14]

In totalitarian nations, there is only one correct way to think. Divergent avenues of thought are closed so that the only information that reaches the inhabitants has been processed by the officially sanctioned channels of communication. The Hitler regime took control of the press, the arts, the film industry, and radio and used them as agencies of indoctrination and propaganda. Hitler established a Reich Chamber of Culture and placed it under the control of Joseph Goebbels, his propaganda minister. Under Goebbel's direction, literature, the press, radio, music, art, and film were used to conduct a concerted propaganda campaign to complete the process of uniformly molding the will.[15] Books that ran counter to the official Nazi *Weltanschauung* were burned. Thus, a complete policy of censorship was inaugurated in Nazi Germany.

The education that Hitler had in mind for the children and youth of Germany was training them to obey orders without questioning them. This training took the form of indoctrinating them to believe they were the offspring of a superior people. Courses in racial hygiene and racial biology mixed a pseudoscientific jargon, a romanticized folk mythology, and a modernized barbarism.

Hitler frequently referred to the need for character- or will-training of German youth. According to him, the character appropriate to Nazi youth was that which encouraged sacrifice for German honor. The meaning of national honor was, of course, interpreted only by the Führer. Training of the will and body was to produce a soldier who welcomed the life of military discipline. The goal of Nazi education was nothing less than the formation of a nation of soldiers who would respond as a single person to the commands of the Führer.

TOTALITARIANISM AND RACISM

Many of history's large monolithic totalitarian political systems such as Fascism, Nazism, and Stalinist Communism fortunately no longer exist. Mussolini's Fascism and Hitler's National Socialism were destroyed in World War II. The Communist system, pioneered by Lenin and consolidated by Stalin, collapsed as a result of its own bureaucratic fossilization. However, totalitarian systems remain in one-party dictatorships. In these cases, schooling is used to reinforce the dictator's cult of personality and to mimic the state-sponsored ideology.

The study of the origins, strategies, and consequences of totalitarianism are instructive in analyzing certain contemporary trends, particularly racism and its political and educational manifestations. Hitler, in Nazi Germany, enshrined Aryan superiority as the key element in his ideology. Racism can be defined as an ideology or attitude that overtly or covertly encourages discrimination based on racial identity, holding some races to be inherently intellectually, socially, or culturally inferior and others superior. Despite concerted efforts to expose and eradicate racism, it continues to be a persistent issue in education and schooling.

In the United States, white racism can be traced to the European, particularly the English, colonization of North America. Cultural superiority was used as a rationale for forcibly removing the Native Americans from their indigenous lands.[16] White colonists regarded themselves to be culturally superior to the Native Americans whom they categorized as savages. The seizure of Native American land was often accompanied by genocide.

The enslavement of Africans, who were forcibly transplanted to the slave states of the United States, reinforced racism. An ideology of white supremacy developed, which relegated Africans to subordinate economic and social positions on the grounds that whites were racially and culturally superior to blacks.

Along with racism against Native Americans and African Americans, immigrants—Irish, Germans, Italians, Jews, Slavs, Japanese, and Chinese, for example—were also subject to ethnic discrimination. The much-debated theories of assimilation, the melting pot, and cultural pluralism are responses to the American multiracial and multiethnic milieu.

While an immense and highly intriguing literature exists on the debate over multiculturalism and multicultural education, our concern in this chapter is to identify racism, today, as a form of incipient totalitarianism in the ideological sense. In U.S. society, there exist small groups, often white but sometimes black or other racial identities, that espouse racial dominance as a goal to be achieved politically, militarily, and educationally. Racist "hate groups" form political organizations and paramilitary units that seek to indoctrinate the young. Although small in membership, they see themselves as having a mission to purify society racially.

While the United States has a problem with racism, it is not unique. Globally, racism is on the rise, especially with the resurgence of ethnonationalism. The persistent conflicts in the former Yugoslavia among Croats, Serbs, and Slavic Muslims are based on themes of ethnic superiority; others—those not of that blood—are regarded as culturally inferior and needing to be purged by "ethnic cleansing." In Africa, tribalism, a primary focus of group identity, too, has often led to extremism. In its extreme manifestation, in Rwanda, tribal conflicts have led to genocide between Hutus and Tutsis.

Racism, in its various manifestations, becomes a kind of primordial irrationalism that is used to unite members of one group against another. Linked with politics, it seeks to purge imagined outsiders. When made a part of schooling, it leads to the indoctrination of the dominant group against others.

Racism occurs when people of one group determine that those of another group, because of pigmentation, ethnicity, language, or religion, are so different that they are of "lesser stock," of lesser worth, or of lesser value as human beings. It reaches its depths when those of one group determine that the differences are so great that members of the other group are less than human beings, or in Nazi-like terms, subhuman. When this occurs, those who regard themselves as superior will set themselves apart from those regarded as inferior by creating ghettos, reservations, or enclaves. Or those who regard themselves as superior may justify attacks and violence against those regarded as inferior, as in the lynchings of blacks that occurred in the United States, the extermination of Armenians by Turks, the holocaust in which Jews were murdered by Nazis, or the ethnic cleansing practiced in Bosnia.

Racism can be customary and based on long-standing prejudices transmitted from generation to generation. An example of customary racism is the code of white supremacy and black inferiority that existed in the American South. This customary code became institutionalized in the legislation of the Black Codes in pre–Civil War America and the "Jim Crow" segregation laws in post-Reconstruction America. Customary racism is learned at home as part of the milieu of growing up. It can be formalized institutionally by law and then reinforced by schooling. Another example of customary racism was the discrimination against Jews in Germany, which during the Nazi period was institutionalized in a legal and ideologically based terminology, and then taught in schools in a curriculum that featured racial history, racial science, and so forth.

The study of totalitarianism, with its "cult of the leader," closure to divergent opinions, highly emotive use of slogans, and division of people into "them and us" is highly instructive in analyzing racism and racist organizations. It reveals a certain kind of leadership–followership psychology that has had tragic consequences.

CONCLUSION

Totalitarianism is a modern system of mind control that seeks to subjugate humans into a single mass collective state. Often accompanied by racism, totalitarians have used education to reinforce their coercive ideology.

The irrationality and totalitarianism exemplified in Hitler's conception of education are relevant for examination by contemporary educators. Hitler's ideology was a misshapen worldview that came from his experiences, from a crude racism, from a superficial Darwinism, and from a contrived mythology. For him, emotional conditioning was substituted for the cultivation of reason.

The irrational base of Nazi education was closely allied to the regime's totalitarianism. In training Germans to respond to Hitler's orders as soldiers respond to the commands of the drillmaster, the Nazi regime deliberately sought to remove the possibilities of alternatives to the National Socialist way of thinking and acting. Totalitarianism's relevance to contemporary educators is that it provides a warning of what happens when irrationality replaces reason and when conformity replaces diversity. Racism, too, is based on irrational beliefs that exalt one racial or ethnic group over another.

DISCUSSION QUESTIONS

1. How does modern totalitarianism differ from older forms of despotism?

2. What is the nature and role of the leader in totalitarian societies?

3. How does indoctrination take place in a totalitarian society?

4. Compare and contrast totalitarianism with other ideological positions.

5. Examine the potential of the mass media to be used as an instrument of indoctrination.

6. Describe the kind of education that is most likely to prepare people to resist totalitarianism.

7. Examine racial, religious, or ethnic storeotyping. How can it lead to the scapegoating used by totalitarian regimes?

8. Define racism and indicate why it remains a significant issue in U.S. society and education?

9. What episodes in the U.S. historical and social experience have contributed to racism?

INQUIRY PROJECTS

* Prepare a research paper that analyzes the personality of a totalitarian leader such as Mussolini, Hitler, or Stalin.
* Read and review George Orwell's *1984* with special emphasis on indoctrination and mind control.
* Prepare a character sketch of the kind of person who would be most susceptible to totalitarianism.
* Prepare a paper that describes and analyzes schooling under a totalitarian regime.
* Review a book written by a person who was persecuted by a totalitarian regime.
* Begin a clippings file of articles from newspapers and magazines that exposes "hate groups."

FURTHER READINGS

Arendt, Hannah. *Eichmann in Jerusalem: A Report on the Banality of Evil.* New York: Viking Press, 1965.

Arendt, Hannah. *The Origins of Totalitarianism.* New York: Harcourt, Brace, & World, 1966.

Azar, Larry. *Twentieth Century in Crisis: Foundations of Totalitarianism.* Dubuque, IA: Kendall/Hunt, 1990.

Bracher, Karl D. *The German Dictatorship: The Origins, Structure, and Effects of National Socialism.* New York: Praeger, 1970.

Bullock, Alan. *Hitler: A Study in Tyranny.* New York: Harper & Row, 1962.

Figueroa, Peter M. *Education and the Social Construction of "Race."* New York: Routledge, 1991.

Frank, Anne. *The Diary of Anne Frank.* New York: Random House, 1956.

Friedrich, Carl J., ed. *Totalitarianism.* New York: Grosser & Dunlap, 1964.

Gregor, A. J. *The Ideology of Fascism.* New York: Free Press, 1969.

Grunberger, Richard. *The 12-Year Reich: A Social History of Nazi Germany, 1933–1945.* New York: Ballantine Books, 1971.

Hitler, Adolf. *Mein Kampf.* Boston: Houghton Mifflin, 1943.

Hoffer, Eric. *The True Believer: Thoughts on the Nature of Mass Movements.* New York: Harper & Row, 1951.

Kandel, I. L. *The Making of Nazis.* Westport, CT: Greenwood Press, 1970. (Originally published in 1935 by Teachers College, Columbia University, New York.)

Kneller, George F. *The Educational Philosophy of National Socialism.* New Haven, CT: Yale University Press, 1941.

Koch, H. W. *The Hitler Youth: Origins and Development, 1922–45.* New York: Stein & Day, 1975.

Lynch, James. *Prejudice Reduction and the Schools.* New York: Nichols, 1987.

Mann, Erika. *School for Barbarians.* New York: Modern Age Books, 1938.

Maser, Werner. *Hitler: Legend, Myth & Reality.* New York: Harper & Row, 1971.

Mayer, Milton. *They Thought They Were Free: The Germans 1933–45.* Chicago: University of Chicago Press, 1955.

Mosse, George L. *Nazi Culture: Intellectual, Cultural and Social Life in the Third Reich.* New York: Grosset & Dunlap, 1966.

Orwell, George. *1984.* New York: Harcourt, Brace, 1949.

Paul, Ellen Frankel, ed. *Totalitarianism at the Crossroads.* New Brunswick, NJ: Transaction Books, 1990.

Schapiro, Leonard. *Totalitarianism.* New York: Praeger, 1972.

Solzhenitsyn, Aleksandr I. *The Gulag Archipelago.* New York: Harper & Row, 1974.

Takaki, Ronald. *A Different Mirror: A History of Multicultural America.* Boston: Little, Brown, 1993.

Taylor, Jay. *The Rise and Fall of Totalitarianism in the Twentieth Century.* New York: Paragon, 1993.

Tormey, Simon. *Making Sense of Tyranny: Interpretations of Totalitarianism.* Manchester, England: Manchester University Press, 1995.

Troya, Barry. *Racism in Children's Lives: A Study of Mainly-White Primary Schools.* New York: Routledge, 1992.

ENDNOTES

1. Leonard Schapiro, *Totalitarianism* (New York: Praeger, 1972), pp. 21–28.

2. George S. Counts, *The Challenge of Soviet Education* (New York: McGraw-Hill, 1957), p. 131.

3. I. L. Kandel, *The Making of Nazis* (Westport, CT: Greenwood Press, 1970), p. 117. (Originally published in 1935 by Teachers College, Columbia University, New York.)

4. Schapiro, *Totalitarianism,* pp. 48–54.

5. George Orwell, *1984* (New York: Harcourt, Brace, 1949).

6. Werner Maser, *Hitler: Legend, Myth & Reality.* (New York: Harper & Row, 1971), pp. 22–38.

7. Ibid. p. 30.

8. Alan Bullock, *Hitler: A Study in Tyranny* (New York: Harper and Row, 1962), p. 379.

9. Hitler, as quoted in Bullock, *A Study in Tyranny,* p. 403.

10. Adolf Hitler, *Mein Kampf* (Boston: Houghton Mifflin, 1943).

11. Hitler, as quoted in Carl Cohen, *Communism, Fascism, and Democracy: The Theoretical Foundations* (New York: Random House, 1972), p. 387.

12. Hitler, *Mein Kampf,* p. 408.

13. George F. Kneller, *The Educational Philosophy of National Socialism.* (New Haven, CT: Yale University Press, 1941), p. 4.

14. H. W. Koch, *The Hitler Youth: Origins and Development, 1922–45* (New York: Stein and Day, 1975).

15. Ernest K. Bramstead, *Goebbels and National Socialist Propaganda, 1925–1945* (East Lansing, MI: Michigan State University Press, 1965).

16. For a treatment of the origins of racism in U.S. history, see Ronald Takaki, *A Different Mirror: A History of Multicultural America* (Boston: Little, Brown, 1993).

► 16

Theory and Education

Chapter 16 is a transitional chapter in which we link the philosophies of education, examined in Chapters 1 through 8, and the ideologies, examined in Chapters 9 through 15, with five related clusters of educational ideas that we will, for purposes of convenience, refer to as *theories*. These theories, examined in chapters 17 through 21 are Essentialism, Perennialism, Progressivism, Social Reconstructionism, and Critical Theory. Although an extensive literature explores the nature of theory and its relationship to government, management, and education, we will stipulate a definition of theory and indicate its relationships to education and schooling.[1] In this chapter, we refer to theory as a grouping or clustering of general ideas or propositions that explain the operations of an institution, such as a school, or a situation, such as teaching or learning; moreover, these ideas and propositions are sufficiently abstract or general that they can be transferred and applied to situations other than those in which they are directly developed.

Theory also means an opinion that originates from trying to establish generalizable patterns from facts, information, or practices. In the sections that follow we examine theories (1) that are derived or deduced from some other bodies of knowledge or thought such as philosophies or ideologies, (2) those that emerge as reactions against such bodies of thought, and (3) those that arise from practice. In some cases, a theory will exhibit elements of all three of these categories.

THEORY AS DERIVATION

Theories of education are often derived from or based on a larger, more comprehensive, and more complete body of thought. For example, Idealism, Realism, and Thomism are speculative philosophies that seek to explain all of reality and the human being's relationship to that reality in terms of being, knowledge, and values. While the philosophers who developed these grand and total philosophical systems may have commented on education, they usually did not attempt to build or create a system of thought that dealt with schooling, curriculum, and instruction in the immediate sense. Other individuals, such as educational philosophers, administrators, or teachers, analyzed these comprehensive philosophies and applied their principles to education and schooling.[2]

Theories of education often exhibit elements of philosophical derivation. For example, Essentialism exhibits elements of Idealism and Realism, Perennialism of Realism and Thomism, and Progressivism of Naturalism and Pragmatism.

Theories of education can also be and often are derived from ideologies. This is particularly true in the case of schooling, which, in most countries, is a national system of educational institutions. The curriculum and styles of instruction, as well as goals and objectives, bear an ideological orientation. For example, schooling in the United States is imprinted with the U.S. version of democracy. Schooling in the former Soviet Union was based on Marxist Leninism. During the Nazi era in Germany and the Fascist period in Italy, schooling was one instrument used to achieve political goals. Again, theories of education exhibit certain elements of an ideological nature, which are also blended with those derived from philosophy. For instance, Social Reconstructionism blends philosophical elements from Pragmatism with ideological elements from Utopianism.

THEORY AS REACTION

Although educational theory is often derived from philosophies and ideologies, it also develops as a reaction to certain social, political, and economic situations, and in a sense is derived from them, or emerges as a reaction against certain ideas and practices. If one considers certain major events in U.S. educational history, the reactive nature of theory can be discerned. For example, after the American Revolution and in the early national period, Thomas Jefferson, Benjamin Rush, and others developed republican theories of education.[3] After the Civil War and the emancipation of the enslaved Africans, theories of educating the freed blacks developed.[4] When an increase in juvenile delinquency occurred after World War II, the theory of life-adjustment education emerged.

Progressive education, while being partly derived from Naturalism and Pragmatism, provides an example of how theory emerges as a reaction to a situation or to certain elements in that situation. At the end of the nineteenth century and beginning of the twentieth century, critics of public schooling in the United States contended that it had become too formal, devitalized, and geared to rote learning. In some of the big cities, school systems were mired in political patronage and corruption. Progressivism as an educational movement and the various experimental schools that it stimulated, including John Dewey's at the University of Chicago, were reactions designed to bring about the reform of U.S. society and education.[5] The revival of basic education, or Neo-Essentialism, in the 1980s provides a useful example of theory arising as a reaction against a political and economic situation and being combined with a particular set of educational ideas. By the late 1970s there was a growing movement, often outside of the schools, for a return to basic skills and subjects, discipline, and traditional values. This "back-to-basics" movement was a reaction against the social and cultural upheavals of the 1960s, the decline of U.S. economic productivity and structural dislocation in the economy, and certain curricular innovations such as the "new mathematics" and "new social studies," for example. By the 1980s, the back-to-basics theory had found support at the federal level in the policies of the Reagan administration and secretaries of education Bell and Bennett. *A Nation at Risk: The Imperative for Educational Reform* called for a curriculum of the "Five New Basics" and the restoration of rigorous academic standards that would reverse "a rising tide of mediocrity" in U.S. schools.[6]

The revived basic education program was also a reaction against certain educational practices that had emerged in the 1960s, especially in secondary schools. The large number of elective courses that had been developed in the 1960s to meet the then-current demands for "relevance" to student interests and social issues were attacked as depreciating and weakening the core of essential, or basic, skills. Curricular requirements in many states were revised to reflect competency in essential subjects such as English, mathematics, and science.

THEORY ARISING FROM PRACTICE

An important phenomenon is how educational theory arises from practice. In the case of the Progressive educator William Heard Kilpatrick, who is treated in Chapter 19, his theory initially emerged from his practice of encouraging cooperative group work, discouraging competition, and discontinuing the practice of marks and grades.

A current manifestation of this phenomenon of theory coming from practice can be found in the "effective schools movement." Certain schools, principals, and teachers are identified as being particularly effective in bringing about high levels of student achievement. An example of generating theory from practice is provided by a Department of Education report entitled *What Works: Research About Teaching and Learning,* which, through an analysis of research, comes to a set of findings or generalizations about effective education. Among the generalizations in *What Works* are the following:

> *Parents are their children's first and most influential teachers. What parents do to help their children learn is more important to academic success than how well-off the family is.*
>
> *Belief in the value of hard work, the importance of personal responsibility, and the importance of education itself contribute to greater success in school.*
>
> *Children learn science best when they are able to do experiments, so they can witness "science in action."*

Teachers who set and communicate high expectations to all their students obtain greater academic performance from those students than teachers who set low expectations.

The most important characteristics of effective schools are strong instructional leadership, a safe and orderly climate, schoolwide emphasis on basic skills, high teacher expectations for student achievement, and continuous assessment of pupil progress.[7]

What Works is based on a research investigation and analysis of school practices. Information about these practices is organized as findings. These findings have sufficient generality about them that they can be applied in various school settings. In other words, they represent an emerging theory of education.

CONCLUSION

In Chapter 16 we have briefly examined educational theory as it is derived from philosophies and ideologies, as it emerges as a reaction to certain situations, and as it arises from school practice. In the following chapters, we examine Essentialism, Perennialism, Progressivism, and Social Reconstructionism, and Critical Theory as theories of education.

DISCUSSION QUESTIONS

1. Based on class discussion, stipulate a definition of educational theory.

2. Examine the relationships among philosophies, ideologies, and theories.

3. Discuss the current expectations that you and your colleagues have of education. Does a theory of education emerge?

4. In your opinion, what constitutes an effective school? After identifying the elements that characterize an effective school, develop a set of generalizations that could be applied to schools. To what degree do your generalizations constitute a theory of education?

5. Reflect on your own educational experiences. Does an educational pattern or theory emerge from your reflections?

INQUIRY PROJECTS

- Examine the bulletin or catalogue of your college or university. Can you deduce a theory of education from its contents?
- Read and review a book on public policy. In a paper, comment on the possibilities of deriving a theory of education from it.
- Read and review a history of U.S. education with particular reference to how educational theories have emerged as reactions to political, social, and economic situations.
- Read and review *A Nation at Risk* or another national report on education. Does this report suggest a theory of education?

- Analyze the teacher education program at your college or university. What are its essential elements? Does it constitute a theory on preparing effective teachers?

FURTHER READINGS

Archer, Margaret S. *Realist Social Theory: The Morphonetic Approach.* New York: Cambridge University Press, 1995.

Feinberg, Walter. *Understanding Education: Toward a Reconstruction of Educational Inquiry.* New York: Cambridge University Press, 1983.

Hare, William. *What Makes a Good Teacher: Reflections on Some Characteristics Central to the Educational Enterprise.* Ontario, Canada: The Althouse Press, 1993.

Jackson, Philip. *Life in Classrooms.* New York: Teachers College Press, Columbia University, 1990.

Kincheloe, Joe L. *Toward a Critical Politics of Teacher Thinking: Mapping the Postmodern.* Westport, CT and London, England: Bergin & Garvey, 1993.

Mason, Robert E. *Contemporary Educational Theory.* New York: David McKay, 1972.

Runciman, W. G. *A Treatise on Social Theory: The Methodology of Social Theory.* New York: Cambridge University Press, 1983.

Silver, Harold. *Good Schools, Effective Schools: Judgements and Their Histories.* New York: Cassell, 1995.

What Works: Research About Teaching and Learning. Washington, DC: U.S. Department of Education, 1986.

ENDNOTES

1. George F. Kneller, *Logic and Language of Education* (New York: John Wiley & Sons, 1966), pp. 157–160, 181–182.

2. Many examples exist of educational philosophies being derived from more comprehensive philosophies. Consult the following examples: J. Donald Butler, *Idealism in Education* (New York: Harper & Row, 1966); William Oliver Martin, *Realism in Education* (New York: Harper & Row, 1969); Van Cleve Morris, *Existentialism in Education* (New York: Harper & Row, 1966); Maxine Green, *Existential Encounters for Teachers* (New York: Random House, 1967).

3. Allen O. Hansen, *Liberalism and American Education in the Eighteenth Century* (New York: Macmillan, 1926).

4. See Henry A. Bullock, *A History of Negro Education in the South, from 1619 to the Present* (Cambridge, MA.: Harvard University Press, 1967).

5. Lawrence A. Cremin, *The Transformation of the School: Progressivism in American Education, 1876–1957* (New York: Alfred A. Knopf, 1962); Robert M. Crunden, *Ministers of Reform: The Progressives' Achievement in American Civilization, 1889–1920* (Urbana, IL: University of Illinois Press, 1984); Ellen Condliffe Lagemann, *A Generation of Women: Education in the Lives of Progressive Reformers* (Cambridge, MA: Harvard University Press, 1979).

6. National Commission on Excellence in Education. *A Nation at Risk: The Imperative for Educational Reform* (Washington, DC: U.S. Department of Education, 1983).

7. *What Works: Research About Teaching and Learning* (Washington, DC: U.S. Department of Education, 1986), pp. 7, 17, 23, 45.

▶ 17

Essentialism and Education

Essentialism is a theory that asserts that education properly involves the learning of the basic skills, arts, and sciences that have been useful in the past and are likely to remain useful in the future. The Essentialist, as the name suggests, believes that there are some essential, or basic, skills that have contributed to human well-being, such as reading, writing, arithmetic, and civilized social behavior that should be found in every sound elementary or primary school curriculum. At the secondary level, the basic curriculum should consist of history, mathematics, science, languages, and literature. The college curriculum should consist of both the liberal arts and science. By mastering these subjects that deal with the natural and social environments, students are prepared to participate effectively in civilized society.

Although perhaps not identified as Essentialism, this theory has had a long history and definite staying power in U.S. education and schooling. When it originated in the nineteenth century, many proponents of public education believed that the goal of the common schools should be the development of a literate, skilled, and productive populace. Schooling was identified with economic productivity and growth. In the early twentieth century, social efficiency educators argued that the public school curriculum should stress those skills and subjects that contributed to economically and socially efficient lives. Periodically in U.S. educational history, concerted efforts have been made to relate education and schools to civic competency, economic skills, and social efficiency.

Clifton Fadiman has stated the case for basic education, another name for Essentialism. Basic education, he says, is concerned with subjects that have "generative power," which means the potency to endow students "with the ability to learn the higher, more complex developments of these master subjects as well as the minor or self-terminating" ones. Such generative subjects deal with "language, whether or not one's own; forms, figures, and numbers; the laws of nature; the past; and the shape and behavior of our common home, the earth."[1]

Among the common Essentialist themes are the following: (1) the elementary curriculum should emphasize basic tool skills that contribute to literacy and numeracy; (2) the secondary curriculum should include history, mathematics, science, literature, and language; (3) discipline is necessary for systematic learning in school situations; (4) respect for legitimate authority, both in school and in society, should be cultivated in students; (5) the mastering of a skill or a subject requires effort and diligence on the part of the learner; (6) the teaching of these necessary skills and subjects requires mature and well-educated teachers who know their subjects and are able to transmit them to students.

In this chapter we examine the Essentialist position, look at Arthur Bestor's curriculum of intellectual disciplines, explore basic education and the Essentialist revival, examine schooling and Essentialism, and inquire into Essentialism's philosophical and ideological relationships.

THE ESSENTIALIST POSITION

Although the basic education position has had a long history, the Essentialist doctrine was formally stated by a group of like-minded educators at the convention of the National Education Association in 1938. Reacting against what they considered the excesses of Progressive education, the Essentialists argued that the primary function of formal education was to preserve and transmit the basic elements, or essentials, of human culture.

In outlining the "Essentialist Platform," William Chandler Bagley, professor of education at Columbia University's Teachers College, stated that (1) U.S. elementary school students were failing to meet the "standards of achievement in the fundamentals of education" attained in other countries; (2) U.S. secondary school students lagged academically behind the eighteen-year-olds of other countries; (3) increasingly large numbers of high school students were essentially illiterate and could not read effectively, and because of deficiencies at the primary and intermediate levels, remedial reading programs had to be instituted in many high schools; (4) in addition to declining literacy, notable deficiencies existed in mathematics and grammar; and (5) despite increased educational expenditures in the United States, there was a noticeable increase in the rates of serious crime.

Bagley identified two specific causes of the United States' educational malaise: (1) dominant educational theories, such as Progressivism, were "essentially enfeebling," and (2) the relaxation of academic standards in many school systems had led to the policy of widespread "social promotion." Bagley chastised Progressives for overemphasizing the child's freedom, interests, and play, and for abandoning discipline, effort, and work. For Bagley, Progressive education had contributed to the "complete abandonment in many school systems of rigorous standards of scholastic achievement for promotion from grade to grade, and the passing of all pupils 'on schedule.' "[2] Instead of a curriculum based on systematic and sequential learning and consecutive, cumulative, and orderly academic development, the Progressives had substituted an undifferentiated program of activities, projects, and incidental learning. Bagley's condemnation of social promotion was similar to today's basic education arguments that students should master minimal competencies before being promoted to a higher grade or being awarded a diploma.

Bagley was joined by other professional educators such as Michael Demiashkevich, Walter H. Ryle, M. L. Shane, and Gary M. Whipple, who, calling themselves Essentialists, urged U.S. schools, teachers, and administrators to return to the basic skills of recording, computing, measuring, U.S. history, health instruction, natural science, and the fine and industrial arts. In taking their stance, the Essentialists asked:

Should not our public schools prepare boys and girls for adult responsibility through systematic training in such subjects as reading, writing, arithmetic, history, and English, requiring mastery of such subjects, and, when necessary, stressing discipline and obedience?[3]

Arguing that progressive education had created discontinuity between the generations, Bagley urged U.S. educators and schools to provide each generation with "possession of a common core of ideas, meanings, understandings, and ideals representing the most precious elements of the human heritage."[4]

Although Essentialists stated their case carefully and consistently, their educational philosophy was not to prevail in the colleges of education, in teacher education, or in the professional literature. Essentialism was either neglected or relegated to a footnote in books on the history of education. Essentialism has recently reappeared in the basic education revival that argues that scholastic standards have fallen, academic rigor and sequence are absent in many schools, and that there needs to be a return to essential skills and subjects.

Bagley and his Essentialists issued a thorough rationale for the Essentialist position. Although early Essentialism has been neglected by philosophers and historians of education, the Essentialist Platform was clearly prophetic of what has proved to be a recurring critique of U.S. education and schools. Like the authors of *A Nation at Risk,* the early Essentialists used comparative and cross-cultural evidence to identify the academic deficiencies of U.S. students. They, like contemporary critics, contended that academic standards had eroded because of permissivism and progressivism. Like current critics, they attributed rising crime rates to indiscipline and a lack of standards in the schools. However, the Essentialism of the 1930s makes an interesting contrast with the contemporary movement. The early Essentialists largely came from within the ranks of professional educators; in fact, several were highly prominent professors of education. Contemporary Essentialism draws much of its support from outside of the educational profession, particularly from business leaders and from Neo-Conservative political forces.

BESTOR'S CURRICULUM
OF INTELLECTUAL DISCIPLINES

The basic education position surfaced again in the 1950s. Just as the earlier Essentialists had challenged Progressive education, critics in the 1950s reacted against a new educational theory called "life adjustment" that emphasized the personal and social needs of U.S. children and youth over academic subjects. Critics such as Max Rafferty, Hyman Rickover, and Arthur Bestor questioned life-adjustment education. Rafferty, who served as Superintendent of Public Instruction in California from 1963 to 1971, wrote two books, *Suffer Little Children* and *What They Are Doing to Your Children,* which attacked Progressive educators for lacking standards and for encouraging a permissiveness that had produced a generation of delinquent, unpatriotic, undereducated "slobs."[5] Admiral Hyman Rickover, who pioneered the first atomic submarine, decried the decline of U.S. academic standards in *Education and Freedom, Swiss Schools and Ours: Why Theirs are Better,* and *American Education—A National Failure.*[6] Rickover argued that U.S. public education had lowered academic standards, ignored the intellectually gifted, and neglected mathematics, science, and foreign-language instruction.

One of the most articulate critics of the 1950s, Arthur Bestor, professor of history at the University of Illinois, published *Educational Wastelands* (1953) and *The Restoration of Learning* (1956) and helped organize the Council for Basic Education.[7] According to Bestor: (1) academic standards in U.S. public schools had declined because of an anti-intellectual educational philosophy that had separated the schools from the scientific and scholarly disciplines; and (2) a narrowly educated group of professional educators, administrators, and department of education bureaucrats at the state level had gained control of entry into the teaching profession by manipulating certification requirements. Bestor urged that the trend to anti-intellectualism be reversed and that the public school curriculum be based on the intellectual disciplines of English, foreign languages, history, mathematics, and science. While the Essentialists were professional educators and the critics of the 1950s primarily were not, their arguments had much in common. Both groups believed that U.S. schools were dominated by an anti-basic education theory. For the Essentialists, it was Progressivism. For the critics of the 1950s, it was life adjustment. Both groups decried falling academic standards, declining literacy, and the absence of rigor and discipline in the schools. Bagley, Rickover, and Bestor saw European schools as having higher academic standards than U.S. schools.

In particular, Bestor's books were part of the movement to restore a basic subject-matter curriculum in the nation's schools. Some comments on his philosophy of education are useful in examining contemporary Essentialist education that emphasizes basic education and a return to intellectual disciplines as the focus of curriculum.

In *The Restoration of Learning,* Bestor established a criterion of education based on intellectual disciplines and indicated that U.S. education was failing to meet the criterion of disciplined intelligence. Strongly implied in Bestor's educational theory is a conception of U.S. democracy based on the rule of reasonable and intelligent citizens. An intelligently functioning democracy is a government of law, orderly parliamentary processes, and democratic guarantees for all citizens. Bestor expressed a definite Essentialist theory of education which provides

> *sound training in the fundamental ways of thinking represented by history, science, mathematics, literature, language, art and other disciplines evolved in the course of mankind's long quest for usable knowledge, cultural understanding, and intellectual power.*[8]

These intellectual disciplines should be fundamental in the school curriculum for they are basic in modern life. In the elementary school, reading, writing, and arithmetic provide indispensable generative skills. The essentials of the secondary school curriculum are science, mathematics, history, English, and foreign languages. These intellectual disciplines, the core of a liberal education, are humankind's most reliable tools in solving personal, social, political, and economic problems.

Bestor sought to achieve his educational ideal through an essential subject-matter curriculum based on history, mathematics, science, foreign languages, and English. Indeed, the years devoted to the pursuit of formal learning are based on these five essential intellectual disciplines. During the first four, five, or six years of schooling, reading, writing, and arithmetic are the necessary generative tool skills. The elementary school student should also be introduced to the structures and methods of the natural sciences, geography, and history.[9]

Junior high school, the grades from seven to nine, marks the beginning of organized and systematic study. A transition is made from arithmetic to the more abstract forms of mathematical reasoning, beginning with elementary algebra. History is to assume a recognized chronological structure. From the generalized natural science studied earlier, a transition is made as the student is introduced to sciences such as biology, physics, or chemistry. Instruction in foreign languages moves forward to grammatical analysis.

Students in the senior high school are expected to pursue a subject methodologically and to use abstract reasoning. Specifically, the study of mathematics is continued through advanced algebra, plane geometry, trigonometry, analytical geometry, and calculus. Systematic work in chemistry, physics, and biology furnishes the needed foundations of scientific knowledge. History's chronological pattern and structure are emphasized. English is employed with accuracy, lucidity, and grace. One foreign language is mastered and another begun.[10]

Bestor's proposed curriculum is prescribed for all students. Once he or she has mastered these essentials, the student can begin vocational or college education. Training in the liberating disciplines prepares a person for intellectual life, citizenship, a vocation, and for a profession.

Bestor feared that U.S. schools were failing to provide the needed intellectual discipline. He charged that some professional educators postulated an erroneous view of a democratic education. Because the intellectual disciplines were once reserved to aristocratic elites, these educators failed to realize that the progress of the modern age now made an intellectual education the prerogative of all.

Bestor charged that professional educators, no longer content with methodology, had usurped curriculum making. Curriculum construction is best exercised by the scholars and scientists who are expert in their academic disciplines. Some professional educators had distorted Progressive education into a "regressive education," according to Bestor. They had watered down the great intellectual disciplines and introduced vocational and life-adjustment courses into the general curriculum to the detriment of the academic subjects. By weakening liberal education, too much of public education had become anti-democratic and anti-intellectual.

Bestor's educational agenda emphasized two fundamental principles: (1) ensuring disciplined intellectual education to every future citizen, and (2) providing opportunity for advanced study to all who possess genuine intellectual capacity and a willingness to develop their intellectual powers.[11]

These two principles serve as the basis of the school's primary responsibilities, which are outlined as follows: (1) the school should provide a standard program of intellectual training in the fundamental disciplines geared to the needs of serious students and to the capacities of the upper two-thirds of the school population; (2) the school should provide special opportunities for exceptionally able students; (3) programs designed for the highest third of the school population should be balanced with adequate remedial programs for the lowest third, the slow learners; (4) a program of physical education for all children should be provided that is distinguished from interschool athletics; (5) the school should diversify its offerings to include certain areas of vocational training; (6) there should be certain extracurricular activities; (7) high-ability students should continue in school; (8) life-adjustment training should be provided only for the least able and least ambitious.[12]

Bestor's proposed reform runs counter to the Progressive views of education. The chief contention is evident in this quotation from Bestor's *The Restoration of Learning:* "The school makes itself ridiculous whenever it undertakes to deal directly with 'real-life' problems, instead of indirectly through the development of generalized intellectual powers."[13]

BASIC EDUCATION AND THE ESSENTIALIST REVIVAL

A recent revival of Essentialism in the United States is the movement for "basic" education. In some respects, this movement, like the earlier Essentialist one, generated from criticisms of U.S. public schools. Basic-education proponents used comparisons with education in other countries, often Germany and Japan, for evidence that U.S. academic standards and achievement had declined. Among the criticisms that proponents of basic education have levied are the following:

1. Permissive, open, and progressive educational methods have neglected basic skills of reading, writing, and arithmetic, and have contributed to a growing functional illiteracy.
2. Schools do not stress fundamental values of industriousness, punctuality, effort, morality, or patriotism.
3. Teachers are ill prepared and undereducated; those teachers who strive for academic excellence find themselves thwarted by inefficient, expensive, and mindless educational bureaucracies.
4. Recent curricular innovations have neglected fundamental skills and subjects. Further, the confusing jargon of the "new math, new social studies, and new science" has made it difficult for parents to be involved in and to monitor their children's education.
5. Social-promotion policies rather than academic achievement have dumped ill-prepared and undereducated high school graduates on the society and the economy.
6. Schools have been used for social engineering and experimentation rather than for basic education. Administrators and teachers perform so many noneducational functions that they neglect the basics.
7. Educational expenses could be contained by reducing nonacademic frills, eliminating electives, and concentrating on required basic skills and subjects.
8. Permissive policies have contributed to violence and vandalism in the schools.
9. Minority groups such as African Americans and Hispanics have been shortchanged by the schools with respect to instruction in the basic skills.
10. U.S. industrial and business productivity has been reduced by undereducated graduates who cannot perform fundamental skills, who cannot read or write effectively, and who lack productive work skills and habits.

The revival of basic education took three lines of development. One, the Council for Basic Education continued to emphasize intellectual content from a liberal arts and sciences perspective. The Council for Basic Education emphasized intellectual content from a liberal arts and sciences perspective. The second line of development emerged from a coalition of some parents, businesspersons, politicians, and occasionally professional educators, who were dissatisfied with public education for a variety of reasons, among them, declining test scores, a decline of traditional patriotic and moral values, increasing drug abuse, and the weakening of the economic position of the United States relative to foreign competitors. Although these critics had varying motives, they were united in demanding a return to basic skills, subjects, and values.[14] The third line of development came under the auspices of the federal government, under the leadership of Terrel Bell, Secretary of Education in the Reagan administration, with the publication in 1983 of *A Nation at Risk*.

Like other reports calling for a return to rigorous academic standards, *A Nation at Risk* warned that "the educational foundations of our society are presently being eroded by a rising tide of mediocrity that threatens our very future as a Nation and a people."[15] Echoing the criticisms of Bagley and Bestor, the National Commission on Excellence reported its findings. Among them were the following:

> *Secondary school curricula have been homogenized, diluted and diffused to the point that they no longer have a central purpose.*[16]

> *In many other industrialized nations, courses in mathematics (other than arithmetic or general mathematics), biology, chemistry, physics, and geography start in grade 6 and are required of all students. The time spent on these subjects, based on class hours, is about three times that spent by even the most science-oriented U.S. students, i.e., those who select 4 years of science and mathematics in secondary school.*[17]

> *In many schools, the time spent learning how to cook and drive counts as much toward a high school diploma as the time spent studying mathematics, English, chemistry, U.S. history, or biology.*[18]

Leaning heavily in the direction of a content-oriented and subject-matter curriculum, the Commission on Excellence recommended

> *that State and local high school graduation requirements be strengthened and that, at a minimum, all students seeking a diploma be required to lay the foundations in the Five New Basics by taking the following curriculum during their 4 years of high school: (a) 4 years of English; (b) 3 years of mathematics; (c) 3 years of science; (d) 3 years of social studies; and (e) one-half year of computer science. For the college-bound, 2 years of foreign language in high school are strongly recommended in addition to those taken earlier.*[19]

and

> *that schools, colleges, and universities adopt more rigorous and measurable standards, and higher expectations, for academic performance and student conduct, and that 4-year colleges and universities raise their requirements for admission. This will help students do their best educationally with challenging materials in an environment that supports learning and authentic accomplishment.*[20]

A Nation at Risk stimulated other national reports and educational recommendations that urged emphasis on basic skills and subjects. For example, the Task Force on Education for Economic Growth, in *Action for Excellence*, stressed basic skills and competencies for productive employment in a structurally and technologically changing society.[21] The College Board in *Academic Preparation for College* identified the basic academic competencies or "broad intellectual skills essential to effective work" in college as reading, speaking and listening, writing, mathematics, reasoning, and studying. Added to this conventional list of tool skills was a basic knowledge of computer processes, terminology, and application.[22] The College Board identified the basic academic subjects that provide "the detailed knowledge and skills" for effective college work as English, the arts, mathematics, science, social studies, and foreign languages.[23]

Essentialism also has reappeared in the arguments of commentators such as E. D. Hirsch, Jr., Chester Finn, and Diane Ravitch who contend that public schools are failing to impart the knowledge needed for cultural and political literacy. For example, E. D. Hirsch, Jr., argues that the average American's declining cultural literacy, the lack of a shared body of common knowledge, is negatively impacting a sense of a national cultural identity and ability to communicate effectively with other Americans. Because the contemporary school curriculum does not deliberately transmit a core to develop cultural literacy, many students complete their formal education without the necessary contextual background that enables them to reference and interpret materials crucial for public communication and for effective functioning in the workplace. A core curriculum designed to promote cultural literacy, Hirsch contends, is needed if citizens are to participate in the institutions and processes of political democracy.[24]

SCHOOLING AND ESSENTIALISM

Essentialism defines the role of schooling in strictly academic terms. For Essentialists, the term *academic,* too, is specifically defined as foundational skills and intellectual subject matters. Essentialists do not like vaguely constructed or broadly defined educational agendas that move the educational process into non-academic areas. This tendency, found among Progressives and Social Reconstructionists, for example, confuses the purpose of the schools, according to Essentialists.

Just as the school's function is specifically defined, the curriculum, too, is specific in terms of generative tool skills and academic subjects. Further, the curriculum is considered too important by Essentialists to be determined by shifting social fads and tendencies and by childish whims. Essentialists argue that educators must carefully structure the curriculum according to scope and sequence. Each grade level should have a particular set of objectives to guide instruction. Each teacher must have a particular set of skills or a well-defined academic subject to teach. It is important that the schools be administered so that each skill or subject is taught in an articulated manner, with one phase of instruction leading to the next. Further, instruction should be cumulative in that each phase builds on the preceding phase and leads to the next.

Essentialists argue that although schools are part of a societal context, they are effective when they fulfill their primary academic function. Knowledge of the social context should help teachers do their academic jobs more effectively and efficiently. It should also help administrators and teachers perform their primary tasks more effectively and efficiently. However, the existence of social problems should not deter teachers from performing their academic tasks, nor should these social issues be allowed to alter the primary function of schools. The Essentialist view is that large social problems are at base political, economic, and social issues that need to be addressed by agencies outside of the school, whose functions are appropriate in dealing with these problems. Although educators need to understand social problems and how they impact education, teachers do not have it in their power to cure society's ills. They do have it in their power, however, to teach reading, writing, history, and science, for example. By providing academic literacy, schools can build a civic knowledge base in an informed citizenry that can then use their informed intelligence to resolve social issues.

For the Essentialist, the examination of social, political, and economic issues are part of the exploration of the academic knowledge base. Here the academic subject either reaches its current or applied state. For example, poverty, drug abuse, and racism might be part of an academic exploration of subject matter. The objective is to understand trends and tendencies in a particular academic subject. The function of the school is to examine issues academically, not to solve them in the school. Indeed, the Essentialist is likely to argue that it is beyond the school's power to solve social problems. The school does its job when it educates an intelligent citizenry and a competent work force by imparting the necessary skills and knowledge of subject matter.

ESSENTIALISM'S PHILOSOPHICAL AND IDEOLOGICAL RELATIONSHIPS

As an educational theory, Essentialism exhibits certain themes that are parallel with the more traditional philosophies of Idealism, Realism, and Thomism discussed earlier. (To review these themes, you may wish to refer to Chapters 2, 3, and 4.) Like these philosophies, Essentialism's educational perspective stresses the transmission to the young of a structured and orderly view of reality. While the Idealist, Realist, and Thomist conceptions of reality are metaphysical, the Essentialist preference for order and structure is primarily social, economic, and cultural. It should be pointed out, however, that some Essentialists derived their position from one of these traditional philosophies.

In terms of an ideological orientation, Essentialism parallels most closely the Conservative view that sees education's primary function as that of transmitting the funded and approved knowledge and values of the culture. It also bears some resemblance to the Liberal perspective, particularly the Classical Liberal variety, which emphasizes the skills, knowledge, and values that enhance social and economic efficiency. Essentialism is highly compatible with those aspects of the contemporary Neo-Conservative ideology that emphasizes a need to (1) enhance U.S. economic productivity in a highly competitive global economy;

(2) restore standards of civility and academic achievement in public schools; (3) structure the curriculum around the fundamental skills and subjects that contribute to social, economic, and political efficiency; and (4) oppose those educators who would weaken the schools' primary academic mission.

The Essentialist position opposes certain aspects of Naturalism, Pragmatism, and Existentialism, which were discussed in Chapters 5, 6, and 7. Unlike the Naturalists, who stress the educational potency of the person's feelings and emotions, Essentialists emphasize the primary importance of the human mind as an instrument best cultivated by intellectual disciplines. While Pragmatists stress an open and evolutionary universe of constant change, Essentialists want education, especially schooling, to provide human beings with a secure and stable reference point. Whereas Existentialists stress human subjectivity and self-definition, Essentialists are more concerned with transmitting an antecedent curriculum to learners.

For the Essentialist, the school has the specific function of transmitting to the young certain generative skills and certain general intellectual disciplines. By transmitting these skills and subjects, the school perpetuates the cultural heritage. Conservatives would concur with Essentialists that the school is to be an agency of cultural continuity and stability. Essentialists would argue that the more the society shows symptoms of social malaise, the more important it is for schools to be stable academic environments for students.

The term *essential* means that the school, in performing its role as a cultural transmitter, identifies and perpetuates the basic cultural elements. It is not to take on nonessential functions such as "social adjustment," career education, consumer education, cooking classes, and other such activities that should be learned elsewhere. For the school to assume responsibility for these nonessentials would mean that the essential core of necessary skills and subjects would be diluted or diminished.

For Essentialists and the contemporary proponents of basic education, the school's primary mission is academic. It is not an agency to promote social engineering, as Utopians or Social Reconstructionists assert. Sharing the Conservative's suspicion of innovation and change, Essentialists would oppose using the schools as experimental laboratories to test curricular or instructional innovations. Untested innovation creates an unsettled atmosphere that weakens the school's essential or basic function.

Primarily an educational theory that focuses on schooling rather than on large socioeconomic issues, Essentialism has a well-defined curricular orientation. Essentialists assert that the curriculum should provide students with a differentiated and organized learning experience rather than an undifferentiated experience that students must organize themselves. The most effective and efficient mode of providing a differentiated educational experience is the subject-matter curriculum in which each subject or intellectual discipline is organized separately from other subjects. Further, each subject is organized according to carefully arranged principles of scope and sequence.

The Essentialists reject curricular innovations, such as Experimentalist problem solving or Progressive projects, which seek to break down subject-matter boundaries. Such undifferentiated curricular designs, contend the Essentialists, are inefficient in that they often force students to "reinvent the wheel" rather than learning and using the fund of knowledge that already exists. Moreover, these undifferentiated educational approaches are presumptuous in that they assume that students can take some elements from a subject without knowing the context from which it comes. Essentialists would condemn the Pragmatist, Reconstructionist, and Progressive approaches to learning as contributing to an academic confusion that weakens intellectual authority and social organization.

Essentialists, like the adherents to traditional philosophies and Conservative ideology, assert that the teacher is an academic authority figure. The teacher is to be a specialist in the content of the subject matter and be skilled in organizing it for instructional purposes. While the Essentialist teacher speaks with the sense of authority that knowledge brings, this should not be confused with authoritarianism. Defenders of intellectual disciplines, such as Arthur Bestor, argue that the liberal knowledge that they contain and convey is the best guarantee for preserving both academic freedom in the school and civil liberties in society.

CONCLUSION

Essentialism is the educational theory that sees the primary function of the school as the preservation and transmission of the basic elements of human culture. It emphasizes (1) a return to systematic subjects, (2) learning as the mastery of basic skills and knowledge, (3) the teacher as a mature representative of the culture and someone who is competent in both subject matter and instruction, (4) education as preparation for work and citizenship, and (5) the preservation of the school's academic function. Above all, Essentialists oppose catering to childish whims or to transitory fads that will cause schools to degenerate into mindless and irrelevant institutions.

DISCUSSION QUESTIONS

1. Define Essentialism and indicate how the term applies to the school and the curriculum.

2. Examine the Essentialist critique. Does it resemble contemporary criticisms of U.S. public schooling?

3. Examine Arthur Bestor's rationale for a curriculum based on intellectual disciplines. Compare and contrast Bestor's proposed curriculum with that recommended in *A Nation at Risk*.

4. Why has there been a resurgence of the basic-education theory in the United States?

5. Reflect on your own educational experience. To what extent does it resemble or differ from an Essentialist or basic-education perspective?

6. Of the philosophies examined in this text, which is most compatible and which is least compatible with Essentialism or basic education?

7. Of the ideologies examined in this text, which is the most compatible and which is the least compatible with the Essentialist or basic-education theory?

INQUIRY PROJECTS

- Identify the key points in the Essentialist critique. In a paper, examine contemporary criticisms of public schooling found in reports such as *A Nation at Risk* and *Action for Excellence*. Do these criticisms parallel those made by the Essentialists?
- Examine and review selected publications of the Council for Basic Education.
- Review a book on education written by one of the following: Arthur Bestor, Max Rafferty, Clifton Fadiman, James Koerner, Hyman Rickover, or Diane Ravitch.
- Collect "letters to the editor" or other public-opinion pieces on education. Determine if these items reflect a basic-education perspective.
- Consult curriculum or methods books used in courses in teacher education at your college or university. To what degree do they reflect or disagree with the Essentialist or basic-education theory?
- Visit several schools and observe the curricular organization and instructional methods being used. To what extent do they reflect or disagree with the Essentialist or basic-education theory?

FURTHER READINGS

Bestor, Arthur E., Jr. *Educational Wastelands: Retreat from Learning in Our Public Schools.* Urbana: University of Illinois Press, 1953.

Bestor, Arthur E., Jr. *The Restoration of Learning: A Program for Redeeming the Unfulfilled Promise of American Education.* New York: Alfred A. Knopf, 1956.

Brodinsky, Ben. *Defining the Basics of American Education.* Bloomington, IN: Phi Delta Kappa Educational Foundation, 1977.

Bunzel, John H., ed. *Challenge to American Schools: The Case for Standards and Values.* New York: Oxford University Press, 1985.

French, Peter A., Theodore E. Uehling, and Howard K. Wettstein, eds. *Studies in Essentialism.* Minneapolis: University of Minnesota Press, 1986.

Gutek, Gerald L. *Basic Education: A Historical Perspective.* Bloomington, IN: Phi Delta Kappa Educational Foundation, 1981.

Hirsch, E. D., Jr. *Cultural Literacy: What Every American Needs to Know.* Boston: Houghton Mifflin, 1987.

Kandel, Isaac L. *William Chandler Bagley: Stalwart Educator.* New York: Teachers College Press, 1961.

Koerner, James D., ed. *The Case for Basic Education.* Boston: Little, Brown, 1959.

National Commission on Excellence in Education. *A Nation at Risk: The Imperative for Educational Reform.* Washington, DC: U.S. Department of Education, 1983.

The Nation Responds: Recent Efforts to Improve Education. Washington, DC: U.S. Department of Education, 1984.

Pursell, William. *A Conservative Alternative School: The A+ School in Cupertino.* Bloomington, IN: Phi Delta Kappa Educational Foundation, 1976.

Rafferty, Max. *Suffer Little Children.* New York: Signet, 1962.

Rafferty, Max. *What They Are Doing to Your Children.* New York: New American Library, 1963.

Rickover, H. G. *American Education—A National Failure.* New York: E. P. Dutton, 1963.

Rickover, H. G. *Education and Freedom.* New York: E. P. Dutton, 1959.

Rickover, H. G. *Swiss Schools and Ours: Why Theirs Are Better.* Boston: Atlantic–Little, Brown, 1962.

Sewall, Gilbert T. *Necessary Lessons: Decline and Renewal in American Schools.* New York: The Free Press, 1983.

Sommer, Carl. *Schools in Crisis: Training for Success or Failure?* Houston, TX: Cahill, 1984.

Task Force on Education for Economic Growth. *Action for Excellence.* Denver, CO: Education Commission of the States, 1983.

The College Board. *Academic Preparation for College: What Students Need to Know and Be Able to Do.* New York: The College Board, 1983.

ENDNOTES

1. Clifton Fadiman, "The Case for Basic Education," in James D. Koerner, ed., *The Case for Basic Education* (Boston: Little, Brown, 1959), pp. 5–6.

2. William C. Bagley, "An Essentialist's Platform for the Advancement of American Education," *Educational Administration and Supervision,* XXIV (April 1938): 241–256.

3. Adolphe E. Meyer, *The Development of Education in the Twentieth Century* (Englewood Cliffs, NJ: Prentice Hall, 1949), p. 149.

4. Bagley, "An Essentialist's Platform," p. 254.

5. Max Rafferty, *Suffer Little Children* (New York: Signet, 1962); *What They Are Doing to Your Children* (New York: New American Library, 1963).

6. H. G. Rickover, *Swiss Schools and Ours: Why Theirs Are Better* (Boston: Atlantic–Little, Brown, 1962); *Education and Freedom* (New York: E. P. Dutton,

1959); *American Education—A National Failure* (New York: E. P. Dutton, 1963).

7. Arthur Bestor, *Educational Wastelands: Retreat from Learning in Our Public Schools* (Urbana: University of Illinois Press, 1953); *The Restoration of Learning: A Program for Redeeming the Unfulfilled Promise of American Education* (New York: Alfred A. Knopf, 1956).

8. Bestor, *The Restoration of Learning,* p. 7.

9. Ibid., pp. 50–51.

10. Ibid.

11. Ibid., p. 358.

12. Ibid., pp. 364–365.

13. Ibid., p. 79.

14. Gerald L. Gutek, *Basic Education: A Historical Perspective* (Bloomington, IN: Phi Delta Kappa Educational Foundation, 1981), pp. 9–13.

15. National Commission on Excellence in Education, *A Nation at Risk: The Imperative for Educational Reform* (Wash-

ington, DC: U.S. Department of Education, 1983), p. 5.

16. Ibid., p. 18.

17. Ibid., p. 20.

18. Ibid., p. 22.

19. Ibid., p. 24.

20. Ibid., p. 27.

21. Task Force on Education for Economic Growth, *Action for Excellence* (Denver, CO: Education Commission of the States, 1983), p. 48.

22. The College Board, *Academic Preparation for College: What Students Need to Know and Be Able to Do* (New York: The College Board, 1983), pp. 7–11.

23. Ibid., p. 13.

24. E. D. Hirsch, Jr., *Cultural Literacy: What Every American Needs to Know* (Boston: Houghton Mifflin, 1987).

▶ 18

Perennialism and Education

The Perennialist theory of education draws heavily from the Realist and Thomist philosophies, examined earlier in this book. Metaphysically, the Perennialists proclaim the intellectual and spiritual character of the universe and the human place within it. Following the Aristotelian premise that human beings are rational creatures, the Perennialists see the school as a social institution specifically designed to develop human intellectual potentiality. The term *Perennialism* comes from the assertion that the important principles of education are changeless and recurrent. For the Perennialist, the educational philosopher's first problem is to examine human nature and to devise an educational program based on its universal characteristics. Among these characteristics are the following: (1) Our human intellect enables us to frame alternative propositions and to choose those that fulfill the requirements of our human nature. Because we can frame and choose between alternatives, we are free agents. (2) The basic human values derive from our rationality, which defines us as human. People everywhere frame their thoughts in symbolic patterns and communicate them to others. (3) Although cultural particularities exist, humans everywhere have framed ethical principles that govern their individual and corporate lives. Throughout the world, people of varying languages and cultures have developed religious and aesthetic modes of experience and expression.

Because human nature is constant, Perennialists assert, so are the basic patterns of education. Foremost, education should aim to cultivate rational powers. Basically, the universal aim of education is truth. And because that which is true is universal and unchanging, a genuine education should also be universal and constant. The school's curriculum should emphasize the universal and recurrent themes of human life. It should contain cognitive materials designed to cultivate rationality; it should be highly logical and enable students to use the symbolic patterns of thought and communication. It should cultivate ethical principles and encourage moral, aesthetic, and religious criticism and appreciation. The Perennialist educational theory seeks to develop the intellectual and spiritual potentialities of the child to their fullest extent through a subject-matter curriculum based on such disciplines as history, language, mathematics, logic, literature, the humanities, and science. These subjects, regarded as bearing the knowledge of the human race, are the tools of civilized people and have a disciplinary effect on the human mind.

Perennialist educational theory emphasizes the humanities as providing insights into the good, true, and beautiful. In these works, humankind has captured a glimpse of the eternal truths and values. Such insights, found in science, philosophy, literature, history, and art, persist as they are transmitted from generation to generation. Works such as those of Plato, Aristotle, and John Stuart Mill, for example, possess a quality that makes them perennially appealing to people living at different times and in different places. Other ideas, which may be popular to a particular time but fail to meet the test of time, are discarded.

These general principles associated with Perennialism can be seen by examining the educational ideas of Robert M. Hutchins and Jacques Maritain. While Hutchins represents a more secular variety of classical humanism, Maritain has been identified with the religious Perennialism associated with Neo-Thomistic philosophy. Although certain important variations exist in the philosophical positions of both Hutchins and Maritain, there is agreement on the following basic principles: (1) a body of truth exists that is universally valid regardless of circumstances and contingencies; (2) a sound education will contribute to the pursuit of truth and to the cultivation of the permanent principles of right and justice; and (3) truth can be taught best through the systematic study and analysis of the human past—as portrayed in the great works of religion, philosophy, literature, and history. In addition to examining the ideas of Hutchins and Maritain, we will also discuss the Paideia proposal as a revival of Perennialism. We will then examine Perennialism in relationship to the other philosophies and ideologies treated in this text.

ROBERT M. HUTCHINS

Robert Maynard Hutchins (1899–1977) was an articulate advocate of the proposition that education is properly devoted to the cultivation of the human intellect. Hutchins received his higher education at Yale University. From 1927 to 1929 he was a professor of law at Yale. At age thirty, he became president of the University of Chicago and served until he became chancellor of that university in 1945.[1] In 1954, Hutchins was named head of the Fund for the Republic. He was associated with the Center for the Study of Democratic Institutions, a nonprofit educational enterprise established by the Fund for the Republic to promote the principles of individual liberty in a democratic society. Hutchins spoke and wrote on liberal education. His major educational works include *The Higher Learning in America* (1936), *Education for Freedom* (1943), *Conflict in Education in a Democratic Society* (1953), *University of Utopia* (1953), and *The Learning Society* (1968).[2]

When asked his opinion as to the ideal education, Hutchins replied:

> *Ideal education is the one that develops intellectual power. I arrive at this conclusion by a process of elimination. Educational institutions are the only institutions that can develop intellectual power. The ideal education is not an* ad hoc *education, not an education directed to immediate needs; it is not a specialized education, or a pre-professional education; it is not a utilitarian education. It is an education calculated to develop the mind.*
>
> *There may be many ways, all equally good, of developing the mind. I have old-fashioned prejudices in favor of the three R's and the liberal arts, in favor of trying to understand the greatest works that the human race has produced. I believe that these are the permanent necessities, the intellectual tools that are needed to understand the ideas and ideals of our world. This does not exclude later specialization or later professional education; but I insist that without the intellectual techniques needed to understand ideas, and without at least an acquaintance with the major ideas that have animated mankind since the dawn of history, no man may call himself educated.[3]*

Hutchins's words reveal some basic principles of his educational philosophy. He believed that: (1) a cultivation of the foundational skills of reading, writing, and arithmetic was indispensable for literate and civilized people; (2) a liberal education should contribute to an understanding of the great works of civilization; and (3) professional and specialized education should be deferred until one has completed general education, an education every person should have as a rational human being.

In 1936, Hutchins published *The Higher Learning in America,* which was a critique of both higher education and general education. Commentary on this work is useful in establishing Hutchins's educational perspective.

Hutchins based his educational philosophy on two basic concepts: (1) humans' rational nature; and (2) a conception of knowledge based on eternal, absolute, and universal truths. His educational theory assumes the presence in human nature of essential and unchanging elements. Believing that human nature was everywhere the same, Hutchins stressed a universal education. Because rationality is the highest attribute of human nature, the cultivation of the intellect is education's highest goal.[4] The intellectual virtues lead to the discovery of the great truths found in the classic works of Western civilization.

Unfortunately, U.S. education has failed to devote its energies to the pursuit of truth and to the cultivation of intellectual excellence. U.S. higher education, in particular, has become misdirected because of confusion that exists in the society external to education. Three factors, Hutchins asserted, have contributed to this general confusion: (1) love of money, (2) an erroneous conception of democracy, and (3) a false notion of progress. Immersed in materialism and catering to the shifting whims of students, donors, business interests, alumni, and politicians, Hutchins claimed that the university had lost its integrity in the frantic search for operating funds. Contemporary America had witnessed the rise of a university that was much like a service station. In contrast, Hutchins argued for a university whose sole purpose was to pursue and discover truth.

Hutchins believed that a confused conception of democracy had resulted in the commonly held belief that everyone should receive the same amount and degree of education. He would reserve higher education for students who have the interest and ability for independent intellectual activity. A false notion of progress had led to the rejection of the wisdom of the past, which had been replaced by a belief that progress comes only from empiricism and materialism. A superficial empiricism had confused knowledge with the mere collection of information and data, according to Hutchins. This confusion had produced an anti-intellectualism that regarded the most worthwhile education as that bringing the greatest financial return.

U.S. higher education was not only beset by confusion from external sources, but it also had its own internal conditions of disintegration, such as professionalism, isolation, and anti-intellectualism. Professionalism, resulting from the surrender of the university to vocational pressures, was motivated by the perverted utilitarianism that equated making money with knowledge. Hutchins's attack on premature professionalism was based on three main arguments: (1) school instruction lags behind actual practice; (2) it is foolish to try to master constantly changing techniques; and (3) direct experience is the most efficient source of practical wisdom.

Overspecialization has isolated specialist from specialist, Hutchins said. Without the integrating core of a common education, specialists lacked the ideas and language that came from shared and communicable experience. Anti-intellectualism stems from an emphasis on the purely utilitarian at the cost of sacrificing theory and speculation. Hutchins asserted that theoretical knowledge was essential to human rationality.

Hutchins claimed that vocationalism and specialized education had entered the curriculum prematurely and had distorted the purposes of general education. An overemphasis on specialization had pushed the liberal arts out of the general curriculum. Some educators had tied education to specific political and social programs that led to either superficiality or indoctrination rather than to critical intelligence.

The Curriculum: The Permanent Studies

Hutchins argued that the curriculum should be composed of permanent studies that reflect the common elements of human nature and connect each generation to the best thoughts of humankind. He particularly recommended the study of the "great books"—classics contemporary in any age. The great books of the Western world embraced all areas of knowledge, according to Hutchins. He believed that four years spent reading and discussing the great books would cultivate standards of judgment and criticism and prepare students to think carefully and act intelligently.

In addition to the great books of Western civilization, Hutchins recommended the study of grammar, rhetoric, logic, and mathematics. Grammar, the analysis of language, contributed to the understanding and comprehension of the written word. Rhetoric provided the student with the rules of writing and speaking needed for intelligent expression; logic, the critical study of reasoning, enabled a person to think and express him- or herself in an orderly and systematic fashion. Mathematics was of general value as it represented reasoning in its clearest and most precise form.

In order to restore rationality in higher education, Hutchins advocated the revitalizing of metaphysics. As the study of first principles, he believed metaphysics pervaded the entire range of intellectual pursuits. Proceeding from the study of first principles to the most current concerns, higher education should examine fundamental human problems. Whereas the social sciences embrace the practical sciences of ethics, politics, and economics, the natural sciences deal with the study of natural and physical phenomena.

Hutchins, who was critical of the specialization that had occurred in teacher education, believed that prospective teachers should have a good general education in the liberal arts and sciences. Such an education contained the basic rules of pedagogy. The liberal arts—grammar, rhetoric, logic, and mathematics—were potent instruments in preparing the prospective teacher to organize, express, and communicate knowledge.

RELIGIOUS PERENNIALISM

The ecclesiastical varieties of Perennialism are found in the educational philosophies of the Neo-Thomists, who are often associated with Roman Catholic education.[5] Like their more secular conferees, the ecclesiastical Perennialists also believe in universal truths and values. These religious Perennialists believe in a permanent or perennial curriculum useful for all people regardless of the contingencies of differing cultures. The religious Perennialists stress that the universe and human beings within it were created by a supreme being who is a knowing and loving God. They see divine purpose operating within the laws of the universe and within human life. The religious variety of Perennialism finds expression in the philosophy of Jacques Maritain, who has also been classified as a Neo-Thomist or Integral Realist.

Jacques Maritain

Jacques Maritain was born in France in 1882 and was educated at the University of Paris. He was born into a Protestant family but became a convert to Roman Catholicism in 1906. Dissatisfied with the skepticism among academic philosophers, Maritain was attracted to the philosophy of Henri Bergson. He later came to urge a reconciliation of faith and reason in philosophy, as exemplified in the works of Thomas Aquinas. Maritain was an astute proponent of Neo-Thomist integral realism and wrote extensively on that subject. His books include such works as *Education at the Crossroads* (1943), *Man and the State* (1951), *On the Use of Philosophy* (1961), and *Integral Humanism* (1968).

Maritain's theory of education is expressed in *Education at the Crossroads,* in which he argued that the purposes of education were twofold: to educate persons to cultivate their humanity and to introduce them to their cultural heritage. Emphasis is given to the cultivation of rationality and spirituality, which define human character. Vocational and professional training he considered subordinate to the cultivation of the intellect.

Like Hutchins, Maritain condemned certain misconceptions that distorted education's true purposes. Influenced by Pragmatism, he believed that modern education, by overemphasizing means, had failed to distinguish between means and ends. The obsession with means had produced an aimless education devoid of guiding principles. Maritain asserted that the proper end of education was to educate people to realize their human potentialities. Genuine education rested on a conception of human nature based on the Judeo-Christian heritage. According to Maritain, education should guide individuals to shape themselves as human persons "armed with knowledge, strength of judgment, and moral virtues" while transmitting the "spiritual heritage" of their "nation and the civilization." Thus, it preserves "the century-old achievements of generations." While the vocational aspect of education is not to be disregarded, it "must never imperil the essential aim of education."[6]

Maritain attacked the "voluntarism" of Naturalists such as Rousseau and the Progressives who exaggerated the human being's emotional and volitional character. In seeking to educate the good-hearted person, the Naturalists neglected or minimized the cultivation of intelligent judgment. In contrast, Maritain argued that a simplistic emotionalism was inadequate. Indeed, he saw the properly functioning person as governed by intellect rather than emotionalism. Even more dangerous than Rousseauean voluntarism, according to Maritain, was the modern emphasis that urged the complete liberation of the emotions and that would make education a matter of feeling rather than thinking.

Maritain viewed the teacher as an educated, cultivated, and mature person who possessed knowledge that the students did not have but wished to acquire.

Good teaching should begin with what students already know and lead them to what they do not know. Maritain saw the teacher as a dynamic agent in the learning process.

The student, a rational and free being possessed of a spiritual soul and a corporeal body, was endowed with an intellect that sought to know. The good teacher should establish an orderly but open climate of learning that avoids the excesses of both anarchy and despotism, for the anarchical classroom rejects any kind of discipline and, with a misguided permissiveness, caters to childish whims. The despotic classroom, through fear of corporal or psychological punishment, reduces students' individuality to a standardized conformity in which spontaneity and creativity are punished as undesirable deviations.

The teacher's task is to foster those fundamental dispositions that enable students to realize their human potentialities. According to Maritain, the basic dispositions to be fostered by education are (1) love of truth, (2) love of goodness and justice, (3) simplicity and openness with regard to existence, (4) a sense of a job well done, and (5) a sense of cooperation. These five basic dispositions are to be cultivated by teachers capable of fostering growth of students' mental lives.

Maritain's Curriculum

Maritain recommended a subject-matter curriculum based on the systematic learned disciplines. Primary education, he contended, was to cultivate the basic skills needed for the successful study of the more systematic disciplines. Maritain argued against the view that the child is a miniature adult. The child's world, instead, was one of imagination. Primary teachers should begin their instruction within the child's own world of imagination and, through the use of stories and storylike narrations, lead the child to explore the objects and values of the rational world. Although the child's initial stimulus is through imagination, he or she gradually comes to exercise intellect in grasping the realities of the external world.

Maritain believed that both secondary education and higher education should be devoted to the cultivation of judgment and intellectuality through the study of the humanities. Secondary education, in particular, was to introduce the adolescent to the world of thought and to the great achievements of the human mind. Among the subjects that Maritain recommended for study in the secondary schools were grammar, foreign languages, history, geography, and the natural sciences.

Maritain divided the college curriculum into four years of study: (1) a year of mathematics and poetry when students study both these subjects and literature, logic, foreign languages, and the history of civilization; (2) a year of natural science and fine arts, which is devoted to physics, natural sciences, fine arts, mathematics, literature, poetry, and the history of science; (3) a year of philosophy, which includes the study of metaphysics, philosophy of nature, epistemology, psychology, physics and natural science, mathematics, literature, poetry, and fine arts; and (4) the last year—the year of ethical and political philosophy, which includes the examination of ethics, political and social philosophy, physics, natural science, mathematics, literature, poetry, fine arts, the history of civilization, and the history of science.

The Relationship between Theology and Philosophy

Maritain was concerned that modern society, with its stress on specialization, had destroyed the sense of integration that gives order and purpose to life. Hutchins, who shared a similar concern, recommended the revitalization of metaphysics to integrate the natural and social sciences. In recommending an education that contributed to the integration of human knowledge, Maritain contended that philosophy, which deals with human relationships to the universe, and theology, which deals with relationships to God, should be at the summit of the hierarchy of learned disciplines. As the most general and integrating of the disciplines, theology and philosophy were to provide the unity that would overcome specialization's disintegrating tendencies.

THE PAIDEIA PROPOSAL: A REVIVAL OF PERENNIALISM

Just as Essentialism is enjoying a revival, Perennialism is also experiencing a renaissance with the "Paideia proposal" designed by Mortimer Adler, a longtime associate of Robert Hutchins. Derived from the Greek, *paideia* refers to the "upbringing of children"; it signifies the general learning that all human beings should have. True to Perennialist principles, the Paideia proposal argues that a genuinely equal educational opportunity should be the same for all children; it should provide the "same quantity," "the same number of years" of schooling, and the "same quality of education."[7] The Paideia proponents argue that to divide students into tracks or to create special programs for some students but not for others is to deny the same quality of education for all.

Stressing the commonality of human nature, Paideia advocates do not propose that schooling be a leveling process that reduces the differences in human capacities to a common denominator. Education's ultimate goal, they assert, is to see that "human beings become educated persons."[8] Construed in Aristotelian terms, schooling not only provides skill and knowledge but also cultivates the habits or dispositions for lifelong education.

Schooling in the Paideia Proposal

For the Paideia proponents, the school, as an institution, provides a one-track rather than a multitrack system of education for all. The issue of a multitrack versus a single-track system raises complicated social, political, economic, and educational dimensions. Advocates of a multitrack system have varying motivations. Some believe that because of students' different intellectual capacities, socioeconomic backgrounds, and physiological–emotional needs, schools need to provide educational options to educate a widely differing student population. Still other advocates of multitrack education, including some Essentialists, believe that schools should sort students according to their academic abilities and should provide the intellectually gifted with a special kind of education that will prepare them as a leadership elite, especially a technological and scientific one. In contrast, Paideia proponents, like Perennialists in general, concentrate on the universality of human nature.

Schooling, according to Paideia proponents, has three major objectives common for all students: (1) it should provide the means of mental, moral, and spiritual growth; (2) it should cultivate the civic knowledge and virtues for responsible citizenship; (3) it should provide the basic skills needed for work rather than particular job training for a single occupation.[9]

Paideia proponents, like the Classical Realists treated in Chapter 3, warn against premature vocational training, which weakens or diminishes general education. Based on the liberal arts and sciences, all people should have a general education to cultivate their human nature and its undergirding rationality. Specialized vocational training, at the expense of general education, limits a person to one economic undertaking which can quickly become obsolete.

The Paideia Curriculum

Paideia advocates argue that all students should follow the same common curriculum for the twelve years of basic schooling. Students, however, would have a choice regarding their second language. The curriculum consists of three related but different learning modes, which have as their goals: (1) acquiring organized knowledge, (2) developing learning and intellectual skills, and (3) enlarging the understanding of ideas and values.[10]

For the acquisition of knowledge, the Paideia proponents, like the Essentialists and the Idealists, Realists, and Thomists, rely on organized subject matter. Their curriculum consists of language, literature, fine arts, mathematics, natural sciences, history, geography, and social studies.

To develop learning and intellectual skills, Paideia proponents emphasize basic skills such as "reading, writing, speaking, listening, observing, measuring, estimating, and calculating."[11] These skills are not taught in isolation but are integral to the entire curriculum. Again, a similarity exists in the identification of basic foundational skills between the Paideia proponents and the Essentialists, who see such skills as "generative" or necessary to other kinds of learning.

In the third area of curriculum, enlarging the understanding, the Paideia proponents return to a basic Perennialist theme—one long associated with Robert Hutchins and continued by Mortimer Adler—that the reading and discussion of the great books or classics are vital to the development of a truly educated person. In Adler's *The Paideia Proposal,* the scope of the great literature encompasses not only the enduring "historical, scientific, and philosophical" works but also the great works in film, drama, dance, and music.[12]

Teaching and Learning in the Paideia School

Teachers in schools following the Paideia theory of education are expected to be liberally educated persons. The methods used by such teachers correspond to the three branches of the curriculum. In teaching the organized subjects that lead to the acquisition of knowledge, the method used is essentially didactic, or instructional, using well-organized narratives. To instruct students to master the essential foundational skills, the teacher uses coaching, which refers to organizing and correcting students to perform skills such as reading or listening correctly. In studying the great works of art and literature that enlarge human understanding, teachers and students enter into the Socratic mode, which uses probing questions and directed discussions.

PERENNIALISM'S PHILOSOPHICAL AND IDEOLOGICAL RELATIONSHIPS

As indicated in earlier sections of this chapter, Perennialism exhibits strong affinities with Realism, especially its classical and Thomistic variations. (See Chapters 3 and 4 for a discussion of these philosophies.) In its curricular orientation and stress on fundamental or essential skills and subjects, it also resembles Essentialism, discussed in Chapter 17. Perennialism has several characteristics that distinguish it from Essentialism, however. Perennialism is distinctively Aristotelian, especially in its assertion that human beings are defined by their essential rationality, which is their universal character. American Perennialism also has been shaped by the strong imprint of Robert Hutchins and the "great books" program and Mortimer Adler's Paideia proposal and program. Although Perennialism, in Western Europe and the United States, has been shaped largely by educators influenced by Aristotelian and Thomist Realism, its principles would also be compatible with Idealism's emphasis on universal truth and values. The Idealist preference for the classics is also highly compatible with Perennialism.

　　Because of its Aristotelian and Realist origins, Perennialism differs from Naturalism, Pragmatism, and Existentialism, examined in Chapters 5, 6, and 7. Unlike Rousseau and other Naturalists, Perennialists give priority to cultivating human rationality through the great works of art, literature, and science. The Perennialist reliance on these great works of Western civilization as a basis for the curriculum differs from the Naturalist emphasis on instincts, feelings, and direct experience. While Perennialists would find much to admire in John Dewey's emphasis on shared experience, they would disagree with the Pragmatist's reliance on the scientific method, stress on change and relativity, and rejection of absolute truths. To the extent that Progressivism (discussed in Chapter 19) neglects foundational skills and the great literary and scientific achievements of the past, Perennialism would oppose it.

Perennialists would agree with certain aspects of Existentialism. They would agree, for example, that human beings should be free to define their projects in order to achieve self-realization. However, Perennialism has an antecedent definition of human beings as rational. Based on this definition, they encourage a sameness or uniformity in the curriculum designed to cultivate their conception of rationality. Existentialists, however, would find this a prior definition that limits human choice and freedom. Perennialists would counter that genuine choice is based on the human power to use knowledge to frame alternatives.

Just as Essentialism has been revived as an educational theory compatible with Neo-Conservatism, Perennialism, too, has enjoyed a renascence. While Essentialism has been used to support arguments for basic skills and subjects that are useful for economic growth, Perennialism's contemporary popularity rests with its emphasis on universal truth and values and its rejection of relativism. Both contemporary Essentialists and Perennialists decry the erosion of academic standards. Perennialists carry the argument further by contending that general intellectual and ethical standards have also eroded because of relativism. For example, Allan Bloom's *The Closing of the American Mind* argued forcefully that relativism in higher education had seriously weakened Americans' sense of intellectual and moral judgment.[13]

Lynne Cheney has argued against relativism in education by asserting that models of excellence in history and literature rest on truths that transcend time and circumstance. These objective truths, which transcend class, race, and gender, are appropriate to all human beings.[14] It is necessary to protect these models of objective truth and value against those who would subvert and use them as ideological tools. Deconstructionists and other postmodern theorists are among those subverting models and standards of objective truth. These critics of universalist standards contend that what is claimed to be objective truth is really a construction of dominant historical and contemporary groups. They argue that the constructed canon in philosophy, literature, and history can be deconstructed and analyzed in terms of its genesis and implication for gender, race, and class descrimination.

Perennialists claim that their educational theory is rooted in universal concepts of truth and justice and is not subservient to any particular ideology. They reject an ideological foundation for education since ideology is tied to particular social, political, and economic contexts, to the contingencies of human culture, rather than its universal character. Claiming that education is designed to cultivate the essential character of a universal human nature, they argue that they can speak about human rights and freedom in universal terms that are transcultural and transnational. They contend that relativistic philosophies such as Pragmatism and educational theories such as Progressivism have weakened the possibility of a truly worldwide or global civilization because they deny the importance of universals. Further, Perennialists claim that Social Reconstructionism and Critical Theory, for example, seek to impose particular ideological frames of reference on education that would lead to political indoctrination.

Critical Theorists counter the Perennialist claim to nonideological purity. They argue that the stress on the great classic books of Western civilization recommended by Hutchins, for example, is really a product of a Eurocentric ideological bias that represents the imposition of the ideology of the dominant culture. Both Reconstructionists and Critical Theorists also contend that the Perennialists' alleged universality is really a culturally based theoretical support of historically dominant institutions.

CONCLUSION

Perennialism asserts certain principles that are foundational to its educational directives. Among them are the following: (1) permanence is of a greater reality than change; (2) the universe is orderly and patterned; (3) the basic features of human nature reappear in each generation regardless of time or place; (4) human nature is universal in its essential characteristics; (5) like human nature, the basic goals of education are universal and timeless; (6) the human being's defining characteristic is rationality, which it is education's task to cultivate; and (7) the funded wisdom of the human race is recorded in certain classic works.

DISCUSSION QUESTIONS

1. Review Chapters 3 and 4. How does Perennialism resemble Realism and Thomism?

2. Define and explain the meaning of the term *Perennialism.*

3. Lead a discussion on one of the "great books" of Western civilization.

4. Debate the Perennialist assertion that vocational and career preparation should not be permitted to interfere with general education.

5. Debate the Perennialist assertion that all students should experience the same curriculum.

6. Does the Perennialist insistence on a common curriculum for all students enhance or retard equality of educational opportunity?

7. Critique Perennialism from the Naturalist and Pragmatist perspectives.

8. Is Perennialism anti-ideological or is it part of an ideological perspective?

9. What trends in society and education would Perennialists identify as eroding standards and values?

INQUIRY PROJECTS

- Read and review a book on education written by Robert Hutchins.
- Read and review a book on education written by Jacques Maritain.
- Using the Perennialist criteria, compile a reading list of the "great books."
- If there is a school in your locality that has adopted the Paideia program, visit it and observe instruction. Report on your observations to the class.
- Read and review a book on the Paideia proposal and program.
- In a character sketch, prepare a paper that describes a Paideia teacher.
- Using one of the "great books," lead a discussion on its important principles.
- Review several of the books being used in the teacher education program at your college or university. Do the authors of these books emphasize universal values or cultural relativism?

FURTHER READINGS

Adler, Mortimer J. *Paideia Problems and Possibilities: A Consideration of Questions Raised by the Paideia Proposal.* New York: Macmillan, 1983.

Adler, Mortimer J. *The Paideia Program: An Educational Syllabus.* New York: Macmillan, 1984.

Adler, Mortimer J. *The Paideia Proposal: An Educational Manifesto.* New York: Macmillan, 1982.

Ashmore, Harry S. *Unseasonable Truths: The Life of Robert Maynard Hutchins.* Boston: Little, Brown, 1991.

Bloom, Allan. *The Closing of the American Mind.* New York: Simon & Schuster, 1987.

Cheney, Lynne V. *Humanities in America: A Report to the President, the Congress, and the American People.* Washington, DC: National Endowment for the Humanities, 1988.

Cheney, Lynne V. *Telling the Truth.* New York: Simon & Schuster, 1995.

Dawson, Christopher. *The Crisis of Western Education.* New York: Sheed & Ward, 1961.

Dawson, Christopher. *The Historic Reality of Christian Culture.* New York: Harper & Brothers, 1960.

Dzuback, Mary Ann. *Robert M. Hutchins: Portrait of an Educator.* Chicago: University of Chicago Press, 1991.

Hopkins, Martin L. *Historical Analysis of Experimentalism and Perennialism in American Education.* Pomona, CA: California State Polytechnic University, Teacher Preparation Center, 1986.

Hutchins, Robert Maynard. *Conflict in Education in a Democratic Society.* New York: Harper and Co., 1953.

Hutchins, Robert Maynard. *A Conversation on Education.* Santa Barbara, CA: Center for the Study of Democratic Institutions, 1963.

Hutchins, Robert Maynard. *Education for Freedom.* Baton Rouge: Louisiana State University Press, 1943.

Hutchins, Robert Maynard. *The Higher Learning in America.* New Haven, CT: Yale University Press, 1936.

Hutchins, Robert Maynard. *The Learning Society.* New York: Praeger, 1968.

Hutchins, Robert Maynard. *Some Observations on American Education.* Cambridge: Cambridge University Press, 1956.

Hutchins, Robert Maynard. *The University of Utopia*. Chicago: University of Chicago Press, 1953.

Klauder, Francis J. *A Philosophy Rooted in Love: The Dominant Themes in the Perennial Philosophy of St. Thomas Aquinas*. Lanham, MD: University Press of America, 1994.

Maritain, Jacques. *Challenges and Renewals*. Notre Dame, IN: Notre Dame University Press, 1966.

Maritain, Jacques. *Education at the Crossroads*. New Haven, CT: Yale University Press, 1943.

Maritain, Jacques. *Integral Humanism*. New York: Charles Scribner's Sons, 1968.

Maritain, Jacques. *Man and the State*. Chicago: University of Chicago Press, 1951.

McNeill, William H. *Hutchins's University: A Memoir of the University of Chicago, 1929–1950*. Chicago: University of Chicago Press, 1991.

ENDNOTES

1. For a discussion of Hutchins's work at the University of Chicago, see William H. McNeill, *Hutchins's University: A Memoir of the University of Chicago, 1929–1950* (Chicago: University of Chicago Press, 1991).

2. Biographies of Hutchins are Harry S. Ashmore, *Unseasonable Truths: The Life of Robert Maynard Hutchins* (Boston: Little, Brown, 1991); and Mary Ann Dzuback, *Robert M. Hutchins: Portrait of an Educator* (Chicago: University of Chicago Press, 1991).

3. Robert M. Hutchins, *A Conversation on Education* (Santa Barbara, CA: Center for the Study of Democratic Institutions, 1963), pp. 1–2.

4. Robert M. Hutchins, *The Higher Learning in America* (New Haven, CT: Yale University Press, 1936), p. 63.

5. Francis J. Klauder, *A Philosophy Rooted in Love: The Dominant Themes in the Perennial Philosophy of St. Thomas Aquinas* (Lanham, MD: University Press of America, 1994).

6. Jacques Maritain, *Education at the Crossroads* (New Haven, CT: Yale University Press, 1960), p. 10.

7. Mortimer J. Adler, *The Paideia Proposal: An Educational Manifesto* (New York: Macmillan, 1982), p. 4.

8. Ibid., p. 10.

9. Ibid., pp. 16–17.

10. Ibid., pp. 22–23.

11. Ibid., p. 26.

12. Ibid., pp. 28–29. Also see Mortimer J. Adler, *The Paideia Program: An Educational Syllabus* (New York: Macmillan, 1984).

13. Allan Bloom, *The Closing of the American Mind* (New York: Simon & Schuster, 1987).

14. For Cheney's ideas on education, see Lynne V. Cheney, *Humanities in America: A Report to the President, the Congress, and the American People* (Washington, DC: National Endowment for the Humanities, 1988); Lynne V. Cheney, *Telling the Truth* (New York: Simon & Schuster, 1995).

Progressivism and Education

In its origins, Progressivism in U.S. education began as a reaction against the formalism, verbalism, and authoritarianism of traditional schooling. While the various phases and nuances of Progressivism will be developed later in the chapter, an initial definition of Progressivism is presented here. Progressivism is the orientation that believes that improvement and reform in the human condition and society are both possible and desirable. Many early Progressive educators were looking for educational innovations that would liberate the child's energies. Other Progressives, identified with John Dewey's Pragmatism, believed that schools were part of a larger framework of institutional and social reform. In the sections that follow, we examine the sources of Progressivism, William H. Kilpatrick's project method, Progressivism's professional impact, and Progressivism's philosophical and ideological relationships.

SOURCES OF PROGRESSIVISM

Although the Progressive Education Association was formally organized in 1919, its antecedents reach back to the eighteenth-century Enlightenment. Like the theorists of the Age of Reason, modern Progressives emphasized the concept of "Progress," which asserts that human beings are capable of improving and perfecting their environments by applying human intelligence and the scientific method to solving social, political, and economic problems. Like Rousseau, the Progressives rejected the doctrine of human depravity and believed that people were essentially benevolent.

Progressivism was also rooted in the spirit of social reform that gripped the early twentieth-century Progressive movement in U.S. politics. As a sociopolitical movement, Progressivism held that human society could be refashioned by political reforms. Such U.S. political programs as Woodrow Wilson's "New Freedom," Theodore Roosevelt's "New Nationalism," and Robert LaFollette's "Wisconsin Idea," although varied in particulars, shared the common concern that the emerging corporate society should be ordered to function democratically for the benefit of all Americans.[1] The leaders in Progressive politics represented what was essentially the middle-class orientation to reform characterized by gradual change through legislation and peaceful social innovation through education.

U.S. educational Progressives could also look to the major educational reformers of Western Europe for inspiration and stimulation. Jean-Jacques Rousseau, author of *Émile,* had written about an education that proceeded along natural lines and that was free of coercion. As an early rebel against traditional schooling, Rousseau argued that learning was most effective when it followed the child's interests and needs.

Progressives could also feel an affinity for the work of Johann Heinrich Pestalozzi, a nineteenth-century Swiss educational reformer, who, as a willing disciple of Rousseau, asserted that education should be more than book learning. It should embrace the whole child—emotions, intellect, and body. Natural education, said Pestalozzi, should take place in an environment of emotional love and security. It should also begin in the child's immediate environment and involve the operations of the senses on the objects found in the environment.[2]

The work of the Viennese psychoanalyst Sigmund Freud was also useful to Progressive educators. In examining cases of hysteria, Freud had traced some mental illnesses to early childhood traumas. He believed that authoritarian parents had caused many children to repress their drives. This repression, especially in the case of sexual drives, could lead to neurotic behavior that had a deleterious effect on the child and on his or her adult life.

While the European educational reformers provided stimulus for Progressive educators, it was John Dewey and his followers who came to exert a profound influence on Progressive education. It should be clear, however, that not all Progressives were Deweyites. Progressive education as a movement was a convenient platform, a rallying point, for those who opposed educational traditionalism rather than a doctrinaire movement.

The Progressive Educational Platform

Before commenting on John Dewey's reactions to Progressive education, a review of the history of Progressive education provides a perspective on the work of the Progressive educators. Certain educators, such as Flora Cooke, principal of the Francis W. Parker School in Chicago, and Carleton Washburne of the Winnetka, Illinois, Schools, had in the early twentieth century developed innovative methods that stressed the child's own initiative in learning. Junius L. Meriam of the University of Missouri had developed an activity curriculum that included excursions, constructive work, observation, and discussion. Marietta Johnson

(1864–1938) had also established the School of Organic Education in 1907 in Fairhope, Alabama. Johnson's Organic Theory of education emphasized the child's needs, interests, and activities. Special attention was given to creative activity that included dancing, sketching, drawing, singing, weaving, and other expressive activities. Formal instruction in reading, writing, and arithmetic was reserved until the child was nine or ten years old. The general method of instruction was that of the free-flowing discussion.

In 1919, a number of Progressive educators met in Washington, D.C., and organized the Progressive Education Association under the leadership of Stanwood Cobb, head of the Chevy Chase Country Day School. To give cohesion to the Progressive educational position, the association stressed the following principles: (1) Progressive education should provide the freedom that would encourage the child's natural development and growth through activities that cultivated his or her initiative, creativity, and self-expression; (2) all instruction should be guided by the child's own interest, stimulated by contact with the real world; (3) the Progressive teacher was to guide the child's learning as a director of research activities, rather than as a taskmaster; (4) student achievement was to be measured in terms of mental, physical, moral, and social development; (5) there should be greater cooperation among the teacher, the school, and the home and family in meeting the child's needs for growth and development; (6) the truly Progressive school should be a laboratory in innovative practices.[3]

At the onset, the Progressive Education Association as a child-centered movement was a reaction against the subject-matter curriculum of traditional schooling. It attracted teachers and parents associated with small, private experimental schools. In the 1920s and 1930s, the Progressive Education Association began to attract professional educators from colleges of education. Many of these educators had been influenced by John Dewey's Experimentalist philosophy of education.

Dewey's Critique of Progressive Education

Although John Dewey's Experimentalism has been discussed elsewhere in this book, the Progressive educational position is made clear by a brief examination of Dewey's critique of the movement, which appeared in *Experience and Education.*[4]

Dewey warned that the controversy between traditional and Progressive educators had tended to degenerate into an assertion of either/or positions. Although sympathetic to Progressivism, Dewey believed that many Progressives were merely reacting against traditional school practices and had failed to formulate an educational philosophy that was capable of serving as a plan of pragmatic operations.

Dewey's analysis of the traditional and the Progressive school is useful in highlighting the contrasts between these two institutions. The traditional school, he said, was a formal institution that emphasized a subject-matter curriculum comprised of discretely organized disciplines, such as language, history, mathematics, and science. Traditionalists, such as Perennialists and Essentialists, held that the source of wisdom was located in humanity's cultural heritage. Morals, standards, and conduct were derived from tradition and were not subject to the test of the scientific method. The traditional teacher regarded the written word as the font of wisdom and relied on the textbook as the source of knowledge and the recitation as the means of eliciting it from students. Traditionalists had attempted to isolate the school from social controversies. Holding to their belief that learning was the transmission and mastery of bodies of knowledge inherited from the past, the traditionalists had ignored the learner's own needs and interests and had deliberately neglected urgent social and political issues. The products of conventional education (namely, the students) were expected to be receptive of the traditional wisdom, have habits and attitudes that were conducive to conformity, and were to be respectful of and obedient to authority.

Although Dewey shared the Progressive antagonism toward the traditional school, he feared that many Progressives were merely reacting against it. Too many Progressives had ignored the past and were concerned only with the present. In their opposition to the traditional school's passivity, some Progressives had come to emphasize any kind of activity, even purposeless activity. Many Progressives had become so antagonistic to education imposed by adults that they had begun to cater to childish whims, many of which were devoid of social and intellectual value.

After urging that Progressive educators avoid the polarization of an either/or educational position, Dewey outlined the philosophy that he believed was suited for the genuinely Progressive school. Progressive education needed a philosophy based on experience, the interaction of the person with the environment. Such an experiential philosophy was to have no set of external goals. Rather, the end product of education was growth—that ongoing experience which leads to the direction and control of subsequent experience.

Truly Progressive education should not ignore the past but rather should use it to reconstruct experience in the present and direct future experiences. For Dewey, education should be based on a continuum of ongoing experience that united the past and the present and led to the shaping of the future.

Dewey also warned that Progressive education should not become so absorbed in activity that it misconstrued the nature of activity. Mere movement was without value. Activity should be directed to solving problems; it should be purposeful and should contain social and intellectual possibilities that contributed to the learner's growth.

The true Progressive educator was a teacher skilled in relating the learner's internal conditions of experience—that is, the student's needs, interests, purposes, capacities, and desires—with the objective conditions of experience—the environmental factors that were historical, physical, economic, and sociological.

Dewey asserted that Progressivism should be free from a naive romanticization of child nature. Although children's interests and needs were always at the beginning of learning, they were not its end. The child's instincts and impulses needed to be refined and developed into reflective social intelligence. Some impulses contained possibilities for growth and development; other impulses would have the opposite result in that their consequences would impede such growth. Impulse became reflective when the learner was able to estimate the consequences of acting on it. By developing an "end-in-view," the learner could conjecture the consequences that would result from action. Understanding the purpose of a particular act involved estimating the consequences that had occurred in similar situations in the past and forming a tentative judgment about the likely consequences of acting in the present. Thus, Progressive education should encourage the cultivation of purposeful, reflective patterns of inquiry in the learner.

Challenging Essentialism and Perennialism, Dewey warned educators against trying to "return to the intellectual methods and ideals that arose centuries before scientific method was developed." Truly Progressive educators would seek systematically to utilize the "scientific method as the pattern and ideal of intelligent exploration and exploitation of the potentialities inherent in experience."[5]

WILLIAM KILPATRICK AND THE PROJECT METHOD

Dewey's plea for a Progressive education based on human experience stimulated William Heard Kilpatrick (1871–1965), who was both an Experimentalist and a Progressive, to construct a methodology of instruction that united purpose and activity and that tested conjectured consequences in action. Kilpatrick, a popular professor at Columbia University's Teachers College, devised the "project method" that came to characterize Progressive education for many U.S. educators.

A brief discussion of Kilpatrick's route to the development of the project method is useful in understanding the Progressive impulse among U.S. educators. Born in rural White Plains, Georgia, the son of a Baptist minister, Kilpatrick received a traditional education. After attending Mercer University, he taught algebra and geometry in the public schools of Blakely in his native state.[6]

As a mathematics teacher, Kilpatrick inaugurated reforms in his classroom. For example, he believed that report cards and grades focused attention on extrinsic rewards that were disconnected from the natural consequences of learning. He abolished the practice of external marks, which he felt encouraged egotism among the achievers and inflicted a sense of inferiority on slower learners. In cultivating freedom in his classroom, he encouraged his students to work collaboratively. Early in his career Kilpatrick revealed a liberal attitude toward classroom discipline, which would later be more theoretically and systematically organized in his project method.

In 1907, Kilpatrick entered Teachers College at Columbia University to continue his professional and academic preparation in education. Here he encountered and accepted John Dewey's pragmatic philosophy.

Later, as a professor of education at Teachers College, Kilpatrick became a noted interpreter of Dewey. His writings and lectures, which espoused themes associated with Experimentalist philosophy and Progressive education, attracted a large and receptive audience. A gifted lecturer, Kilpatrick clarified many of Dewey's more difficult theoretical concepts, He was not, however, merely an interpreter. He also advanced his own educational philosophy, which synthesized Progressivism and Experimentalism into the "purposeful act," or the "project method."[7] Because he reached a large number of teachers in his classes, Kilpatrick exerted a shaping influence over U.S. educational theory and practice.

Kilpatrick's project method rejected traditional education's reliance on a book-centered instruction. Although not an anti-intellectual, Kilpatrick asserted that books were not a substitute for learning through living. The most pernicious form of bookishness was found in the textbook's domination of conventional teaching. Too frequently, teachers relied exclusively on information in textbooks. This often led to mechanically organized, secondhand experiences. The student who succeeded in the traditional school was frequently of a bookish inclination and successful in memorizing but not always in understanding what was read. Because of its stress on bookishness and memorization, conventional schooling had degenerated into devitalized mechanical routines in which teachers assigned lessons from textbooks, drilled their students on the assignments, heard recitations of memorized responses, and then evaluated them on their recall of the material. Such schooling, in Kilpatrick's view, stifled individual creativity, led to boredom, and lacked collaborative social purposes.

In contrast to the rote nature of traditional book-centered education, Kilpatrick's project method was designed to elaborate a constructive Progressivism along Experimentalist lines. In the project method, students were to choose, plan, direct, and execute their work in activities, or projects, that would stimulate purposeful efforts. In its theoretical formulation, the project was a mode of problem solving. Students, either individually or in groups, would define problems that arose in their own experiences. Learning would be task centered in that success would come by solving the problem and testing the solution by acting on it. Action from purposeful planning would meet the pragmatic test and be judged by its consequences.

Kilpatrick recommended that the school curriculum be organized into four major classes of projects. First, the creative, or "construction," project involved concretizing a theoretical plan in external form. For example, the students might decide to write and then present a drama. They would write the script, assign the roles, and actually act out the play. Or, the creative project might actually involve the design of a blueprint for a library. The test would come in the construction of the library from the plan devised by the students. Second, the appreciation, or "enjoyment," project was designed to contribute to aesthetic enjoyment. Reading a novel, seeing a film, or hearing a symphony were examples of projects that would lead to aesthetic appreciation. Third, the "problem" project was one in which the students would be involved in resolving an intellectual problem. Such problems as the resolution of racial discrimination, the improvement of the quality of the environment, or the organization of recreational facilities were social problems that called for disciplined intellectual inquiry. Finally, the "specific learning" project involved the acquiring of a skill or an area of knowledge. Learning to type, swim, dance, read, or write were examples of the acquisition of a specific skill.

Kilpatrick's project method should be interpreted both in terms of its suggested social consequences and its strictly educational aims. To be sure, the project method had educational objectives, such as improvement in creative, constructive, appreciative, intellectual, and skill competencies. However, acquiring these competencies was only a part of Kilpatrick's plan for educational reform. Kilpatrick believed, as did Dewey, that education as a social activity was a product of human association and collaboration. In a free society, democratic discussion, debate, decision, and action depended on the willingness of individuals to use the methods of open and uncoerced inquiry. Kilpatrick believed that the project method lent itself to group work, in which students could collaboratively pursue common problems and share in associative inquiry. Such was the essence of the democratic processes. Even more important than the acquiring of specific skills was the student's need to acquire attitudes appropriate to a democratic society.

The person that Kilpatrick envisioned as a result of education based on purposeful collaboration was the democratic man or woman. Such a person would possess an experimental attitude and would be willing to test inherited traditions, values, and beliefs. Through the project method, students would learn to use democratic methods of open discussion, carefully reasoned deliberation, decision making that respected both the rights of the majority and the minority, and action that resulted in peaceful social change.

Kilpatrick's model of the democratic citizen was much like that envisioned by the middle-class Progressives in politics and in education.[8] This person would use a democratic methodology and would expect opponents to use the same procedure. As a reconstructive person, this Progressively educated man or woman would believe that social institutions were creations of human intelligence and could be periodically renovated when the situation required it. The democratic citizen would be open to using the scientific method and would discard theological, metaphysical, political, and economic absolutes as dogmatic impediments that blocked human inquiry into the conditions of life. Above all, Kilpatrick wanted to educate individuals who shared a common framework of democratic values. Such men and women would be wholehearted and willing participants in the democratic community.

PROGRESSIVISM'S PROFESSIONAL IMPACT

As indicated, Progressive educators such as Kilpatrick sought to reconceptualize the U.S. school curriculum and methods of instruction along more open-ended, experimental, and collaborative lines.[9] However, the degree to which Progressive education actually was felt in educational practice has been much debated. Historians such as Cremin argue that certain Progressive educational innovations became so commonplace in the schools that they no longer appeared to be reforms. Critics of Progressivism, such as Essentialists, Perennialists, and Neo-Conservatives, have argued that Progressivism exercised a pervasive but deleterious influence on public schools in that it contributed to the lowering of academic standards and achievement.

Arthur Zilversmit, in *Changing Schools,* posed the question, Did Progressive philosophy actually impact educational policy and practices in local schools? He argues that the impact of any educational philosophy, including Progressivism, needs to be assessed in terms of U.S. public schooling's basic organizational reality. Public schools are local agencies, governed by local boards of education, administered by local superintendents, and taught by teachers who serve local populations. For Zilversmit, the impact of Progressivism must be assessed in terms of local personalities, their social and educational attitudes, and available community resources. While Progressivism had an impact on schools, Zilversmit found that it was more eclectic and less systematic than was generally assumed. According to his analysis, some Progressive educators inaugurated curricular and methodological reforms while others, primarily school administrators, emphasized efficiency, effectiveness, and economical organization, structures, and scheduling. Indeed, Winnetka's superintendent, Carleton Washburne, was a Progressive exemplar who competently blended curricular and administrative Progressivism.[10]

Progressivism entered schools eclectically in the administration of superintendents who were professionally prepared in what was called the "modern" philosophy of education. Concurrent with the Progressive movement and Progressive ideology, the modern, as contrasted with the traditional, philosophy selectively incorporated Progressive principles. The modern philosophy of education was an essential feature of many university programs of professional education. In the modern approach, key features were (1) larger schools facilitating more class sections and more curriculum diversity; (2) curriculum diversity enhancing educational enrichment; and (3) a propensity to create junior high or middle schools as distinct schools. These features were often endorsed by Progressives and became part of the modern school administrator's ideology.[11]

In addition to its eclectic implementation in schools, Progressivism influenced the educational profession, especially in its professional organizations and journals. In the case of U.S. educational philosophy, its origins coincided with the more general Progressive movement. Kaminsky, in *A New History of Educational Philosophy,* relates the origins of educational philosophy to reformist tendencies that provided a critique of "America's version of Victorianism."[12] Progressives took the lead in the American Social Science Association to free social inquiry from metaphysically based formal constraints. Dewey and other Progressive intellectuals worked to make educational philosophy a weapon of social and educational reform against Herbert Spencer's entrenched Social Darwinism.

Progressives were members of a complex and interlocking network of professional organizations such as the National Educational Association, the Progressive Education Association, the John Dewey Society, and the Philosophy of Education Society, and published in professional journals such as *Progressive Education, The Social Frontier,* and *Educational Theory.*[13]

The Progressive Teacher

Progressive education called for a teacher who was different in temperament, training, and techniques from teachers in more traditional schools. Although the Progressive teacher needed to be competent in the content and methods of inquiry of such academic disciplines as history, science, mathematics, and language, instruction in the Progressive classroom required more than a chronological or a systematic subject-matter presentation of the various learned disciplines. The Progressive approach was interdisciplinary. Problems were not specifically located within a particular learned discipline but rather intersected them in interdisciplinary fashion.

Because the Progressive classroom was oriented to purposeful activity, the Progressive teacher needed to know how to motivate the students so that they initiated, planned, and carried out their projects. As learning was centered in the participating group, the Progressive teacher needed to know how to use collaborative processes.

Perhaps the most difficult challenge for the teacher was to act as a guide rather than the center of learning. The skilled teacher, in the Progressive context, did not dominate the classroom as its focal point. Rather, he or she made the interests of the learner central. The teacher was properly a guide to discussing, planning, and executing learning.

PROGRESSIVISM'S PHILOSOPHICAL AND IDEOLOGICAL RELATIONSHIPS

As a theory of education, Progressivism draws heavily from the philosophies of Naturalism, examined in Chapter 5, and Pragmatism, examined in Chapter 6. From Naturalists, such as Rousseau, Progressives borrowed the doctrine that children should be free to develop according to their interests and needs. As indicated, the Experimentalists who were part of the Progressive persuasion disagreed when the child-centered Progressives exaggerated children's interests to the point of ignoring or discounting the educative role of society.

The child-centered Progressives' emphasis on children's needs and interests led them to conclude that the curriculum should develop from the child and that the most effective school environment was a permissive one in which children were free to explore and act on their interests. From the origins of Progressivism to the present, Progressives have stressed children's directly expressed needs and interests over academic subject matter.

While some Progressives were influenced by Naturalism, others drew their educational rationale from the Pragmatism or Experimentalism of John Dewey. Although they could agree that children should be liberated from repressive schooling, they disagreed on the extent to which education was a social force or involved some degree of social imposition. Believing that human intelligence was shaped by social interaction, Deweyan Progressives gave a greater role to the group and to social issues and problems. Deweyan Progressives also empha- sized the power of the scientific method to achieve complete and reflective thought. Deweyan Progressives would see Rousseau's isolation of the child from society and complete reliance on the child's freedom to be a romanticization of the child's nature and an abandonment of the educator's social responsibility. Thus, Progressivism's philosophical reliance on both Naturalism and Pragma- tism has caused internal tensions.

Progressivism rejects the more traditional philosophies of Idealism, Realism, and Thomism and their emphasis on antecedent reality, hierarchical categories, and subject matter. It should be pointed out, however, that the Idealist emphasis on child growth, exemplified in Froebel's kindergarten, was an early influence on many Progressives. Moreover, the Idealist concern for social integration had an impact on Dewey's thought.

Ideologically, Progressivism is most compatible with Liberalism, in both its classical and more modern forms, than with other ideologies. Liberalism's concern for individual rights and freedom finds an educational corollary in Progressivism's emphasis on the individual child. The freedom to inquire and test ideas, exempli- fied by Liberal theorists such as John Stuart Mill, is also stressed by Progressives.

The Progressive inclination toward change rather than stasis is much like the Liberal orientation. Progressivism is seen by Conservatives as threatening cul- tural continuity, eroding the power of tradition as a stabilizing factor, and jeop- ardizing legitimate authority. Conservatives fear that Progressive permissiveness, like Liberal individualism, will weaken standards.

The Liberal emphasis on representative institutions and gradual incremental reform rather than sweeping Utopian grand designs or Marxist revolution is com- patible with Progressive social reform. Progressive social reformers such as Jane Addams, Woodrow Wilson, and Theodore Roosevelt worked within the social and political system. Their efforts at reform were designed to improve the system by using representative institutions and processes to remedy its internal weak- nesses. Progressive reformers, like Liberals in general, prefer open-ended reform, which has limited ends-in-view rather than the preconceived ends found in both Utopian and Marxist ideologies.

Deweyan Progressives, while sharing many Liberal attitudes, reject the com- petitive ethic associated with Classical Liberalism and Social Darwinism. The old Liberalism was judged to be personally egotistical and socially and econom- ically wasteful by Dewey, who condemned it and called for a new Liberalism that encouraged cooperation, social planning, and scientifically directed human experience.

Progressivism, like Experimentalism and Liberalism, is incompatible with both political and social totalitarianism and with the authoritarianism in education that flows from it. The Progressive emphasis on freedom to follow one's interests violates the totalitarian requirement that subordinates individual interests to the will of the leader or to the dictates of the state or party. The Progressive emphasis on experimentation and the testing of ideas and values in experience encourages a questioning attitude that is contrary to the totalitarian rule for unquestioning obedience.

Progressivism, as a theory of education, opposes many of the concepts and practices associated with Essentialism and Perennialism. The points of disagreement become clear by contrasting the positions of the basic educator and the Progressive educator. The basic educator, whose pedagogical position reflects the more traditional and conservative Essentialism and Perennialism, advocates the following:

1. Learning the general cultural tool skills that are foundational to other kinds of learning. For example, reading, writing, and arithmetic are identified as basic, foundational, and generative of other school subjects and out-of-school activities. Early on, the advocates of basic education construe schooling to be literary and book centered.
2. Organizing the curriculum around well-defined essential skills and subject matters. There is a general opposition to ill-defined, undifferentiated, and amorphous curricular patterns that emphasize open education, learning through field experiences, projects, activities, and other unstructured kinds of learning.
3. Identifying the school, its administrators, and teachers as academic experts who have knowledge of content and of instructional methods. The basic education proponent opposes using the school as a vehicle for social change, innovation, and experimentation. The classroom is dominated by the teacher and instruction is planned and directed by the teacher.

The Progressive educator, in contrast, takes the following pedagogical posture:

1. Rather than introducing basic skills directly, it is better to have children acquire methods of learning and investigating by solving their problems and satisfying their needs. For example, John Dewey argued that children learned to think by using the scientific method to solve problems. William Heard Kilpatrick stressed learning by means of collaborative activities in his project method. In other words, learning, the curriculum, and instruction come from the child's interests.
2. The school should be immersed in social issues and in advancing social change. Externally, school administrators and teachers should break down

the theoretical and political walls that separate the school from society. They should also demolish the inner walls of school organization that divide it into subject areas, grade levels, and departments.

3. Teachers should be project directors, stimulators of learning, counselors, and learning consultants rather than transmitters of information. Instruction should be varied and often indirect.

CONCLUSION

Progressive education urges the liberation of the child from a pedagogical tradition that emphasizes rote learning, lesson recitations, and textbook authority. In opposition to the conventional subject-matter disciplines of the traditional curriculum, Progressives seek to develop alternative modes of curricular organization. They encourage such varied but related alternatives as activities, experiences, problem solving, and the project method. Progressive education is characterized by (1) a focus on the child as the learner rather than on subject matter, (2) an emphasis on activities and experiences that are direct rather than an exclusive reliance on verbal and literary skills and knowledge, (3) the encouragement of collaborative group-learning activities rather than competitive individualized lesson learning. In its broad social directions, Progressivism in education encourages democratic procedures designed to create community participation and social reform. It also cultivates a cultural or ethical relativism that critically appraises and often rejects inherited traditions, attitudes, and values.

DISCUSSION QUESTIONS

1. Identify and analyze the sources of Progressivism in terms of their theoretical compatibility and internal consistency.

2. Compare and contrast the traditional and the Progressive schools.

3. Compare and contrast the Progressive and Conservative views of the past and their applications to instruction.

4. Using Kilpatrick's project method as a case study, analyze how theory is formulated from practice.

5. Identify the elements in Kilpatrick's project method that are derived from either Naturalism or Pragmatism.

6. Review Essentialism treated in Chapter 17. Using the Essentialist preference for differentiated learning, critique Kilpatrick's project method.

7. Using the Neo-Marxist concept of the "hidden curriculum," examine Kilpatrick's project method.

8. Compare and contrast the Progressive and basic education (Essentialist and Perennialist) conceptions of curriculum and instruction.

INQUIRY PROJECTS

* Prepare a paper that identifies and analyzes the antecedents of Progressivism.
* Prepare a biographical sketch of a Progressive educator such as Francis Parker, Jane Addams, Carleton Washburne, Junius Meriam, Marietta Johnson, William Heard Kilpatrick, or Harold Rugg.
* Based on the principles of Progressive education, prepare a character sketch of a Progressive teacher.
* Review Lawrence Cremin's *The Transformation of the School: Progressivism in American Education.*
* Review John Dewey's *Experience and Education.*
* Devise and prepare a lesson plan based on Kilpatrick's project method.
* Visit a school that embodies Progressive methods in its program. Report your observations to the class.
* Review national reports on education such as *A Nation at Risk* and *Action for Excellence.* Do these reports reflect an anti-Progressive point of view?

FURTHER READINGS

Blum, John M. *The Progressive Presidents: Roosevelt, Wilson, Roosevelt, Johnson.* New York: W. W. Norton, 1982.

Cremin, Lawrence A. *The Transformation of the School: Progressivism in American Education, 1876–1957.* New York: Alfred A. Knopf, 1961.

Crunden, Robert M. *Ministers of Reform: The Progressives' Achievement in American Civilization, 1889–1920.* Urbana: University of Illinois Press, 1984.

Dewey, John. *Experience and Education.* New York: Collier Books, 1963.

Graham, Patricia A. *Progressive Education: From Arcady to Academe: A History of the Progressive Education Association, 1919–1955.* New York: Teachers College Press, 1967.

Kaminsky, James S. *A New History of Educational Philosophy.* Westport, CT: Greenwood Press, 1993.

Kilpatrick, William H. *Education for a Changing Civilization.* New York: Macmillan, 1925.

Kilpatrick, William H. *The Foundations of Method.* New York: Macmillan, 1925.

Kilpatrick, William H. *Philosophy of Education.* New York: Macmillan, 1951.

Kilpatrick, William H. *The Project Method.* New York: Teachers College Press, 1921.

Kliebard, Herbert M. *The Struggle for the American Curriculum, 1893–1958.* Boston: Routledge & Kegan Paul, 1986.

Lauderdale, William B. *Progressive Education: Lessons from Three Schools.* Bloomington, IN: Phi Delta Kappa Educational Foundation, 1981.

Pratt, Caroline. *I Learn from Children.* New York: Simon & Schuster, 1948.

Ravitch, Diane. *The Troubled Crusade: American Education, 1945–1980.* New York: Basic Books, 1983.

Reese, William J. *Power and the Promise of School Reform: Grassroots Movements During the Progressive Era.* Boston: Routledge & Kegan Paul, 1986.

Rugg, Harold O., and Ann Schumaker. *The Child-Centered School.* New York: World Book Co., 1928.

Tanner, Daniel. *Crusade for Democracy: Progressive Education at the Cross-*

roads. Albany: State University of New York Press, 1991.

Tenenbaum, Samuel. *William Heard Kilpatrick: Trail Blazer in Education.* New York: Harper and Brothers, 1951.

Washburne, Carleton. *What Is Progressive Education?* New York: John Day, 1952.

Zilversmit, Arthur. *Changing Schools: Progressive Education Theory and Practice, 1930–1960.* Chicago: University of Chicago Press, 1993.

ENDNOTES

1. For a discussion of Progressivism in U.S. politics, see John Morton Blum, *The Progressive Presidents: Roosevelt, Wilson, Roosevelt, Johnson* (New York: W. W. Norton, 1982).

2. For a discussion of Pestalozzi's educational theory and its significance for Progressivism, see Gerald L. Gutek, *Pestalozzi and Education* (New York: Random House, 1968).

3. For the definitive treatment of the Progressive Education Association, see Patricia Albjerg Graham, *Progressive Education: From Arcady to Academe—A History of the Progressive Education Association, 1919–1955* (New York: Teachers College Press, Columbia University, 1967); the definitive history of Progressive Education in the context of U.S. Progressivism can be found in Lawrence A. Cremin, *The Transformation of the School: Progressivism in American Education, 1876–1957* (New York: Alfred A. Knopf, 1961).

4. John Dewey, *Experience and Education* (New York: Collier Books, 1963).

5. Ibid., pp. 85–86.

6. For a study of Kilpatrick's life, educational philosophy, and influence, see Samuel Tenenbaum, *William Heard Kilpatrick: Trail Blazer in Education* (New York: Harper and Brothers, 1951).

7. William Heard Kilpatrick, "The Project Method," *Teachers College Record,* XIX (1918): 319–335, and *The Project Method* (New York: Teachers College Press, 1921).

8. For a discussion of middle-class Progressivism, see Robert M. Crunden, *Ministers of Reform: The Progressive's Achievement in American Civilization, 1889–1920* (Urbana: University of Illinois Press, 1984).

9. Herbert M. Kliebard, *The Struggle for the American Curriculum, 1893–1958* (Boston: Routledge & Kegan Paul, 1986).

10. Arthur Zilversmit, *Changing Schools: Progressive Education Theory and Practice, 1930–1960* (Chicago: University of Chicago Press, 1993), pp. 38–56.

11. Ibid., pp. 168–183.

12. James S. Kaminsky, *A New History of Educational Philosophy* (Westport, CT: Greenwood Press, 1993), pp. 19–23.

13. For a history of the John Dewey Society, see Daniel Tanner, *Crusade for Democracy: Progressive Education at the Crossroads* (Albany: State University of New York Press, 1991).

▶ 20

Social Reconstructionism and Education

Social Reconstructionism sharply contrasts with the conservative Essentialist and Perennialist theories, which Reconstructionists regard to be reflective theories that mirror inherited social patterns and values. Reconstructionists assert that educators should originate policies and programs to reform society. Teachers, they say, should use their power to lead the young in programs of social engineering and reform.

Social Reconstructionists claim to follow John Dewey's Pragmatism, which emphasized the need to reconstruct both personal and social experience. Seizing on Dewey's emphasis on reconstructing experience, Reconstructionists stress the reconstruction of social experience and the culture.[1]

Although Social Reconstructionists differ on particulars, they agree on premises such as the following: (1) all philosophies, ideologies, and theories, including educational ones, are culturally based and emerge from specific cultural patterns that are conditioned by living at a given time and in a particular place; (2) culture, as a dynamic process, is growing and changing; and (3) human beings can refashion culture so that it promotes human growth and development.[2]

Rather than being abstract or based on speculative philosophy, educational theories, Reconstructionists contend, should shape social and political policies. Reconstructionists are suspicious of universalist or cosmic theories of education that emphasize highly abstract categories of unchanging reality, human nature, truth, and value. This suspicion can be traced to their Pragmatist origins and their rejection of the dualism found in Realism and Thomism and the educational theories derived from them, Perennialism and Essentialism.

Social Reconstructionists view contemporary society as facing a severe crisis resulting from humankind's unwillingness to reconstruct institutions and values to meet the needs of modern life. Human beings entered the modern technological and scientific era with attitudes and values derived from the rural, preindustrial past. To resolve the crisis, human beings need to examine their heritage and identify the viable elements that will help to resolve the present crisis. If people examine their heritage, deliberately plan the direction of change, and implement the plan, they can create a new social order. The school's task is to examine the cultural heritage critically and to emphasize the elements that can be used in the needed reconstruction of society. In the sections that follow, we examine cultural crisis and reconstruction; the pioneering work of George S. Counts; development theory and futurism; and issue-oriented schools; and consider Reconstructionism in its philosophical and ideological relationships.

CULTURAL CRISIS

Reconstructionism asserts that modern society is experiencing a profound crisis caused by an unwillingness to engage in fundamental cultural reconstruction. The symptoms of cultural crisis are many. There are great variations in economic levels of life, both in the United States and throughout the world. While a few people enjoy wealth, the vast majority struggle at a subsistence level that borders on dire poverty. In the United States, large numbers of people, especially members of minority groups, have been victimized by decades of poverty and discrimination. Internationally, two-thirds of the world's population is barely surviving. The Reconstructionist regards the contradiction between wealth and poverty as a residue of the prescientific past.

The world is plagued by international tensions and war or the threat of war. In an age of potential nuclear destruction, military conflict with the threat of escalation into worldwide holocaust jeopardizes humankind's continued existence on this planet. Further, the Reconstructionists point to myriad unresolved conflicts and to the wastage of human potential. Such problems as overpopulation, environmental pollution, violence, and terrorism are symptoms of the pervasive crisis.

At the root of the crisis is the severing of human values from social and economic realities. The human creative genius has developed dynamic scientific and technological instruments that contribute to further change. At the same time that the dynamic forces of science and technology have changed the material environment, an inherited conception of an idealized past seeks to preserve the status quo. While Reconstructionists examine the past to find viable elements in the cultural heritage that can be used instrumentally, they disdain theories that urge us to go back to the "good old days." For them, the nostalgia for a problem-free past is often an ideological camouflage used by Neo-Conservatives to preserve the status quo.

Cultural Reconstruction

Reconstructionists believe that modern society and human survival are intimately related. To ensure human survival and to create a more humane civilization, human beings need to become social engineers who can plan the course of change and use science and technology to achieve desired goals. Hence, Reconstructionist education should cultivate (1) a critical examination of the cultural heritage, (2) a commitment to work for deliberate social reform, (3) a planning attitude capable of plotting the course of cultural revision, and (4) the testing of the cultural plan by enacting programs of deliberate social reform.

Reconstructionists believe that all social reform arises in existing life conditions. Students are expected to define the major problems facing humankind and to recognize the dynamic forces of the present. Students should be able to detect the customs, beliefs, and values that impede social reconstruction. Values that are merely customary should be reconstructed. The moral and ideological culture is permeated with residues of the prescientific and pretechnological age. Customary and stereotypical ways of thinking that lead to intolerance, discrimination, and superstition should be identified and discarded.

THE PIONEERING WORK OF GEORGE S. COUNTS

A clear statement of the need for educators to resolve social problems was made by George S. Counts in his book *Dare the School Build a New Social Order?* George S. Counts (1889–1974) was an educator who stimulated Social Reconstructionist theory. Born in rural Kansas, Counts witnessed the geographical closing of the American frontier and believed that new frontiers needed to be forged in human ideas and social institutions. Counts, who earned his doctorate at the University of Chicago in 1916, applied social theory to educational issues. During his active life, Counts was a professor of education at Columbia University's Teachers College, a president of the American Federation of Teachers, a leader of New York's Liberal Party, and a determined advocate of civil liberties. He was also a distinguished comparative educator who developed pioneering insights into Soviet society and education. Although Counts was on the radical cutting edge of social change in the United States, he became a determined anti-Communist. He early detected the totalitarianism inherent in Stalinism in the Soviet Union.[3]

Although Counts did not formally identify with those who called themselves Social Reconstructionists, an analysis of his educational theory clarifies themes of central concern for Reconstructionist educators. Counts's still unanswered question—"Dare the school build a new social order?"—created a ferment that continues today.

A photograph of George S. Counts (1889–1974), author of *Dare the School Build a New Social Order?* and a leading Reconstructionist theorist.

For Counts, the great crises of the twentieth century were symptoms of profound transition and rapid change. Acute cultural change occurred as U.S. society moved between two very different social patterns. The older, agrarian, rural, neighborhood community had been displaced by a rapid rush into a mode of life that was highly complex, industrialized, scientific, and technological. From a loose aggregation of rural households and neighborhoods, the nation, under the impetus of technological change, became a mass society characterized by minute structural and functional differentiation. While these rapid changes appeared to be primarily material, the social, moral, political, economic, religious, and aesthetic aspects of life were also affected.

Change itself did not necessarily provoke crisis. Rather, crisis occurred when individuals were unprepared to cope with and order the processes of change. Counts believed that educational systems had failed to equip people, both cognitively and attitudinally, to deal with pervasive social and cultural changes. The crisis was further aggravated because change occurred multilaterally. That is, alterations in one area accelerated changes and compounded crises in other areas of life. Because of people's unwillingness to reconstruct society, turmoil and maladjustment characterized the current period of profound change.

Counts's analysis used the cultural-lag theory, which asserted that a lag occurred when human technological inventiveness outdistanced moral consciousness and social organization. An institutional crisis resulted from a whole series of maladjustments between inherited attitudes and values on the one hand, and technological innovations on the other.

One of the most serious dislocations was in the economy, where inherited values of rugged individualism impeded the establishing of a planning, cooperating, and coordinating social order. The Reconstructionist distinguished between a *planning* society and a *planned* society. In a planning society, the social design was never really completed but was continually refashioned by human creative intelligence. In contrast, a planned society, which followed a master blueprint for social change, was often locked into a predetermined mold which prevented innovative reconstruction of the plan. Thus, it was more important to use planning as a process than to arrive at a desired social destination.

To Counts, the crucial problem was to formulate a theory of education to prepare people to resolve social crises by reconstructing ideas, beliefs, and values in the light of changing conditions. In *Dare the School Build a New Social Order?* Counts challenged educators to create an educational system that recognized the emergence of a world society.[4]

U.S. education's task was twofold: (1) reconstruction of the theoretical foundations based on the U.S. cultural heritage, and (2) the experimental development of school programs that could deal with problems of acute cultural crisis and social disintegration.

Because education was always relative to a given society, U.S. education was a product of its unique heritage. For U.S. education to serve broad social needs, these needs had to be examined in terms of the cultural heritage. Then, the heritage could be reconstructed in view of social problems. In his book *The Social Foundations of Education* (1934), Counts argued that "education is always a function of time, place, and circumstances" that reflects "the hopes, fears, and aspirations of a particular time in history."[5]

Counts reasoned that a viable conception of the U.S. cultural heritage rested on two necessary conditions: (1) affirmation of the values in the democratic tradition, and (2) recognition of the dominant contemporary reality—the emergence of a technological civilization. On these two conditions, U.S. educators could create an educational theory that encouraged fundamental social reconstruction. Based on a concept of cooperative behavior in an essentially cooperative society, a synthesis of the viable elements of the democratic heritage and the requirements of science would harness scientific and technological powers for democratic purposes. The reconstruction of a comprehensive educational theory encompassed the entire range of human activities. Labor, income, property, leisure, recreation, sex, family, government, public opinion, race, ethnicity, war, peace, art, and aesthetics were appropriate to educational reconstruction.

When he challenged educators to fashion a cultural philosophy of education for modern American life, Counts was also urging them to assume the responsibilities of "educational statesmanship." Counts defined an educational statesman as a leader, a proponent of vital ways and means, a person of ideas, and an initiator of broad policy. For too long, teacher education had concentrated on mechanics and had neglected major social and economic problems. In formulating educational philosophies and programs, the educational leader was to provide national direction.

Counts's conception of the democratic ethic was uniquely associated with the U.S. experience and exalted the frontier and the popular democracy associated with Andrew Jackson, the Progressivism of Woodrow Wilson, the Liberalism of Franklin D. Roosevelt, and the attempts to create a planning society as found in the New Freedom, the New Deal, the Experimentalism of John Dewey, and the historical relativism and economic interpretations of Charles Beard.[6] In emphasizing the Progressive-Liberal strand of U.S. tradition, Counts rejected the more conservative Hamiltonianism, Social Darwinism, economic individualism, and rugged competitive capitalism. U.S. democracy was not only a political expression but was and should continue to be a product of the economic, social, moral, and aesthetic forces operating within the heritage. Democracy rested on an egalitarian social base and had to penetrate all areas of life. Inequalities of opportunity caused by wealth, race, color, or religion were subversive to the democratic ethic.

The Importance of Technology

A reconstructed program of U.S. education was directly related to a technological civilization. The application of science to the modes and techniques of life had created a new cultural force—technology—which was "the art of applying science and mechanics to the various departments of human economy." A practical and purposeful instrument, technology was marked by an emphasis on precise, orderly, and defined relationships. While its experimental character concerned the practical application of knowledge, technology was not limited to material processes and products. It was also a process, a method of solving problems and of viewing the world.

Because technology applies science to life, the role of science in a reconstructed educational philosophy should be examined. Counts saw science as humanity's most accurate instrument and method of problem solving. As a method of intelligence, science produced ordered and precise knowledge. Terming science "a method of organized and critical common sense," Counts described this method in the following manner: (1) the scientific method begins with an hypothesis growing out of previous experience, knowledge, and thought; (2) the hypothesis is tested by a process of accurate and adequate observation employing the most precise instruments; (3) data are compiled and the hypothesis proved or rejected on the basis of empirical and public verification.[7]

In commenting on science as a cultural instrument, Counts examined the characteristics of technology—the application of science to the modes and techniques of life. Technology was rational, functional, planful, dynamic, and efficient. Technological rationality rested on its freedom from tradition. Embracing immediately relevant ideas and methods that served human purposes, technology observed, inquired, and accurately and mathematically described. As quantitative reasoning tested the outcomes of technology and predicted their consequences, humanity's freedom of action increased. As it came to occupy larger areas of life, the inherent rationality of science would penetrate into society.

Because it was functional rather than purely abstract, technology was basically utilitarian. And because it was capable of being planned, technology required carefully formulated purposes, determination of directions, and conception of projected actions prior to their undertaking. The technological mode opposed impulse and caprice. The technological age required a planning and cooperating society.

Technology was dynamic. One invention or discovery initiated an ever-greater, unending cluster of new inventions. The acceleration of change initiated by inventions and discoveries was not solely material but quickly spread into the nonmaterial culture and caused subsequent economic, political, moral, and social alterations. The dynamic character of technology had accelerated social change.

Efficiency was technology's most pervasive characteristic. Technological processes achieved the greatest possible end with the least expenditure of waste and energy. Originating in the machine, the ideal of efficiency extended first to economic production and then to the entire society. Technology placed a premium on professional competence. For without the expert knowledge of the specialist, the entire productive mechanism might fall into disorder. As technology advanced, inexpert opinion yielded to trained intelligence.

Technology placed great power in human hands. Like science, it was a neutral instrument that could serve humane and enriching purposes or be an instrument of ruthless exploitation. In a nuclear age, it could be an instrument of liberation or of destruction. This powerful instrument was not a mere additive to civilization; rather, it was a system of relationships that continually altered social patterns. The technological age required continual reconstructions of the economy, society, education, government, and morality.[8]

Counts's examination of U.S. civilization affirmed two essential strains: a basic egalitarian democratic ethic, and the emergence of a scientific-industrial-technological society. These two strains were elements in a reconstructive synthesis that became the basis of his "civilizational" philosophy for U.S. education. Rather than prescribe the design of the emergent society, Counts preferred open-ended and experimental social engineering. The American people would shape their own destiny, using their own elastic democratic temperament. Counts wrote that the course of U.S. democracy depended on the ability of the people

to learn from experience, to define the problem, to formulate a program of action, to discover, appraise, and marshal the apparent and latent, the actual and potential resources of American democracy.[9]

The School and Cultural Reconstruction

In formulating a viable educational philosophy, the Reconstructionist educator gave careful attention to the school as a cultural agency. However, caution was exercised so that the school's potentiality as an instrument of reconstruction was not exaggerated. It was necessary to distinguish between education and schooling. More informal education referred to the total process of enculturation. The school as a specialized social agency was established to bring children into group life through the deliberate cultivation of socially preferred skills, knowledge, and values.

Counts believed that Americans had not sufficiently recognized the differences between education and schooling. They had identified the school with progress and regarded schooling as an unfailing solution to all problems.

However, world crises had multiplied during the period of the greatest expansion of schooling. Instead of directing social change, the school was driven aimlessly by external forces. The immature American faith in the power of schooling was based on a concept of education as a pure and independent entity isolated from social, political, and economic conflicts. This uncritical attitude inhibited the serious examination of education's moral and social foundations. Although Americans associated education solely with democracy, history demonstrated that an appropriate education existed for every society or civilization. In the twentieth century, the totalitarians proved extremely adept at using education to promote their particular ideologies. German education under the Nazis and Soviet education under the Communists demonstrated that the school could serve many masters.

Some educators, including many Progressives, erroneously believed that the school was capable of reconstructing society without the support of other social institutions. Because the school was only one of several educative social institutions, educators had to be constantly aware of the changing functions and structures of the society that determined its task. An educational theory based solely on schooling lacked reality and vitality.[10] Counts believed that the school, while important, was only one of many cultural agencies. When he asked educators to "build a new social order," Counts was urging educators to examine the culture and ally with those social forces and groups that exemplified the democratic ethic in technological use. Although educators could not reform society without the support of others, "educational statesmen" could provide leadership in building a new society. While a limited type of educational origination, it differed from the reflective theory, which held that the school should merely mirror society. Mere reflection meant that powerful pressure groups could dominate the school for their own special interests. Counts's educational theory also opposed the "four walls philosophy of the school," which asserts that educators should be concerned only with schooling and should ignore social issues.

In outlining a democratic educational program, Counts emphasized two major objectives: (1) the development of democratic habits, dispositions, and loyalties; and (2) the acquisition of knowledge and insight for intelligent participation in democratic society. Public education was to develop a feeling of competency and adequacy in the individual; an allegiance to human equality; brotherhood, dignity, and worth; loyalty to the democratic methodology of discussion, criticism, and decision; a mentality characterized by integrity and scientific spirit; and respect for talent, training, and character.[11]

Counts attacked the doctrines of educational impartiality and neutrality that demanded the teacher's complete objectivity. All education is committed to certain beliefs and values. Some criteria are necessary to guide the selection or rejection of educational goals, purposes, subjects, materials, and methods. At no point can the school assume complete neutrality and at the same time be a concrete functioning reality. For every society, there was an appropriate, distinctive education. The primary obligation of U.S. educators was to clarify the underlying assumptions and guiding principles that gave commitment and direction to the school.

As each new generation was brought into social participation, it mastered society's skills, knowledge, and attitudes. Without this transmission and perpetuation, the particular society perished. The release of human energy occurred, not by freeing individuals from tradition, but by introducing them to a vital and growing tradition.

Counts challenged both the more traditional Essentialists and Perennialists and the child-centered Progressives. Traditionalists, like the Perennialists, stressed education as purely intellectual and universal rather than involved in solving social problems. For them, the school should cultivate intellectual skills, knowledge, and habits. In the pursuit of pure knowledge, teachers were not to become involved in economic, political, and social controversies.

In addition to opposing educational traditionalism, Counts challenged child-centered Progressives. He attacked the notions of some Progressives who believed it possible to have a completely neutral school in which children were never imposed on but were totally free to develop according to their own interests. Counts held that only as social participants could children grow through their experiences. As a cultural participant, the child was imposed on by the culture and in turn made an imprint on the culture.

DEVELOPMENT THEORY AND FUTURISM

Two contemporary movements that bear a relationship to Reconstructionism are Development theory and Futurism. Development theorists and Futurists are concerned with creating a new world order.

Contemporary Development educators are concerned with bringing about worldwide change. They are especially concerned with "empowering" the economically impoverished and often politically suppressed peoples of the developing third-world nations in Asia, Africa, and Latin America. Unlike the Development theories of the 1960s that emphasized modernization from the top down by centralized government agencies, grassroots Development educators stress initiatives, planning, and implementation by people at the local level.[12]

Still another approach to using education to create a new social order comes from Futurists, educational theorists who attempt to predict the course of social and technological change and to educate for it. Their goal is not only to reduce the lag between technological change and social adaptation to it, but also to provide human beings with the knowledge and methods to control and to direct change. Futurists, such as Alvin Toffler, author of *Future Shock,* maintain that the school curriculum not only lags behind social and technological change but is also anachronistic in that it is geared to an era that has already passed.[13] While Counts argued that schools in the industrial era were still educating as if they existed in an essentially rural and agricultural society, Futurists find schools educating for the industrial rather than the postindustrial needs of the so-called information society.[14]

ISSUE-ORIENTED SCHOOLS

As noted, Social Reconstructionist educators see the schools as centers in which teachers and students grapple with society's pressing issues, not merely for academic inquiry but to engage in action-oriented research and solution. In such inquiry-oriented schools, the focus is on large social, political, economic, and educational issues. The Social Reconstructionist seeks to (1) locate schools in a social, or societal, context; (2) use schools as instruments or agencies of directed social change and reform; and (3) identify society's current social, political, economic, and educational problems. Because of their action-oriented position, the Reconstructionists encounter opposition from Perennialists, Essentialists, and even some Progressives, who fear that the schools would become politicized. These critics contend that, if applied, Social Reconstructionism would lead to the indoctrination of students for particular political purposes.

Countering the objections of their educational opponents, Social Reconstructionists contend that contemporary U.S. schools are immersed in profound social issues that daily impact their educational mission, activities, and performance. Problems such as poverty, racism, sexism, homelessness, drug abuse, and violence are social pathologies of endemic proportions in the United States. The Social Reconstructionists argue that schools cannot ignore these problems. Not only do they have an impact on society, politics, and the economy, but they also profoundly affect schools, students, and teachers. Further, these profound problems have even shaped the relationship between the school and society. For example, if students are victims of poverty, sexism, and racism, if they are hungry, and if they attend schools in a state of anxiety due to the fear of violence, then their attitudes, dispositions, and expectations about schooling will be negatively impacted. If teachers, too, feel the impact of these debilitating conditions either directly or through the lives of their students, then teaching and learning— the heart of schooling, will be affected as well. In other words, social issues outside of the school are part of the context that shape what goes on in schools.

The Social Reconstructionist's issues-oriented school is based on a belief that a definite intersection exists between the school and society. The larger society's unresolved tensions and strains have an impact on schools, teachers, and students. For Reconstructionist educators, social issues, rather than an exclusive emphasis on academic subjects and skills, constitute the underlying base of the curriculum and the educational experiences that derive from it. The school becomes a societal laboratory in which students, by engaging in action-oriented problem solving, become self-empowered agents of directed social change. From such a perspective, curriculum construction is continuous rather than a process that can reach completion. Unlike the Perennialist who envisions a curriculum of eternal verities that remains unchanged in its key features, the Reconstructionist sees the curriculum as being continually reconstructed in terms of society's changing socioeconomic and political needs.

Educators who follow the Social Reconstructionist theory would see social issues problematically. For them, information about an issue is important in the research phase. However, the problem would need to be acted on and resolved by students and teachers in an active mode of learning.

In a problem-centered and action-oriented approach to major social issues, the Social Reconstructionist would ask the following focusing questions: (1) What are the viable elements in the culture and what are the areas of knowledge that explain these elements? (2) What are the problematic areas—the issues—that are impacting the society? (3) How can the problem areas be resolved so that the solutions become part of a reconstructed culture and society?

A social issue, or problem, that affects society and schooling can be analyzed in two dimensions: societally (structurally) and personally. A problem such as drug abuse may exist at the national, in some cases international, level and be found to be affecting social, political, economic, and educational institutions and infrastructures. Living in a society that exhibits major strains produces personal dissonance as well. At the local school level, drug-addicted students not only suffer the consequences of addiction but also exert a negative impact on the school, teachers, and other students. In analyzing a major social issue such as drug abuse, it becomes evident that what we consider to be a national issue, while perhaps more acute in the United States, is an international or global issue as well that affects the societies and people of other countries. While drug abuse is used as an example of a major issue, other national—and perhaps global—problems are poverty, racism, sexism, homelessness, terrorism, and violence.

Reconstructionists argue that educators—administrators and teachers alike—need to be knowledgeable about the social context in which schooling occurs. This knowledge will aid them to first understand the social situation and then to develop strategies for its reconstruction.

RECONSTRUCTIONISM'S PHILOSOPHICAL AND IDEOLOGICAL RELATIONSHIPS

Social Reconstructionism has been influenced by Pragmatism, especially John Dewey's Experimentalism. Reconstructionists believe that by using the insights of the social sciences and the scientific method, they can create a new society. Whereas Pragmatism is open-ended, Reconstructionism tends to offer a version of the new society. Critics of the theory argue that the Reconstructionist preconceptions interfere with experimental inquiry and could lead to indoctrination in the schools.

In terms of ideology, Reconstructionists have been influenced by Liberalism, especially its modern variety, and Utopianism. Modern Liberalism, with its predilection for social reform through government regulation and intervention, is compatible with the Reconstructionist emphasis on social engineering and planning. However, the Reconstructionist proposals for a new society based on comprehensive social planning exceed the Liberal orientation to incremental reform and change.

In their desire for comprehensive social change and planning, the Reconstructionists have been influenced by the grand designs of the Utopian theorists. Although Reconstructionists have a vision of the new society, they do not regard themselves as visionaries.

Social Reconstructionists have some interesting relationships to Progressives. In fact, the socially oriented wing of the Progressive education movement was the base from which Reconstructionism emerged. George Counts and other socially oriented Progressives charged that child-centered Progressives were ignoring significant social issues and problems. For the Reconstructionists, a truly Progressive theory of education needed to examine the nature of social crisis and resolve the problems that aggravated that crisis. Child-centered Progressives countered that the Social Reconstructionists were politicizing schools and attempting to indoctrinate children according to their particular ideological creed.

Many parallels exist between Social Reconstructionism and Critical Theory, which is examined in the following chapter. Both theories agree that schools should be used to develop students' critical consciousness and ability to analyze social problems. They concur on the need to achieve a more equitable distribution of economic goods and services and to eliminate discrimination based on race, ethnicity, class, and gender. However, the historical origins of the two theories are different. Social Reconstructionism arose from the Pragmatic and Progressive temper for social, economic, and political reform. In many respects, its economic analysis was informed by Charles A. Beard's historical interpretations and George Counts's educational analyses. While economic forces certainly condition politics, society, and schooling in Reconstructionist analysis, these institutions and agencies are not completely economically determined. Although schools as institutions might be controlled by favored economic classes, schooling, even in a capitalist society, as an educational process still has liberating possibilities.

Because of its emphasis on the school as an agency of social change and social engineering, Reconstructionism is opposed by the traditional philosophies of Idealism, Realism, and Thomism, which construe education in intellectual terms. It also draws the opposition of Conservatives, Essentialists, and Perennialists, who claim that it negates the power of tradition, promotes social instability, and neglects the cultivation of essential skills and subjects. Reconstructionists, they contend, would use schools to test their social theories and turn children into sociological and pedagogical guinea pigs.

CONCLUSION

Social Reconstructionism is a theory that seeks to use the school to create a new society. A primary function of schools is to aid in the diagnosis of the crisis of modern society. Schools are to identify the major social problems that contribute to the cultural crisis and are to create the skills and attitudes that will resolve these problems. For Social Reconstructionists, teachers should not fear a committment to building a new society. Discounting charges of indoctrination, they claim that all education is a product of a particular culture. Originating with the socially oriented wing of Progressive education, Reconstructionism continues in various contemporary forms such as Development education and Futurism.

DISCUSSION QUESTIONS

1. Identify and analyze the symptoms of cultural crisis. Can and should schools seek to resolve these issues?

2. Critique Social Reconstructionism from the perspectives of Essentialism, Perennialism, and Progressivism.

3. Compare and contrast the Conservative and the Social Reconstructionist conceptions of tradition.

4. How would a Marxist critique Social Reconstructionism?

5. Indicate the ways in which Social Reconstructionism resembles ideology.

6. To what extent is Social Reconstructionism a conflict theory?

7. Examine the dynamic impact of technology on society. Use the computer, television, or the automobile as case studies.

8. Critique Counts's statement that "education is always a function of time, place, and circumstances" from the perspective of a Perennialist such as Hutchins or Adler.

9. Describe the kind of teacher that would be needed in a Reconstructionist issue-oriented school.

10. Identify the kinds of social, economic, and political problems in contemporary society that Reconstructionists would use in an issues-oriented curriculum.

INQUIRY PROJECTS

- In a paper, identify and analyze the areas of social and economic disparity and tension in the United States.
- Prepare a map that identifies areas of conflict in the world.
- Using statistics from the United Nations or the World Bank, estimate the number of people on the earth who suffer from malnutrition and extreme poverty.
- Do a content analysis of selected social studies textbooks used in secondary schools. Identify the socioeconomic problems that these books discuss. Do the authors suggest solutions to these problems?
- Review a book by George S. Counts, Theodore Brameld, William O. Stanley, or another Reconstructionist educator.
- Review a book by Alvin Toffler or another Futurist author, with special reference to education and schooling.
- Develop a unit for classroom instruction that follows the Reconstructionist approach.
- Arrange a debate on the following resolution: Resolved, the public schools will adopt a Social Reconstructionist orientation.

FURTHER READINGS

Brameld, Theodore. *Education for the Emerging Age: Newer Ends and Stronger Means.* New York: Harper & Row, 1965.

Brameld, Theodore. *Toward a Reconstructed Philosophy of Education.* New York: Holt, Rinehart and Winston, 1956.

Cernea, Michael M. *Putting People First: Sociological Variables in Rural Development.* New York: World Bank/Oxford University Press, 1985.

Coombs, Philip H. *The World Crisis in Education: The View from the Eighties.* New York: Oxford University Press, 1985.

Counts, George S. *Dare the School Build a New Social Order?* New York: John Day, 1932.

Counts, George S. *Education and American Civilization.* New York: Bureau of Publications, Teachers College, Columbia University, 1952.

Counts, George S. *Education and the Foundations of Human Freedom.* Pittsburgh: University of Pittsburgh Press, 1962.

Dennis, Lawrence. *George S. Counts and Charles A. Beard: Collaborators for Change.* Albany: State University of New York Press, 1989.

Dennis, Lawrence J., and William E. Eaton, eds. *George S. Counts: Educator for a New Age.* Carbondale: Southern Illinois University Press, 1980.

Farganis, Sondra. *Social Reconstruction of the Feminine Character.* Totowa, NJ: Rowman & Littlefield, 1986.

Gutek, Gerald L. *The Educational Theory of George S. Counts.* Columbus: Ohio State University Press, 1970.

Gutek, Gerald L. *George S. Counts and American Civilization: The Educator as Social Theorist.* Macon, GA: Mercer University Press, 1984.

Heilbroner, Robert I. *The Future as History.* New York: Harper & Row, 1968.

Honneth, Axel, ed. *Cultural-Political Interventions in the Unfinished Project of Enlightenment.* Cambridge, MA: MIT Press, 1992.

James, Michael E., ed. *Social Reconstruction Through Education: The Philoso-*

phy, History and Curricula of a Radical Ideal. Norwood, NJ: Ablex, 1995.

Miller, William C. *The Third Wave and Education's Futures.* Bloomington, IN: Phi Delta Kappa Educational Foundation, 1981.

Stanley, William B. *Curriculum for Utopia: Social Reconstructionism and Critical*

Pedagogy in the Postmodern Era. Albany: State University of New York Press, 1992.

Toffler, Alvin. *Future Shock.* New York: Random House, 1970.

Toffler, Alvin, ed. *Learning for Tomorrow: The Role of the Future in Education.* New York: Random House, 1972.

ENDNOTES

1. For the history of Social Reconstructionism, see Michael E. James, *Social Reconstructionism Through Education: The Philosophy, History and Curricula of a Radical Ideal* (Norwood, NJ: Ablex, 1995).

2. Significant examples of Social Reconstructionism can be found in Theodore Brameld, *Toward a Reconstructed Philosophy of Education* (New York: Holt, Rinehart and Winston, 1956); and William O. Stanley, *Education and Social Integration* (New York: Bureau of Publications, Teachers College, Columbia University, 1953).

3. Counts's realization of the totalitarian nature of Soviet Communism can be found in George S. Counts, *The Challenge of Soviet Education* (New York: McGraw-Hill, 1957).

4. George S. Counts, *Dare the School Build a New Social Order?* (New York: John Day, 1932), pp. 17–18.

5. George S. Counts, *The Social Foundations of Education* (New York: Charles Scribner's Sons, 1934), p. 1.

6. Lawrence J. Dennis, *George S. Counts and Charles A. Beard: Collaborators for Change* (Albany: State University of New York Press, 1989).

7. George S. Counts, *Education and the Promise of America* (New York: Macmillan, 1946), pp. 87–88.

8. Counts, *Social Foundations,* pp. 70–73.

9. George S. Counts, *The Prospects of American Democracy* (New York: John Day, 1938), pp. 350–351.

10. George S. Counts, *The American Road to Culture* (New York: John Day, 1930), p. 18.

11. George S. Counts, *The Schools Can Teach Democracy* (New York: John Day, 1939), pp. 16–17.

12. Philip H. Coombs, *The World Crisis in Education: The View from the Eighties* (New York: Oxford University Press, 1985), pp. 3–31.

13. Alvin Toffler, *Future Shock* (New York: Random House, 1970), p. 353.

14. Alvin Toffler, ed., *Learning for Tomorrow: The Role of the Future in Education* (New York: Random House, 1974); also see William C. Miller, *The Third Wave and Education's Futures* (Bloomington, IN: Phi Delta Kappa Educational Foundation, 1981).

▶ 21

Critical Theory and Education

In the history of educational philosophy and theory, Critical Theory is one of the more recently developed theories to appear. Although one can most likely trace part of its theoretical lineage to the great protestors of the past, we will emphasize contemporary contributors.

ORIGINS AND PROPONENTS
OF CRITICAL THEORY

It is possible to detect many parallels between Marxism, particularly Neo-Marxism, and Critical Theory. Marx's analysis of class struggle over the control of the means and modes of economic production is significant for the concept of conflict theory, a central theme in Critical Theory.[1] While the Critical Theorists have borrowed themes such as class conflict from Marx, they have not been associated with the totalitarian legacy of statist Communism, which occurred when Marxism was implemented in the Soviet Union by Lenin and Stalin. In Western Europe, Neo-Marxist theoreticians such as Antonio Gramsci and Juergen Habermas developed a form of Neo-Marxist analysis that was divorced from the version of Marxism implemented in the Soviet state. A leading group of theoreticians associated with the Frankfurt School of sociology used selected Marxist concepts for social analysis. The Frankfurt School influenced some educational theorists in the United States as they developed a Neo-Marxist interpretation of U.S. education.[2]

In addition to theoretical currents emanating from Europe, others originated in Latin America. Ivan Illich in *Deschooling Society* argued that Westernized schooling had become an instrument of neocolonialist expropriation and repression in less technologically developed societies in Asia, South America, and Africa.[3] Paulo Freire, too, designed a liberation pedagogy, which sought to raise the consciousness of disempowered and dispossessed people.[4]

In the United States, the forces of change unleashed by events during the late 1960s have exerted a continual impact on analyses of U.S. society and education. The civil rights, ecological, feminist, counterculture, gay and lesbian, and anti-war movements stimulated a critique of U.S. culture, society, and education. Persistent themes developed during the counterculture movement of the late 1960s, such as racism, classism, and sexism, form an important part of the Critical Theory critique. By the 1980s, however, a Neo-Conservative reaction had mobilized as an opposing force to the countercultural trends. Neo-Conservativism, actually a hybrid of Classical Liberal economics and religious fundamentalism, emphasized economic competition, deregulation, fundamentalist values, and basic education. (See Chapter 12 for a discussion of Neo-Conservatism.) By the 1990s, battle lines were formed between the two opposing camps in what has been called the culture wars.

Overriding Concerns

Critical Theory focuses on two related elements in education: critique and reform. As a critique, it examines the issue of who—what class—controls educational institutions and processes and establishes educational goals and priorities. It asks the critical questions, Who controls the schools? Who makes policies that govern schools? Who determines the ethical, social, and economic goals of education? Who establishes the curriculum? Once these questions of control are answered, then the analysis turns to an examination of the controllers' motives, purposes, and agenda. Critical Theorists do not ask these questions in the abstract, metaphysical sense of the more traditional educational philosophies such as Idealism or Realism. Rather, they contend that the crucial educational issues rest on the power of one group to control another and to hold it in subordination. The power holders in society seek to impose their views of knowledge, schooling, curriculum, and teaching on those who lack economic and political power. Important instruments of control are the authoritative documents, the texts, which serve to legitimize such control. In contemporary, postmodern society, the power holders (those who possess wealth) control the corporate sector, dominate major political parties, and shape the media's electronic messages.

Traditionally, the economic power brokers have been capitalists. However, power currently resides in the highly complex organizational form of multinational global corporations rather than in the notorious nineteenth-century robber barons. In addition, the power holders in the United States traditionally have been white males of European ancestry. The historically dispossessed have been women and Asian, African, and Native Americans. Among the disempowered are unskilled workers, small farmers, and underpaid service employees. It is possible to extend the critique internationally. Globally, in a world dominated by multinational corporations, even nations can be divided into the powerful industrial corporate ones and those, often in the southern hemisphere, that are less technologically developed and therefore exploited. While the Critical Theorists have been preoccupied with critique, they also have developed an agenda for using education and schooling to empower those who lack control over their own lives and destinies.

Similar to Marxists, Critical Theorists focus on the dynamics of socioeconomic conflicts found in politics, culture, and education. Conflict Theory holds that dominant classes use social institutions, such as schools, to reproduce the exploitative conditions that sustain their favored position. Subordinate classes, if conscious of their condition, can struggle to overthrow the oppressors who exploit and disempower them.[5] In the social conflict, Critical Theorists are squarely on the side of oppressed subordinate classes and groups. Raising the consciousness of subordinate groups is crucial for equipping them to wage the struggle. Conventional schooling, controlled by the dominant class power structure, seeks to maintain and reproduce the social, political, and economic status quo. Critical Theorists believe we must work against the cultural agents that reproduce the status quo.

A Question of Timing Phrases

Critical Theorists want to create a "new public philosophy" for the "postmodern era."[6] A consideration of these phrases—*postmodern era* and *new public philosophy*—helps to position the theory.

Some academic commentators call the contemporary period the postmodern era. The term *postmodern,* while difficult to define, has great currency among contemporary theorists. It is an unusual term coined by those who see themselves as participants in a new era rather than by historians, who, for example, retrospectively coined the terms *classical period* to refer to the ancient Greek and Roman civilizations and *medieval period* to refer to the Middle Ages. In contrast, those who use the term *postmodern* seem to sense that they are participating in a new era.

Perhaps the term *postmodern* can be clarified by considering some trends of the late twentieth century that appear significant for the twenty-first century. Among them are the following: (1) a change in the economies of Western nations from heavy industries to technology, information, and service; (2) the ending of the bipolar Cold War between the United States and the former Soviet Union; (3) the questioning and abandonment of traditional lifestyles and values and the overt surfacing of alternative lifestyles and values in Western nations; (4) the collapse of the Communist system in the Soviet Union and eastern Europe; (5) the surfacing of a fundamentalist religious orientation in the Islamic world and also in Western societies; and (6) profound debate about authority and legitimacy, particularly in educational institutions. Whether these trends signify the end of the modern era, the beginning of the postmodern era, or a transition to an age whose contours remain indeterminate is an open question. However, a significant group of theorists, who have determined that we live in a new historical reality, have opted for the term *postmodern.*

In seeking to define what they regard as a new era in history, certain theorists, particularly in the field of literature but also in the fields of philosophy and social science, have critically analyzed the major literary and philosophical works of what they regard as the old order. Rather than seeing these works as enduring elements in the culture, as do Idealists, Realists, Essentialists, and Perennialists, they see them as the constructed works that dominant groups used at a given time in history to give them a sense of legitimacy and authority. As constructed works of a given time and place, they can be analyzed and deconstructed. In the process of deconstruction, they become historical literary residues rather than canons of authority. In academic circles, a great debate has occurred between "constructionists" and "deconstructionists" over what constitutes the bases of culture, value, and education. This struggle becomes particularly crucial for curriculum construction. For example, should the U.S. curriculum be rooted in the important works of Western civilization? Or are these works period pieces that represent the cultural control of one group over another? Should the curriculum be deconstructed and reconceptualized to include the cultures of hitherto under-represented groups and their cultural styles?

Part of the postmodern movement, Critical Theorists, like Social Reconstructionists, provide a critique of the two major political forces in U.S. life: Conservatism and Liberalism. They see modern U.S. Neo-Conservatism, such as that embodied in the Reagan and Bush administrations and the "Contract with America" of Newt Gingrich—and educational agendas based on them—as a means to keep the dominant socioeconomic classes in power and other groups subordinate to them. Critical Theorists attack the following features of the Neo-Conservative educational platform: (1) identifying the cultural foundations of U.S. education as based in Western civilization; (2) stressing a curriculum of basic education and skills training, especially for disadvantaged groups; and (3) re-affirming authoritarian controls in schooling in the name of efficiency and productivity for the marketplace. For Critical Theorists, these planks in the Neo-Conservative educational platform reinforce the structures of oppression in educational institutions.

Somewhat like the Philosophical Analysts, Critical Theorists are concerned with language. They want to develop a critically affirmative language with a vocabulary of sufficient power to examine education and schooling as species of cultural politics. Similar to contemporary Deconstructionists, they devote energy to examining the texts—the sources and documents—that give legitimacy to educational authority. While many Philosophical Analysts are concerned with applying empirical processes to clarify language, Critical Theorists critique texts as sets of "historically and socially constructed practices."[7] They reflect how authors at a given time constructed "knowledge" and by this construction used the text as an instrument of power. By analyzing texts as instruments that expressed power at a given time, it is possible to deconstruct them.

The term *public philosophy* is also instructive regarding the Critical Theorists' educational position. Used in the Progressive era by journalist-philosophers such as Walter Lippman, public philosophy meant that the public should be educated about the broad issues of the day in order to exercise an informed role in shaping public policies. The Critical Theorists have moved the concept of creating a public philosophy into the arena of conflict between the power holders and the disempowered. They see the debates over public philosophy as part of a wider and deeper struggle for democracy.

EDUCATION, SCHOOLING, AND TEACHING

Critical Theorists place the schools squarely in the arena of cultural politics and conflict. According to their analysis, schools historically have been controlled by and used by economically, socially, and politically dominant groups to impose their preferred versions of knowledge as means of social control. For the children of the dominant groups, this imposition confirms their social, political, and cultural position of power. Children of subordinate groups, usually economically disadvantaged and politically disorganized ones, are taught that they live in a society in which economic, social, and political institutions are functioning correctly. They are given textbooks and other instructional materials that confirm, or legitimatize, this dominant-class-constructed version of social reality. This process of educational imposition or legitimization helps the dominant groups to maintain their positions, to have hegemony, over subordinate groups. Schools, therefore, are not neutral academic institutions but are political agencies that empower some and disempower others. The empowerment–disempowerment strategy is one of a controlled reproduction of predefined social and economic roles based on the functioning of the world marketplace.

Based on their critique, Critical Theorists seek to reform schooling so that schools can become "democratic public spheres" that will awaken young people to their genuine moral, political, economic, and civic rights and responsibilities.[8]

Teaching

Critical Theorists seek to redefine the teacher's role and the nature and purpose of teaching. As they critique the forces that disempower large groups in U.S. society, they also identify those trends that, in the name of educational legitimacy and effectiveness, have disempowered teachers. Among them are standardized testing, the mechanics of teacher competency assessment, and top-down administrator-controlled schools. These mechanisms take away the teachers' power to design and conduct instruction and give that power instead to others such as administrators or legislators.

Critical Theorists argue for what they call a transformative rather than reactive agenda for teacher empowerment. Like the Social Reconstructionist concept of "educational statesmanship," the Critical Theorist reform agenda reconceptualizes the teachers' role so they can become "engaged and transformative intellectuals." Key to transforming teachers' roles is to encourage reflection on the ideological principles that sustain practice and that connect educational theory to wider social, economic, and political issues. The Critical Theorist reform agenda includes the following teacher roles:

1. Working for real school reforms that will enable them to exercise power over education.
2. Engaging in collaboration with other teachers to improve instruction.
3. Interacting with the people in the communities whose children they educate, and organizing for collaborative community action.
4. Engaging in critical dialogues with students about the political, economic, and cultural issues of U.S. society.
5. Working to redistribute power in schools between teachers and administrators by giving teachers, students, and community members a larger role in educational policymaking.
6. Recognizing that problems such as drug abuse, teenage pregnancy, illiteracy, malnutrition, and inadequate health care cannot be ignored by schools.[9]

Learning

Critical Theorists call for learning that recognizes and encourages students' cultural diversity. Supportive of multicultural education, they emphasize that learning should begin with the students' own autobiographies and family and community experiences. Their affirmation of cultural diversity opposes the concept that schools should structure learning around a Western culture core, a common Neo-Conservative theme. It also runs counter to the consensus-building style advocated by Experimentalists and Liberals. An important outcome of learning is acquiring a critical language for analyzing major contemporary social, political, economic, and educational issues.

Curriculum

Critical Theorists would begin the process of curricular reconceptualization with a critique of the existing curriculum. The curriculum exists in at least two dimensions: the overt curriculum of identified skills and subjects and the "hidden curriculum" that covertly shapes values, attitudes, and behaviors. The overt curriculum tends to reinforce the status quo that favors the dominating minority in that it constructs their version of knowledge as the legitimate version for all students. For example, it tends to enforce a monolingual language policy that disempowers students who do not have English as their first language. It constructs subjects such as literature, history, geography, and social studies in terms that support the existing power structure.[10] The hidden curriculum, with its emphasis on competition, consumerism, and private property, further reinforces the socioeconomic status quo. For example, the practice of homogeneous grouping contains both overt and hidden elements. As a school-engineered way of streaming students, it tends to reproduce the socioeconomic, and often sexist, status quo. Even though homogeneous grouping reproduces social strata in the school, the rationale for ability grouping is alleged to rest on academic criteria. Covertly, grouping can be part of the hidden curriculum in that it reproduces the existing social structure and conditions students to accept the legitimacy of a socially divisive structure.

Emphasizing the educational richness of diverse cultures and styles of learning, a Critical Theorist curriculum would use the students' unique multicultural experiences to develop new skills and knowledge. Such a curriculum would stress (1) the study of the students' histories, languages, and cultures; and (2) an analysis of the persistent issues of U.S. life, particularly those that empower some and disempower others.

CRITICAL THEORY'S PHILOSOPHICAL AND IDEOLOGICAL RELATIONSHIPS

As a recent educational development, Critical Theory parallels Pragmatism and its revived form called Neo-Pragmatism. Like Pragmatists such as Peirce and Dewey, Critical Theorists tend to reject the large universalizing concepts found in Idealist and Realist metaphysics. Also, like earlier Pragmatists such as John Dewey and John Childs, Critical Theorists seek to spark a public debate over education. They seek to resurrect a broad-based public discussion that relates education, schooling, and the curriculum to social, economic, and cultural issues. Despite these parallels, Critical Theory appears to clash with Pragmatism, especially Dewey's Experimentalism, in three areas: (1) the primacy of the scientific method as the basis of the Complete Act of Thought; (2) the impulse to create larger and more inclusive shared communities through consensus-building strategies; and (3) Experimentalism's open-endedness which asserts that education's sole end is growth for the sake of further growth.

Critical Theorists have redefined and adapted several Marxist principles. They emphasize that schools, like other agencies in society, rest on an economic base and that schooling in a capitalist society, through the overt and hidden curricula, legitimizes the dominant group's control of that base. They also tend to see political and educational issues as expressing a clash between contending polarized groups.

Several Social Reconstructionist themes have been revitalized by Critical Theorists. They see education and schooling in broad social, political, and economic, rather than strictly academic, terms. Like the Social Reconstructionists who want teachers to become educational statespersons, Critical Theorists urge teachers to become engaged in socially and politically transformative roles. Rather than reflecting and transmitting the cultural heritage, transformative teachers would seek to reconceptualize the heritage to empower not only themselves but those who are disempowered by the society's political and economic structures. Just as Social Reconstructionists have used Utopian thought to envision possible educational reform and change, Critical Theorists, too, have considered Utopian thought to be useful in designing preferred futures.[11]

Critical Theory has many philosophical, ideological, and educational opponents. Idealist and Realist philosophers and Essentialist and Perennialist theorists would attack Critical Theory as a position that is neither critical nor theoretical. These more traditional philosophies and theories are based on universalizing tendencies that produce large generalizations about education. This tendency to universalization has been attacked by postmodern theorists, including Critical Theorists, as a form of dominant-group-constructed social control. In defense of their universalist positions, the more traditional philosophers and theorists would see Critical Theory as primarily a political and economic ideology that would politicize schooling and teaching to achieve a political agenda of creating some kind of undefined democratic socialism. Rather than decontrolling schools, opponents would contend that Critical Theorists are establishing new controls. They would look on the Critical Theorist critique as one that would abandon the school's primary role as an intellectual and academic agency that places education in the context of the cultural heritage.

Conservatives and Neo-Conservatives would clash ideologically with Critical Theorists on many issues. They would charge that Critical Theorists would create cultural rootlessness by abandoning the educational foundations of Western civilization, and would create an unskilled society by reducing the importance of generative skills needed for social efficiency.

Liberals would find Critical Theory a very perplexing ideology. While Liberals might support the goals of a more equitable distribution of wealth, a political education to raise the consciousness of minority groups, and multicultural education, they would rely more on experimental incremental processes. Reform for Liberals would come from a gradual reform of existing conditions in an incremental process rather than by the radical transformation urged by the Critical Theorists. Liberals would also oppose what they regard as the polarizing language and tactics of Critical Theorists. Historically, Liberals have acted as consensus builders, both politically and educationally, who create a large middle or moderate group.

While Philosophical Analysts would likely commend the Critical Theorists' concern with language and creating a socially conscious vocabulary, they would find certain phrases used by Critical Theorists to be highly emotive and slogan-like. Words such as *empowerment, disempowerment, transformative, pedagogical silencing, structures of oppression,* and *emancipatory vision,* for example, would need analysis to render them verifiable propositions.

CONCLUSION

Critical Theory, a recent development in educational thought, has exercised a significant role in contemporary analyses of society, education, and schooling. Critical Theorists, through their analyses of educational institutions and situations, have developed a vocabulary of terms such as *hegemony, social control, conflict theory, hidden curriculum,* and *empowerment* that are found in contemporary educational discourse. They see schools, curriculum, teaching, and learning as agencies and activities that transcend the exclusively academic and have important political, economic, social, and educational meanings and implications. Critical Theorists argue for a bold educational agenda that would transform not only schools but also society.

DISCUSSION QUESTIONS

1. Examine the origins of Critical Theory. What are the relationships to Marxism, Neo-Marxism, and Social Reconstructionism?

2. Define the concepts of conflict theory, hegemony, dominant and subordinate classes, social control, and hidden curriculum. Then, use these concepts to analyze the condition of contemporary U.S. education.

3. Are we living in the postmodern era? What is the meaning of *postmodernism*?

4. Using the concept of the hidden curriculum, identify its impact on your own education.

5. Analyze the teacher education program in your college or university in terms of Critical Theory.

6. Using Critical Theory as a mode of analysis, determine who establishes educational goals and the school curriculum in your college.

7. Analyze the universalist propositions found in Idealism, Realism, and Thomism from the position of Critical Theory.

8. Analyze current proposals for educational reform from the perspective of Critical Theory.

9. According to Critical Theory, what constitutes a valid authority for curriculum construction?

INQUIRY PROJECTS

- As you do your clinical or field study, observe the school and classroom settings in which you are involved. Do you find evidences of social control, dominant class culture, and the hidden curriculum?
- Review several textbooks used in the teacher education program at your college or university. Based on Critical Theory, determine the books' perspectives.
- Arrange a debate between two teams, one taking the Critical Theory and the other the Neo-Conservative perspective, on the proposition: Resolved, the curriculum core of U.S. secondary education will feature the Western cultural heritage.
- According to Critical Theory, prepare a profile of a transformative teacher.
- Read and review a book on Postmodernism, Poststructuralism, or Critical Theory.
- Invite a Critical Theorist philosopher to speak to your class on the application of the theory to schooling.

FURTHER READINGS

Aronowitz, Stanley, and Henry A. Giroux. *Education Under Siege: The Conservative, Liberal, and Radical Debate Over Schooling.* Westport, CT: Bergin and Garvey, 1985.

Aronowitz, Stanley, and Henry A. Giroux. *Postmodern Education: Politics, Culture, and Social Criticism.* Minneapolis: University of Minnesota Press, 1991.

Bailey, Leon. *Critical Theory and the Sociology of Knowledge: A Comparative Study in the Theory of Ideology.* New York: Peter Lang, 1994.

Calhoun, Craig J. *Critical Social Theory: Culture, History, and the Challenge of Difference.* Cambridge, MA and Oxford, England: Blackwell, 1995.

Gibson, Rex. *Critical Theory and Education.* London: Hodder and Stoughton, 1986.

Giroux, Henry A. *Border Crossings: Cultural Workers and the Politics of Education.* New York: Routledge, 1992.

Giroux, Henry A. *Teachers As Intellectuals: Toward a Critical Pedagogy of Learning.* Westport, CT: Bergin and Garvey, 1988.

Giroux, Henry A., and Peter L. McLaren. *Between Borders: Pedagogy and the Politics of Cultural Studies.* New York: Routledge, 1993.

Habermas, Jurgen. *The Philosophical Discourse of Modernity.* Cambridge, MA: MIT Press, 1987.

Hoy, David C., and Thomas McCarthy. *Critical Theory.* Cambridge, MA and Oxford, England: Blackwell, 1994.

Ingram, David. *Critical Theory and Philosophy.* New York: Paragon House, 1990.

Kellner, Douglas. *Critical Theory, Marxism, and Modernity.* Baltimore: Johns Hopkins University Press, 1989.

Kincheloe, Joe I. *Toward A Critical Politics of Teacher Thinking: Mapping the Postmodern.* Westport, CT: Bergin & Garvey, 1993.

Lankshear, Colin, and Peter L. McLaren, eds. *Critical Literacy: Politics, Praxis, and the Postmodern.* Albany: State University of New York Press, 1993.

McCarthy, Thomas. *The Critical Theory of Jurgen Habermas.* Cambridge, MA: MIT Press, 1989.

McLaren, Peter L. *Schooling As Ritual Performance: Toward a Political Economy of Educational Symbols and Gestures.* London and New York: Routledge, 1993.

McLaren, Peter L., and Colin Lankshear. *Politics of Liberation: Paths from Freire.* New York and London: Routledge, 1994.

McLaren, Peter L., and Peter Leonard, eds. *Paulo Freire: A Critical Encounter.* London and New York: Routledge, 1993.

Peim, Nick. *Critical Theory and the English Teacher: Transforming the Subject.* London and New York: Routledge, 1993.

Poster, Mark. *Critical Theory and Poststructuralism: In Search of a Context.* Ithaca, NY: Cornell University Press, 1989.

Roblin, Ronald, ed. *The Aesthetics of the Critical Theorists: Studies on Benjamin, Adorno, Marcuse, and Habermas.* Lewiston, NY: E. Mellen Press, 1990.

Stanley, William B. *Curriculum for Utopia: Social Reconstructionism and Critical Pedagogy in the Postmodern Era.* Albany: State University of New York Press, 1992.

ENDNOTES

1. For a discussion of Marxism and Critical Theory, see Douglas Kellner, *Critical Theory, Marxism, and Modernity* (Baltimore: Johns Hopkins University Press, 1989).

2. For a discussion of Habermas and the Frankfurt School, see Robert E. Young, *A Critical Theory of Education: Habermas and Our Children's Future* (New York: Teachers College Press, Columbia University, 1990); Richard Wolin, *The Terms of Cultural Criticism: The Frankfurt School, Existentialism, Poststructuralism* (New York: Columbia University Press, 1992).

3. Ivan Illich, *Deschooling Society* (New York: Harper & Row, 1971).

4. Paulo Freire, *Pedagogy of the Oppressed* (New York: Continuum, 1984).

5. Martin Carnoy, "Education, State, and Culture in American Society," in Henry A. Giroux and Peter L. McLaren, ed., *Critical Pedagogy, The State, and Cultural Struggle* (Albany: State University of New York Press, 1989), pp. 6–7.

6. Henry A. Giroux and Peter McLaren, "Schooling, Cultural Politics, and the Struggle for Democracy," in Henry A. Giroux and Peter McLaren, eds., *Critical Pedagogy,* p. xi.

7. Ibid., p. xii.

8. Ibid., p. xxi.

9. Ibid., p. xxiii.

10. For a discussion of applying Critical Theory to the curriculum, see Nick Peim, *Critical Theory and the English Teacher: Transforming the Subject* (New York: Routledge, 1993).

11. Henry A. Giroux and Peter McLaren, "Schooling, Cultural Politics, and the Struggle for Democracy," p. xiii.

Index